ENVIRONMENTAL LAW AND POLICY

FOURTH EDITION

by

JAMES SALZMAN
Samuel Fox Mordecai Professor of Law
Nicholas Institute Professor of
Environmental Policy
Duke University

BARTON H. THOMPSON, JR.
Robert E. Paradise Professor of Natural Resources Law
Perry L. McCarty Director,
Woods Institute for the Environment
Stanford University

CONCEPTS AND INSIGHTS SERIES®

FOUNDATION
PRESS

© 2003 FOUNDATION PRESS
© 2007, 2010 THOMSON REUTERS/FOUNDATION PRESS
© 2014 LEG, Inc. d/b/a West Academic
    444 Cedar Street, Suit 700
    St. Paul, MN 55101
    1–877–888–1330

Printed in the United States of America

ISBN: 978–1–60930–305–1
Mat #41387791

To my parents, with gratitude for encouraging me to look beyond the horizon and follow my star.

J.E.S.

In memory of my parents, Bart and Lorraine Thompson, for everything they taught me.

B.H.T.

PREFACE

Environmental law is critically important and endlessly fascinating. To see its importance, just imagine the United States today without federal regulation of air and water quality, pesticide use, and solid waste disposal. No matter how far the nation has come in addressing environmental issues, there remains much to do. Federal and state laws have only begun to address such important environmental issues as global climate change, non-point water pollution, indoor air pollution, groundwater depletion, and over-fishing. Scientific uncertainty, risk tradeoffs, cognitive biases, and fundamental policy disagreements, moreover, make it extremely difficult to agree on solutions to many of these remaining problems. Environmental law already has picked the low hanging fruit. The remaining problems continue to challenge even the wisest and most patient policy experts.

In many environmental law books, the important concepts and issues underlying the regulatory schemes can get lost amid a myriad of legal details. The purpose of this book is to provide a conceptual overview of environmental law and policy in a concise, readable style. The book covers all of the major environmental statutes and cases, but from a broader and more policy oriented perspective than traditional casebooks, hornbooks, treatises, and student guides. Our goal is to introduce the reader to the major themes and frameworks of environmental law, not to overburden the reader with minutiae. The book should be useful as a basic text for courses and seminars on environmental law and policy, as a readable and stimulating supplement to traditional law school casebooks, and as a primer for professionals wishing a quick, user-friendly survey of environmental law.

The book is divided into four parts. Part I introduces the major themes and issues that cross-cut environmental law, such as scientific uncertainty, market failures, and problems of scale. Part I also covers major legal concepts in the environmental field such as enforcement, standing, citizen suits, takings, the commerce clause, and administrative procedure. Later chapters use the themes and conceptual framework introduced in Part I to integrate the discussions of individual statutes into a broader portrait of the law. Part II offers overviews of each of the major federal pollution statutes. As in the rest of the book, the focus is on the ideas and debates underlying the statutes. International pollution issues such as ozone depletion, climate change, and transboundary waste disposal are integrated with their domestic counterparts. Part III examines a number of issues concerning the protection and use of natural resources, including the public trust doctrine, two of the major natural resource statutes—the Endangered Species Act and section 404 of the Clean Water Act—and energy. Part IV addresses environmental impact statements, focusing on the National Environmental Policy Act, the model for environmental assessment legislation around the world.

In the fourth edition, we have thoroughly updated the chapters and made two significant additions. To provide students a deeper understanding of how environmental law works in practice, we have added a new Chapter 4 on Enforcement. We have also added a series of in-depth problem exercises throughout the book describing a legal or policy conflicts and asking students to identify and assess solutions. To assist teachers using the book in their classroom, the accompanying Teacher's Manual has been revised to reflect these changes. We hope this book conveys the excitement that we have long felt in teaching in this area.

We are grateful for the helpful review of chapters by Craig Oren, John Applebaum, Alex Klass, Bill Cohen, Bill Funk, Craig Oren, Ralph Cavanagh, and David Driesen; the substantive contributions of Lewis Grossman, Josh Eagle, Durwood Zaelke and David Hunter; the hospitality of Andy Beattie at the Key Centre for Biodiversity and Donna Craig and Michael Jeffery at the Macquarie Centre for Environmental Law; the creation of diagrams by Robert Starner; and the student research assistance of Sean Roberts, David Wright, George Quinton, Jimmy Michaels and Ben Jacobs. Some of the text on ozone depletion and climate change was adapted from material in David Hunter, James Salzman, and Durwood Zaelke, International Environmental Law and Policy (4th ed., 2011) and some of the text on enforcement from J.B. Ruhl, John Nagle, James Salzman and Alexandra Klass, Practice and Policy in Environmental Law (2nd ed. 2010). Finally, we are indebted to our colleagues in law schools throughout the nation, who have helped develop the theories and analysis on which the nation's environmental policy and this book are built, and to our students, who keep the field fresh and alive.

J.E.S.

B.H.T.

TABLE OF CONTENTS

TABLE OF CONTENTS

ENVIRONMENTAL LAW AND POLICY

FOURTH EDITION

Part 1
TOOLS OF THE TRADE

Chapter 1

AN INTRODUCTION TO ENVIRONMENTAL LAW AND POLICY

I. Why Study Environmental Law?

The simplest definition of "environmental law and policy" might read: "the use of public authority to protect the natural environment and human health from the impacts of pollution and development." While accurate, this definition suffers from two fatal flaws—(1) it's deadly boring and (2) it fails to capture why environmental law matters.

Instead of laboring over a precise definition, pick up today's newspaper and see if you find any of the following types of headlines—"3,000 Scientists tell Government to 'Act Now' on Climate Change," "Grizzly Bear Defenders Fight Logging Projects," "Environmental Protection Agency Tangles with Texas in Battle over Air Quality," "Are Pesticides in Our Drinking Water?", "Fracking Causes Local Concern." Environmental law and policy are a part of everyday life, no matter where you live. It is more than protecting cuddly pandas or clamping down on Dickensian factories that belch smoke and churn out barrels of waste. Indeed the field cuts a remarkably broad swath—taking in climate change, water pollution, wetlands conservation, wildlife protection, green spaces, ozone depletion, smog alerts, recycling, international trade, etc.

While every field jealously claims for itself primacy as "the most important area of the law," environmental law has as good a claim on that title as any. Why should we care about environmental law? Because, taken together, the challenges to environmental quality have a critical influence on where we live, our quality of life and, perhaps most important, the kind of world our children and their children will live in. These things matter. Consider how sea level rise will affect a coastal community, what soil erosion means to a farming community, what the collapse of a fishery does to a fishing community, and how long it will take to reverse these impacts, if they even can be reversed.

Not only does environmental law matter, it's also difficult, controversial, and fascinating. Our regulation of endangered species, to take an example, challenges deeply held convictions across the political spectrum. Do endangered species have rights

3

that we should respect? How do we balance the benefits of saving an endangered salamander against the costs of an industrial development that can provide jobs to an economically depressed town? Do some species deserve more legal protection than others? We may be willing to protect a bald eagle, but who really cares about the Delhi Sands flower loving fly?

The long-time debate over drilling for oil in the Arctic National Wildlife Refuge is no less challenging. On the one hand are the arguments that drilling could bring much needed economic development to impoverished Eskimo communities, that it will reduce America's dependence on foreign oil and that, with modern technology, it may be possible to drill with little impact on the landscape. Opposed are those who counter that drilling will threaten the Porcupine Caribou Herd and, even with best efforts and technology, despoil one of America's great remaining natural areas. How can the law mediate between these opposing views? And why do opponents of drilling care so much, given the fact that it's unlikely they'll ever meet someone who has ever been to the Refuge, much less go themselves?

This is not to suggest that opposition to drilling (a position shared by most Americans) is irrational but, rather, that whatever drives this view resonates widely and defies simple explanation. Indeed it may seem odd to describe the environmental field as contentious at all, given the fact that virtually all Americans consider themselves environmentalists. Poll after poll shows that 80% and more of those surveyed believe that environmental protection should be a high governmental priority. Scratch the surface beneath the trite phrase that "environmental protection is good," though, and this seeming consensus dissolves into difficult questions of how much environmental harm we should accept, how much we as a society are willing to pay for certain levels of environmental protection, and who should bear these risks and costs. This chapter and the next provide a series of frameworks through which to consider these questions—historical, economic, ethical, equitable, etc. While these perspectives and modes of analysis may not provide definitive solutions, they will explain why so many people find the field exciting, important, and difficult.

Before proceeding further, it is worth noting that the broad subject of environmental law is often viewed as comprising two quite distinct fields—pollution law and natural resources law. In some respects, these really are different. Laws such as the Clean Air Act and Clean Water Act focus primarily on sources of pollutants, threats to human health, and risk levels, for example, while wildlife conservation, forest management, and wetlands protections concentrate more on land use and ecological concerns. As Chapter 2 makes clear, however, despite their differences in emphasis, both fields share fundamental similarities and can usefully be viewed as protecting different aspects of the environment, whether clean air and water or species and their habitat.

II. A Short History of Environmental Protection

One cannot understand current conflicts over allocation and protection of our nation's natural resources—whether water, timber, wilderness, or rangelands—and potential solutions without some grasp of the changing values of those resources over the course of our nation's history. Nor do the approaches taken in our pollution statutes make sense unless understood in their historic context. While the histories of natural resource protection and pollution control are interwoven in places, as the stories below explain they have important differences, as well.

A. Natural Resources

Wilderness holds a special place in the American consciousness. The stillness of a remote forest lake or the imposing crags of a mountain peak provide for many both a sense of connection to a larger world and a sense of inner wonder. Wilderness is also big business. It primes our economy through eco-tourists paying top dollar for trips to Antarctica, backpackers buying high-tech gear for hiking the Appalachian Trail, families enjoying Disneyworld's Jungle Cruise, and even kids having birthday parties in the Rainforest Café. The environment holds a strong grip on our collective imagination and, as the above examples make clear, the marketplace provides a dizzying number of ways for us to enjoy a range of "wilderness experiences."

Our love affair with things wild, however, is quite recent. To the Europeans who first came to America, eagerly seeking out the wilderness would have been incomprehensible. Indeed for most of the last two millennia, wilderness has been viewed more often with repugnance, as something dangerous and even an affront to civilization. The roots of this view go back to the Bible and earlier. After Adam and Eve have tasted the forbidden fruit, for example, their punishment is exile from the Garden of Eden into the wilderness. This is the same harsh, inhospitable region where Moses and the tribes of Israel must wander for forty years, where Jesus is sorely tempted by the Devil for forty days.

The Biblical wilderness is unforgiving, a wasteland of physical hardship and spiritual testing that forges iron faith.

The later folk traditions in Europe reflected this harsh view. In many of the fairy tales of the Brothers Grimm, for example, when the protagonists leave the village bad things surely follow. For Hansel and Gretel, the forest is a place of monstrous beasts and creatures, surely no place for innocent children to wander. In the same manner, William Bradford, the first governor in Plymouth Plantation, described the surrounding forests as "hideous and desolate." To be fair, he had his reasons. The world outside his settlements posed very real threats to survival, hiding wild animals and potentially hostile and, to his eyes, heathen tribes. Faced with this absence of morality and civilization, the Pilgrims and their successors felt both a religious and practical compulsion to "civilize" the wilderness.

This is not to say, however, that the natural environment had no positive characteristics for early Americans. The goal of conquering the wilderness was usually not to convert it into cities but, rather, to a rural, pastoral state—a controlled, managed nature. Thus was wasteland converted to garden. One could have too much civilization as well as too little. The city—a pure civilized state—was viewed equally by many as immoral and disconnected from God. To the degree that the earliest Americans did admire the unspoiled landscape, these were either areas that reminded them of cultivated landscapes in England, or particular aspects of the landscape—birds, flowers— that could be incorporated into a garden view.

To the early settlers, it seemed that much of Europe had gone too far toward the pole of civilization to achieve the ideal pastoral state. But it wasn't too late for America. Thus early American writers, such as Crevecoeur, despised wild areas but praised the improved, managed nature of the rural landscape. As he described, "I will revert into a state approaching nearer to that of nature, but at the same time sufficiently remote from the brutality of unconnected savage nature." Thomas Jefferson's ideal citizens were those yeoman farmers who labored on the earth (unlike city dwellers and industrial laborers). They were virtuous, close to God, independent—the moral center of democratic society.

In the Westward expansion and development that long accompanied America's growth, the frontier mantra was largely one of taming the environment. Wilderness posed a barrier to progress and prosperity. It was an obstacle, something to be conquered. As naturalist Aldo Leopold later wrote of the 1930s,

"A stump was our symbol of progress." But the era of frontier settlement coincided with the rise of a broader appreciation for wilderness. In 19th century art and literature, the presence of a grand and ancient wilderness came to assume a role as a distinctive source of American identity and superiority. This nationalist embrace of wilderness as a replacement for the long history of European culture was evident in the poetry of William Cullen Bryant, the novels of James Fenimore Cooper, the art of Thomas Cole, Asher Durand, Albert Bierstadt, and, most famously, in the writings of Henry David Thoreau.

The best known of the Transcendentalists, Thoreau's writings sprang from his belief that God could be found in nature through intuitive contemplation. For Thoreau, modern industrial society, by cutting people off from nature, was cutting them off from God. The commercial spirit of civilization kept people from contemplation of the divine. Nature was a source of vigor, inspiration, and strength. It stripped life down to its essentials. As Thoreau simply stated, "In Wildness is the preservation of the world." Yet Thoreau's terrifying account of climbing Mount Katahdin in Maine leaves little doubt that he believed one could experience too much wilderness as well as too little. In fact, Thoreau's ideal was really a middle landscape rather than pure wilderness, a life alternating between wilderness and civilization or residence in "partially cultivated country." This middle landscape is the essence of *Walden*, a subsistence farming existence just a few miles outside of Concord, Massachusetts.

Thoreau was not particularly influential in his day, however, and the notion of preserving wilderness was not a serious option. Indeed the opposite was true. Throughout most of the Nineteenth Century, federal policies sought to settle the western wilderness with Jefferson's virtuous yeoman farmers. A series of preemption and donation acts followed by the Homestead Act of 1862 and a variety of other statutes gave successive waves of settlers title to millions of acres of public lands. Often the statutes required some effort to cultivate the land before title would vest. It's important to note that despite publicizing these lands as "virgin" and "uninhabited," that was rarely the case; rather, the Native Americans already living there were often moved off the land.

To the extent there was federal supervision of the often chaotic process, it was to assure that wilderness was being tamed, not protected. And if wilderness could not necessarily be turned to farmland, particularly in the arid lands between the 100th Meridian and the Sierra Nevada and Cascade mountain ranges, its natural resources could at least be developed and exploited. Cattle were allowed freely to graze the public grasslands and miners were promised exclusive control of minerals they were able to discover on the public lands. At the same time that public lands were being granted for agriculture, mining, and other development, Congress was granting railroads millions of acres of alternating sections of public lands in an effort to speed the process along.

While this mass transfer of land from public to private ownership was taking place, halting steps toward preserving wilderness began, albeit from very modest beginnings. George Catlin, a painter of Native Americans and prairie life, had proposed in 1832 the concept of preserving Indians, buffaloes, and their wilderness home in a park. And there was some early action. In 1832, Arkansas Hot Springs was set aside as a national reservation; in 1864, the federal government granted Yosemite Valley to California as a park "for public use, resort, recreation"; in 1872, President Grant signed an act creating Yellowstone "as a public park or pleasuring ground for the benefit and enjoyment of the people"; and, in 1885, New York State created a huge forest reserve in the Adirondacks "to be forever as wild lands." Yet few of these acts were motivated by the aesthetic, spiritual, or cultural values of wilderness. The Adirondacks forest reserve was created to ensure clean water for New York City. Arkansas Hot Springs and Yellowstone were given protection primarily to prevent commercial exploitation of curiosities such as geysers. These were museum for freaks of nature.

As the Nineteenth Century drew to a close, though, public attitudes began to change about wilderness preservation. As Frederick Jackson Turner famously observed in 1893, "The frontier has gone, and with its going has closed the first period of American history." To Turner and many others, wilderness in American history had served as a fundamental source of democracy and rugged individualism. Ironically, the success of the frontier movement had raised the fear that wilderness, and the prized social values it had come to represent, might be lost. If the frontier were vanishing, preservation of the remaining wild areas was now a valid public concern.

The dominant personality of the "preservationist" movement was a remarkable Scot named John Muir. Like Thoreau, Muir celebrated the presence of the divine in wilderness. It was not trite for him to proclaim that forests were temples on earth and mountains their steeples. He and other preservationists praised wilderness as a source of toughness and ethical values. Indeed he argued that many of the nation's difficulties could be attributed to *too much* civilization and the effete, corrupt urban culture. Unlike the earlier transcendentalists, however, Muir had no ambivalence about pure wilderness. He was the first great public defender of wilderness for its own sake. When asked what a rattlesnake is good for, Muir famously replied, "It is good for itself." Founder of the Sierra Club, Muir was enough of a pragmatist to realize that the public and politicians needed to be persuaded of the wisdom of preserving wilderness.

An early and important ally of Muir was the equally impressive figure, Gifford Pinchot. The first American professionally trained as a forester in Europe, Pinchot became the consummate Washington insider. He was made the first Chief of the U.S. Forest Service by Teddy Roosevelt and later helped found the Yale School of Forestry, the first of its kind in America. Like Muir, Pinchot opposed the wholesale exploitation of public lands, but for very different reasons. While Muir championed the preservation of the nation's sublime landscapes, Gifford Pinchot's views rested on a philosophy of "wise use"—the view that expert management should ensure the optimal use of natural resources. The key words here are "management" and "use." Pinchot recognized that there would always be competing demands for natural resources, and thus supported the strategy of multiple use. From this "conservationist" perspective, the natural resource expert might manage parts of the public lands for their wilderness values (as Muir would demand) or, equally, for forestry, grazing, hunting, or water power. The guiding principle in this decision was ensuring the greatest good for the greatest number of people.

The great battle that catapulted the preservationist and conservationist movements into national prominence involved the Hetch Hetchy Valley in Yosemite National Park. From 1901 through 1913, there were repeated calls for damming the Tuolomne River in Hetch Hetchy Valley to increase San Francisco's water and electricity supply. From a conservationist perspective, there seemed a pretty good argument in favor of damming the river if one weighed the water needs of a city of 400,000 against the interests of those few who would benefit from Hetch Hetchy's preservation. Despite support of the dam by the President, Congress, and Pinchot, however, Muir led a more effective opposition campaign than anyone anticipated. Against the claims of dam supporters praising the beauty and potential recreational uses of a reservoir, Muir and grassroots supporters denounced as wasteful and sinful this "destruction" of a valley they claimed was more sublime than Yosemite Valley. In response, the pro-dam *San Francisco Chronicle* ridiculed Muir's supporters as "hoggish and mushy esthetes," setting the tone for the many similar battles that have followed. The preservationists lost and Hetch Hetchy was dammed, but through the process of a sustained political campaign preservationists gained many supporters and popularized the wilderness ethic.

Following World War II, the growth of America's middle class, and construction of the interstate highway system, America's public lands became both more familiar and cherished. While there had been only a handful of conservation groups at the time of the Hetch Hetchy dispute, by the early 1950s there were over 300. Thus when the battle of dams was rejoined, the results were different. In 1954, a dam was proposed at Echo Park that would threaten Dinosaur National Monument on the Colorado–Utah border. This time, the far larger preservation movement enjoyed greater support and created an unprecedented grassroots campaign against development. Mail to Congress was almost eighty-to-one against the dam. After five years, the dam proponents gave up.

The first great preservation victory behind them, environmental groups continued to organize and keep up their pressure on Congress. The 1960s saw passage of landmark laws such as the Wilderness Act of 1964, the Land and Water Conservation Act of 1965, the National Historic Preservation Act of 1966, and the National Wild and Scenic Rivers System in 1968. Totally unlike earlier laws that had encouraged disposal of the public lands, this new wave of legislation took the opposite approach of retention and preservation. Recent conversion of public lands into national monuments is only the latest example of this counter-trend.

In the 1970s, the nation turned its attention to the importance of preserving environmentally valuable lands and waters that are in *private* hands or part of the more general public domain. In 1973, Congress passed the Endangered Species Act, which both constrains those federal actions, such as the construction of dams and highways, that might jeopardize the continued existence of endangered species and restricts private land development that might kill or harm endangered species. This remains the strongest legal protection of biodiversity in the world. Then, in 1977, Congress amended the Clean Water Act to strengthen protections of privately held wetlands. Unlike prior federal laws that focused on the spectacular (e.g., national parks such as Yellowstone) and the special (e.g., wilderness areas), these laws recognized that even lands that appear to many humans to be relatively "ordinary" can provide valuable habitat for biodiversity and other important ecosystem services such as water purification and flood control.

Application of these laws has proven controversial, often pitting environmentalists against property rights advocates who argue that restrictions on the use of their property should be compensated. Nor has passage of these laws resolved the conflict between conservationists and preservationists. The decade-long debates over oil drilling in the Arctic National Wildlife Refuge and logging in private, old growth forests are proof of that.

Today our natural resource policies must continue to ford the raging confluence of distinct historical perspectives—the view of wilderness and nature as obstacles to human welfare and resources to be developed and managed for society's benefit, in one stream, and the role of wilderness and nature as sacred, essential to defining who we are as a people, and providing important ecosystem services, in the other. As Wallace Stegner succinctly described, our position is unique. "No other nation on Earth so swiftly wasted its birthright; no other, in time, made such an effort to save what was left."

B. Pollution

Ever since the rise of farming and settled populations, pollution has been a concern of human society. The classic method of managing waste was one of dilution. Population densities were low and the environment could generally assimilate the largely organic wastes. As city populations rose, however, the harms from pollution and its links to public health became clearer in the public's eye. Thus a London proclamation in 1306 threatened those responsible for air pollution from coal burning with "grievous ransoms." Forty years later, Londoners could be fined two shillings if they did not remove waste from outside their homes. It's fair to say, though, that even up to the turn of the 20th century, despite the construction of city sewers and early attempts at controlling air and water pollution, London still had "killer fogs" and Chicago's rivers still congealed from the run-off of its slaughterhouses. As a practical matter, pollution regulation simply didn't exist.

Instead, legal responses to pollution relied on the common law doctrines of trespass and nuisance. As described in Chapter 3, however, these legal remedies were retrospective, compensated only property losses, and required proof of proximate causation, often difficult to come by in pollution cases. Despite the obvious weaknesses of relying on the common law to protect the environment, there was very little national political concern over pollution through the first half of the 20th century. Following World War II, though, the nature of pollution began to change. In particular, the field of organic chemistry took off, with mass distribution and use of synthetic compounds such as plastics and many modern pesticides. Viewed as technological wonders (which these new compounds truly were), there was little understanding of their impacts on the environment or human health. While worth a chuckle when viewed in retrospect, there were serious proposals in the early 1960s to use (small) nuclear bombs to build canals. If a single event can be linked to triggering the erosion of this naive acceptance, it would be the publication and uproar that surrounded publication of Rachel Carson's book, *Silent Spring*, in 1962.

Known for her wonderful writings about the natural history of the ocean and seashore, Carson, a marine biologist with the U.S. Fish and Wildlife Service, was an unlikely pioneer of the environmental movement. Well aware that attacking a popular chemical product would be controversial, Carson spent four years of research prior to publication of *Silent Spring* carefully documenting the health and environmental effects of the pesticide DDT. The magazine, the *New Yorker,* published *Silent Spring* in a three-part series. Even prior to publication, the chemical industry mounted a high-profile attack on the book and its author, dismissing Carson as a nature-nut and unscientific. Ironically, the strength and hostility of the attacks on *Silent Spring* caught the interest of President Kennedy, who formed an advisory group to investigate the use and control of pesticides. This, in turn, spurred Congressional studies on pesticide regulation. Suffering from cancer at the time her book was published, Carson died in 1964, but the concerns aroused by *Silent Spring* continued to grow, spawning new advocacy-based organizations.

The group Scenic Hudson, for example, was formed in 1963 and, in an early grassroots victory, successfully opposed plans to develop Storm King Mountain in the Hudson Valley into the world's largest pumped-storage hydroelectric plant. The case, *Scenic Hudson Preservation Conference v. Federal Power Commission*,[1] marked the first time environmental groups had been granted standing, the ability to bring a lawsuit before a court. The Environmental Defense Fund, another grassroots organization, was founded in 1967 to ban use of the pesticide DDT in Long Island.

---

[1] 407 U.S. 926 (1972).

SCENIC HUDSON PRESERVATION CONFERENCE V. FEDERAL POWER COMMISSION

354 F.2d 608 (2d Cir.1965)

In March 1965, the Federal Power Commission granted a license to Consolidated Edison Company of New York, Inc. to construct a hydroelectric power plant on the west side of the Hudson River at Storm King Mountain in Cornwall, NY. Intended to provide additional electricity to New York City during peak use periods, the proposed project would have included a storage reservoir, a powerhouse, and transmission lines. Building the plant, however, threatened to remove part of the mountain near the river and flood an adjacent forest for the reservoir. Several local residents, as well as hikers' groups and conservation groups, opposed the project, fearing that it would destroy the natural beauty of the region and decimate the fish populations in the Hudson. These groups banded together to form the Scenic Hudson Preservation Conference and, along with several towns that would be impacted by the project, sued the Commission to stop the project and force consideration of alternative plans.

In a hearing before the Second Circuit, the court granted standing to Scenic Hudson and the towns. Noting that Section 10(a) of the Federal Power Act required all projects licensed by the Federal Power Commission be adapted to serve beneficial public uses, including "recreational purposes," the court found that the Federal Power Commission had not adequately studied alternatives or compiled a sufficient record to support its decision. Thus the court remanded the case, sending it back to the agency to conduct the license process properly. At the rehearing in 1971, the court held that the Federal Power commission had adequately considered the environmental and recreational impacts of the project.

The circuit court decision had three major consequences. First, despite winning its case in 1971, Consolidated Edison continued to face opposition to the Storm King project and, in 1979, ultimately abandoned plans to construct even a scaled-down plant. Second, the case provided a clear example of the benefit of forcing agencies to consider the environmental impacts of their decisions, inspiring passage of National Environmental Policy Act in 1969. Third, by granting standing to the local groups comprising Scenic Hudson and allowing them to sue on behalf of the public interest, the court opened the door for environmental groups to challenge agency decisions and laid the foundation for the development of citizen suits.

Over 20 million people participated in the first Earth Day in 1970, and pollution control was firmly set on the national political scene. Creation of the Environmental Protection Agency and enactment of the Clean Air Act in 1970 was closely followed by the Clean Water Act in 1972, as President Richard Nixon and presidential candidate Senator Edmund Muskie competed with one another for the newly important environmental vote. The Resource Conservation and Recovery Act followed in 1976 and Superfund in 1980. Events such as Love Canal and the nuclear accident at Three Mile Island ensured that the public interest in environmental issues remained high. Taken together, these laws and those that have followed are known as the era of "modern environmental law." In contrast to earlier regulation of pollution, all of these laws established uniform, tough, national standards.

The same era witnessed the birth of international environmental law. The UN-sponsored Stockholm Conference on the Human Environment in 1972 was the first gathering of the world's heads of state for environmental protection. Creating the United Nations Environment Program, the Stockholm Conference launched two-decade wave of international agreements, including the Convention on International Trade in Endangered Species (1972), the moratorium on whaling (1982), The Montreal Protocol on Ozone Depleting Substances (1987), and the Basel Convention on Transfrontier Movement of Hazardous Wastes (1989), to name just a few.

When looking back to 1970 from today's vantage, it is easy to point out flaws in these laws. Congress was consistently over-ambitious, setting goals that could not be met, such as clean water or air within a decade, and shifting pollution from one medium to another (e.g., burning solid waste to reduce landfill pressure but increasing air pollution). Nonetheless, the modern era of environmental law stands out as a great success. Despite a larger population and greatly increased levels of economic activity, most of our nation's air and water are far cleaner than four decades ago. Our rivers no longer burn and the mountains around Denver and Los Angeles are clearly visible to residents.

Environmental interest has grown and subsided over this period, as has opposition to environmental protection. Indeed, environmental law has undergone constant change since the 1970s. Growing partisanship over environmental issues slowed the pace of new federal legislation in the late 1990s and the first decade of the 20th century. The result has been legislative stagnation. Congress refused to ratify the Kyoto Protocol or pass domestic climate change legislation. When Barack Obama took his second oath of office in January 2013, almost two decades had passed since the last significant amendments to major federal environmental legislation—the 1990 Clean Air Act Amendments (which reduced emissions of sulfur dioxide contributing to acid rain), the 1996 Food Quality Protect Act (which strengthened the Federal Insecticide, Fungicide, and Rodenticide Act), and the 1996 Safe Drinking Water Act Amendments.

Opposition to environmental law has become more strident and partisan. In the 2012 presidential campaign, three of the major Republican candidates openly called for the abolition of the Environmental Protection Agency. Many Republican members of Congress, as well as some Democrats, have successfully campaigned on platforms opposed to environmental laws, criticizing them as "job-killing," too costly, or otherwise ill conceived. Environmental groups, meanwhile, are complaining that the administration has not moved fast enough. However the current political dynamic plays out, environmental law and policy will surely remain at the forefront of the public debate, an exciting, important, and complex field.

QUESTIONS AND DISCUSSION

1. Do you consider yourself an environmentalist? Do you have stronger views on environmental protection when thinking about pollution, threats to natural areas, or threats to endangered species? Why do you think most people hold different views about pollution and nature conservation?

2. John Muir, Gifford Pinchot, Aldo Leopold, and Rachel Carson have rightfully taken their place as recognized heroes of the environmental movement. A more modern list might include people like John Adams (co-founder of the Natural Resources Defense Council), Bill Reilly (former head of the World Wildlife Fund and EPA Administrator), Bill McKibben (author and founder of the group, 350.0rg), Jane Lubchenco (marine ecologist and former head of NOAA), or Ray Anderson (founder and chairman of Interface, a leading environmentally-conscious carpet producer), among others. Whom would you include in a list of today's environmental heroes and why?

3. The popular conception of wilderness has evolved throughout American history—from a threatening untamed force, to an abundant economic resource, to an inspiring spiritual resource, to a basic part of our American identity. Is the conception of wilderness still evolving? How would you describe the popular conception of wilderness today? How is this reflected in popular images and in the marketplace?

4.   In considering the recent debates over climate change, how would you characterize the environmentalist position? How would you describe the industry position? Which aspects of these positions do you support and why?

5.   If you were Administrator of the U.S. EPA today, what would be your highest priorities? Why?

Chapter 2

PERSPECTIVES ON
ENVIRONMENTAL LAW AND POLICY

I. Basic Themes of Environmental Law

In seeking to provide client counsel, all too often environmental lawyers look first to the law rather than to the problem itself. To be sure, the law creates the framework within which environmental problems are resolved. But one cannot intelligently apply the law without also understanding the forces that created the problem in the first place. Consider, for example, the seemingly different threats posed in the newspaper headlines described in the introduction to Chapter 1—climate change, protection of an endangered species' habitat, air pollution, and fracking. All of these stories share a similar trait, of course, since they directly relate to environmental protection. But the similarities run far deeper. While the actors, the location, and the nature of the concerns are quite different in the particulars, the *underlying* causes of the environmental problems may be understood as simple variants on common themes.

This section introduces the basic themes that run throughout environmental law and policy—the themes of scientific uncertainty, market failure, mismatched scale, cognitive biases, and nontraditional interests. It is no exaggeration to say that these resonate throughout the entire field of environmental law and policy, irrespective of the particular issue. Understanding their implications is a critical first step in understanding the field and resolving environmental conflicts.

A. Scientific Uncertainty

In many respects scientific uncertainty is *the* defining feature of environmental policy. Most environmental problems involve complex technical and economic issues. But policy makers rarely have anything approaching perfect knowledge when asked to make specific decisions. Certainty may come too late, if ever, to design optimal legal and policy responses.

In the context of climate change, for example, the detailed mechanisms of global warming are still only partly understood. Will increases in the earth's temperature lead to greater cloud formation, acting as a negative feedback to warming? Are measured temperature increases over the last century due to increased carbon in the atmosphere, the onset of an unrelated global warming trend, or a combination of the two? If atmospheric carbon dioxide concentrations continue to increase, what will the mean global temperature be in 20, 30, and 40 years, and what will this mean for sea level rise and local climates?

All of these questions bear directly on our decisions *today* to regulate emissions of greenhouse gases or introduce carbon taxes. The UN's Intergovernmental Panel on Climate Change has provided estimates based on the best judgment of over 2,000 scientists researching these issues from around the globe, but no one can claim these are correct. They are simply the best projections we have.

Similarly in the case of using pesticides near drinking water sources, experiments may show that exposing mice to very high levels of a pesticide causes cancer. But we typically have little baseline data to understand what happens to humans exposed to the pesticide at everyday levels, orders of magnitude lower than those that harmed the mice. And mice, of course, aren't people, so perhaps the effects observed in mice would not occur in larger mammals.

Troubling levels of uncertainty are present when conserving natural resources, as well. Perhaps developers have proposed setting aside an acre beside a new mall to provide habitat for an endangered salamander population otherwise threatened by the mall. Will an acre provide sufficient habitat for its survival? Is the main reason for the salamander population's collapse not loss of habitat but, rather, predation by cats? We do not know enough about the salamander's life history or recent population declines to be certain, yet such information is critical to designing effective policy responses to specific proposed actions such as a new mall.

Another source of uncertainty lies in the complex interrelations among causes of environmental harms. Rather than resulting from a single, identifiable action, many environmental harms are caused by cumulative, multiple actions. Addressing one cause may have little effect or, even worse, exacerbate another problem. Take the example of endangered salmon in the Pacific Northwest. Why are so many stocks collapsing? One can point to overfishing, damming of rivers, logging practices that lead to erosion and silt in the rivers, coastal pollution, and over-reliance on hatchery fish. To conserve and restore salmon populations, we must address most, if not all, of these causes, yet there is enormous debate over which particular action will be most effective. And solving one problem may cause another to appear somewhere else. Or consider acid rain. Did the emissions of a particular coal-fired plant in the Ohio Valley contribute to the acidification of a mountain lake in the Catskills?

Most likely yes, but good luck figuring out *how much* harm it contributed and, therefore, how much its emissions should be reduced.

In fact, uncertainties over the magnitude of environmental problems, their causes, and future impacts bedevil law and policy. What we would like to know as policy makers rarely approaches our actual knowledge. But if we do not understand well the current situation, then how can we predict the future impacts of our laws and policies? Does prudence dictate waiting until we have better information or taking early action in the face of potentially serious threats?

In the climate change debate, for example, some industry-sponsored trade groups have argued that scientific uncertainty counsels prudence. The "problem" of global warming has not been rigorously established, they argue, and our limited knowledge of atmospheric physics severely restricts our ability to predict future temperatures or climates. And even if global warming is happening, there are enormous unknowns over how much warming will occur and at what rate. If the threat of global warming turns out to have been an exaggerated threat, then actions taken today to reduce fossil fuel consumption will have been an overreaction. Spending money to reduce fossil fuel use, it follows, may cause more harm than good because of increased unemployment and diversion of resources away from other worthy causes. The best response is more research and development. After all, how can one craft an effective policy without clearly understanding the problem we're trying to solve?

The obvious response to such arguments is that waiting for more scientific certainty, if it ever comes, imposes costs of its own. In the face of a credible and significant threat, the opposing argument goes, we must act today so as to avoid the present and future harms (which may well be greater) imposed by delay. To employ a nautical metaphor, we should be bailing water out of our sinking ship as fast as possible, not standing on the deck studying the angle and rate of descent.

The exact same dynamic is at work in the examples of pesticides and endangered species. Delay while we study the toxicology of a pesticide may result in an increase in cancers that could have been prevented. Delay in the case of an endangered species may lead to greater understanding, but of a now-extinct species. Yet, as the voices of caution warn, overreaction imposes its own real costs in the form of higher prices and scarce public monies that could have been better spent elsewhere. In these and countless other examples, there are good reasons to wait and reduce the uncertainty, and good reasons to avoid potential future costs by acting now. Thus perhaps the first question of environmental law and policy is how to act in the face of uncertainty.

There are two basic strategies to address this intractable problem. The first is to develop better information. As we shall see later in the book, many environmental statutes require generation of considerable information to provide a surer basis on which to create policy. A second strategy is known as the *precautionary principle*. Influential in the field of international environmental law, in its simplest form the principle counsels caution in the face of significant but uncertain threats. It's hard to argue against such an obvious rule of conduct but people differ significantly over how the principle should be applied in practice. In its most extreme form, the principle would forbid any activity that potentially could produce significant harms, regardless of the likelihood that these harms may occur. The problem, though, is that such a view counsels inaction in the face of uncertainty, no matter what the cost. The strategy, moreover, is paralyzing in the context of risk-risk choices, where every alternative poses significant risks and one must choose among them. Such risk-risk choices arise commonly in the environmental field, such as deciding whether to build a nuclear power plant or a coal-fired plant. Each option poses environmental concerns and potential harms.

In the international context, the precautionary principle generally has been viewed as shifting the burden of proof from those who would challenge an offending activity to those who wish to commence or continue the activity. This shift in burden could shorten the time period between when a threat to the environment is recognized and a legal response is developed. In the climate change context, for example, the burden would fall on oil companies to establish that global warming is not a serious and credible threat before drilling new wells. In the salamander example, the developer would shoulder the burden of proving that the loss of habitat will not threaten the salamander's survival before clearing land for a mall. Chemical manufacturers would bear the responsibility of justifying that the use of particular pesticides would pose no significant health risks before allowing the pesticides to be sold and used.

This shift in burden changes the tenor and nature of the debate over *how well understood* the problem must be before taking action. But it does not shed light on an equally important question—*how serious* the problem must be before taking action (i.e., which risks are worth addressing), much less the appropriate action to take. As we shall see below, these are fundamentally political, not scientific, questions, and they pose additional levels of uncertainty.

B. Market Failures

Misaligned incentives underlie most environmental conflicts. While protecting the environment often provides a net benefit to society, the economic interests of individual parties involved often can encourage harmful activities. Thus a basic challenge for environmental policy lies in understanding the reward structures of the parties and then changing incentives so that environmental protection reinforces rather than collides with the parties' self-interest. In the following examples, consider how costs and benefits are allocated.

- In the case of climate change, a company may choose voluntarily to reduce its greenhouse gas emissions, but it may end up raising its operating costs and losing market share if its competitors do not reduce their emissions as well.

- A neighbor of a factory may be having constant sore throats because of particulate emissions, but the bother isn't worth the cost of bringing a lawsuit.

- All of her neighbors have sore throats, too, but they can't seem to come together to negotiate with or sue the factory.

On its face, one might think that the market would automatically promote environmental protection. The most basic principle of economics, after all, is supply and demand. As the supply of a valuable good becomes scarce, its price rises. Since clean air and water are clearly valuable, one would expect that as they become scarcer their price should also rise, making it more expensive to pollute. Yet this clearly does not happen in real life. The market has somehow failed, as it does when the company fails to reduce its greenhouse gas emissions and the factory's neighbors can't agree to sue the factory. To correct these market failures and craft an effective legal response, we first need to understand the distortions at play.

1. Public Goods

Try to buy some clean air. Sure, you can buy real estate in the wilds of Alaska where the air is clean, but you own the land there, not the air. In fact, your neighbor can breathe it right after it blows through. It turns out that many environmental amenities, such as clean air and scenic vistas, are called *public goods*. Their benefits can be shared by everyone, but owned by no one. No one owns the air. No one can sell it or prevent others from using it.

The same is true for *ecosystem services*. Largely taken for granted, healthy ecosystems provide a variety of critical services.

Created by the interactions of living organisms with their environment, these ecosystem services provide both the conditions and processes that sustain human life—purifying air and water, detoxifying and decomposing waste, renewing soil fertility, regulating climate, mitigating droughts and floods, controlling pests, and pollinating plants. Not surprisingly, recent research has demonstrated the extremely high costs to replace many of these services if they were to fail. Looking at just one ecosystem service that soil provides, the provision of nitrogen to plants, serves as an example. Nitrogen is supplied to plants through both nitrogen-fixing organisms and recycling of nutrients in the soil. If nitrogen were provided by commercial fertilizer rather than natural processes, the lowest cost estimate for crops in the U.S. would be $45 billion; the figure for all land plants would be $320 billion.

The value of $320 billion is estimated by calculating replacement costs—what we'd have to pay to replace the ecosystem service of nitrogen fixing by other means. But what are these natural goods and services *really* worth? Perhaps surprisingly, in the eyes of the market they are not worth anything. We have no shortage of markets for ecosystem goods (such as clean water and apples), but the services underpinning these goods (such as water purification and pollination) are free. Make no mistake, these environmental amenities are valuable—just ask yourself how much it's worth to you to breathe unpolluted air—but they have no *market value*. There is no market to exchange public goods such as ecosystem services and, as a result, they have no price. This explains the riddle of why pollution does not become expensive as clean air is "used up." Because there's no market for clean air or climate stability, there are no direct price mechanisms to signal the scarcity or degradation of these public goods until they fail. Hence, despite their obvious importance to our well being, ecosystem services largely have been ignored in environmental law and policy. Partly as a result, ecosystems are degraded.

2.   The Tragedy of the Commons

Imagine you are a shepherd who grazes twenty sheep on a village common. Along with your pan pipes and bag lunch, you herd your flock to the common every day. So long as the number of sheep on the common remains small, the grass remains plentiful and the sheep contentedly munch away. Assume, though, that shepherds from over the mountain have heard of the wonderful grass in the common and bring their flocks. With each hour these sheep graze, there is less grass available for future grazing. In fact, you soon realize that this increased level of grazing will soon nibble the grass down to the roots, with the result of not enough forage in the future for anyone's flock, including your own. Yet you and the other shepherds will likely continue to allow your sheep to overgraze. Why?

The answer lies in the economic incentives. The more the sheep graze the fatter and more valuable they will be when they come to market. You could stop your flock's grazing, of course, to try and preserve the pasture for other days; but there is no guarantee your fellow shepherds will be similarly conscientious. In that case, you're a chump, sacrificing your own interests for no benefit. As a result, you may well encourage your sheep to graze *as much as possible*, and your neighbors will do the same. "Might as well get the grass in my sheep's tummies before it disappears in others'," you think. The result is individually rational in the short term—if the resource will be depleted, you might as well ensure you get your fair share—but collectively disastrous in the long term. It would be far better for each shepherd to restrain her flock's grazing, but seeking to maximize immediate economic gain ensures long term economic— and environmental—collapse.

This same phenomenon, known as *the tragedy of the commons*, can be identified in many open access resources, as farmers race to pump water from a shared underground aquifer, fishing boats with ever larger nets chase fewer and fewer fish, and wildcat drillers race to pump out oil as fast as they can. In each case, individually rational behavior is collectively deficient. Individuals' personal incentives work *against* the best long-term solution.

3. Collective Action and Free Riders

So what is to be done? Perhaps you could negotiate with all the shepherds and collectively agree to graze less. This may work when there are a handful of shepherds who all come from the same village. But it becomes increasingly difficult to reach agreement as the number of shepherds increases (and more difficult still if they come from different places without shared cultural norms and informal means of enforcement). This obstacle is known as a *collective action problem* and is due to the increased transaction costs in negotiating solutions as the number of parties increases. At a certain point, it's simply too expensive and difficult to reach consensus agreement. To see this in action, try to decide on which movie to see or settle a restaurant check with more than four friends.

Perhaps, as a last resort, in frustration at the inability to agree on a common solution, some of you decide to stop grazing your flock so that the grass on the common can grow back. Noble intent, no doubt, but there is a risk that other shepherds will take advantage of your generosity and keep their sheep on the common. More food for their flocks, they may smirk. These shepherds benefiting from your sacrifice are known as *free riders*. A similar phenomenon might occur even if all the shepherds agreed to graze less. New shepherds might come in and start grazing all the time, free-riding off of your sacrifice. Thus any solution to commons problems must overcome both the high transaction costs in reaching agreement among many parties (collective action) and counterproductive behavior by parties outside the agreement (free riders).

4.   Externalities

Assume you have sold your sheep, moved on from the now trampled and scraggly common, and own a chemical factory. When you balance your firm's financial books, you notice something odd. In figuring out your bottom line, you subtract your costs to operate (such as labor, materials, utilities, etc.) from the revenue you earn from selling your chemicals. But the pollution from your smokestacks does not reduce your bottom line. Make no mistake; your factory *is* causing real costs in the form of acid rain, smog, and reduced air visibility. But, as described above, because clean air is a public good you do not have to pay as you "use up" the clean air. It acts as a sink for your pollution at no cost. As a result, in seeking to maximize short-term economic gain, you do not consider the cost of your pollution. You can "overuse" the clean air and continue polluting. The costs from damage to forests, increased respiratory ailments, and reduced pleasure in clear vistas from your pollution are very real, but they are *external* to the costs you currently pay to operate. These costs are borne by the public and known as *externalities*.

If, on the other hand, your factory has to pay for the external harm it causes, then it will pay for its pollution and likely reduce it. The process for forcing the factory to recognize environmental and social costs is known as *internalizing externalities* and reflects a basic lesson of economics—when we have to pay for something, we use less of it than if it is free. By internalizing externalities, we correct the market failure by charging for environmental harms and providing more accurate price signals to buyers.

This works both ways. Assume that you own a wetland beside your factory. The wetland provides a nursery for young fish to spend their first few months in relative safety before entering the adjacent river. The outdoors enthusiasts who fish along the river and the sporting good stores who sell fishing tackle all benefit from the services your wetland provides, but they don't pay you for them. While your factory's pollution generates *negative externalities*, your wetland provides *positive externalities*. Just as the fact that you don't have to pay for the costs caused by your pollution removes any incentive to reduce pollution so, too, does the fact that you are not paid for the benefits provided by the wetland remove any incentive to conserve rather than pave it over for a parking lot.

If all negative externalities were internalized—if all costs imposed on the environment were borne by the polluting party— then environmentally harmful products and processes would be relatively more costly and the market would reinforce environmental protection. Equally, if positive externalities were internalized—if benefits generated by ecosystem services such as flood control and water purification were paid for by the recipients—then habitat conservation would be truly valued in the marketplace. A central problem, of course, is "getting the prices right." Even if we had the authority to charge a factory for the damage its pollution caused, how much would that be? As with clean air, there are no markets for environmental harms, either; thus their costs must be estimated. But even rough estimates would be an improvement over the current situation where negative externalities are costless to polluters and positive externalities are not rewarded. One of the key goals of environmental law is thus to bring environmental externalities into the marketplace; we discuss policy instruments to internalize externalities later in the chapter.

C.   *Mismatched Scales*

Natural boundaries rarely track political boundaries. A map of the western United States shows states and counties with straight lines and right angles. Map the region's watersheds, ecosystems, or forests, however, and nary a straight line will appear. Ecological concerns were, not surprisingly, far from the politicians' and surveyors' minds when these political jurisdictions were created, but the mismatch of natural and political scales poses difficult challenges for environmental management. Air pollution, water pollution, and wildlife certainly pay no heed to state (or national) borders, with the result that often the generator of the pollution is politically distinct from those harmed.

Acid rain was hard to control in the 1970s and 1980s because of political jurisdictions. The costs of reducing emissions downwind were borne by those who received no benefit and, similarly, those benefiting from reduced pollution upwind did not have to pay for it. Midwestern power plants were far removed from the polluted lakes and forests of the Northeast and Canada. New York, Vermont, and certainly Canadian voters couldn't vote in Ohio or Pennsylvania. Thus those with the greatest cause for concern did not live in the areas where their concerns could be most effectively expressed. Similar problems of scale are evident in wildlife protection, where draining or filling prairie potholes in the Great Plains, for example,

may benefit the local farmers but imperils migratory birds from
Mexico to Canada. Pumping carbon dioxide in the air may not seem
significant to a company operating a coal-fired power plant in
Montana, but to an islander on a low-lying Pacific atoll the
prospects of sea-level rise are a good deal more unsettling.

As a result of these *geographical spillovers* across jurisdictions,
transboundary environmental problems often pose the challenges of
collective action (the high transaction costs to bring differing
parties together), equity (ensuring that the parties enjoying the
benefits of environmental protection also bear a share of the costs),
and enforcement (monitoring compliance at a distance from the
source of authority). This is as true with national laws as with
international.

Mismatched political and natural boundaries also pose
challenges of management authority. This is often expressed as a
problem of federalism. Who should control pollution and natural
resource management: local or national authorities? Locals are
closer to the problems, often understand them better, and have to
live with the consequences of the environmental policy. At the same
time, if the problem is one of transboundary pollution, the locals
don't live with the consequences of their pollution. Those
downstream do.

With natural resources, locals may well feel an entitlement.
Their parents and grandparents may have grazed their herds on
the same government land that some bureaucrat in Washington
now wants to fence off from cattle. But public lands belong to the
nation as a whole, so shouldn't they be managed at the national
level? If public lands are being degraded by locals' over-use, then
the federal government must restrict use, the argument goes,
regardless of local tradition or expectations. This conflict has no
simple solution, and has led in the past to violent intimidation of
federal officials and broad political movements such as "the
sagebrush rebellion" in the 1970s and the "wise use" movement
today.

In another variant of this problem, political and economic
scales can be mismatched as markets encompass multiple political
jurisdictions. Imagine, for example, that in order to attract business
Arkansas decides to lower its standards for air pollution. All else
being equal, lower compliance costs for environmental regulations
should translate into corporate higher profits. This not only poses a
transboundary concern for the border states of Louisiana and
Alabama; it also pressures states with similar industries, such as
North Carolina, to lower their standards, in order to prevent
industry relocation. The dynamic of local jurisdictions competing

with one another by lowering environmental standards to attract industry is known as the *race-to-the-bottom*.

Realize, as well, that concerns over the race-to-the-bottom can not only pressure jurisdictions to lower their standards but can also *chill* efforts in states seeking to strengthen standards (because industry will threaten to relocate if their costs of regulatory compliance are increased). If this is the case, then nationwide standards seem necessary. The same phenomenon can occur in the international context as well, as nations compete with one another for business investment.

The fact that companies choose their locations based in part on costs of doing business is indisputable. There is a strong debate, however, over the extent to which a race-to-the-bottom really occurs in the environmental field. For one thing, states can compete on many grounds, perhaps lowering tax rates or workplace safety requirements to attract business. Hence it's not a given that they would reduce environmental standards to attract industry. Indeed, because environmental quality is an important amenity, there's an argument that local jurisdictions are more likely to engage in a "race-to-the-top," competing for industry by offering *higher* environmental quality. The data on international industry relocation suggest that stringency of environmental regulation is less important to companies than proximity to markets, labor costs, raw material costs, political stability, etc. And this makes sense, since environmental costs are usually a small percentage of total business costs. In those industries where environmental costs are relatively high, though, such as in the chemicals sector, there is evidence that companies have relocated with environmental compliance costs in mind. Perhaps more important, though, is the fact that many regulators believe the race-to-the-bottom occurs, whether that is borne out in fact or not, and act accordingly.

Problems of scale occur in time as well as in space. Decisions must be made today that may prevent harm ten or twenty years from now or, indeed, in generations not yet born. Ozone depletion and climate change are two examples. CFCs (which are the major cause of stratospheric ozone depletion) and greenhouse gases we emit today will cause impacts over the next 50 years or longer. The same distributional asymmetry is at play here as with physical scale. The costs of refraining from an action fall on us today, while the benefits are enjoyed (most likely by others) far later. Yet these future beneficiaries can't express their preferences in today's voting booth or courtroom. Indeed, the temporal scale of many environmental problems makes it difficult even to hold current elected officials accountable, since many of the harms from their actions will not be felt until they have left office. Supporting overfishing today may keep a local politician in office, for example, while the stark impacts may not be evident until years later when the stock has collapsed. As a result, many environmental advocates claim to be acting on behalf of the interests of future generations, but deciding what the proper sacrifice today should be for future benefits that may or may not be appreciated is easier said than done.

D.   Cognitive Biases

To complicate matters further, people do not think about environmental options in the way that a classical economist would predict a "rational" person would. Everyone suffers from cognitive limitations and biases that affect our views about the environment and environmental policy. In some cases, these limitations and biases undercut efforts to reduce pollution and to protect the environment. In other cases, these limitations and biases lead us to overestimate environmental risks and to demand policy measures that may not be "rationally" justified.

Part of the problem is that people just are not very good with numbers. Start with probabilities. Assume, incorrectly, that the federal government requires all new chemicals to be tested to see if the chemicals are carcinogenic (i.e., cause cancer). And assume, again incorrectly, that the federal government has developed a new toxicity test that is highly reliable in testing for carcinogens: if a chemical is carcinogenic, the test will be positive 95 percent of the time, while if a chemical is not a carcinogen, the test will be negative 95 percent of the time. If a chemical tests positive, what is the probability that it really is a carcinogen? Most people would estimate that the odds are very high (probably 95%) and urge that the chemical be regulated immediately. But the probability depends on the distribution of carcinogens within the universe of all chemicals. If there are 10,500 chemicals in total, and only 500 are carcinogens, for example, a chemical that tests positive has less than a 50–50 chance of being a carcinogen. If only 100 of the chemicals are carcinogens, a chemical that tests positive has about a 15 percent chance of causing cancer.[1]

People also are not very good at evaluating environmental tradeoffs, particularly when the tradeoffs require them to compare costs and benefits across time. For example, economists have

---

[1] For those readers who need numbers to be convinced of this point, if 500 chemicals are carcinogens, 500 of the non-carcinogens (5% of 10,000) would test positive, while only 475 of the carcinogens (95% of 500) would test positive, so a chemical that tests positive is more than likely not a carcinogen. If only 100 chemicals are carcinogens, 520 of the non-carcinogens (5% of 10,400) would test positive, while 95 of the carcinogens (95% of 100) would test positive, so the odds that a chemical that tests positive is a carcinogen is 95/615 or 15.4%.

studied how much more people will voluntarily pay to buy energy-efficient appliances that will reduce the buyers' future energy bills. The surprising answer for most consumers is "not much," even when the future savings are significant. Economists have found that the average consumer chooses cheaper, energy-guzzling appliances even when the future "returns" on an energy-efficient appliance are equivalent to a 25% to 75% return on a bank account! Even when buyers receive information about the energy savings, they often have a hard time figuring out the exact amount of money they will save in the future and then comparing those savings with the difference in purchase prices. Buyers therefore focus on the one piece of information that is certain and obvious—the energy-efficient appliance cost more today than the energy guzzler.

The problems go far beyond being bad at numbers. Consider how people evaluate potential risks from pollutants and toxic substances. People may reach very different conclusions based solely on how information is conveyed. Psychologists, for example, have found that people are less likely to be concerned if told that a substance is 95 percent likely to be safe than if told that the same substance poses a five percent risk of causing cancer. In psychology terminology, this is known as a *framing effect*. People also find it difficult to evaluate very small risks, so that a one-in-a-thousand risk sounds bigger to most people than a purely numerical analysis would suggest. Familiarity plays a role in risk perception, as well, with people underestimating the risk of familiar events (e.g., driving or breathing polluted air). More importantly, we tend to overestimate unfamiliar risks about which we have recently read or heard negative news. Psychologists attribute this to an *availability heuristic* in which the availability of examples makes people believe that something is more likely to occur. Where stories about a potential risk get told and retold, and perhaps even highlighted by the press or others, an *availability cascade* may lead to mass public concerns about relatively small risks. (News stories in the past, for example, have caused widespread concern over the risk of an asteroid hitting the earth or flesh-eating diseases). Finally, once people decide that something is risky, an *anchoring effect* makes it very difficult to change their minds, even by showing them contrary evidence. These psychological heuristics can lead the public to demand that even insignificant risks be regulated.

Other cognitive biases, however, can undermine efforts to regulate significant environmental risks. People, for example, tend to be overly optimistic about their ability to overcome environmental risks that they voluntarily confront. Fishermen rarely believe that overfishing will lead to the collapse of their fisheries; most sun lovers are convinced that they can bake for days under the sun without contracting skin cancer. As a result of what psychologists call *self-enhancing attributional biases*, moreover, few people believe that they are to blame for environmental problems. It's always the other guy's fault. Car drivers believe that factories are to blame for smog; farmers believe that they are better at conserving water than city residents. When it comes time to decide how to solve an environmental problem, people similarly believe that others should bear most, if not all, of the burden of the solution. Developing nations believe that the industrialized world should solve the problem of global climate change, while the United States argues that developing nations also must do their "fair share." To use the technical terminology, people (and nations) suffer from *egocentric interpretations of fairness*.

E. Protected Interests

As should be evident by the examples provided above, environmental protection inevitably causes a clash of competing interests. In addition, the protected interests frequently do not have a voice of their own. We already have discussed the importance of future generation' interests in the preceding section on mismatched scales. If we could make use of a time-travel machine and bring them back from the future, they surely would have strong views on how decisions taken by us today will impact their health and welfare. Absent such science fiction technology, though, their theoretical interests can only be voiced by those in the present. This is sometimes described as a matter of "intergenerational equity."

Endangered species litigation is brought technically on behalf of an affected person (perhaps a researcher of the species) but in reality is brought on behalf of the species as well. It goes without saying, of course, that these entities cannot bring a lawsuit on their own behalf, much less appear in court. (Well, perhaps one could carry a bird or a fish into court for dramatic effect, but what are you supposed to do with future generations?) Proxies therefore must bring the litigation on their behalf. It is no surprise then that the most significant standing cases over the last four decades have been environmental cases. The injury-in-fact requirement for standing traditionally has required physical or economic injury to the plaintiff. Should it be extended to include recreational or aesthetic injuries as well? *Sierra Club v. Morton*[2] and subsequent cases say it should. In a classic law review article, Professor Chris Stone provocatively asked, "should trees have standing?"[3] In environmental law, in some contexts they really can.

---

[2] 405 U.S. 727 (1972).

[3] Christopher D. Stone, Should Trees Have Standing: Toward Legal Rights for Natural Objects (1974).

This innovative inclusion of interests, however, poses its own challenges. To paraphrase the Lorax of Dr. Seuss, who should speak for the trees? And how should nonhuman interests be balanced against those of flesh and blood people? The Spotted Owl conflict in the Pacific Northwest often pitted environmentalists against logging communities, with loggers complaining that environmental groups cared more about animals than people. While "win-win" compromises can often be found, so long as environmental protection extends beyond peoples' immediate health and wallets, such conflicts will be inevitable.

Thus to someone new to environmental law, it may seem odd that our wildlife conservation laws protect endangered species that most people would squash if found crawling in their kitchens. It may give pause to realize that our natural resource management laws protect parks and refuges that no one you know will ever visit. The simplest explanation of these observations is that there clearly is something at stake in the environmental field beyond classic protection of human health and economic interests. The underlying perspectives that drive environmental attitudes are explored in the next section.

II. Four Analytical Frameworks

Imagine that the government is trying to decide whether to permit a new pesticide to be manufactured and sold in the United States. What criteria would you use to make this decision? Should the United States ever permit the sale of a pesticide that would injure human health? What if the pesticide would not injure humans but might harm wild animals that come into contact with the substance? Would you consider the benefits of the pesticide? Should it matter, for example, if the pesticide would increase crop yields? Reduce the costs of food? Can such benefits "outweigh" harm to humans or the environment? Assuming that the pesticide could harm human health, does the distribution of the harm among individuals matter? Should harm to farmworkers, many of whom are poor and Hispanic, be viewed differently than harm to consumers? If you decided to ban use of the pesticide within the United States, would you allow its manufacture here and sale to developing countries where use is legal?

In evaluating environmental decisions such as these, most policymakers and analysts use one of four general frameworks. Some policymakers and analysts focus on ethics (*environmental rights*). Some try to ensure that both environmental protection and development interests are meaningfully addressed (*sustainable development*). Others take an empirical approach and balance the risks posed by environmental problems against the cost of controlling them (*utilitarianism*). Yet others look to see whether the costs and other burdens of environmental harms and solutions are equitably distributed among individuals and groups throughout our society and future interests (*environmental justice*).

In the pesticide hypothetical, the "ethicist" would want to know whether the pesticide would injure humans, in violation of their "right" to a healthy environment, and perhaps whether it would harm other animals and plants. The "sustainable development" advocate would seek to ensure that the policy makers consider the impacts of their decisions both for environmental protection and local communities. The "utilitarian" would want to know more specifically whether and how the pesticide would benefit society and then weigh those benefits against the health and environmental costs. Those individuals concerned with distributional equity would be interested in whether the harms from the pesticide use would fall primarily on minorities or less powerful members of society, such as farmworkers and future generations.

These frameworks do not exhaust all of the potential modes for analyzing environmental issues, nor are they necessarily mutually exclusive. Some environmental writers, for example, have suggested that the law should follow a "pragmatic" philosophy that borrows and balances among all of these frameworks. Yet other writers have urged an "ecological economics" approach that evaluates the long-term sustainability of activities such as pesticide use or irrigated agriculture, as well as the sustainability of the overall scale of the economy. Virtually every argument found in contemporary environmental debates, however, builds off of one or more of the basic frameworks outlined above.

Whenever you hear or read an environmental argument, you should ask yourself which policy framework is being used. Disagreements over environmental policy often stem more from disagreements over the correct framework than from disagreements over the facts or how the facts should be applied under a framework. At their base, many environmental conflicts are driven by conflicting values. For example, in deciding whether to reduce the airborne emissions of a pollutant, environmental groups may stress the right of people to a healthy environment, while businesses may emphasize the high economic costs of the emission-control equipment and the right to development. To complicate matters, most policymakers and analysts do not say what framework they are using, let alone explain why they are using one framework rather than another. Instead, the policymakers and analysts simply assume that everyone agrees with their framework. As a result, they fail to confront the real source of their disagreement with others. Even worse, some policymakers and analysts use multiple and even inconsistent frameworks, using one and then another as best befits their goals. In reading the sections that follow, you will gain a clearer understanding of why certain policy disputes are so difficult to resolve—the parties are basing their positions on fundamentally different assumptions.

A.   Environmental Rights

Environmental law often reflects a strong, if not well elaborated, view that humans have a right to environmental protection. Even before the first Earth Day, Senator Gaylord Nelson of Wisconsin proposed an amendment to the United States Constitution in 1968 that would have recognized an "inalienable right to a decent environment" and required both the federal and state governments to "guarantee" that right. Nelson's proposal and numerous other efforts to add an environmental right to the United States Constitution have failed. Yet both international law and the constitutions of a handful of states acknowledge rights to various environmental amenities. At the international level, the 1972 Stockholm Declaration of the United Nations Conference on the Human Environment states the "common conviction" that people have a "fundamental right to freedom, equality, and adequate conditions of life, in an environment of a quality that permits a life of dignity and wellbeing," as well as a "solemn responsibility to protect and improve the environment for present and future generations."[4] At the state level, the Hawaiian constitution proclaims that every person has the "right to a clean and healthful environment."[5] The constitutions of Massachusetts, Montana, and Pennsylvania set out similar rights.

Both judicial opinions and statutes often speak in the language of rights. The Ninth Circuit has written that is "difficult to conceive of a more absolute and enduring concern than the preservation and, increasingly, the restoration of a decent and livable environment. Human life, itself a fundamental right, will vanish if we continue our heedless exploitation of this planet's natural resources."[6] The environmental advocates who pushed for new federal environmental legislation in the late 1960s and 1970s often unabashedly compared environmental protection to civil rights and the constitutional proscription of cruel and unusual punishment. The idea of environmental rights proved very powerful and helped encourage Congress to aggressively address environmental problems.

---

[4] Report of the United Nations Conference on the Human Environment, U.N. Doc. A/CONF. 48/14/rev. 1, U.N. Pub. No. E.73.IIA14, at 4, Principle 1 (1974).

[5] Haw. Const. art. XI, § 9.

[6] *Stop H–3 Ass'n v. Dole*, 870 F.2d 1419, 1430 (9th Cir.1989).

The concept of environmental rights tends to push policy toward absolute positions. If the population has a right to a healthy environment, for example, the cost of eliminating health risks would seem irrelevant. Because environmental rights arguments drove passage of many of the major federal environmental statutes, these laws often appear to call for absolute protection of human health without consideration of costs. The Clean Air Act, for example, mandates ambient air quality standards that are "requisite to protect the human health," apparently irrespective of cost.[7] The original goal of the Clean Water Act was to eliminate the discharge of all pollutants into the nation's waterways by 1985.[8]

Although environmental-rights arguments have encouraged the passage of environmental statutes that often seem to call for absolute protections, reality has tempered what the government has been willing to do in practice. Consider, for example, the proposition that every person has a right to be free from air pollution that could harm his or her health. Although this might sound reasonable, even small levels of exposure to most major air pollutants will injure a small population of sensitive individuals. Only a zero pollution standard would ensure everyone a safe environment. Because that could seriously undermine the economy, the federal EPA establishes ambient air quality standards that protect most, but not all people. Similarly, although the Clean Water Act talked of eliminating all pollutants by 1985, the nation has come nowhere close to meeting this goal. As explained in Chapter 6, most facilities that discharge effluent into the nations' waterways need reduce their discharges only to the degree technologically feasible, and some pollution sources such as farms enjoy broad exemptions from the Act.

The rights discussed so far are *anthropocentric*. They address the rights of current and future generations of humans to a healthy and livable environment, however that might be defined. Some philosophers and ethicists have suggested that other living organisms, and perhaps nature more generally, enjoy independent rights. *Biocentric* rights concern the rights of plants and animals other than humans. In passing the Endangered Species Act, Congress took a primarily anthropocentric view of the importance of protecting plants and animals. According to Congress, endangered and threatened species often "are of esthetic, ecological, educational, historical, recreational, and scientific value to the Nation and its people."[9] To advance these human interests, the Endangered Species Act protects imperiled species; individual

---

[7] 42 U.S.C. § 7409(b)(1).

[8] 33 U.S.C. § 1251(1)(a).

[9] 16 U.S.C. § 1531(a)(3).

members of a species are protected only when necessary to preserve the species. But many environmentalists argue that species, and individual animals and plants, have a right to preservation even if the animals and plants are of no practical importance whatsoever to humans. The influential wildlife ecologist, Aldo Leopold, for example, believed that humans are not separate from the other animals and plants, but part of a community with them. As part of this community, humans should respect a "land ethic" based on the notion that a "thing is right when it tends to preserve the integrity, stability, and beauty of the biotic community. It is wrong when it tends otherwise."

Taking an even broader *ecocentric* perspective, some environmentalists argue that nature as a whole has a right to protection. Under this view, strip mining of a mountainside raises much the same concerns as clear cutting a forest or extirpating the last known population of an endangered animal species. In all these cases, humans are interfering unethically with natural processes and creations.

To other people, discussion of biocentric and ecocentric rights is mere silliness. In their view, humans are different from most other animals (and certainly from plants and rocks). Humans are intelligent, sentient creatures. Because animals, plants, and rocks cannot talk, moreover, their interests and preferences remain unknown. In the view of such critics, people who assert that biota and the rest of the physical world have "rights" are merely expressing their own policy preferences for conservation—giving their own preferences an extra push by claiming that they are protecting the moral rights of entities that cannot communicate. Critics also question why, given the constant change in the world through extinction and speciation, the existing geological configuration and assortment of species have any special claim to preservation. Finally, critics observe that people do not think or act as if most animals, plants, or rocks have broad rights to existence and preservation. While most people would oppose cruelty to animals, few would oppose fishing a non-threatened stock of fish, killing a rabid animal, exterminating household "pests," or weeding the garden.

Rights arguments, moreover, do not always favor greater environmental protection. While environmental proponents argue that regulation is needed to protect people's right to a healthy and livable environment or to protect biocentric or ecocentric rights, landowners often assert that regulations of their land use intrude on their property "rights." Businesses, unions, and other economic interests argue that proposed regulations will interfere with "rights" of employment or the "rights" of a local community to determine for itself how to use local resources and determine its own future. Some of these "rights" have taken on international or constitutional dimensions. After announcing the fundamental environmental right quoted earlier in this section, the Stockholm Declaration of the United Nations Conference on the Human Environment also affirms the "sovereign right" of all nations to "exploit their own resources pursuant to their own environmental policies."[10] As discussed in Chapter 3, environmental regulations that conflict with existing property rights might rise to the level of unconstitutional takings. In whatever context the rights are raised, legislators, judges, and other policymakers must decide how to balance the varied rights that are asserted.

B.   *Sustainable Development*

Economic development has long been a defining goal of governments. Economic expansion has been considered fundamental to ending poverty in the developing world and raising standards of living worldwide. For decades, international institutions, foreign aid programs from developed countries, and non-profit organizations have expended tremendous resources to develop the energy, transportation, education, and institutional infrastructure necessary to fuel economic growth in the developing world. At the same time, most developed countries have sought to maximize economic growth within their own borders. And why not? Ever-expanding global and national economies suggest more wealth to go around, and ideally, ever higher standards of living for everyone, from the very poor to the very rich.

As global warming, loss of biodiversity, crashing fisheries, ozone depletion, and other recent environmental crises make clear, however, the current pace and manner of economic expansion may be incompatible with environmental protection.

The development goal cannot, however, be abandoned. Poverty still must be reduced and standards of living raised throughout the developing world, as well as in the poorest sections of industrialized nations. For both political and equity concerns, development cannot simply be subordinated to environmental protection. Instead, development and environmental protection must be integrated, and this process of integration lies at the core of the concept of *sustainable development*.

The principle of sustainable development provided the core message for the 1992 Earth Summit in Rio de Janeiro (the largest international governmental meeting ever held). Sustainable

---

[10] Report of the United Nations Conference on the Human Environment, supra note 4, at Principle 21.

development was defined as "development that meets the needs of the present without compromising the ability of future generations to meet their own needs." Sustainable development provides an important overarching theme for three reasons.

First, in historical terms, sustainable development tied together two disparate fields—development and environmental protection. Prior to the 1990s, those working in the development world saw their goal primarily as poverty alleviation and those in the environmental field as environmental protection, with little overlap between the two. As a result, development projects often had unnecessarily destructive environmental impacts and environmental protection efforts too often took little heed of local economic impacts. Creating a park in a developing country might be viewed as a conservation success, for example, despite the potentially adverse economic consequences for the local community. Indira Gandhi is said to have remarked that poverty is the greatest polluter. By linking environmental protection and poverty alleviation to economic development, sustainable development forged the key insight that development and environmental protection efforts must be mutually reinforcing.

Second, sustainable development contradicts the common assumption that growth is good. Importantly, "growth" is not the same thing as "development." In order to create a sustainable economy—one that provides goods and services to ensure a positive quality of life into the future—the model cannot be one of growth, for the simple reason that no natural system can accommodate indefinite growth—trees don't climb to the sky. Our natural systems cannot forever continue to assimilate the impacts of growth. Climate change provides a case in point. Thus, central to the concept of sustainable development is the importance of limits— that we must develop within the constraints of natural systems. Hence to many environmental policy experts, the greatest challenge posed by sustainable development is that of re-orienting our economies so they develop (providing greater value and standards of living) while remaining within physical limits in terms of resource consumption and pollution.

Third, sustainable development focuses both on *intragenerational equity* (allowing members of the present generation to meet their needs) and on *intergenerational equity* (the interests of future generations). Thus sustainable development lengthens the geographic and time horizons of decisions, ensuring that both long and short-term interests are considered. What this means for foreign aid policies and nonrenewable resources remains contentious, as does the matter of deciding what future generations would want us to do, but these are important policy debates that otherwise might not be considered.

The earliest proposals for a constitutional guarantee of environmental rights typically stressed the rights of current humans to a healthy environment. But claims to environmental rights go considerably farther. For example, philosophers and ethicists have argued that future generations of humans also have rights to a livable environment and an equitable share of the Earth's natural resources. Such rights would call for limiting the current exploitation of groundwater, petroleum, hard minerals, and other scarce resources and for regulating actions, like the emission of greenhouse gases or the storage of nuclear waste, that could have serious impacts in decades to come.

Few people would disagree that public policy should take into account the needs and interests of future generations. The tough questions are how and to what degree. How should an exhaustible resource be allocated among current and future generations? Is the current generation free to use up a natural resource if they use the resource to produce capital amenities, such as roads and factories, of value to future generations? How can we even determine the preferences of future generations?

C.　*Utilitarianism and Cost–Benefit Analysis*

Neo-classical economists have long advocated a very different approach that balances the costs and benefits of contemplated environmental policies. In the eyes of economists, environmental problems are the result of market failures, and the goal of the law should be to correct these failures. No rational person would pay more for a product than the product is worth to her. Neither should the government regulate an environmental problem if the cost of the regulation exceeds the benefits to society. Such a regulation would unjustifiably waste society's resources even though some people might benefit from the regulation.

The government compares the costs and benefits of regulations in several different ways. In a full cost-benefit analysis, the government uses market prices, surveys, and other devices to place a monetary value on the environmental benefits that the regulation hopes to achieve—e.g., avoided medical costs, lives or species saved, the aesthetics of cleaner air or preserved wetlands. The government then compares these benefits against the costs of the regulation— e.g., employment loss, reduced industrial production or land development, the cost of needed pollution control equipment. Under traditional economic logic, the government should proceed with the regulation only if the expected monetary value of the benefits exceeds the monetary costs.

Where a regulation is designed primarily to save human lives, the government sometimes conducts a simpler analysis that calculates the cost of the regulation per life saved. The government again calculates the costs of the regulation, but rather than placing a monetary value on the benefits, the government merely estimates the likely number of lives saved. By dividing the costs by the expected number of lives saved, the government obtains the cost per life saved. The government then can compare this cost to the price of similar regulations or to economic estimates of the value of a human life to decide whether to pursue the contemplated regulation.

The executive branch of the federal government has long touted cost-benefit analyses as a means of choosing among alternative environmental policies. Every president since Richard Nixon has required EPA and other regulatory agencies to conduct cost-benefit analyses before adopting major regulations that could impose a significant cost on the economy. Under the current executive order, federal agencies must quantify, "to the extent feasible," both the benefits and costs of potential regulatory actions and, to the extent the law gives the agencies any discretion, "propose or adopt a regulation only upon a reasoned determination that the benefits of the intended regulation justify its costs." Agencies also must adopt the most "cost-effective" approach where different regulations could accomplish the same goals but at different costs.[11]

Congress, by contrast, has not been as receptive to arguments for cost-benefit analysis. A handful of federal environmental statutes call for explicit cost-benefit comparisons. Thus the two major federal environmental statutes regulating direct human exposure to toxic products—the Federal Insecticide, Fungicide, and Rodenticide Act, which regulates agricultural chemicals, and the Toxic Substances Control Act, which regulates other toxins—both require EPA to balance the benefits that a product would provide against the human and environmental risks that the product would pose. A number of other statutes permit EPA and other regulatory agencies to give at least some consideration to cost in regulating the environment. The Clean Water Act, for example, allows costs to be considered in deciding whether to permit the filling of a wetland and in setting limits on some discharges of pollutants into a waterway. In many important instances, however, Congress has forbidden agencies from considering cost to any degree. EPA cannot consider cost in setting national ambient air quality standards. Nor can a federal agency consider cost in deciding whether to move

---

[11] Executive Order 12866, 58 Fed. Reg. 51735 (1993).

forward with an action that might jeopardize the continued existence of an endangered or threatened species.

Why has Congress been reticent to embrace cost-benefit analysis in the environmental field? Part of the reason may be that Congress believes that people have a moral right to a clean environment. As emphasized earlier, where rights are at stake, the costs of enforcing those rights arguably has little, if any, role to play. But part of the reason is also the conceptual and practical problems that plague the application of cost-benefit analysis to environmental issues.

Start with the question of fairness. Most people are not troubled when individuals voluntarily choose to make a tradeoff between their health and other goals of importance to them, so long as the choice does not harm someone else. When the government is deciding whether to regulate an environmentally risky activity, however, one group of people generally bears the risk, while a different segment of society enjoys the benefits of the activity. Is it fair to compare the risks and benefits to these separate groups and to tolerate the risks if the benefits to the latter group are large? Imagine, for example, that a factory emits a toxic pollutant that kills one person each year from the local population. The only way to eliminate the pollution is to shut down the factory, but the product that it ships to other parts of the country produces $100 million dollars in social value. Even if you believed that the $100 million outweighs the "value" of the life saved (a difficult calculation to which we will return in a minute), is it ethically permissible to let one person die so that *other* people can economically benefit?

Although it might be tempting to conclude that such tradeoffs are never permissible, consider the implications of that conclusion. Given that some people are sensitive to even low levels of air pollutants, the only way to avoid *any* environmental injuries or damage might be to shut down industry entirely. Yet most people would find this solution unacceptable because the cost of the solution would seem too great for the benefits received. If closing down all industry is an unacceptable price to pay for protecting even the most sensitive members of society from air pollution, however, where should policymakers draw the balance? While environmental law provides many examples of "win-win" situations, in which environmental protection efforts actually can increase both efficiency and social wealth, we live in a world of limited resources, and tradeoffs often are unavoidable. Cost-benefit analyses are one obvious means of choosing among such tradeoffs.

Assuming that cost-benefit analysis is ethically acceptable, however, practical problems of implementation still loom large. To begin with, to what degree are the costs and benefits involved in environmental regulation *commensurate*—i.e., readily comparable? To many people, environmental risks such as the death of a person or the loss of a species cannot be quantified in the same dollar terms as the costs of installing pollution-control equipment or of a reduction in new housing. Nor can such risks be directly compared to the costs.

Even if placing a dollar figure on these risks is theoretically acceptable, how does one determine the value of a life, an endangered species, or an old-growth forest? Economists have developed techniques for trying to determine such values. To measure the value of a life, for example, economists sometimes use the salary premium that employees demand for working in a particularly risky occupation. But the techniques are controversial and often generate a wide range of numbers depending on the assumptions used.

Efforts to place a value on endangered species have also generated great controversy. Some species (e.g., salmon) are bought and sold in the marketplace and thus have a direct *market* value. But many species do not have market values, and market values often reflect only part of the value of a species to society. In many cases, a species' most significant or only values are its *nonuse* values: the values that people gain not from using the species or its services today but from having the option to use the species or its services in the future (*option value*), simply knowing that the species exists in the world (*existence value*), or knowing that their kids and grandkids will be able to enjoy the species (*bequest value*). Economists try to determine nonuse value by *contingent valuation methodology* ("CVM"), in which surveyors ask a random sample of people how much they would pay to save a species. Although CVM generates a dollar value, the reliability of that value is open to challenge on numerous grounds. The phrasing of questions in the survey often dramatically affects the value that people report. People also may overstate the value they place on species, both to sound altruistic and because they do not need to back up their answer with an actual monetary contribution toward saving the species.

The intertemporal quality of many environmental issues further complicates cost-benefit analyses. As noted earlier, the costs of environmental regulation are often immediate while at least some of the benefits typically accrue in the future. Reducing emissions of carbon, for example, costs money today but may generate climate benefits for decades to come. Standard economic analysis states that these future benefits should be *discounted*—i.e., given a reduced value compared to current costs and benefits—

because (1) most people would prefer a dollar today over a dollar next year and (2) any monies saved today by not adopting a regulation can be invested to generate a larger dollar sum in the future. Economists, however, disagree on the appropriate discount rate for environmental analyses. Some analysts, moreover, argue that discounting is inconsistent with society's obligation to future generations: while discounting might be useful to an individual deciding whether to save money for a vacation next year, one generation does not have the right to discount the benefits or costs to another generation. Other analysts, while acknowledging the appropriateness of discounting traditional costs and benefits, object to the discounting of lives that a regulation will save in the future. Why, they argue, should society care more about saving lives today than saving lives in the future? Whether a regulation saves five lives today or five lives in twenty years should not matter in their view.

Scientific uncertainty also makes cost-benefit analyses more problematic. As already discussed, scientific uncertainty plagues environmental issues. Scientists typically cannot tell us with any degree of certainty how many people will die or become sick after being exposed to a hazardous substance or the likelihood that an endangered species will go extinct if a particular tract of habitat is developed. Economists try to address such uncertainties in several ways. First, they calculate *expected values* for those costs and benefits that are uncertain: all of the potential values are weighted by their probabilities and then summed to obtain a mid-range estimate. Economists also conduct *sensitivity analyses* in which they see how various changes in the assumed costs and benefits would affect the ultimate conclusion of whether the benefits of the regulation outweigh the costs. Economists similarly perform *worst-case scenarios* in which they assume that a pollutant or activity will have the worst possible impact on health and the environment. None of these approaches, however, eliminates the underlying uncertainty.

The practical problems of cost-benefit analysis suggest that cost-benefit analyses, at a minimum, should be interpreted with appropriate caution. The practical problems involved in cost-benefit analyses, however, do not mean that the government should ignore the costs of regulation. Many individuals who oppose using formal cost-benefit analyses to decide environmental policy still believe that cost is relevant: the resources that society is willing to spend on environmental issues are scarce, and the government therefore should focus on environmental goals that have the greatest benefit and on the regulatory policies that accomplish these goals at the lowest cost.

D. Environmental Justice

A final framework is environmental justice. Here the focus is on how the burdens of environmental harms and regulations are allocated among individuals and groups within our society. Environmental law historically ignored distributive issues. Supporters of strong environmental laws emphasized environmental rights, while those more sympathetic to economic concerns argued for greater consideration of costs; virtually no one asked how environmental harms or regulatory costs were distributed. This began to change in 1978 when Governor James Hunt of North Carolina proposed disposing of soil tainted with polychlorinated biphenyls (PCBs) in a new waste dump to be opened in Warren County, a poor region in the northeastern part of the state with a population that was sixty-four percent African American and Native American. Joined by national civil rights leaders, local residents blocked the entrance to the dump site for over two weeks, arguing that the county had been chosen for the site because it was a minority community with little political power. Although the demonstration ultimately failed to keep the PCB-laced soils from the site, the demonstration attracted national attention to the issue of environmental justice and forced the governor to support state legislation prohibiting additional landfills in Warren County.

A wide range of studies conducted since the Warren County demonstrations indicate that poor and minority communities bear a disproportionate share of environmental burdens. For example, African-Americans and Hispanics disproportionately populate communities that are host to treatment, storage, and disposal facilities for hazardous waste. Minority communities disproportionately suffer from substandard air quality and are home to a higher number of Superfund sites that are contaminated by hazardous substances. Minorities also suffer environmental injuries, such as lead poisoning and pesticide exposure, to a greater degree than do Caucasians. Although the statistical reliability of a number of the studies is questionable, the sheer number of studies, and the consistency of their results, suggests a disturbing maldistribution of environmental burdens in the United States.

Environmental justice focuses both on the distribution of environmental burdens and policies (*substantive* environmental justice) and also on the process by which environmental decisions are made in the United States (*procedural* environmental justice). In the view of most advocates of environmental justice, local communities should have a significant, if not controlling voice in decisions and activities that impact their residents' lives. Decision making processes in turn should be open to all residents, and everyone should have access to the scientific and other resources needed to understand and assess policy proposals. Environmental justice advocates thus push for decisions to be made at the local level through democratic processes. This runs counter to the modern emphasis in American environmental policy on *federal* decision making by *expert* agencies. Environmental justice advocates also typically have little faith in traditional environmental groups, which tend to have few minority employees and accomplish much of their work in the courts and the halls of Congress rather than in local communities.

The key policy questions are why the burdens are not equally distributed and how, if at all, the maldistribution can be corrected. Much of the debate over environmental justice in the United States has focused on the siting in minority communities of waste dumps and industrial facilities that could adversely affect the health of local residents. Many residents of minority communities believe that racism is at work and have fought efforts to locate facilities in their communities, labeling such efforts *environmental racism*. Regardless of whether the governmental agencies that oversee the siting and permitting of such facilities intentionally discriminate, minority communities frequently have less political power and may be at a number of procedural disadvantages. Local residents may find it difficult to attend relevant hearings, which may be held in state or county capitals hundreds of miles away from the affected community; the siting agency might not publish notices and other materials in Spanish and other locally spoken languages or provide interpreters for hearings; few minority communities have the resources to hire scientists and other experts needed to rebut the claims of the facility owners.

Discriminatory siting decisions may not be the only or even the principal reason why environmentally dangerous facilities end up located disproportionately in minority communities. Although virtually all studies agree that minority and poor communities host a disproportionate share of industrial and waste facilities, they disagree as to why. A number of regional studies have suggested that housing dynamics are instead at fault: after a facility is located in a community, those who can relocate to other neighborhoods move out of the area and housing prices fall, making the community more attractive to minorities and poorer individuals who previously could not afford to live there.[12] To the degree that more systemic problems such as housing underlie the greater exposure of

---

[12] *See* Vicki Been and Francis Gupta, *Coming to the Nuisance or Going to the Barrios? A Longitudinal Analysis of Environmental Justice Claims*, 24 Ecology L.Q. 1 (1997).

minorities and the poor to industrial and waste facilities, changes in environmental policies by themselves will unfortunately not eliminate distributional inequities. Other studies have found a close correlation between the siting of undesirable land uses and a community's voting rate, with less politically active communities suffering greater environmental justice problems.[13]

In response to such concerns, the federal government has taken a number of steps to address environmental inequity. In 1994, President Bill Clinton issued an executive order, still in effect, that requires all federal agencies to incorporate environmental justice into their decision making "by identifying and addressing, as appropriate, disproportionately high and adverse human health or environmental effects."[14] Some governmental agencies also have adopted their own policies designed to reduce the chances that their decisions will impact minority communities on a disproportionate basis. In licensing nuclear facilities, for example, the Nuclear Regulatory Commission engages in an environmental equity analysis designed to identify and avoid both intentional discrimination and disproportionate burdens. In 1997, the Commission rejected an application to build a uranium enrichment plant in the African American community of Homer, Louisiana, because the Commission's staff had not adequately examined whether racial discrimination had played a role in the site selection process.[15]

Community members seeking to keep an environmentally hazardous facility out of their neighborhoods increasingly have tried to use Title VI of the Civil Rights Act of 1964 to address issues of environmental racism.[16] Title VI prohibits any program or activity that receives federal funds from discriminating on the basis of race, color, or national origin; most state and local environmental programs receive some federal funding and thus are subject to Title VI. Although a plaintiff who sues in court under Title VI must prove intentional discrimination, federal agencies may adopt a lower burden of proof for administrative proceedings. EPA prohibits disproportionate impacts, whether or not caused by intentional discrimination, in programs receiving EPA funding. In 2000, faced by an increasing number of Title VI complaints, EPA issued a Draft Revised Guidance for investigating administrative complaints alleging violations of Title VI. The interim guidance proved

---

[13] James T. Hamilton, *Testing for Environmental Racism: Prejudice, Profits, Political Power?*, 14 J. of Policy Analysis and Management 107, 127 (1995).

[14] Executive Order 12,898, 59 Fed. Reg. 7629 (1994).

[15] In the Matter of Louisiana Energy Services, L.P., Decision of the Nuclear Regulatory Commission Atomic Safety and Licensing Board, May 1, 1997.

[16] 1342 U.S.C. §§ 2000d et seq.

controversial with state and local governments, and EPA has yet to adopt a final guidance document.

Although environmental justice discussions have focused on the siting of industrial and waste facilities, environmental justice also provides a framework for addressing environmental policy more broadly. Many advocates of environmental justice, for example, observe that the law provides greater protection for environmental amenities of importance to affluent white populations, such as biodiversity, than threats of far greater concern to rural poor, such as pesticide exposure. The Endangered Species Act thus does not consider cost in protecting endangered species; but the Federal Insecticide, Fungicide, and Rodenticide Act permits cost to be considered in deciding whether to allow pesticides to be used in the United States.

Environmental justice advocates also suggest that the government should consider distributional impacts in choosing and designing its regulatory tools. As discussed in Chapter 4, for example, the government has adopted tradable emission credits under the Clean Air Act. Under the trading program, a factory that finds it relatively inexpensive to reduce its air emissions can reduce its emission by more than the regulations require and then sell its "excess credits" to a factory that finds it more expensive to reduce emissions; the second factory can then use the credits to help meet its regulatory requirements. Emissions trading can achieve the same overall emission reduction at a lower cost and is thus economically efficient. But if the trading system is not carefully designed and implemented, factories in poorer areas of a region might become net purchasers of the pollution credits—resulting in more pollution in the poorer areas at the same time as the air becomes cleaner in other areas, so-called "hotspots."

CASE STUDY: FRACKING

Hydraulic fracturing, popularly known as "fracking," is a method for extracting natural gas from deep within shale formations. Traditionally, natural gas drillers have sunk pipes straight down into gas deposits. In fracking, special technology allows the drill to change directions from vertical to horizontal, running along shale formations miles below the surface. To fracture the shale, blasts and a special mixture of water, sand, and chemicals is injected at very high pressure through holes in the well casing and into the rock. The combined impact of blasts and forced fluids creates fissures releasing natural gas (also known as shale gas or methane) that has been trapped in the shale formations for millions of years. The fracking fluids flow back up the well through steel pipes encased in concrete to the surface, opening a passage for the natural gas to follow.

The potential of fracking is enormous, turning assumptions about America's energy security upside down. Reports of massive stores underneath parts of the East Coast, many in areas with struggling economies, have led some to predict that fracking could satisfy the nation's need for natural gas for fifty or one hundred years.

Natural gas is familiar to us as the blue flame used on gas stove tops and water heaters. It can generate electricity and even power cars, buses, and trucks, dramatically reducing America's dependency on foreign oil while creating domestic jobs. Natural gas produces fewer greenhouse gases than other fossil fuels, so there could be climate change benefits, as well. As a result, in a modern-day miners' rush, investment is pouring into the field, and we could see thousands upon thousands of new wells across the country in the next few decades.

Fracking raises at least four basic concerns about water, in addition to seismic and air pollution issues. The first is that the fracking fluids blasted thousands of feet below the surface are finding their way into shallow aquifers that provide drinking water. The composition of fracking fluids is regarded by companies as a confidential business secret but they likely contain toxic and carcinogenic fluids. The second is that methane is escaping from well casings as it is brought back to the surface. The third is that the recovered fracking fluid is polluting local water sources. And the last is the sheer amount of water needed for fracking.

There are currently more questions about the threats posed by fracking than answers. Research to date has found that water samples near fracking sites contained higher levels of methane than distant drinking water sources, and some of this methane has been sourced to thermogenic methane that only occurs deep within the earth, most likely brought to the surface through leaks in the concrete casing of the drilling rigs. There is little evidence to date that the fracking fluids are making their way up to shallow aquifers from the point of injection over a mile underground. Disposal of the fracking fluid that comes back up to the surface, though, has raised serious concerns, particularly in watersheds that provide drinking water.

The U.S. EPA has started to get involved, but only in a limited manner. Indeed, it has been prevented from doing so. In the 2005 energy bill, text was adopted that specifically exempted fracking from coverage under the Clean Water Act and the Safe Drinking Water Act. Some have dubbed the exemption the "Halliburton Loophole." Regulation and enforcement therefore primarily occur at the state level but these have been very uneven, administered by agencies with stretched resources. Nor is methane regulated in drinking water. It is not thought to be harmful to health, but there is very little research on the topic.

Assume that you are the Secretary of the Environment for your state and the legislature has mandated you to establish a set of policies for granting fracking permits. How could the four analytical frameworks described above guide your decision? Would you allow fracking to take place? What restrictions would you impose?

QUESTIONS AND DISCUSSION

1. As noted in the text, uncertainty can cut both ways—acting today to address an uncertain future harm may prove to be an overreaction, causing immediate economic and social harm; yet not acting in the face of an uncertain future harm may prove an underreaction, causing economic and social harm at a later date. Discuss the issue of nuclear power in terms of uncertainty and policy choices. Does the uncertain, though potentially massive, harm from climate change suggest we should move with all deliberate speed to shift toward non-carbon energy sources, including nuclear power? Or does the potential harm from the operation of nuclear power plants and dangers from transport and disposal of hazardous waste caution against its use? How should policy makers balance these competing sources of uncertainty? Should the accident at the Fukushima nuclear reactor in Japan influence this decision?

2. Explain the problem of climate change in terms of market failures. How do the concepts of public goods, the tragedy of the commons, collective action, free riders, and externalities all contribute to climate change and, in turn, present obstacles to reducing greenhouse gas emissions?

3. Some states and municipalities have tried to limit the importation for disposal of hazardous waste from other states. The Supreme Court, however, has consistently ruled that states cannot ban the import of waste solely on the basis of its origin in another state. Explain this "flow control" problem in terms of mismatched scales and externalities.

4. A recurring issue in the environmental field is the relative role of experts and the public in deciding which risks to address and how. Should scientific experts, for example, decide which chemical products to allow on the market? Or should public officials, guided by expert views but also by public attitudes and concerns, make such decisions? Use concepts from this chapter, such as cognitive biases and environmental justice, to address this issue.

5. Institutional arrangements can play a subtle but important role in the development of law and policy. The text noted that cost-benefit analysis is required under the Toxic Substances Control Act and the Federal Insecticide, Fungicide and Rodenticide Act, but not under any other environmental laws. Why the difference? For one thing, these two laws were drafted by the House and Senate agriculture committees while the more traditional pollution laws were drafted by the environmental and public works committees. Why do you think this might matter?

6. How would you resolve the following questions using three of the analytical frameworks set out in this chapter (environmental rights, utilitarianism, and environmental justice)? How would you personally go about resolving the questions?

a. A Native American tribe, faced by high unemployment and poverty on its reservation, decides to open a hazardous waste disposal site on its reservation close to its border. The facility will produce significant income and employment. A small town just outside the reservation objects to the environmental risks posed by the hazardous waste site.

b.   Cars that sit idling in traffic produce significant pollution. Every morning, traffic piles up for miles trying to get on the bridges going into Bay City. To reduce both congestion and pollution, Bay City proposes charging significantly higher tolls for use of the bridges during the peak commute hours of the morning and late afternoon. The higher tolls will pose a problem for the working poor, who will not be able to afford the higher tolls and do not have jobs with flexible working hours.

c.   U.S. law prohibits the use of the pesticide, Dimethyl Terrible. This is an inexpensive chemical that is very effective at protecting crops but has been linked to increased incidence of birth defects and cancer among field workers and even people living in the vicinity of the farms. Should companies be allowed to produce this pesticide in America and sell it overseas to poorer countries where the pesticide's use is legal? Should it depend on whether the pesticide leaves residues on fruits and vegetables that are then exported back to the United States (sometimes know as the "circle of poison")?

Chapter 3

THE PRACTICE OF ENVIRONMENTAL PROTECTION

I. Instrument Choice

Americans believe they are environmentalists. As noted earlier, polls show up to 80% or more of Americans agree with the statement that environmental protection should be a high priority. The Environmental Protection Agency (EPA) estimates that we spend about 2.5% of gross national product on environmental protection. If this is such a high priority, though, why not spend more? The obvious answer is that there are other important pressing needs, as well, and a finite pool of resources to draw from. This public policy trade-off is sometimes described as the "choice between guns and butter." Should a country spend more of its resources on the military or on social services? Should a country spend more of its resources on environmental protection or economic development? Depending on their situations and values, different countries choose very different allocations.

Determining the proper level of environmental protection is not solely a scientific decision. A scientist can tell us the likely health impacts of regulating Dimethyl Terrible to 10 parts per million, and an economist can tell us the likely costs and benefits of this regulation, but neither can tell us the "correct" level of regulation. In a world of competing resource needs, the key question for policy-makers is the "socially best" level of protection. Setting the appropriate level of environmental protection is expressly a *political* decision for the simple reason that there are other competing needs. We could bring Los Angeles quickly into compliance with the Clean Air Act, for example, by drastically reducing the use of cars but this is not a trade-off citizens currently are willing to accept.

In choosing the "right" level of environmental protection, many consider the key issue to be what level of risk we are willing to accept, and at what cost. There are precious few risk-free activities in life. And though we surely can reduce the risks to us and to nature from industrial activities or development, these can come at a cost. We may well decide to bear these costs, either based on a hard-nosed cost-benefit assessment or on an ethical judgment that our national parks should have clear vistas or that the impacts of air pollution should not fall disproportionately on inner-city children, but these decisions are ultimately judgments over what we should protect and how much. How "safe" is safe enough? How

51

"clean" is clean enough? Because these questions are so value-laden, environmental law and policy are deeply contested areas. Indeed, in order to make such judgments it is hard to see how the field could be any other way.

Determining the level of resources we should commit to environmental protection (versus other pressing social needs) and the levels of protection we should set (e.g., whether in the case of air pollution we should seek to protect the average person, asthmatics, or severe asthmatics) will never be easy. Regardless of how these determinations are ultimately made, however, everyone would agree that we should achieve a particular level of environmental protection at lowest social cost. But *how* to do this? Reliance on the common law? Regulations? Market instruments? Implementing environmental policy is where the rubber meets the road and it has provided some of the most innovative regulatory instruments in all of American law.

A.   The Regulatory Toolkit

As described in the history section of Chapter 1, prior to the rise of the "modern era" of environmental law in the 1970s, the traditional response to pollution had relied on the common law doctrines of trespass and nuisance. In the 1904 *Madison v. Ducktown Sulphur, Copper & Iron Co.* case,[1] for example, Georgia farmers filed suit against a nearby copper smelter in Tennessee. The farmers claimed that air pollution from the smelter had ruined their crops and made worthless their timber. For its part, the smelter responded that it had already spent close to $200,000 to reduce its emissions. Added to the mix was the fact that the smelter served as the economic linchpin for the community, supporting growth of the surrounding areas from 200 to 12,000 people. As compensation for the farmers' loss, the court found the smelter liable for the nuisance but refused to issue an injunction. Balancing the equities, the court ordered the smelter to pay the farmers $1,000 for their damage suffered. Given the setting, how could the result have been any different? Would any court have been willing to destroy half of the taxable value of the county in a nuisance suit brought by some out-of-state farmers?

Whether or not one agrees with the result in *Madison*, upon reflection the limits of such nuisance actions are clear. First, what about future damages? Under this type of retrospective remedy, those suffering injury must bring a lawsuit every time *after* they have been harmed. There is no direct, prospective protection. Although courts can try to address this problem by awarding

---

[1] 83 S.W. 658 (Tenn. 1904).

permanent damages that cover both past and future expected harm, courts must guess at the future harm, so the permanent damages ultimately are likely to prove either too low or too high. Second, imagine there is not only a smelter but also a textile factory and ironworks upwind of the farmers as well. The farmers may still suffer the same amount of damages, if not worse, but whom should they sue? Can they prove it was the pollution from the smelter that caused the damage rather than that from the other factories? And if the damage came from all three, how can the farmers demonstrate the relative culpability? When there are multiple sources of pollution, establishing proximate cause becomes difficult. Finally, private nuisance actions may only be brought to remedy damage to private property. Remedies for damage to common resources, such as the fish in a river or trees in a public forest, can be sought only by bringing a *public* nuisance action, and that generally can be brought only by the state. Thus fishermen could not bring a nuisance suit against a factory polluting the river, even if it led to mass fish kills and threatened their livelihood.

[margin handwritten note:] difficult to prove single entity caused harm

Through this vantage, the benefits of a regulatory approach become clear. First, regulating conduct provides prospective rather than retrospective protection. Regulations limiting air or water emissions, for example, prohibit certain activities *before* they can cause significant harm. Thus, in principle, injured parties need not sue afterwards for compensation because they won't be harmed in the first place. Second, a regulatory approach makes unnecessary the need to show causation. Because pollution is regulated as it occurs at the source, there is no need to determine which factory's emissions caused specific harms. Again, if the regulatory limits are well set, there will be no harms that need to be compensated. Regulations also make irrelevant the distinction between harm to public or private resources, since regulation occurs prospectively at the source, regardless of who owns the downwind and downstream properties. Finally, regulations limiting pollution avoid tort debates over whether the polluting parties acted negligently or exercised due care. With regulation, they must meet the objective standards, period. Given these relative advantages, it should be no surprise why the era of modern environmental law ushered in uniform, national pollution control standards.

Simply choosing a regulatory approach over reliance on the common law, however, still leaves fundamental questions unanswered. The most basic of these is what type of regulatory instrument to use. To explore the range of possible instruments, let's return to the classic environmental problem—the tragedy of the commons.

Imagine again that you have a herd of sheep that grazes on the public common. The common, though, is an open access resource. This means that anyone can graze as many sheep as she likes. So long as the resource is under little pressure (i.e., few sheep are grazing) there is no need for regulatory intervention because there is no problem of scarcity. Once significant competing uses of the resource develop, however, then the need for state action arises. In the context of the common, once more and more people graze more and more sheep, the common is in danger of becoming overgrazed and denuded. So we need to do something, but how should we best overcome the tragedy currently in the making?

There is a range of policy approaches to overcome the tragedy of the commons. An easy way to remember these is as the "**Five P's**"—**P**rescriptive Regulation, **P**roperty Rights, **P**enalties, **P**ayments, and **P**ersuasion. Each of these approaches has advantages and disadvantages. The challenge is determining which is appropriate under a particular set of circumstances. Some familiarity with these tools will help you understand the policy options available for addressing the specific environmental problems discussed in the chapters that follow.

1. *Prescriptive Regulation*

By far the most common way to internalize costs is indirectly, through prescriptive regulations mandating what parties can and cannot do. In the case of the commons, for example, the government might limit access, perhaps restricting the number of sheep that may graze or the amount of time or season the sheep may graze. The government may set aside areas for re-vegetation, etc. Such prescriptive regulation, also referred to as *command-and-control regulation*, can be very effective but there is considerable debate over its efficiency.

Economists and industry, for example, often criticize prescriptive regulations as inefficient and unwieldy. They argue that this approach provides little reason for innovation because once the regulated party has achieved the emission standard, the law creates no incentive to reduce pollution further. Unless the technology standards regularly change, there exists little incentive for a facility to reduce pollution beyond the BAT requirements. "So long as the regulations require use of Filter X, we've bought Filter X and it's working properly, there's no reason to go further." This supposedly encourages reliance on traditional, proven control technologies rather than pollution prevention strategies and new technologies.

It is important to note, however that, by forcing better environmental performance, prescriptive regulations can also

increase efficiencies and productivity, resulting in a net gain to the
company. Indeed, noted economist Michael Porter has argued that
strict environmental regulation encourages production process and
design innovations.[2] These cost savings, the Porter Hypothesis
contends, can exceed both the compliance and innovation costs,
resulting in greater competitiveness.

2.   Property Rights

A classic solution to the tragedy of the commons is the creation
or recognition of property rights in the environmental resource.
These property rights can be vested in individuals or in
communities (as is the case in many indigenous cultures).
Returning to the grazing example, assume the state carves up the
common into square parcels of land and grants fee simple title for
each parcel to the individual shepherds using the common,
including you. Are you still as eager to overgraze as before?

All of a sudden, your previous incentive to use up the resource
as fast as possible (before everyone else does) is no longer relevant.
Instead, your interests are best served by carefully tending your
part of the common so it remains fertile long into the future—so it
is *sustainably managed*. In a variant of the privatization approach,
assume the entire common now belongs to you. What would you do?
You may well charge other shepherds to use the common, or even
let them on for free, but you would do so only to the extent that the
resource base remains intact and productive—i.e., so long as the
common is not overgrazed. In financial terms, to maximize profits
you will safeguard your asset over the longer term. Moreover, this
approach has low administrative costs. The government simply
creates the property rights, allocates them initially, and steps back,
leaving future allocations to the market. Some commentators have
called for far greater reliance on property rights approaches to
environmental protection. Sometimes called "Free Market
Environmentalism," this strategy would privatize as many
environmental resources as possible, in the belief that markets are
better mechanisms for allocation of goods than governmental
regulators.

Implicit in a property rights approach is the importance of
technology. To enforce your rights, you need both to know someone
is making use of your resource (an issue of monitoring capacity) and
to have the ability to exclude others' use. As an example, consider
the history of the American West. It was only with the invention of
barbed wire that settlers could effectively exclude cattle from
grazing on their lands. Prior to this technology, there was no

---

[2] Michael E. Porter & Claus van der Linde, *Towards a New Conception of the Environment–Competitiveness Relationship*, J. Econ. Perspectives, Fall 1995, at 97.

affordable way to keep cattle from grazing wherever they wanted—hence the short-lived though much-fabled cattle drives. In a more modern context, decoders have allowed satellite television channels to privatize the airwave commons. Unless satellite channel providers could exclude other's use through scrambling their signals, there would be no way for them to sell their product (since people could use it for free).

Despite the increasing interest and application of property rights approaches to environmental protection, there are some significant obstacles. The first is that many environmental resources are not easily amenable to commodification. When resources have significant public goods aspects (such as major watersheds or biodiversity), privatization may not lead to the socially most beneficial use of the land. Private property owners typically value only those uses that provide monetary remuneration. In these cases, the important positive externalities will not be valued. Perhaps the new owners of the common wish to use it for mini-golf while the sheep starve. If the government wants to ensure the important public goals of a secure food supply or supporting the agricultural sector, it will need to step in. Property rights advocates would approve of this course of action, so long as the government paid the property holders.

There may be normative concerns, as well, that rub against privatization of national parks or other environmental amenities in the public domain. For example, the government could try to "privatize" wildlife by equipping each animal with a collar or tag that identifies its "owner." Yet wildlife in the process would lose part of their "wildness," the quality that gives them a unique and valuable identity.

Practically, there also are difficult allocation issues for the initial privatization of environmental resources. Using the commons as an example, assume that the government has divided up the land into 50 separate parcels. Whom should be given title? Should the land be auctioned to the highest bidder? This could favor wealthier newcomers and corporate interests. Giving more respect for traditional users, perhaps the allocation should be based on historic use or current levels of consumption. Yet this puts newcomers at a disadvantage and favors those who have been the most profligate in the past. If we can't decide among these competing users, should we just have a random drawing? Any allocation mechanism will tend to favor some groups at the expense of others. Whom should be favored comes down to a contentious political decision.

a.   Tradable Permits

A variant of creating property rights is the use of tradable permits. Here, property rights are created in the form of marketable use, emission, or extractions rights—for example, the right to graze in a certain area, emit a ton of sulfur dioxide, or catch a lobster. Trading systems use the market to make prescriptive regulation more efficient. The government decides how much of a harmful activity (such as pollution) to permit, awards private rights to engage in the activity up to the regulatory cap, and then permits those rights to be traded. The market thus does not play a role in determining the level of environmental protection; that is the role of the regulatory regime.

By letting the market rather than regulators determine individual actors' emissions, profit-motivated agents who can control pollution at low cost may reduce emissions more than needed to comply with permit limits. They can then sell surplus allowances at a profit to higher-cost agents. Thus, the greatest share of reductions will come from agents who can do so at the cheapest cost, allowing each polluter to weigh the marginal cost of abatement against the cost of buying credits and make an efficient individual decision. If the cap is set appropriately, marketable permits achieve the same level of protection as command-and-control alternatives at a lower cost. The net result allows the regulated community to select appropriate control strategies and encourages innovative practices and technologies.

One downside of trading is similar to that for private property approaches—the difficulty of initially allocating permits. Moreover, constructing smoothly functioning markets is not simple. There must be a sufficient and well-defined marketplace and a community of market participants. There also must be a refined currency of trade, one that is fungible and reflects the desired environmental quality. For example, it would be a stretch to consider allowing coastal developers in Florida to "trade" wetland values they eliminate for reductions in phosphorous emissions in Oregon. But where the environmental good (or bad, so to speak) can be captured in a measurable unit (whether that be tons of pollutant or kilos of fish) and market service areas and participants are well-defined, trading programs have had demonstrable success in a variety of contexts, increasing the efficiency and flexibility of prescriptive instruments.

To make this more concrete, imagine how a trading program would work with grazing on the common. Government policy makers decide that the common can sustain no more than 400 sheep grazing per year. The government therefore creates 400 permits. Each permit entitles the holder to graze one sheep for the calendar year listed on the permit. Unless the shepherd has a separate permit for each sheep grazing on the common, she is breaking the law. The government then allocates the permits in some fashion (which, as noted above, has significant distributional consequences) and lets trading commence. In theory, those for whom grazing is most valuable will pay the highest price to buy the permits from those who value them less, ensuring that the common is dedicated to the most valuable market use.

3.   Financial Penalties

The most direct way to internalize externalities is through charges, taxes, or liability. In theory, environmentally harmful activities should be charged the cost of the harm imposed. By increasing the costs of polluting activities, such penalties discourage unnecessary pollution and waste. In economic terms, the penalty should be set so it equals the marginal environmental damage at the socially optimal level of pollution. Also known as a Pigouvian tax, this policy instrument ensures that each actor now has a direct incentive to regulate her own behavior according to how valuable the polluting activities are.

In theory this is very attractive. One could levy the penalty on pollution (whether emissions or solid waste), on the feedstock (e.g., a carbon tax on oil or coal), or on the final product (e.g., a gas-guzzling car), but there are two practical obstacles. The first lies in getting the price right. Markets are efficient only when the prices for goods accurately reflect their full environmental and social cost. A key aspect in internalizing externalities, then, is valuation. If one agrees that externalities should be internalized—that polluters should pay—the obvious question is "how much"? We might all agree that CFC emissions, for example, harm the ozone layer, but how much monetary harm is caused by releasing a kilogram of CFCs? One dollar? One penny? One-hundredth of a penny? Because there is no market for the ozone layer, these values must necessarily be estimated. The second challenge is political. Increasing taxes is never easy, and environmental charges seem to be harder, still. President Clinton proposed a carbon tax at the start of his presidency, but the proposal quickly died in a hailstorm of political opposition. The cap-and-trade legislation proposed in 2010 similarly failed in the Senate, lambasted by its critics as "cap-and-tax." This is not to say that environmental taxes are never passed. They have become common in Europe and may be found in the United States, for example, on CFCs. But levying them at charges high enough to significantly influence behavior is easier said than done. In many cases, the charges have been more intended for revenue-raising than serious behavior modification.

4.   Financial *Payments*

As noted above, government can discourage certain polluting activities through penalties but, equally, can encourage beneficial activities through subsidizing them. California has embarked on a major program of tax benefits for property owners who install solar panels. While government payments for environmentally-friendly activities have great potential, most government payments have negative environmental impacts. In the commons example, shepherds could be paid *not* to graze their sheep.

In addition to internalizing the environmental costs that are now outside the market, getting the price right so that resources can be allocated efficiently also requires the elimination of price distortions, which typically occur in the form of government subsidies. The World Resources Institute has estimated that U.S. farmers who receive federal reclamation water repay only 17 percent of the full cost of the water projects. Nor is this solely an American concern. Subsidies from around the globe to agriculture, fossil fuel exploration and extraction, road transportation, dam building, logging, and other extractive activities amount to hundreds of billions of dollars, dwarfing subsidies for environmental protection.

5.   *Persuasion*

If prescriptive regulation and market instruments represent "hard" regulatory approaches, then a softer approach may be found in laws requiring information production and dissemination. Sometimes described as *reflexive laws,* the theory behind such approaches is that the government can change people's behavior by forcing them to think about the harm they are causing and by publicizing that harm. In the context of the commons, the government might require shepherds to record and publish the number of sheep they graze or the amount of forage the sheep eat. The government also may try to educate the shepherds with brochures or presentations on the causes and dangers of overgrazing. In these cases, the government is "nudging" people to engage in better ways rather than directly regulating them.[3] Such information approaches are often used when there is either inadequate political support to impose market or regulatory instruments or such instruments are ill suited to the problem. In a number of cases, particularly in the case of pollution, requirements

---

[3] For more on nudging, *see* Richard H. Thaler & Cass R. Sunstein, Nudge: Improving Decisions About Health, Wealth, and Happiness (2009).

to collect and disseminate information have led to significant change in the behavior of regulated parties, even in the absence of overt prescriptive regulation.

B.　Putting the Toolkit to Work

While many of the examples above have related to the tragedy of the commons, one can apply this toolkit of regulatory instruments to virtually any environmental problem. Taking the example of climate change, for example, consider the range of legal instruments you could use to reduce greenhouse gas emissions as well as their potential shortcomings. If you were head of the EPA, what would your proposed greenhouse gas law look like?

Reliance on the common law would prove difficult because causation—the link between discrete emissions and harm (whether in the form of sea level rise or aberrant weather patterns)—could not be established easily. It's hard to see how nuisance or trespass doctrines would work with such attenuated causation and multiple sources, though lawyers are trying (we describe common law climate suits in Chapter 6).

Prescriptive regulation seems more workable. In the greenhouse gas context, regulation could take the form of emission controls, limiting the amount of pollution a source may emit. Financial penalties seem a good potential fit, as well. One could levy emission fees based on the amount of greenhouse gases emitted. These would encourage each actor to look for ways to reduce his emissions and to regulate his behavior according to how valuable the polluting activities are. Conversely, one could rely on payments, providing tax credits for research and development on energy efficient technologies, or tax deductions for energy-efficient purchases or one could remove subsidies for oil and coal exploration.

Relying on property rights, one could establish a trading market for greenhouse gases. In the typical *cap-and-trade-program* for pollution, policymakers would establish a socially desirable level of aggregate greenhouse gas emissions, determine a formula for initial allocation of emissions among sources, and issue permits to members of the regulated community that entitle each bearer to emit a given quantity of that pollutant. The political battle would focus on the overall cap, which is included in the trading market, and how allocations are allocated.

Finally, persuasion through information disclosure also might work well. One could, for example, require firms to collect and publish over the web data on their greenhouse gas emissions. Perhaps not surprisingly, such proposals have been strongly opposed by many in industry. Similarly, one might create an eco-labeling or independent certification program, providing a seal of approval for those companies or goods that achieve significant greenhouse gas reductions. The theory behind such programs is to provide green consumers with reliable information on which to base their purchases and favor environmentally friendlier companies in the marketplace.

C. Instrument Design Issues

In the context of instrument choice, there are three longstanding issues worth keeping in mind. The first is the debate over relative efficiency. As noted above, there has long been criticism of prescriptive regulations as inefficient both because the government (rather than the market) generally determines the best available technology and because there is little incentive for a firm to reduce its pollution beyond what the government requires. In place of prescriptive regulation, critics contend, there should be greater reliance on market instruments because these allow the regulated parties to choose the most economically efficient means of compliance.

While this is an important debate, the way it has been described above is both misleading and incomplete. It's misleading because many market instruments necessarily rely on prescriptive regulation. For example, tradable permits can increase efficiency, but they require prescriptive regulation to establish the market, to set the cap. Trading programs work only because regulated parties are forbidden from engaging in certain activities unless they have an adequate number of permits, whether that be grazing sheep or emitting greenhouse gases. The description above is incomplete because it considers only costs to the regulated community. There are costs of administration to consider, as well.

The second major issue in instrument design—the relevance of administrative costs—has played out most clearly within the category of prescriptive regulations and the choice between technology-based and health-based standards. Assume, for example, you are crafting a regulation that will limit emissions of dimethyl terrible. Should the regulatory standard mandate use of best available technology (perhaps a particular filter the company places on its smokestack) or a health-based standard? The health-based standard might mandate, for example, that a facility's emissions of Dimethyl Terrible cannot increase the risks of cancer above one in a one million (i.e., a chance that one person in a population of one million will contract cancer because of the dimethyl emissions). From a pure efficiency perspective, the health approach is appealing. Why mandate uniform emission controls when we know that in many cases such standards will be over-protective? Take the example of a chemical plant on an ocean peninsula with a strong steady breeze out to sea. If this plant's emissions will not come into contact with people (and assuming it is not toxic to ocean life), then why force it to pay for control technology that provides no benefit?

The classic response to this argument is that, while a health-based standard may theoretically be more efficient, in practice a technology-based standard is not only more protective but much easier for EPA to administer and enforce. A health-based standard necessarily relies on modeling. What level of exposure will people downwind of the plant experience? Based on toxicological studies (generally done on mice), how many cancers is this exposure likely to cause in people? Needless to say, there are a lot of assumptions and extrapolations necessary in such a calculation and therefore, environmental critics charge, lots of room for fudging results to favor industry interests and lower levels of protection. Moreover, EPA can monitor whether a company is using required technology more easily than it can monitor a company's emissions and the effect of those emissions. As described above, so long as the regulations require use of Filter X, if the company has bought Filter X and it's working properly, neither the company nor EPA has any worries.

This conflict between health-based and technology-based standards occurs throughout pollution control legislation and is a theme we will re-visit often. When crafting its regulations, EPA typically faces a fundamental trade-off between regulatory strategies that are inflexible but relatively easy to administer (e.g., technology-based requirements) and those that are more complex but flexible (e.g., risk-based).

A third issue worth noting is that, in some respects, the choice of regulatory target is as important as choice of instrument. To illustrate why, assume you are charged to come up with a brand new regulatory strategy to address the potential harms from pesticide use. In approaching this problem, before choosing to rely on prescriptive regulation, property, penalties, payments, or persuasion, you must first determine the appropriate entity to regulate since this will, in turn, determine which instruments work best. Which potential parties should you regulate? If focusing on the chemicals used in pesticides, should you direct your attention to manufacturers of these goods or their retailers (those who sell the chemicals on the market)? Large retailers such as Walmart often have a great deal of power over manufacturers, so perhaps they are best suited to act as a filter, refusing to sell goods that are not "environmentally friendly" or shown to be "safe" in use. At the same time, manufacturers know their chemicals better than anyone, so perhaps they should be directly regulated so they can shoulder the direct responsibility for re-formulating their pesticides. In a more indirect approach, perhaps the best regulatory target would be farmers. An information disclosure requirement could require them to inform buyers of the chemicals applied to their crops. Superfund, discussed in Chapter 8, takes a similar approach by holding land owners responsible for the safe disposal of hazardous waste on their property. As the above example makes clear, there are pressure points throughout the product chain to influence pesticide design and use, and selection of the regulatory target partly dictates which instruments will be most effective.

In any complicated problem, which environmental issues surely pose, potential contributors may have to be left out of the regulatory scheme for sheer practicality. The government simply can't regulate everyone. But this raises political problems—charges of favoring one group over another. Indeed environmental law offers clear examples of such political picking-and-choosing. As Chapter 7 on the Clean Water Act explains, most nutrients in water pollution come from agriculture (as "nonpoint source" pollution). Yet, largely because of the agricultural lobby's political clout, farm runoff is effectively unregulated.

D.   Where to Go from Here?

Since the 1970s, environmental protection has progressed from reliance on the common law, to reliance on prescriptive regulatory commands, to reliance on market instruments and information. In comparison to other areas of the law such as torts, property, or even corporate law, however, environmental law is still a very young field, just over 40 years old. While the current structure and approach to environmental protection offers clear advantages over its predecessors, the entire field remains remarkably dynamic and in flux, with major reforms proposed in Congress virtually every year. Environmental law is surely contentious, as well, and widespread criticism has prompted many of these proposed reforms.

A major criticism of environmental law is inefficiency. Environmental law's requirements are too rigid, critics charge, and its rules too restrictive, resulting in protection that could be achieved at less cost or should not be required at all. In 1990, EPA's Scientific Advisory Board ranked major threats to the environment and human health. In its report on "Reducing Risk," the Board found little connection between EPA's budget priorities and the scientists' risk rankings (indeed it was close to an inverse correlation).[4] EPA spent large sums on risks that the Board ranked as comparatively low and small amounts on risks ranked as comparatively higher. EPA's largest budget item, treatment of contaminated land, for example, was rated as a low priority while high priorities, such as radon exposure and ecosystem protection, received much less funding. *Reducing Risk* and subsequent studies have led many people to call for stronger reliance on cost-benefit analysis and risk assessment when drafting and implementing environmental laws. Defenders of EPA's priorities have responded that scientific risk estimates do not take into account all of the characteristics of risk that are important to the public (e.g., whether businesses cause the risk or the risk naturally occurs) and that EPA's expenditures closely parallel the public's perception of risks.

Another cause of inefficiency can be the laws themselves. A number of environmental laws could be described as "management by crisis." Following public outcry over an event, Congress rushes to address the problem and enacts hastily drafted legislation. The clearest example of this is in the Superfund law governing the remediation of contaminated land. Following media coverage of widespread contamination from chemical barrels buried beneath the homes in Love Canal in upstate New York, Congress drafted Superfund in a matter of months. The bill's passage was even more hurried because it was adopted in the lame duck Congress between the election of Ronald Reagan over Jimmy Carter and Reagan's inauguration.

Moreover, as many environmental law students find in their first few classes, environmental law can be quite complex and ambiguous. In some areas, particularly the field of hazardous waste law, the regulations can be dauntingly opaque. To be sure, many of these criticisms represent industry lobbying for more lenient treatment or weaker standards, but simply dismissing such critiques as industry whining misses the point that the system of environmental law raises compliance barriers all on its own. Consider, for example, that there are over 11,000 pages of federal environmental law, not to mention state and local laws, and the number of environmental provisions is growing.

Another major concern raised by environmental law is that of unintended consequences. The simplistic ecological maxim that "everything goes somewhere" has a grain of truth. Actions taken to resolve one problem often may exacerbate or create another problem. Thus restricting land disposal of hazardous waste in the

---

[4] Environmental Protection Agency, Reducing Risk: Setting Priorities and Strategies for Environmental Protection (1990).

1980s reduced that problem but created a new one. In an example of "media shifting," greater volumes of hazardous waste were burned in incinerators instead of being buried, and the danger from air toxics increased. Another classic case of an unintended impact is Superfund's expansive liability regime for contaminated land sites discouraging development of downtown industrial sites (known as "brownfield sites") and, instead, driving businesses to so-called "greenfield sites" in the suburbs, exacerbating the problems of urban sprawl.

Such cases present examples of *risk/risk problems*. Reducing one risk often increases another risk. Given that we live in a closed system and that everything really does go somewhere, it's crucial that we manage risk/risk decisions more intelligently since they are inevitable. One way to do so involves taking more of a *life-cycle approach*, identifying where the pollution or resource goes, straight from its creation all the way to its ultimate disposal.

A final major criticism of environmental law is that of fairness. As described earlier, determining who should bear the burden of environmental protection is a controversial subject. Why should a company that complied fully with environmental laws at the time it disposed of its waste be potentially liable under Superfund for cleaning up an entire site that was mismanaged and largely contaminated by others? Is it fair that private landowners should be uncompensated if they cannot develop their land because of the chance presence of an endangered species?

Despite its shortcomings, in its brief four decades environmental law has accomplished a great deal, yielding a fertile seedbed for regulatory innovations, trading programs, environmental taxes, and performance-based regulation, not to mention the experiments currently underway at the state level.

II. The Administration of Environmental Protection

In order to understand the practice of environmental law one must first grasp the broader legal framework within which it operates. While media-specific statutes such as the Clean Air Act or resource-specific laws such as the Endangered Species Act determine what regulated parties may or may not do, these operate within more general constraints on what the government is allowed to do. Administrative law sets the parameters for how agencies may implement these statutes and constitutional law sets the limits of governmental authority. Vast subjects in themselves, the remaining sections of this chapter provide a brief primer on the roles of administrative and constitutional law in environmental protection, as well as the unique role of non-state actors in the environmental field and their use of citizen suits to shape environmental law.

A.   Basics of Administrative Law

Administrative law is held up as one of the great inventions of the American experience and, in many respects, it truly is. Administrative law makes government activity more open, accountable, and responsive to the public than in any other country. Administrative law concerns *how agencies operate*—the processes and procedures they use to perform their functions—and the *separation of powers*—the competitive relationship and respective powers between the legislative and executive branches of government and the role of courts in refereeing this constant battle. Writ large, the field is about government, what government does, and what it can and can't do. In some ways, administrative law represents the flip side of corporate law. Just as corporate law regulates the conduct of private organizations, administrative law serves as the law of public organizations.

Why is understanding the law of agencies crucial to understanding environmental law? As a short answer, one cannot identify an environmental issue that is *not* managed by an agency. Air and water pollution? Look to EPA. Wetlands? The Department of Defense (through the Army Corps of Engineers). Forests? Department of Agriculture (Forest Service). Endangered Species? Department of Interior (Fish & Wildlife Service). Marine fisheries? Department of Commerce (National Marine Fisheries Service). The list could, and does, go on and on and on. Agency action is where environmental protection happens.

Hardly a new creation, the first three administrative departments were established in 1789 (State, Treasury, and War). Along the way, other well-known departments such as Interior, Treasury, Justice, Commerce, and Labor have been added with growth spurts during the New Deal in the 1930s and the Great Society in the 1960s. President Richard Nixon created the Environmental Protection Agency in 1970 in response to growing interest in the environment. Hard to believe, but the Code of Federal Regulations' Alphabetical List of Agencies now runs over nine pages of fine print!

This alphabet soup of government agencies plays many different roles. Agencies can issue rules, conduct inspections, award licenses, adjudicate disputes, demand information, hold hearings, and give and take money, just to name a few activities. As a result of these varied roles, agencies maintain an uneasy position within the three branches of government. As we all learned in high school, the Executive Branch faithfully executes the laws, the Legislative

Branch creates laws and controls the purse strings, and the Judicial
Branch interprets the law and applies the Constitution. So where in
this scheme do agencies fit in? All agency actions must be
authorized by Congress, which effectively delegates some of its
authorities. But, from the brief description above, it seems that
agencies fit in all three branches—making rules, investigating
compliance, punishing violations, and hearing appeals. This
combination of tasks leads to tension within the Executive and
Legislative branches as they compete with one another to influence
agency behavior.

The judiciary is supposed to act as a referee in this turf war,
determining if agencies (generally located within the Executive
branch) have followed Congressional intent closely enough. Making
this determination depends critically on the court's vision of the
agency itself. Consider two very different models of administrative
agencies. In one model, which is called *scientific expertise*,
technocrats in white jackets populate the agency. These agency
personnel are experts in what they do, faithfully carrying out the
will of Congress by relying on their best professional judgment. This
model views agencies as efficiently implementing the mandates of
government.

The contrasting model, known as *interest group representation,*
views agencies as mini-legislatures. As in Congress, special
interests battle it out to influence the implementation of laws. In
this model, agencies are simply a microcosm of the larger political
debate, with the same political processes taking place within
agencies. This is not necessarily a bad thing, but raises the specter
of two dangers. The first is known as *agency capture*. Agencies may
so closely align themselves with the industries they're supposed to
regulate that the public interest is lost in the process. Perhaps the
clearest example of this was the decision by the U.S. Forest Service
that the best "multiple use" of the Tongass National Forest, given
the competing interests of recreation, wildlife protection,
preservation, and logging, was to dedicate *100%* of the forest to
logging.[5] Such one-sided decisions can be explained by *public choice
theory*, which predicts that the efforts of concentrated interests
directly impacted by government policy (e.g., timber companies
logging in National Forests) will more effectively influence the
political process than more diffuse, though larger, interests (such as
the general public).

A second danger is that of agency self-interest. In order to
increase its power and perpetuate itself, the argument goes,

---

[5] *Sierra Club v. Hardin*, 325 F. Supp. 99 (D. Alaska 1971), rev'd sub nom.
Sierra Club v. Butz, 3 Envtl. L. Rep. 20292 (9th Cir.1973).

agencies may act more out of bureaucratic self-interest than in the public interest. This charge is often levied against the Army Corps of Engineers, for example, for pushing environmentally harmful, expensive construction projects that are popular in Congressional members' home districts.

Which model one believes best describes agency action has a huge influence on the appropriate judicial role in administrative law. If scientific expertise is the accurate model, then judicial review should be deferential since, after all, the agency officials are the real experts. If, however, interest group representation better exemplifies agency action, then little deference should be granted by judges and strict review should be used to uncover hidden deals, rent seeking, and self-interested decisionmaking.

The last broad point to note about agencies is the importance of the Administrative Procedure Act (APA).[6] Passed in 1946, the APA operates for agencies in some respects the way the rules of civil procedure do for trial judges and lawyers. For our purposes, the APA sets out procedures agencies must follow when promulgating rules and adjudicating conflicts. It also establishes the standard of judicial review (which varies depending on the type of action) when agency actions are challenged in court. The next two subsections briefly explain the APA requirements and case law governing (1) agency rulemaking and (2) adjudication. Understanding these two common types of agency action is important because the main line of attack against agency action is just as often procedural (e.g., the proper notice requirements for rulemaking were not complied with) as substantive (e.g., the Clean Air Act forbids this agency action).

1.   *Rulemaking*

As just noted, the APA breaks most agency actions into two broad categories—rulemaking and adjudication. As its name suggests, rulemaking describes agency decisions that affect general classes of people. Rulemaking concerns prospective policy decisions and produces rules of general applicability. Adjudication, by contrast, concerns agency decisions over claims of disputed facts that require particularized application and produces what are called "orders." An agency decision, for example, to establish the level of sulfur dioxide that oil-fired power plants may emit would be rulemaking. If a particular plant challenged the rule's applicability to its operations, the agency decision would be an adjudication. In general, differentiating between rulemaking and adjudication is straightforward, but it's an important distinction because the APA's requirements for the two procedures are significantly different.

---

[6]   5 U.S.C. §§ 551 et seq.

Where do agency rules come from? Usually they come from statutory mandates. In most environmental laws Congress simply passes broad framework legislation, leaving it up to the agency to fill in the (often extensive) details. As described in Chapter 5, when the Clean Air Act requires EPA to "protect the public health with an adequate margin of safety," EPA must decide which *specific pollutants* to regulate and their permissible *levels* of emission. In RCRA, Congress leaves it up to EPA to determine which substances should be regulated as solid hazardous waste. These are technical decisions with immense practical impact. Not all agency rulemaking is statutorily driven, though. Some rules may come from public petition; some may result from political pressure from Congress or the White House. All are published in the Code of Federal Regulations.

In reaching these decisions, the agency must comply with the APA's procedural requirements for rulemaking. In the environmental context, we need only concern ourselves with the APA's requirements for what is known as *informal rulemaking* (sometimes referred to as *notice-and-comment* rulemaking). The term *informal*, though, can be misleading. Informal rulemaking is still a rigorous procedure, not just Bob and Sue sitting around an office saying, "You want to make a rule?" "Sure. You go ahead and write it. I'm going to get some donuts."

Section 553 of the APA requires agencies to provide notice of a proposed rule in the Federal Register, including the agency's source of authority to issue the rule, a description of the proposed rule, and notice to interested persons of the location and time of public hearings, as well as opportunity to submit comments. The agency also must publish the final rule in the Federal Register, including responses to the categories of submitted comments, justifying the rule's final form. This is a far more rigorous process for agency action than in any other country in the world and seeks to ensure that agency rules are well-crafted, transparent, and consider the views of affected parties.

When final rules are challenged (as many of EPA's are), the key question for the courts is what the standard of review should be. The APA states that courts must ensure the agency action is not arbitrary and capricious or an abuse of discretion. Although this standard might sound very deferential to agencies, federal courts in the 1970s used it to take a "hard look" at agency actions. In *Citizens to Preserve Overton Park v. Volpe*,[7] the Secretary of Transportation provided no justification for approving the construction of a highway through a park in Memphis, despite the fact that the

---

[7] 401 U.S. 402 (1971).

relevant law forbade use of public funds to construct highways through public parks if a "reasonable and prudent" alternative route was available. In remanding the case back to the agency, the D.C. Circuit Court of Appeals held that it could not determine if the agency's action was arbitrary and capricious absent evidence that the agency's decision had resulted from a thorough, probing, in-depth review. This and similar decisions forced agencies to create more thorough records of decision in anticipation of judicial review.

In its 1978 decision in *Vermont Yankee Nuclear Power Corporation v. Natural Resources Defense Council, Inc.,*[8] the United States Supreme Court put an end to this trend and announced that courts generally should not add new procedural requirements. In challenging an action by the Atomic Energy Agency, the Natural Resources Defense Council argued that it should have been able to engage in cross-examination, discovery, and other procedures prior to issuance of the rule. The D.C. Circuit agreed, holding that the agency's procedures had been inadequate. On appeal, the Supreme Court told lower courts to knock it off. Courts, the Supreme Court held, cannot impose procedural requirements that are not required by statute unless there are extremely compelling circumstances or constitutional constraints.

The United States Supreme Court appeared to further limit judicial oversight of agency actions a few years later in the classic administrative law case of *Chevron U.S.A., Inc. v. Natural Resources Defense Council.*[9] *Chevron* concerned EPA's interpretation of the term "stationary source" under the Clean Air Act. The case is described in the box on the next page and turned on whether the EPA's interpretation of this statutory language represented a permissible interpretation of the Clean Air Act. If Congress had provided little guidance to the text's meaning, how much deference should be given to the agency's interpretation of the statutory requirement?

The approach to statutory interpretation that the Court adopted in *Chevron*, sometimes referred to as the "*Chevron* two-step," asks two questions. First, has Congress spoken directly to the precise question at issue? If the statutory language is clear or Congress' intent is otherwise clear, then the issue is simple. The court must determine whether the agency action conforms to the unambiguous Congressional mandate. The court exercises a

---

[8] 435 U.S. 519 (1978).

[9] 467 U.S. 837 (1984). It's interesting to note that the most important administrative law cases (*Overton Park, Vermont Yankee, Chevron, and Lujan*) are environmental cases. And a helpful hint—if you're taking administrative law, the teacher asks you a question about judicial review, and you have no idea what the answer is . . . offer up "*Chevron*" and there's a good chance you'll be right.

completely independent judgment with no deference to the agency. If, though, as is far more often the case, Congress has not directly addressed the specific question, or is silent, or ambiguous, or has expressly left a gap for the agency to fill, the second step kicks in. In this instance, the court must decide only whether the agency's answer is based on a "permissible" construction of the statute. The agency's interpretation need not be the best or most reasonable in the eyes of the Court; it simply must be reasonable and not arbitrary, capricious, or an abuse of discretion. In *Chevron*, the Supreme Court concluded that the Clean Air Act was ambiguous but that EPA's interpretation of the term "stationary source" was reasonable and thus permissible.

CHEVRON U.S.A. INC. V. NATURAL RESOURCES DEFENSE COUNCIL, INC., ET AL.
467 U.S. 837 (1984)

One of the major changes of the 1977 amendments to the Clean Air Act was a revision of the "New Source Review" provisions for states that were not in compliance. Facilities in these non-attainment areas that wished to add new sources or make major modifications to existing sources of air pollution would have to obtain a state permit and employ specific control technologies.

A key question that arose in implementing these modified rules was what constituted a "source." In the past, the EPA had relied on different definitions of a stationary source, sometimes treating each individual unit of equipment as a source (i.e., each individual smokestack), and at other times regarding an entire plant facility as a source. This latter approach was known as "bubbling," because it essentially bundled all of the separate units within a plant under a conceptual bubble, treating the total emissions as a single source of pollution. This concept allowed companies to manage their compliance more efficiently, distributing emissions reductions among the various smokestacks to reduce total costs, all the while ensuring the total emissions did not increase. Initially, the EPA adopted the dual definition of "source," and required each new or modified unit to meet the new source review provisions. However, in 1981, after the Reagan Administration came into office, the EPA adopted the bubble approach.

In 1982, the Natural Resources Defense Council (NRDC) challenged the new EPA definition in the appeals court of the D.C. Circuit. The D.C. Circuit ruled against the new EPA interpretation of "stationary source." A number of industry groups, including Chevron Inc., supported the new EPA regulation, and joined the government in appealing the case to the Supreme Court. As part of its case, NRDC argued that the "plain meaning" of the 1977 amendments required that each unit in a plant be considered an individual source, because the definition of "major stationary source" included references to any "building" or "structure," and these could not refer to an entire plant. The government argued that the EPA decision should be given deference, and that the entire plant approach would allow states to balance the Clean Air Act goals of improving air quality and encouraging industrial growth.

In a unanimous decision, the Supreme Court upheld the EPA's plantwide definition of a stationary source. The Court concluded that Congress' intended definition of "stationary source" was not obvious from the statute. It held that the EPA's designation of an entire plant as a source was reasonable, and therefore the Court must defer to the agency's decision and uphold the plantwide definition. In applying this two-part test for evaluation of agency decisions, the Court established a fundamental part of administrative law.

There are, of course, many reasons why Congress might leave issues open by using vague statutory language. It might consciously desire the agency to make a policy choice; it may not have considered the specific issue (as was the case in *Chevron*); it may have been unable to reach a compromise so it passed over the issue. On its face, *Chevron* placed great power in the hands of agencies since it seemed to call for strong deference. This is consistent with arguments that unelected judges should back off and let agencies do what they do best (i.e., apply their expertise) so long as the procedures are followed. In practice, though, *Chevron* has not led to a massive increase in favorable agency decisions. Courts still overturn agency rules, almost always relying on Step One (that Congressional intent was clear and the agency got it wrong) rather than the more deferential Step Two. This practice is more consistent with the interest representation model—because of agency capture and self-interest, agencies may make decisions contrary to the facts or statute and courts must provide the first line of protection against this. We will see these arguments play out in Chapter 10's discussion of *Babbitt v. Sweet Home Chapter of Communities for a Great Oregon*,[10] upholding the Department of Interior's interpretation of the Endangered Species Act.

As a final insight on rulemaking, it is important to note that one class of rules is not subject to the APA requirements for informal rulemaking at all. Known as nonlegislative rules or

---

[10] 515 U.S. 687 (1995).

THE PRACTICE OF ENVIRONMENTAL

publication rules, these include guidance documents and interpretive rulings (such as tax forms and how to fill them out, or guidance to prosecutors on how various violations should be punished). Such nonlegislative rules are far more voluminous than either the statute or informal rules they support. As an example, there are roughly 20 feet of shelf space for informal rules issued under the Clean Air Act. Agencies can issue these rules without any notice or public comment for the simple reason that, technically, these rules are not legally binding. Agencies, however, usually follow them as a matter of practice, placing regulated parties at the risk of violating requirements on which they never had an opportunity to comment. The standard of judicial review for such nonlegislative rules is known as *Skidmore* deference, a lower level of deference than the *Chevron* standard.[11]

2.   Adjudication

While rulemaking concerns prospective decisions affecting a class of people, adjudication is more often retrospective and covers a broad range of agency actions, from license denials and revocation to the agency's enforcement of its rules. As with rulemaking, the key challenges to adjudication decisions are often procedural, i.e., was the proper process followed?

For most environmental issues, the relevant procedures are set out in the requirements for informal adjudication in section 555 of the APA. Fairly minimal, these requirements include the right to counsel, to appear before the agency, and to receive a decision within a reasonable time. Agencies usually set additional procedures and publish these in the Federal Register. All of these requirements supplement, of course, the Constitutional requirements of the 5th and 14th amendments for due process if there is deprivation of liberty or property.

3.   Final Agency Action

Agencies obviously take many actions that are neither rulemaking nor adjudication, such as issuing a permit to hold a parade in a national park or failing to consider the appropriate factors in denying a petition to list a species under the Endangered Species Act. Administrative law prevents challenges to agency actions in court until the doctrines of finality (i.e., the action has been decided within the agency), ripeness (the issue is ready for judicial resolution) and exhaustion (the challenging party's opportunities for review within the agency process are exhausted). When agency actions can be challenged in court, APA Section 706 directs the judge to "compel agency action unlawfully withheld or

---

[11] *United States v. Mead Corp.*, 533 U.S. 218, 234–38 (2001).

unreasonably delayed" as well as "hold unlawful" actions found to be "arbitrary, capricious, an abuse of discretion, or otherwise not in accordance with law."

III. Constitutional Issues in Environmental Policy

The United States Constitution dictates what the federal and state governments can and cannot do. In this section, we explore the powers that the federal Congress can use to protect the environment, the degree to which Congress and state legislatures can delegate decisions to expert administrative agencies like EPA, and the constitutional "takings" provisions that restrict the degree to which the federal and state governments can protect the environment by regulating private property.

One other constitutional issue also looms large in the environmental field and is covered at various points later in this book. The supremacy clause of the United States Constitution gives Congress the power to preempt state environmental regulations. Congress has largely eschewed its power to preempt more restrictive state regulations, leaving states free to go beyond the environmental standards set by the federal government. However, Congress has occasionally chosen to limit stronger state regulation. As discussed in Chapter 5, for example, most states are not free to set whatever automobile standards they wish.

A.   *Congressional Powers*

In passing environmental laws, Congress has relied primarily on its *commerce power*.[12] For years, this seemed a fairly safe bet because the courts permitted Congress to use this power to regulate virtually any activity that had the remotest possible relationship to interstate commerce. Think of virtually any environmental regulation, and it is easy to imagine some way, although sometimes attenuated, that the regulation will affect interstate commerce. In a series of cases in the 1990s, however, the Supreme Court held that there are limits to Congress' authority, raising new questions about the constitutionality of some federal environmental laws.

Of greatest importance is *United States v. Lopez*.[13] Alphonso Lopez, a high school student, was convicted of violating the federal Gun-Free School Zones Act which banned the possession of firearms within 1000 feet of any school. By a slim 5–4 majority, the Supreme Court reversed the conviction and held that the Act was not within Congress' commerce power. According to the Court, Congress can use its commerce power to regulate only (1) the "use of the channels

---

[12] Art. I, § 8 ("The Congress shall have Power. . . . To regulate Commerce . . . among the several States. . . . ").

[13] 514 U.S. 549 (1995).

of intrastate commerce," (2) activities that threaten the "instrumentalities of interstate commerce, or persons or things in interstate commerce," and (3) "activities having a *substantial* relation to interstate commerce" (emphasis added). *Lopez* focused on whether the Gun-Free School Zones Act met the third of these tests. The Court concluded that carrying a gun near a school does not substantially affect interstate commerce and therefore is not a legitimate subject of federal regulation. The majority refused to "pile inference upon inference in a manner that would bid fair to convert congressional authority under the Commerce Clause to a general police power of the sort retained by the States."[14] In the Court's view, Congress cannot regulate an activity merely because it has some impact on interstate commerce, however remote.

Even as restricted by *Lopez*, the Commerce Clause provides Congress with very broad authority over the environment. Virtually all of Congress' efforts to regulate pollution or hazardous substances would seem constitutional. The Federal Insecticide, Rodenticide, and Fungicide Act and the Toxic Substances Control Act regulate products such as pesticides and asbestos that are bought and sold in interstate commerce, and thus fall within Congress' authority to regulate the use of the channels of interstate commerce. The traditional pollution statutes, such as the Clean Air Act and Clean Water Act, regulate commercial activities or products, such as automobiles, that again are sold in interstate commerce. Congress' efforts to hold generators of hazardous waste and disposal facilities responsible for the cleanup of contaminated land arguably protects interstate commerce from the dangers of pollution. Indeed, the Supreme Court has explicitly held that the commerce power is "broad enough to permit Congressional regulation of activities causing air or water pollution, or other environmental hazards that may have effects in more than one state."[15]

Federal laws that regulate local land use, however, such as the Endangered Species Act or the wetlands provisions of the Clean Water Act, have a less certain constitutional footing. First, land use decisions historically have been the province of local government, making Congress look more like an interloper when it becomes involved. Second, and more importantly, the linkage between land use regulations and interstate commerce often is remote. The connection between interstate commerce and a small seasonal wetland or the habitat of an endangered species that is

---

[14] *Id.* at 567.

[15] *Hodel v. Virginia Surface Min. & Reclamation Ass'n*, 452 U.S. 264, 282 (1981).

geographically confined is far less obvious than the relationship between pesticides and interstate commerce.

To date, challenges to federal land use regulations all have failed. Federal courts of appeal repeatedly have rejected constitutional challenges to federal regulation of wetlands under the Clean Water Act. The Supreme Court granted certiorari in *Solid Waste Agency of Northern Cook County v. United States Army Corps of Engineers*[16] to consider whether Congress could regulate isolated wetlands that are not connected to navigable waterways, but ultimately decided that Congress had not intended to regulate such wetlands, avoiding the constitutional issue. The Court warned, however, that broad jurisdiction under the Clean Water Act would "result in a significant impingement on the states' traditional and primary power over lands and water use" and raise "significant constitutional and federalism questions." In finding again five years later that Congress had not intended to regulate certain isolated wetlands, the Court repeated its warning that a broad interpretation of the Clean Water Act "stretches the outer limits of Congress's commerce power and raises difficult questions about the ultimate scope of that power."[17]

A number of federal appellate courts have upheld the federal government's ability to protect the habitat of purely intrastate species under the Endangered Species Act, but the judges have had a difficult time agreeing on a rationale. By an extremely fractured vote, for example, a three-judge panel of the D.C. Circuit rejected a constitutional challenge to the federal government's efforts to protect the few hundred acres of remaining habitat, all in a limited area of Southern California, of the Delhi Sands flower loving fly.[18] After a local county found that it could not reconstruct an intersection to meet the needs of a new hospital because the construction might jeopardize the fly, the county sued to challenge Congress' authority over the fly and its habitat. One judge concluded that the federal government could protect the fly both because the fly someday might be found to have genetic value of interstate importance and because, absent federal regulation, states might compete for businesses by lowering their protections of biodiversity. A second judge concluded that Congress had adequate authority because the objects of regulation—the hospital and the traffic intersection—had "an obvious connection with interstate commerce." The third judge dissented, finding no connection with interstate commerce.

---

[16] 531 U.S. 159 (2001).

[17] *Rapanos v. United States*, 547 U.S. 715, 738 (2006).

[18] *National Ass'n of Home Builders v. Babbitt*, 130 F.3d 1041 (D.C. Cir. 1997).

Other Congressional powers also may support particular environmental legislation. For example, the Property Clause, which gives Congress the "power to dispose of and make all needful Rules and Regulations respecting . . . Property belonging to the United States,"[19] justifies laws designed to protect the environment on federal lands, even when the laws regulate activities on nearby private property. Congress also may be able to use its spending power both to pay for environmental amenities and, by refusing to grant federal funds to states or private entities that fail to adopt various environmental measures, encourage states or private entities to adopt policies that they otherwise might not. Congress, for example, requires states to meet specified ambient air standards if the states wish to receive federal highway funds.

B.   Legislative Delegation

Expert administrative agencies like the federal EPA are critical to modern environmental regulation. Congress does not have the expertise, time, or resources to work out all the details of environmental regulation—for example, the appropriate ambient air quality standard for sulfur dioxide, or the proper habitat to protect for the endangered snowy plover. Congress unavoidably must rely on EPA and other agencies to determine these regulatory details. As emphasized earlier, moreover, environmental regulation is plagued by uncertainty and beset by change. Even if Congress could establish all the details of a regulatory regime at one point in time, new scientific, economic, and social information would require Congress constantly to revise the details. Congress can best deal with uncertainty and change by setting out broad policy directives that are not dependent on assumptions that are likely to change and then letting administrative agencies implement the directives on an evolving basis.

The Constitution, however, establishes Congress as the legislative, or policy-making, branch of the government. As Congress provides EPA and other agencies with greater discretion, the question arises whether, at some point, Congress is unconstitutionally delegating its legislative authority to administrative agencies.

Every federal environmental statute delegates policy decisions to EPA or other federal agencies. Consider, for example, the Clean Air Act's mandate that EPA set ambient air quality standards at a level "requisite to protect the human health" and allowing for "an adequate margin of safety."[20] At first glance, this Congressional

---

[19] Art. IV, § 3.

[20] 42 U.S.C. § 7409(b)(1).

directive might seem relatively specific. But any effort to apply this directive to a particular pollutant raises scores of policy questions. If even a slight level of pollution would injure a small population of sensitive people, should EPA set a zero standard, or can EPA focus on the average member of the population? How should EPA handle scientific uncertainty: if a minority of scientists believe that a pollutant is more dangerous than the current consensus view, what should EPA assume? What is an "adequate margin of safety"?

Does the Constitution require Congress to provide administrative agencies with a minimum level of policy guidance? The temptation is to say "yes." Otherwise, Congress could escape making any controversial policy decisions and delegate to an administrative agency the authority to issue whatever regulations the agency wishes to adopt. Yet drawing a line between permissible and unconstitutional delegations is exceptionally difficult since any delegation gives an agency some policy discretion. By limiting Congress' ability to delegate regulatory authority, moreover, the courts risk undermining the effectiveness of the modern administrative state.

During the New Deal era, the Supreme Court invalidated a number of statutes for unconstitutionally delegating legislative authority to an administrative agency. In *Yakus v. United States*,[21] however, the Court upheld the Emergency Price Control Act of 1942, even though it gave the federal Office of Price Administration the authority to fix commodity prices at a level which, in the judgment of the Administrator, would be "generally fair and equitable and will effectuate the purposes of this Act." Broader delegations are hard to imagine, and the Court has never used the unconstitutional delegation doctrine to invalidate Congressional legislation since. In *Whitman v. American Trucking Associations, Inc.*,[22] the Supreme Court held that Congress had not unconstitutionally delegated its legislative power to EPA by authorizing the agency to set national ambient air quality standards that, "allowing an adequate margin of safety, are requisite to protect the public health." According to the Court, a "certain degree of discretion, and thus of law making, inheres in most executive or judicial action," and this standard is "well within the outer limits" of the Court's nondelegation precedent.[23]

In contrast to the federal courts, approximately a third of the state judiciaries still carefully police legislative delegations under their own constitutions. These courts typically require the state

---

[21] 321 U.S. 414 (1944).
[22] 531 U.S. 457 (2001).
[23] Id. at 474–475.

legislature to provide "adequate standards" or an "intelligible principle" to constrain an agency's decisions. These state courts worry that, absent any constraint, legislatures will be tempted to duck tough policy decisions, abdicating their constitutional responsibility.

C. Regulatory Takings

The *just compensation provisions* of the United States Constitution, which prohibit the federal and state governments from "taking" private property without the payment of just compensation, also constrain environmental regulation. Although courts could have read the provisions as applying only to physical expropriations of property for highways and other governmental uses, the Supreme Court has held for over a century that regulations may also constitute takings for which compensation must be paid. The difficult trick, as courts have learned, is determining *when* a regulation goes too far and becomes a taking. Perhaps not surprisingly, many of the principal cases addressing this issue have involved environmental regulations.

The question of what constitutes a *regulatory taking* is one of the most difficult legal issues around. Take, for example, the argument that a landowner should be compensated for loss in property value because the federal government will not let her develop part of her property on which an endangered species lives. Part of the problem is that neither courts nor academic scholars can agree on *why* the Constitution should require the government to pay compensation for regulations that reduce the value of a landowner's property. Taking an economic approach, some judges and scholars argue that, absent compensation, the government may suffer from what has been labeled *fiscal illusion*. If the government does not have to pay compensation, it may conclude that its regulations are costless, even where they destroy significant property value; as a consequence, the government may over-regulate property. Other courts and scholars, by contrast, argue that compensation is a matter of fairness: a property owner should not have to bear the cost, for example, of preserving the habitat of an endangered species when neighboring landowners bear no cost at all and the habitat will benefit the general public. The arguments for providing compensation are multiple, and each unfortunately points to a different test for identifying regulatory takings.

For every argument in favor of compensation, moreover, there is a counter-argument. In response to the argument that the government will suffer from fiscal illusion if it does not have to pay compensation, some academic scholars have observed that property

owners generally enjoy significant political power and are likely to
make the cost of a proposed regulation very evident to the
legislature. Legislatures thus are more likely to under-regulate
property than to over-regulate it. As for the fairness argument,
many courts and scholars would respond that property owners do
not have the right to develop their land if it would destroy a species'
essential habitat. By prohibiting the development, the government
is not imposing a cost on the property owner but simply preventing
the landowner from injuring the environment in a way that never
was permissible.

Even assuming that there is a good argument for providing
compensation, one has to worry about the potential costs of
providing compensation. Environmentalists, for example, fear that
Congress might hesitate to protect the environment if the
government has to pay every property owner who claims that his or
her land will decline in value as a result. To many conservatives,
this simply shows that the benefits of the environmental
regulations do not justify their costs. But environmentalists would
reply that the legislative process is not always rational and that
large compensation payments may deter legislation even when the
benefits exceed the costs. The government, moreover, must raise
taxes to pay for any compensation, and economic studies have
demonstrated that many types of taxes generate high social losses
(e.g., by discouraging people from working).

Given these complexities, it should not be surprising that the
Supreme Court has had trouble devising an easy test for when a
regulation constitutes a taking and requires compensation. Indeed,
in the late 1970s, the Court appeared to give up any hope of
developing general guidelines for determining when a regulation is
a taking. In *Penn Central Transportation Co. v. New York City*,[24]
the Court confessed that it had been "unable to develop any 'set
formula' for determining when 'justice and fairness' require that
economic injuries caused by public action be compensated by the
government, rather than remain disproportionately concentrated on
a few persons." The Court concluded that regulatory takings cases
should be analyzed instead on an ad hoc, fact-specific basis in which
courts balance (1) the extent of interference with "distinct
investment-backed expectations," (2) the nature of the interference,
and (3) the purposes of the governmental regulation. Over a quarter
of a century of experience with the *Penn Central* balancing
standard, however, has led to few regulations being overturned.
Given latitude, most courts appear to be unwilling to encumber
governmental efforts to protect the environment and other public

---

[24] 438 U.S. 104 (1978).

amenities by requiring the government to pay compensation if it wishes to regulate the actions of property owners.

In an attempt to bring greater certainty to regulatory takings doctrine (and perhaps to add a bit of backbone to the law), the Supreme Court in the late 20th century announced two "categorical takings tests" to supplement the *Penn Central* balancing standard. First, the Court held that regulations constitute takings if they interfere with a property owner's "core" right to exclude others from her land. Thus, regulations that permit members of the public onto someone's property or that otherwise authorize a *permanent physical occupation* of the property are takings for which compensation must be paid. Second, in *Lucas v. South Carolina Coastal Council*,[25] described on the next page, the Court also held that a regulation constitutes a taking if it deprives a landowner of *all* the economically viable use of her property. Because only preservation statutes are likely to deprive a landowner of the total economic use of her property, environmentalists worried that *Lucas* reflected an anti-environmental bias on the part of the Court.

The Supreme Court today does not appear anxious to apply these categorical takings tests to a broad set of regulations. Tellingly, landowners have never argued that pollution-control statutes such as the Clean Air Act are takings. By restricting the way in which property owners can use their land, pollution-control statutes potentially can reduce the value of some parcels. But no one contends in our society today that a landowner has the right to pollute. Because pollution-control statutes do not take any property right from the landowner, pollution-control statutes do not constitute takings, even if they lower the value of someone's land. By contrast, many landowners do believe that they have the right to develop their land even if it contains wetlands, habitat for endangered or threatened species, or other environmentally valuable resources. In their eyes, governmental protections of these lands therefore do raise takings issues.

LUCAS V. SOUTH CAROLINA COASTAL COUNCIL
505 U.S. 1003 (1992)

In 1984, David Lucas became involved in Wild Dunes, a real estate development project involving 2500 condominiums and several golf courses and marinas on a South Carolina barrier island known as the Isle of Palms. Lucas sold his interest in Wild

---

[25] 505 U.S. 1003 (1992).

Dunes in 1986, but bought back two waterfront lots—one for a personal residence, and the other for investment. The land was in an "unstabilized inlet" and had suffered over the years from flooding and erosion. In the face of growing concerns over beach erosion, South Carolina subsequently passed a Beachfront Management Act that prohibited construction or reconstruction in a no-build zone extending 20 feet landward of the point of furthest erosion over the previous three decades. Large portions of Lucas' land fell within the no-build zone.

Lucas challenged the Act as an unconstitutional taking of his property, claiming that the Act prevented him from developing his land and rendered the property valueless. The trial court agreed that the Act had stripped Lucas' land of all economic value and awarded him $1.2 million in compensation. Pending review of the case by the South Carolina Supreme Court, Hurricane Hugo battered the South Carolina coast, severely damaging and flooding much of the Isle of Palms. The state supreme court subsequently reversed the lower court's decision, holding that the Act sought to avoid a public harm and therefore was constitutional. No one, according to the court, is entitled to use land in a way that is harmful to the public.

The United States Supreme Court disagreed. According to the Court, the state supreme court's approach was unworkable because it is impossible to differentiate between regulations that prevent a harm and those that confer a benefit. "One could say that imposing a servitude on Lucas' land is necessary in order to prevent his use of it from 'harming' South Carolina's ecological resources; or, instead, in order to achieve the 'benefits' of an ecological preserve." Because the Act eliminated all the economically viable use of Lucas' land, the Act was a taking unless developing the land would be a common law nuisance or otherwise unlawful under "background principles" of state property law.

On remand, the South Carolina supreme court found that state common law did not limit the development of Lucas' property and that Lucas was therefore entitled to compensation. South Carolina settled the litigation in 1993 by purchasing Lucas' lots for just under $1.6 million. A year later, the state sold Lucas' lots, and a home was built on one of the lots. The construction was permissible because, in 1990, South Carolina had amended the Beachfront Management Act in response to the demands of coastal landowners who, in the aftermath of Hurricane Hugo, demanded the right to rebuild their homes. Coastal erosion continues to threaten homes on the Isle of Palms. Lucas, meanwhile, has become a conservative spokesperson for the property rights movement.

Landowners have tried a variety of arguments in favor of compensation in these settings. In challenging federal and state endangered species protections, for example, landowners have argued that the government has authorized an unconstitutional physical occupation of their property by the endangered species. If the government cannot permit people to invade someone's land, landowners reason, how can the government authorize endangered species to do the same? Courts have rejected this argument on the ground that the species are native to the land and thus not the same as marauding members of the public. A case might turn out differently if the government decided to transplant a species onto land that had not recently served as habitat or perhaps had never been habitat.

More commonly, property owners have challenged regulations as preventing them from developing a portion of their property and thus depriving them of all the economically viable use of that land in violation of *Lucas*. These challenges have raised the so-called "denominator question": can a landowner raise a *Lucas* claim regarding part of her property even if she can develop the rest? The government seldom prohibits a landowner from developing all of her land; as a result, the landowner retains some value in the portion that can be developed. Unless *Lucas* applies to the specific subparcel of land that cannot be developed, the landowner thus loses.

In *Tahoe–Sierra Preservation Council v. Tahoe Regional Planning Agency*,[26] the Supreme Court held that courts should examine the "parcel as a whole" in applying *Lucas*. In *Tahoe–Sierra*, the Tahoe Regional Planning Agency imposed a lengthy moratorium on the development of land near Lake Tahoe while the agency tried to determine how to protect the lake's water quality. The landowners challenged the moratorium, arguing that it temporarily deprived them of all the economically viable use of their land and therefore violated *Lucas*. The Court disagreed, rejecting the view that the land could be "conceptually severed" into different temporal pieces. Because the property retained longterm value, *Lucas* did not apply. In a similar vein, regulations that prohibit development of only a portion of a parcel of land are generally not categorical takings under *Lucas*. In such cases, the regulation is a taking only if it fails the multi-factored *Penn Central* standard.

---

[26] 535 U.S. 302 (2002).

Should it matter in environmental takings cases if landowners purchase their property after a governmental regulatory system is already in place? Assume, for example, that a landowner buys land in 1990—long after Congress awarded the Army Corps of Engineers authority to regulate wetlands—and is told in 2005 that she cannot develop any of her property because it contains valuable wetlands. The landowner argues that she's entitled to compensation under *Lucas.* Is it fair to award her compensation given that she knew or should have known of the regulatory authority? On the other hand, is it fair to let the government "off the hook" because the land changed hands? In *Palazzolo v. Rhode Island,*[27] the Supreme Court held that landowners who purchase property after a regulatory system is in place are not automatically barred from pursuing a takings claim. In concurring opinions, however, Justices O'Connor and Scalia disagreed on the relevance of the timing of the purchase. Justice O'Connor thought the timing should be relevant but not conclusive, while Justice Scalia argued that timing is totally irrelevant.

IV. How Citizen Groups Shape Environmental Law

Ask what has contributed the most to the development of a strong system of environmental regulation in the United States, and the most knowledgeable people are likely to point to the existence of a dynamic and forceful environmental movement. The United States has hosted an active environmental movement since soon after Henry David Thoreau moved to Walden Pond. When the Audubon Society (a predecessor to today's National Audubon Society) was formed in 1886, almost 40,000 people joined. Within the next fifty years, conservationists formed such important national organizations as the Sierra Club, the Izaak Walton League, and the Wilderness Society. By 1960, over 300,000 Americans belonged to major conservation organizations. These organizations helped to establish the vast system of national parks, forests, and wilderness areas that grace the United States today and to pass early environmental legislation.

The first Earth Day in 1970, however, saw a major change and expansion in the American environmental movement. The number of environmental organizations grew geometrically. The focus of the environmental movement, moreover, broadened to include pollution and toxic substances. Borrowing from the Civil Rights movement, environmental groups also adopted a more activist stance, filing litigation and aggressively lobbying Congress and administrative agencies. A number of the new environmental organizations

---

[27] 533 U.S. 606 (2001).

specifically emphasized legal change. Among the most prominent were the Environmental Defense Fund (formed in 1967 to get DDT banned), the Natural Resources Defense Council (formed in 1969 to help improve federal pollution laws), and the Sierra Club Legal Defense Fund (now Earthjustice, organized in 1971 to litigate cases on behalf of the environment).

The American environmental movement has played an essential role in the passage and implementation of effective environmental laws. Few political scientists would have predicted that the federal government would pass as strong laws as it has. Industrial opponents of environmental laws are typically well organized and can afford to invest substantial resources to defeat or weaken legislation. Few members of the general public, by contrast, have a sufficient enough interest in any particular piece of environmental legislation to devote equivalent resources to ensuring the legislation's passage. When asked to participate in a collective lobbying effort, moreover, many member of the public may be tempted to decline, presuming that they can "free ride" on the lobbying efforts of other members of the public.

The major environmental organizations in the United States have found effective means of overcoming these "collective action" obstacles. Environmental groups have raised substantial money from the public both by framing environmental issues in moral terms and by perfecting mass mailing campaigns. Although many people still free ride on others' donations, environmental groups have used their limited resources efficiently. Unlike industrial lobbyists, environmental organizations have been able to focus their resources entirely on environmental issues. Through coordinated lobbying campaigns, the organizations have provided Congress and state legislatures with valuable scientific and legal expertise. Through member communications and skilled use of the media, environmental organizations also have mobilized voters. As a result, the imprint of environmental organizations can be found throughout environmental law. The Natural Resources Defense Council, for example, helped pass the Clean Water Act. The Environmental Defense Fund helped devise the acid rain provisions of the 1990 Clean Air Act Amendments, including the provisions establishing a trading program in SO_2 emissions.

Environmental organizations have played an equally important role in shaping and strengthening environmental law through litigation. We explore their use of *citizen suits* and the doctrine of *standing* in our discussion of Enforcement in Chapter 4.

QUESTIONS AND DISCUSSION

1.   Do you agree that the proper level of environmental protection for air pollution and water pollution is fundamentally a political decision? If so, what does this mean about an ethical obligation to protect the environment?

2.   If there is no single "right" level of environmental protection and we must rely on our political process to determine these issues, then the proper working of political decisionmaking becomes critically important. Do you think political processes tend to favor environmental protection or favor economic development? Do you think certain interests tend to dominate the political process? Are these interests more likely to be environmental groups or extractive and polluting industries? Or does it depend on the issue? Why might one interest generally do better than the other?

3.   Apply the Five P's from the regulatory toolkit to a local environmental problem such as loss of wetlands or water pollution of a nearby lake or river. Do all five of the Five P's apply to the case of protecting an endangered species?

4.   As noted in the text, Free Market Environmentalists argue that the market can provide for better pollution control and natural resource management than government regulation. Some have even argued that the national parks should be sold at auction. While politically an unlikely event, what are the strongest policy arguments in favor of privatizing our national parks?

5.   Should the government provide compensation to the property owners in the following hypotheticals *as a matter of policy*? Are the property owners entitled to compensation under the United States Supreme Court's case law?

   a.   Best Chemicals, Inc., owns the patent on one of the most popular pesticides on the market, DiePest, which brings in over $350 million in income each year. The federal government has just decided to ban the production and sale of DiePest because of a new test showing that DiePest is carcinogenic in lab mice.

   b.   Over the past 25 years, new residential developments in Suburbia have destroyed 99 percent of the historic habitat of the 8–toed horned-headed lizard. As a result, the lizard population has dropped from an estimated 100,000 lizards in 1980 to just 57 today, and the government has just listed the lizard as endangered under the Endangered Species Act. Roberta Stilts owns the last 10 acres of lizard habitat. Stilts would like to develop her property just like all of her neighbors have previously developed their land, but the government has told her that it will not permit her to develop the land (although they will permit her to construct a small single-family residence on ¼-acre of the property that is not prime habitat).

Chapter 4

ENFORCEMENT

I. The Challenges of Enforcing the Law

Environmental enforcement is a critically important topic. The mere fact of a law's existence is no assurance of its implementation. Rules on the books can prove meaningless if they are not enforced. At a minimum, an effective system of enforcement should achieve both the *force* of law (compliance) and the *rule* of law (fair application to everyone). Yet ensuring the force and rule of law is by no means a given. Indeed, many countries around the world lack one, the other, or both.

Effective enforcement does not mean that *all* parties will comply with *all* relevant regulations *all* of the time. The federal tax system has a strong enforcement program. Yet what taxpayer does not blanch when receiving notification of an Internal Revenue Service audit? A fine-tooth inspection of any tax return will likely reveal some filing or calculation error, as will searching audits in any highly regulated field, whether securities, insurance, or others. Some noncompliance may be unintentional, and some knowing. Just think about your own driving. How often do you drive above the speed limit—whether because you are late, it seems safe, or others are driving fast too? One issue in enforcement therefore is what rate of compliance to seek. The government always can increase compliance by increasing the probability of detection and the size of fine or imprisonment, but these come with costs—the funding needed for more inspectors or the potential unfairness of raising fines or imprisonment terms even higher for relatively minor infractions.

Enforcement strategies may differ depending on the reason for noncompliance. Some regulated parties violate the law because it is in their economic interest. A company, for example, may be able to save money by dumping its effluent into a local stream without treating it first. These violators are *amoral calculators* who decide whether or not to comply with the law based on what is in their economic best interest.[1] In these cases, the government may want to impose a fine or prison sentence in order to deter violations. When the government fines a company for violating the Clean

---

[1] For an interesting discussion of the various reasons why regulated parties violate the law, and the implications for appropriate enforcement policy, *see* Robert A. Kagan & John T. Scholz, *The "Criminalization of the Corporation" and Regulatory Enforcement Strategies*, in Enforcing Regulation 67 (Keith Hawkins & John Thomas, eds. 1984).

Water Act, it discourages the company from violating the law again. This is known as *specific deterrence*. The fine also sends a signal to other companies that they risk a financial penalty if they violate the Clean Water Act, thus deterring a broader set of businesses from violating the law. This broader effect is known as *general deterrence*.

Companies and individuals, however, may violate environmental law for reasons other than saving money. Some regulated parties, for example, might be *political citizens* who are willing to comply with laws that they consider to be just, but believe that a particular environmental law either is unprincipled or is being enforced in a capricious and unfair fashion. To increase compliance among political citizens, the government needs to convince them of the appropriateness of the law and ensure that the law is being applied in a fair and even fashion. Other regulated parties may be *incompetent*; even though they want to comply with the law, they are unable to do so for technical or organizational reasons. In this last situation, the government can increase compliance only by helping the regulated party overcome its lack of capacity.

The problem, of course, is that violators can be any or all of these types—and it often will be difficult to differentiate among them. This makes it difficult to choose the correct strategy. To avoid the risk that amoral calculators will get by "scot-free," the government may be tempted to fine everyone. But this could backfire with political citizens (who may view this policy as unfair) and will do no good with incompetents (who are simply unable to comply). The government often will have no good option and must try to differentiate among violators as best it can. If the government does not fine political citizens or incompetents, however, amoral calculators will have an incentive to try to disguise themselves as one of those two types.

How well does U.S. environmental enforcement work? In terms of overall environmental metrics, the answer appears to be quite positive. With few exceptions, the air is cleaner, water less polluted, and waste more safely handled than twenty and thirty years ago. The sheer level of enforcement activity in the U.S. is also large. In 2011, the EPA initiated over 3,200 civil enforcement cases and opened 371 new environmental crime cases, not to mention the many actions filed by state authorities and many more independently-filed citizen suits. EPA claimed its enforcement actions resulted in 1.8 billion pounds of reduced pollution and $19 billion of investments by regulated parties to reduce pollution, clean up contamination, and fund environmentally beneficial projects.

Taken together, these are big numbers, and indicate a lot of enforcement activity.

Yet, if one focuses on what is not being monitored, the success of the nation's enforcement efforts becomes less clear. On average, EPA conducts about 22,000 inspections per year leading to over 3,000 civil actions; and states (who do the lion's share of enforcement) conduct 146,000 inspections and 9,000 enforcement actions on their own.[2] Impressive numbers, until one realizes that there are roughly eight *million* regulated parties subject to environmental laws. In other words, a regulated party has about a 2% chance of being inspected (and a 0.16% chance of being sanctioned) in any given year.

Indeed, certain areas of environmental law still face significant levels of noncompliance. A 2009 series of articles in the *New York Times* reported more than half a million violations of the Clean Water Act by 23,000 different companies since 2004. Roughly 40 percent of the nation's water systems, serving almost 25 million Americans, provided water that violated Safe Drinking Water Act standards. The reporter's conclusion was damning: "The violations range from failing to report emissions to dumping toxins at concentrations regulators say might contribute to cancer, birth defects and other illnesses. However, the vast majority of those polluters have escaped punishment. State officials have repeatedly ignored obvious illegal dumping, and the Environmental Protection Agency, which can prosecute polluters when states fail to act, has often declined to intervene."[3] Nor is this a new problem. EPA's own *Enforcement Alert* newsletter noted over a decade ago that "when EPA looks closely at an industry sector, usually it discovers a high rate of noncompliance."[4]

Should we be troubled by this level of noncompliance? According to the New York Times, at least some of the violations are paperwork violations. Does this matter? What can be done to strengthen compliance?

II. The Players

Enforcement of federal environmental law involves the close cooperation of different actors at both the federal and state level. How much to centralize or decentralize enforcement is itself an

---

[2] Jon Silberman, *Does Environmental Deterrence Work? Evidence and Experience Say Yes, But We Need to Understand How and Why*, 30 Envtl. L. Rep. 10,523, 10,528 (2000).

[3] Charles Duhigg, *Clean Water Laws Are Neglected, at a Cost in Suffering*, New York Times, Sept. 12, 2009, at 1.

[4] Office of Regulatory Enforcement, U.S. EPA, Compliance with Permitting Critical to Clean Air Act Goals: EPA Concerned About Noncompliance With New Source Review Requirements, Enforcement Alert 4 (Jan. 1999).

important policy choice. Government personnel at the state or local level may have a better feel for the regulated community and why particular companies or individuals are not complying. At the same time, federal officials often worry that state and local officials may be too close to the regulated community and overly tempted to let violators off too easily. Greater centralization also can ensure more consistent enforcement policies across the nation.

The U.S. EPA wields the primary implementation and enforcement authority for most environmental statutes. The Washington, D.C., EPA office, known within the agency as "Headquarters," interprets how the laws and regulations should be applied, determines enforcement priorities, issues penalty guidelines, and serves as the institutional check on state enforcement of federal environmental laws. The agency's ten regional offices generally have divisions for each program—air, water, solid waste, pesticides, etc.—with their own enforcement personnel. Their activities are overseen by the headquarters Office of Enforcement and Compliance Assurance (OECA). This group seeks to coordinate nationwide enforcement initiatives, strategically targeting certain sectors and companies. OECA also ensures consistency by the requirement that it sign off on all judicial filings and consent decrees entered into both at headquarters and in regional offices.

Despite EPA's central role in enforcement, it does not have independent authority to litigate cases. The Department of Justice (DOJ) serves as EPA's lawyer, filing actions on its behalf and representing the agency in court. As with EPA's regional offices, many of EPA's cases are litigated around the country by attorneys in DOJ's regional offices.

While DOJ serves as EPA's lawyer, the relationship is more complicated than the standard attorney-client model, for DOJ is first and foremost the government's lawyer. This dual loyalty can become problematic in three circumstances: (1) when EPA wants to file an action that DOJ believes is inconsistent with other governmental priorities, (2) when EPA and another agency (such as the Department of Transportation) take different views on litigation, and (3) when EPA wants DOJ to appeal an adverse decisions but DOJ lawyers decide not to, concerned over the precedential effect of an adverse ruling at the appellate level. It is not surprising that agencies take different views on what constitutes the best interests of the government, but DOJ sits in the middle, ultimately exercising its judgment over the view of any single agency.

EPA also partners with states, whose environmental agencies play a major role in enforcement on the ground. Indeed, most environmental laws provide for delegation of enforcement authority to state programs. With limited resources, EPA has made use of this opportunity, delegating significant enforcement authority to the states for the administration and enforcement of many features of the major environmental laws. These delegations are premised on the adoption of state statutes and regulations that are substantially equivalent to or no less stringent than EPA's program under the federal statute.

In many respects, this arrangement benefits both parties. EPA has limited resources and cannot practically carry out the inspections and enforcement actions necessary to ensure adequate deterrence throughout the country. State and local authorities not only can provide these resources, but as noted, are generally closer to both the actors and the impacts of pollution, and thus are likely to better understand the specific challenges and opportunities surrounding particular enforcement actions.

At the same time, however, there has been increasing tension between EPA and many state environmental agencies over the proper balance between compliance facilitation and sanction in the face of violations. While an oversimplification, many states favor compliance facilitation and seek to assist companies to achieve better compliance. As discussed above, this "good apple" view of noncompliance contrasts with the sanction strategy against "bad apples," and EPA often worries that state enforcement may go soft on local companies, not because of a fundamental difference of opinion on the appropriate approach to compliance, but out of concern over impacts on the local economy.

As an example of the concern over sweetheart deals between local business and regulators, consider the facts of *Friends of the Earth, Inc. v. Laidlaw Environmental Services (TOC), Inc.*[5] The South Carolina Department of Health and Environmental Control (DHEC) entered into a settlement with Laidlaw for hundreds of Clean Water Act violations in the North Tyger River. Laidlaw agreed to pay a $100,000 civil penalty. The settlement was challenged by an environmental group and, digging deeper into the issue, the federal District Court found that "Laidlaw drafted the state-court complaint and settlement agreement, filed the lawsuit against itself, and paid the filing fee. . . . [T]he settlement agreement between DHEC and Laidlaw was entered into with unusual haste, without giving the Plaintiffs the opportunity to intervene. . . . [And] in imposing the civil penalty of $100,000

---

[5] 528 U.S. 167 (2000).

against Laidlaw, DHEC failed to recover, or even to calculate, the economic benefit that Laidlaw received by not complying with its permit."[6]

Given the risk of state enforcement authorities catering to local industry interests, EPA retains the ability to step in and intervene in enforcement actions, even if the state has already imposed a sanction. In a practice known as "overfiling," EPA can seek to impose penalties in addition to the state's sanctions if the state has not taken "timely" and "appropriate" enforcement action. In simple terms, if EPA officials determine that the state's response to noncompliance was too slow (i.e., not within 90–120 days from the date of discovery of the violation) or too lenient (i.e., an inadequate response given the severity of the violation), it can seek to increase the penalties or impose other appropriate remedies, so long as they are consistent with the substantive law of the state in which the violation took place (since the state program was approved by EPA in lieu of the federal program).

III. The Enforcement Process

The enforcement process involves a series of discretionary decisions—how to monitor for and detect noncompliance; whether to prosecute noncompliance; whether to rely on administrative or judicial processes; whether to pursue civil or criminal sanctions. And each of these decisions masks many smaller decisions (e.g., which type of civil sanction to pursue, and at what level).

A.   Detection

While discussions of enforcement generally focus on punishment—whether to impose fines, an injunction, or criminal sanctions—it is important to keep in mind that enforcement authorities must first learn that a violation has occurred. Though often taken for granted, monitoring for noncompliance is an essential first step in the enforcement process.

Indeed, environmental enforcement policy involves two fundamental and interrelated decisions—how diligently to monitor for violations, and how to punish violators who are discovered. The expected cost to regulated parties of violating an environmental law reflects the interaction of these two decisions. If there is a very high probability of detection because the government carefully monitors everyone, the government may be able to deter people without setting a very high penalty. As the probability of detection drops, however, penalties must rise in order to provide the same

---

[6] *Friends of the Earth, Inc. v. Laidlaw Envtl. Servs. (TOC), Inc.*, 890 F. Supp. 470, 491 (D.S.C. 1995), *vacated,* 149 F.3d 303 (4th Cir. 1999), *rev'd,* 528 U.S. 167 (2000).

level of deterrence. There are practical limits on both monitoring and penalties. High levels of monitoring may be prohibitively expensive, and high fines may raise concerns about fairness.

Officials become aware of violations of environmental laws from a wide range of sources. These include reports from neighbors, disgruntled employees, environmental groups, and local response agencies such as police or fire departments, as well as referrals from state regulatory personnel. EPA may also discover violations during inspections of facilities or as part of a broader investigation of a targeted industrial-sector or multi-facility company.

Perhaps surprisingly, however, the primary source of information on environmental noncompliance is not gained through government inspections but, rather, through the polluters themselves. Self-reporting reduces the government's enforcement costs. And self-reporting can raise the awareness of regulated parties, so that they catch violations before they occur. As a result, self-reporting requirements are found throughout environmental law. Under the Clean Water Act, for example, owners or operators of point sources (i.e., discrete sources of water pollution such as pipes) must regularly sample and report their effluents. The Clean Air Act similarly authorizes EPA to require any person who owns or operates an emission source to establish and maintain records; make reports; install, use and maintain monitoring equipment or methods; and sample emissions as EPA prescribes.

As a result of these requirements, inspections are much more likely to find so-called "paperwork violations" than physical violations (i.e., finding improperly filled out or missing reports rather than illegal discharges during the inspection). While such a heavy reliance on self-reporting has advantages, a moment's reflection makes clear that it also creates the potential for cheating. Why should a company admit it has violated the law when no one is looking?

There are two basic strategies to address the incentives for cheating when self-reporting. The first is to require facilities to use monitoring technologies that are tamper-proof or provide real-time reporting. This has been difficult in the past, but with technological developments is increasingly viable. The second, and more common strategy, is to make cheating extremely painful. Under the major environmental statutes, paperwork violations are treated no different than physical violations. The Clean Air Act, for example, provides for civil penalties of up to $25,000 *per day of violation*. Knowing violations can lead to criminal penalties.

PROBLEM EXERCISE: AUDIT IMMUNITY POLICIES

The internal audit is a key aspect of compliance assurance. Knowing the law is important, but knowing whether or not you are in compliance is even more important. Internal audits are investigations that a company conducts of its own operations to ensure that it is in compliance with all relevant environmental laws. In some respects, it is analogous to the annual tune-up you give your car. It is not required by law, but provides reassurance that your car is in good working order. If a company's review of its records, operating policies, and personnel uncovers violations, presumably it will then remedy them. Moreover, audit procedures allow management to set environmental performance goals. A manufacturing team cannot be rewarded for reducing waste by 20% if there are not tracking mechanisms in place both to establish a baseline and to measure performance over time. The old business adage, "What gets measured gets done," is surely true in the case of environmental management.

The challenge for enforcement officials is what to do about past periods of noncompliance revealed by voluntary audits. Since EPA issued its original Audit Policy in 1995, twenty states have adopted policies for self-disclosure of environmental violations, wrestling with the issue of how to treat internal environmental audits when prosecuting a company. As a general matter, enforcement authorities have conflicting goals. They want to encourage audits by companies but, at the same time, do not want to hamper their enforcement efforts.

You are the head of your state's environmental enforcement agency and have been asked to write a memo analyzing the implications of creating an "audit immunity" policy. There exists a number of possible audit immunity approaches, ranging from total protection from prosecution for violations discovered by an internal audit, to lesser penalties, to no protection at all. Not surprisingly, at one end of the spectrum, industry lobbyists are pushing for total protection from penalties while, on the other end, some prosecutors are arguing for no protection at all.

Moreover, there are many factors that may counsel in favor of greater or lesser immunity. Your memo should consider, for example, how (or whether) the level of immunity should be dependent on each of the following specific concerns:

- Whether the audit was voluntary or legally required;

- Whether the noncompliance was discovered through a systematic audit or by chance;

- How soon after discovery the company reported the noncompliance to the environmental authorities;

- How soon after discovery the company corrected the noncompliance;

- Whether the facility is a small business; and

- Whether there have been past violations of the same type at the facility.

Do you think certain types of violations should be treated differently (or perhaps never be eligible for immunity), or that the type of immunity should vary depending on the statute?

B. Civil Enforcement

Once a potential violation has been detected, the enforcement agency must decide whether and how to proceed. With limited resources, neither EPA nor the state can pursue every violation through administrative or judicial processes. For many violations, simply notifying the manager of the violation and how it can be corrected may be all that is needed. Informal responses as simple as phone calls, site visits, or notice of violation letters may be sufficient to return the party into compliance. Light slaps on the wrist, though, will obviously not always be adequate to ensure widespread compliance. And sometimes a message needs to be sent to the broader regulated community.

1. Administrative versus Civil Proceedings

The majority of enforcement actions are *civil proceedings*, and the vast majority are *administrative hearings* conducted within the agency rather than in the court system. The benefits of relying on internal agency adjudication rather than courts are obvious—easier to administer, less costly in terms of time and personnel, no need to coordinate with the Department of Justice, and an administrative judge who is familiar with environmental statutes. The proceedings start with a *complaint* filed against the defendant, identifying the environmental violation and the sanction. If the defendant contests the charge or proposed penalties, it files an *answer* and there is a hearing before an Administrative Law Judge (ALJ), who reviews the written materials and may hear witnesses or documentary evidence. The ALJ files a decision, which may be appealed within the agency to the Environmental Appeal Board.

At this point, upon exhausting agency procedures, the parties can go to court and engage in *civil litigation*, where the EPA is represented by DOJ attorneys. Civil litigation generally takes longer and is more expensive than administrative enforcement. As a result, far fewer cases are resolved through courts than through the administrative process.

Why would EPA ever go to court rather than handle all enforcement through administrative hearings? A different range of civil options are available to a district court judge than to an administrative law judge and, while not always the case, a district court typically can impose higher penalties than an administrative law judge. Despite the much smaller number of enforcement actions pursued in court, judicial cases result in much higher overall penalties.

2.   Fines and Other Penalties

Remedies represent the "so what" of the enforcement process. At the end of the day, remedies determine how effective enforcement will be. The most common civil penalty involves fines. This is appropriate if one seeks to punish the party or simply remove the economic benefit of noncompliance.

When the government decides to seek civil penalties, it must calculate the appropriate level of monetary penalty. The government has a great deal of discretion in setting fines. The maximum is usually set by the statute and can be extremely high (e.g., $25,000 per day per violation for some violations of the Clean Water Act). The minimum is the lowest level that can still be considered a deterrent, i.e., eliminating any economic benefit achieved by violating the statute. The proposed damages are important not only for the court case but also for the negotiations preceding a trial, particularly since about 95% of enforcement actions never go to trial.

EPA has adopted *penalty policies* for each of the major environmental statutes to guide the setting of civil penalties in particular cases. Such policies carry a variety of benefits. They ensure consistency and thus fairness across different cases; they also help EPA to justify the penalties that it imposes when a penalty is challenged. What factors should EPA consider in setting a penalty? Most of the penalty policies start by focusing on two factors: (1) the gravity of the violation, and (2) the amount of money that the regulated party saved by not complying with the environmental law. EPA believes that violators, at a minimum, should disgorge any savings from their illegal action, and graver violations deserve higher penalties. To ensure that penalties are fair, EPA also considers the degree to which a violation was willful or negligent, the violator's prior history of compliance, the degree to which the violator cooperated with authorities, and the violator's ability to pay. Finally, to encourage swift compliance, EPA also considers whether a violator has already taken steps to avoid future violations—and similar factors.

In some circumstances, an injunction can be far more costly to a violator than even heavy fines, particularly when the injunction delays a large development project where loans must continue to be paid, permits may expire, and stopping one action may have the result of halting many related activities. The scope of an injunction can vary. So can its length. A permanent injunction ceases all activity indefinitely. A temporary injunction might provide protection until an Environmental Impact Statement or some other process has been completed. Some courts may choose not to issue an injunction when other effective remedies are available.

3.   Other Compliance Measures

The last few years have witnessed significant growth of nontraditional, flexible agreements between environmental enforcement agencies and regulated parties. This has been most evident in the enforcement arena with the growth of *supplemental environmental projects* (SEPs). In general, SEPs are part of negotiated settlements between the government and violators for "beyond compliance" environmental activities either in place of or in addition to monetary penalties. Put simply, SEPs represent a negotiated deal that trades off a reduced penalty for an environmentally beneficial action that is not mandated by law. SEPs have ranged from purchasing lead paint abatement kits for schools and restoring endangered species habitat to installing a closed-loop wastewater recycling system. SEPs may provide more direct environmental benefit than payment of a fine to the U.S Treasury, and may be more appropriate for violators that are not acting out of pure economic self-interest.   However, some have expressed concern over companies gaining inappropriate benefits. As a result, violators whose SEPs involve public awareness projects are required to state that the project is part of the settlement of a government lawsuit. Moreover, funds paid for SEPs are not tax deductible.

A final sanction available to EPA for civil actions includes so-called *contractor listings*. Under both the Clean Air Act and Clean Water Act, convicted facilities can be placed on EPA's "List of Violating Facilities." Facilities on this list cannot receive contracts, subcontracts, grants or loans from the federal government. The sanction applies only to the facility, not the entire company, but if a facility depends on government contracts this can be a severe punishment.

C.   Criminal Enforcement

The key statutes governing air, water and solid waste all provide for criminal sanctions. Heavy civil fines and injunctions already provide powerful deterrents to regulated parties, and you can hardly put a corporation behind bars, so why include criminal provisions in environmental laws? Criminal sanctions send a very different message both to the regulated community and to the public. Put simply, criminal sanctions are not regarded as just another cost of doing business. Criminal sanctions, whether in the form of imprisonment or monetary penalties, are the exclamation point at the end of the sentence, "You will comply, or else!"

Despite their greater deterrent force and powerful rhetoric, criminal sanctions can be problematic in an environmental context. We have already discussed the difficulty of achieving full compliance all of the time. There are over 300,000 federal environmental regulations, so if enforcement officials want to find instances of noncompliance at a company, chances are they can. The key question then becomes when criminal charges should be brought instead of or in addition to civil charges.

If one looks across the criminal environmental cases that have been brought, typical charges include falsifying documents, tampering with monitoring or control equipment, and repeated violations. But this doesn't tell us why criminal charges were brought rather than civil. As all law students learn in their criminal law class discussion of *scienter* and *mens rea*, the key to criminal enforcement is intent—a person or organization has knowingly and willingly committed the illegal act. This simple requirement can be problematic in a technical, highly regulated field such as environmental law. Does criminal sanction for environmental violations require intent only to commit the act, or is it necessary to commit an act *and* have knowledge that the act is illegal? Is it enough to know that you are discharging a liquid, or do you also have to know that this discharge violates the Clean Water Act? Cases have gone both ways.

Another question is who within an organization to criminally charge. Many environmental criminal actions are brought against companies and/or company employees. With long chains of command and many people involved at different stages of decisions, the guilty party for a specific action may not be obvious. For example, what if a boss tells her engineer that it is too expensive to send the waste in tanks to a treatment facility, to "do something about it," and the engineer disposes of the waste illegally?

Under a theory known as the "Responsible Corporate Officer Doctrine," criminal liability can be imposed on corporate managers or officers who were in a position to know about and prevent a violation, even if they were not the ones who actually committed the illegal act. Mere knowledge is not enough. A person liable as a responsible corporate officer must also have had the ability or authority to influence the corporate conduct causing the violation. The government has successfully used this doctrine to convict high-level corporate officers (even presidents) for environmental violations by lower-level employees.

IV. Citizen Suits

Up to this point, we have focused on the government's role in enforcement, but environmental organizations have played an equally important role in enforcing environmental law through litigation. As explained in Chapter 3, environmental groups can obtain judicial review under the Administrative Procedure Act when EPA or other federal agencies take administrative actions that are inconsistent with the law or facts. Under *citizen suit* provisions in most federal environmental statutes, environmental organizations also can typically bring enforcement actions when the federal and state governments do not do so.

A.   *Statutory Authorization*

Virtually every major federal environmental law passed since 1970 has contained a *citizen suit* provision. (The lone exception is the Federal Insecticide, Fungicide, and Rodenticide Act, which the agricultural committees in Congress, rather than the more receptive environmental committees, drafted.) Under the citizen suit provisions, individuals and organizations can pursue two new categories of lawsuits not authorized by the Administrative Procedure Act. First, they can sue anyone or any organization, either public and private, alleged to be in violation of an environmental law, serving in effect as private attorneys general. Environmental groups have actively used this opportunity both to supplement the government's limited enforcement resources and to pursue violations that the government is ignoring. When governmental enforcement efforts declined at the beginning of the Reagan Administration in the early 1980s, groups such as the Natural Resources Defense Council organized enforcement campaigns to take up the slack. Second, individuals or groups can sue the EPA administrator or other relevant governmental officials who are failing to carry out a non-discretionary statutory obligation, such as the promulgation of a required regulation. Environmental organizations used this provision frequently in the 1970s and 1980s to enforce deadlines that Congress had set in the major environmental statutes.

Although deadline lawsuits are less important today given the maturity of most environmental laws, the opportunity to bring private prosecutions remains extremely important. Statutes in other fields, such as antitrust and securities regulation, permit private individuals to sue for damages where the plaintiffs have been injured by violations. In authorizing citizen suits under the federal environmental statutes, however, Congress for the first time called on private citizens to play a direct public role in enforcing the law. The purpose of citizen suits is not to provide compensation to the plaintiffs for injuries but to ensure more effective enforcement of environmental laws.

In authorizing individual citizens and environmental groups to serve as private prosecutors, Congress has been cautious not to make citizen suits into profit-making opportunities. Most of the citizen suit provisions permit citizens and environmental groups to pursue only injunctive relief. A few statutes authorize courts to impose monetary penalties in citizen suits, but the penalties are payable to the United States, not the private prosecutor. In practice, however, plaintiffs often settle their citizen suits on terms that include not only the cessation of violations, but also (1) the payment of monies to the plaintiff or other organizations and (2) agreements to engage in supplemental projects of benefit to the environment.

Citizen suit provisions do not permit private plaintiffs to prosecute every violation of an environmental law. First, for largely political reasons, Congress purposefully has excluded some violations from the purview of citizen suits. The Clean Air Act, for example, does not permit lawsuits to enforce many automobile emission standards. Second, the Eleventh Amendment precludes plaintiffs from pursuing citizen suits against states if the suits seek monetary penalties, although purely injunctive actions are still permissible. Finally, most of the citizen suit provisions authorize lawsuits only against persons "alleged to be in violation" of the underlying act. In *Gwaltney of Smithfield, Ltd. v. Chesapeake Bay Foundation*,[7] the Supreme Court unanimously interpreted this language to preclude citizen suits alleging purely past violations; to prevail, a plaintiff must demonstrate a "state of either continuous or intermittent violation"—that is, "a reasonable likelihood that a past polluter will continue to pollute in the future." In response to *Gwaltney*, Congress in 1990 amended the citizen suit provision in the Clean Air Act to permit citizen suits against defendants "alleged to have violated (if there is evidence that the alleged violation has been repeated) or to be in violation."[8] Most federal environmental statutes, however, retain the original wording interpreted in *Gwaltney*.

In authorizing citizen suits, Congress also worried about the confusion and conflicts that could result if the government and private plaintiffs simultaneously sued over the same violation. As a result, citizen suit provisions prevent private plaintiffs from filing a lawsuit if the federal or state government has commenced and is "diligently prosecuting" a civil or criminal action or, under some

---

[7]   484 U.S. 49 (1987).

[8]   Clean Air Act § 304(a)(1), 42 U.S.C. § 7604(a)(1).

statutes, has initiated at least some forms of administrative enforcement proceeding. To give the government an opportunity to pursue its own enforcement relief and to give the defendant a chance to clean up its act, private plaintiffs also must provide the federal government, any involved state, and the alleged violator with notice of the alleged violation at least sixty days before filing a citizen suit. Courts are split on what happens if the government does not initiate an enforcement action before a citizen suit is filed, but subsequently enters into a consent decree with the defendant while the citizen suit is pending. Most courts have concluded that the consent decree bars the citizen suit if the decree reasonably ensures that the violation will not recur.

To help promote citizen suits, Congress has authorized courts to order defendants to reimburse prevailing plaintiffs for their litigation costs, including "reasonable" attorney fees. Courts calculate fee awards by taking the reasonable time that the plaintiff's attorney has spent on the citizen suit and then multiplying this figure by a reasonable attorney fee rate to get an amount known as the "lodestar." According to the Supreme Court, the reasonable rate for a public interest attorney is the rate that she would bill if in private practice, not the much lower amount that the attorney's environmental organization pays her. Although courts occasionally award more than the lodestar if the lodestar does not fully reflect the quality or competence of council or the case is particularly novel, the Supreme Court has indicated that such "multipliers" should normally not be awarded.

B. Standing

Whenever an environmental group or individual seeks judicial review or files a citizen suit, one of the first questions that the court will ask is whether the plaintiff has standing to sue. According to the Supreme Court, an individual generally must demonstrate four facts to establish standing. The first three requirements are constitutionally required by Article III of the United States Constitution. First, the plaintiff must demonstrate that the challenged action has or will cause the plaintiff "injury in fact." Second, the plaintiff must show that this injury can be traced to the challenged action. Third, the plaintiff must show that the court, through some form of available relief, can redress the injury. The fourth requirement for standing is only "prudential," and therefore Congress can eliminate or alter it: the injury must be within the "zone of interests" that the underlying substantive statute is designed to protect. Where an organization sues, the organization must show not only that one or more of its members satisfy these standing requirements but also that the goal in seeking judicial relief is "germane to the organization's purposes." Thus, the Minnesota Elk Breeder's Association might have standing problems suing the National Marine Fisheries Service for failure to list a tuna species as endangered.

Are all these standing requirements truly needed? Some academics have argued not. In their view, the question should be whether Congress has authorized individuals or organizations to seek judicial review or other relief in federal court. For example, where Congress has authorized "any person" to pursue environmental violators, as Congress has done in virtually every citizen suit provision, the courts should not erect roadblocks in the way of potential citizen prosecutors. A majority of the current Supreme Court, however, has suggested that the existing standing rules are important for several reasons. First, standing requirements such as "injury in fact" ensure that there is justification for involving the courts in what otherwise might be a largely academic question. If no one has been hurt, judicial intervention is unnecessary. Second, the standing requirements ensure that the plaintiff has sufficient interest in the lawsuit to provide adequate representation of the public interest. Finally, standing is a means of ensuring the separation of powers; absent injury in fact and the other standing requirements, courts would interfere unnecessarily in the discretion of the executive branch. Whether you agree with these arguments, and each has its critics, they have led federal courts to throw a number of citizen suits and other cases out of court. Indeed, environmentalists have worried at times that the courts have been trying to use standing to roll back decades of environmental activism.

Injury in Fact. Most standing disputes focus on the first requirement of injury in fact. The Supreme Court helped to promote environmental litigation in the early 1970s, and thus usher in stronger environmental protection, by adopting a broad view of what constitutes an injury in the environmental field. In *Sierra Club v. Morton,*[9] the Sierra Club challenged the Forest Service's approval of Walt Disney Enterprises' plan to develop a ski resort in the Sequoia National Forest. The Supreme Court held that the Sierra Club had not established standing to sue because it had not alleged that any of its members actually used the area of the proposed development and thus would be affected by Disney's plan. But the Court emphasized that standing did not require a showing of *economic* injury. For standing purposes, injuries can "reflect 'aesthetic, conservational, and recreational' as well as economic values" and can be widely shared among the population. All the

---

[9] 405 U.S. 727 (1972).

Sierra Club needed to do therefore was to allege that its members would suffer aesthetic or recreational injury as a result of the proposed development (and that's exactly what the Sierra Club did on remand). Justice William O. Douglas would have gone further and allowed law suits to be filed "in the name of the inanimate object about to be despoiled, defaced, or invaded by roads and bulldozers and where injury is the subject of public outrage." In Douglas' view, trees and wildlife, not just people, should have standing in court.

For almost two decades after *Sierra Club v. Morton*, the Supreme Court showed no interest in constructing standing barriers to environmental litigation. In its 1992 decision in *Lujan v. Defenders of Wildlife*,[10] however, the Court showed a new willingness to scrutinize standing claims. In that case, an environmental organization sought review of the Department of the Interior's decision that the Endangered Species Act does not extend to U.S. agency actions that affect endangered species overseas. Two of the organization's members submitted affidavits stating that they had previously traveled to overseas areas in which species were threatened by U.S. agency actions and that they hoped to go again. The Court concluded that such inchoate plans to return to the areas are inadequate to establish standing; only present and definite plans to return provide the type of "actual or imminent" injury required for standing. The Court also held that a plaintiff does not have standing simply because he or she has a professional or personal interest in studying or seeing an endangered species.

A critical question in *Lujan v. Defenders of Wildlife* and similar environmental cases is the degree to which Congress can provide standing for parties who would not meet the traditional injury-in-fact requirement. In *Defenders of Wildlife*, the lower court had held that the plaintiffs had suffered a "procedural injury": the Endangered Species Act required agencies to consult with the Department of the Interior before taking actions that might jeopardize an endangered species, giving all citizens a "procedural right" to insist on a consultation. Four members of the Court concluded that a plaintiff has standing to vindicate such a procedural right only where disregard of that right also impairs "a separate concrete interest." While agreeing that the plaintiffs had not established standing, Justices Kennedy and Souter suggested that "Congress has the power to define injuries and articulate chains of causation" that otherwise would not provide standing, but "Congress must at the very least identify the injury it seek to

---

[10] 504 U.S. 555 (1992).

vindicate and relate the injury to the class of persons entitled to bring suit."

LUJAN V. DEFENDERS OF WILDLIFE
504 U.S. 555 (1992).

The Endangered Species Act requires each federal agency to consult with the Secretary of the Interior to ensure that the agency's actions will not jeopardize any endangered or threatened species. The Department of the Interior originally decided that this requirement extends to U.S. agency actions in foreign countries, only to change its mind in 1986. Under regulations issued in 1986, agencies must confer with the Secretary of the Interior only in connection with actions in the United States or on the high seas. Environmentalists argue that this regulation is inconsistent with the Endangered Species Act, that the Act applies to all agency actions whether domestic or overseas, and that the 1986 regulation will lead to the extinction of species in foreign countries.

Defenders of Wildlife, a major environmental organization dedicated to protecting wildlife, brought a lawsuit challenging the 1986 regulation. To show that the new regulation injured its members and the Defenders therefore had standing, the environmental group relied on affidavits filed by two of its members, Joyce Kelly and Amy Skilbred. Kelly stated that she had traveled to Egypt in 1986 and observed the habitat of the endangered Nile crocodile. She claimed that she intended to return to Egypt in the future to view the crocodile itself, but that U.S. involvement in the Aswan Dam project would harm the crocodile and deprive her of the opportunity to see the animal in the wild. Skilbred stated that she had traveled to Sri Lanka and observed the habitats of endangered species such as Asian elephants and Sri Lanka leopards. She also intended to return to see the animals themselves, and she worried that U.S. involvement in the Mahaweli development project would further jeopardize these species.

The Court of Appeals for the Eighth Circuit concluded that Defenders had standing to sue and that Congress had intended the Endangered Species Act to apply to foreign projects. On appeal, the United States Supreme Court reversed. The Court never reached the validity of the regulation, concluding by a 6–3 vote that Defenders did not have standing to challenge the regulation. Because Kelly and Skilbred had no immediate and definite plans to travel to Egypt or Sri Lanka to view endangered species, the Court argued that the challenged regulation did not threaten the type of actual and imminent injury needed for standing. According to the Court, the women's "'some day' intentions—without any description of concrete plans, or indeed even any specification of *when* the some day will be—do not support a finding of the 'actual or imminent' injury that our cases require."

The 1986 regulation remains in place today. Both the Aswan Dam and Mahaweli development projects proceeded with U.S. assistance. The Nile crocodile, Asian elephant, and leopard have not gone extinct so far, though they all remain endangered. As for Joyce Kelly and Amy Skilbred, it is unknown whether they ever took their trips and, if they did, whether they saw any of the species that they hoped to view.

Redressability. The requirement that injuries be redressable by judicial action also occasionally trips up environmental plaintiffs. The Supreme Court, for example, has held that a plaintiff does not have standing to bring a citizen suit for environmental violations that have occurred entirely in the past, because neither of the remedies potentially available to the plaintiff (an injunction or a civil penalty payable to the government) could remedy any injury that the plaintiff has suffered as a result of the past violation.[11] In a subsequent decision, however, the Court held that an environmental organization has standing to seek civil penalties in the face of ongoing violations, even though any penalties awarded go to the government, because the penalties will deter future violations.[12]

Zone of Interests. The "zone of interests" requirement, as noted, is purely prudential, and courts have often held that citizen suit provisions have overridden it under specific laws. In *Bennett v. Spear*,[13] for example, ranchers and irrigation districts, upset by the Department of Interior' decision to reduce their water deliveries because of endangered-species concerns, filed a citizen suit under the Endangered Species Act (ESA) claiming that the department had failed to perform nondiscretionary duties—using the "best scientific data available" and considering the economic impact of designating a particular area as "critical habitat" for a species. Although a lower court held that the ranchers and districts did not have standing because the purpose of the ESA is to protect the environment, the Supreme Court reversed. The Court emphasized that the citizen suit provision grants a right to file a citizen suit to "any person" and found that Congress contemplated that industry

---

[11] *Steel Co. v. Citizens for a Better Environment*, 523 U.S. 83 (1998).

[12] *Friends of the Earth v. Laidlaw Environmental Services*, 528 U.S. 167 (2000).

[13] 520 U.S. 154 (1997).

groups might use the provision to avoid "overenforcement" of the law. By contrast, courts have sometimes rejected industry efforts to challenge federal regulations designed to improve the environment on the ground that the government did not prepare an environmental impact statement under the National Environmental Policy Act (NEPA). Unlike most environmental statutes, NEPA does not contain a broad citizen suit provision.

Climate Change. Lawsuits brought to address climate change have raised new and unique standing issues because of the difficulty of linking specific damage to climate change (not to mention to particular contributors to climate change) and the challenge of remedying climate change through any single action or policy. In *Massachusetts v. Environmental Protection Agency*,[14] the Supreme Court upheld the standing of Massachusetts to challenge EPA's failure to regulate greenhouse gas emissions under the Clean Air Act by a close 5–4 vote. For injury in fact, the majority relied on unchallenged affidavits stating that sea levels had already risen in the 20th century as a result of global warming and "begun to swallow Massachusetts' coastal land." According to the dissent, however, there was no evidence of "actual loss of Massachusetts coastal land" other than a "single conclusory statement," and the risk of *future* loss of coastal land from sea level rise was not sufficiently imminent and impending to satisfy constitutional standing requirements.

The majority and dissent also disagreed on causation and redressability. Noting that motor vehicle emissions in the United States are only one of the sources of greenhouse gases (a "bit part"), the dissent concluded that the linkage between motor vehicle emissions and Massachusetts' claimed injury was "far too speculative to establish causation." Redressability was "even more problematic" because "any decreases produced by petitioner's desired standards are likely to be overwhelmed many times by emission increases elsewhere in the world." The majority, by contrast, noted that no one in the case disputed the "causal connection between man-made greenhouse gas emissions and global warming." And a favorable ruling for Massachusetts would reduce the risk of climate change. "While it may be true that regulating motor-vehicle emissions will not by itself *reverse* global warming, it by no means follows that we lack jurisdiction to decide whether EPA has a duty to take steps to *slow* or *reduce* it." The majority also suggested that states enjoy a lower standing threshold in the case of climate change because of their "parens patriae" status—acting on behalf of their citizenry.

---

[14] 549 U.S. 497 (2007).

QUESTIONS AND DISCUSSION

1.   In an era of tight and shrinking government budgets, how much should we spend on environmental enforcement? Given that speeding causes more deaths than violations of environmental laws, should more resources be dedicated to traffic enforcement than environmental enforcement? Do you think that cost-benefit analysis should determine how we spend scarce enforcement resources?

2.   Assume you are a state environmental official, and a state inspector has just informed you that Belching Industry, Inc., exceeded its air-pollution standards for six days earlier in the month. In the 1990s, Belching often violated environmental law and, as a result, was fined several million dollars. Since a change of management in 2000, Belching has been highly compliant with environmental laws, but is rumored to be losing money and cutting corners to stay in business. Belching voluntarily brought the most recent violation to the inspector's attention and reports that the violation was due to equipment failure that will not occur again. What steps would you take in response to this information?

3.   While overfiling represents a potential stick for the EPA to bring states in line, EPA also has a big club that it can swing in the form of withdrawing a state's delegated authority to operate a program. EPA can give and EPA can take away. In practice, however, EPA only rarely threatens to exercise this authority. Why do you think EPA is reluctant to withdraw delegated authority from states?

4.   Given the sheer number and complexity of environmental laws and regulations, as well as its "aspirational" character of setting ambitious goals, what do you think is the appropriate role for criminal sanctions? Assume a person is convicted under the Clean Water Act for discharging gasoline from an underground storage tank. What factors would you want to consider in deciding whether to recommend the defendant be sent to prison?

5.   What role should environmental groups and private individuals play in enforcing environmental laws? If the government uses its prosecutorial discretion not to seek an injunction or penalty against a company that has violated the Clean Water Act, should an environmental group be able to sue? Why might this lead to inefficient environmental policy?

6.   Should Congress encourage citizen suits by allowing courts to award civil penalties to environmental groups or individuals who successfully sue a company for violating an environmental law? Should the government pay bounties to groups or individuals who provide the government with information showing that a company is violating an environmental law and leading to the company's conviction? What are the downsides to creating such incentives for citizen suits?

7.   Should Congress add citizen suit provisions to other federal laws (e.g., tax laws, drug laws, or immigration laws)? Are there aspects of environmental law that make citizen suits particularly appropriate in the environmental context?

8. Do you agree with the Supreme Court in *Massachusetts v. EPA* that Massachusetts had standing to challenge EPA's refusal to regulate greenhouse gases under the Clean Air Act? Should the Supreme Court be addressing issues as complex, broad, and multifaceted as climate change or, as the dissenters argued, should the Supreme Court leave such issues up to Congress and the Executive Branch?

Part 2
POLLUTION

_____

Chapter 5

THE CLEAN AIR ACT

I. The Challenges of Regulating Air Pollution

Amidst our many environmental laws, the Clean Air Act Amendments of 1970[1] (the CAA) stand apart. A massive law, the CAA was also historic. Unlike earlier laws passed by Congress, the CAA boasted *uniform, national standards* covering a wide range of pollutants and sources. Passed just one year after we put a man on the Moon, the CAA reflected both the technological optimism of the times and the frustration with poor air quality in our cities (it was apparently joked at the time that Pittsburgh's air was so dirty you had to floss your teeth after breathing).

With the passage of the CAA, it was hoped that our nation's clean air problems would be largely solved within the decade. Over four decades and billions of dollars later, however, the CAA presents a curious contradiction. Overall, the air we breathe is cleaner than in 1970. With few exceptions, the concentrations of major air pollutants have dropped despite greatly increased economic activity. Yet many of our largest cities still fail to meet the clean air requirements of the CAA. Indeed over one-half of our population lives in areas out of compliance with the CAA. We have come a long way, yet still have far to go.

A review of the CAA provides a fascinating study of cooperative federalism, strategic choice of regulatory targets, and cutting-edge environmental policy instruments. To understand the CAA's structure, however, first requires a basic understanding of the air pollution problem. As with most environmental issues, the air pollution "problem" is actually a combination of many different problems. There are many kinds of air pollutants with varying environmental and health impacts. Some are highly mobile, some highly reactive. Apart from toxic air pollutants such as vinyl chloride and small particulates, air pollution alone generally does not produce fatalities. More often, air pollution aggravates health problems through chronic exposure, increasing the incidence and severity of respiratory diseases such as bronchitis, pneumonia, and asthma.

In cities, we are most concerned about the health effects from breathing smog (O_3), produced by reactions of nitrogen oxides (NO_x) with volatile organic compounds (a broad class of hydrocarbons

---

[1] 42 U.S.C. §§ 7401–7671.

known as VOCs) and from fine particulate matter that lodges in
lung tissue. While some might dismiss the health threats from air
pollution as a bothersome nuisance, we're not just talking about
occasional sore throats and coughs. The American Lung Association
reports that lung disease is the third-leading cause of death in the
United States every year, killing almost 400,000 people. More than
35 million Americans currently suffer from chronic lung disease
and, over the last five years, the death rate for lung disease has
remained steady while the other leading causes of death have
decreased significantly. Recent studies have also identified a strong
correlation between fine particles and premature death.

Other common pollutants such as NO_x and sulfur dioxide (SO_2)
combine to form "acid rain," as well as contributing to the formation
of fine particles. Beyond health concerns, acidic compounds formed
by pollution deposit many miles from the original emission source
and can seriously injure trees and aquatic ecosystems. The German
name for the impacts of acid rain, "Waldsterben," tersely describes
the problem—"forest death."

From a regulator's perspective, the air pollution problem is
made difficult because these air pollutants (and many others) arise
from different sources. Vehicle emissions are responsible for over
half of total CO emissions, about half of NO_x and over one-quarter
of VOCs. Power plants are important emitters of SO_2 and NO_x.
Incinerators and industrial sources are major sources of hazardous
air pollutants but, perhaps surprisingly, so are small sources and
motor vehicles (which EPA says account for half of all cancers
attributed to outdoor sources of air toxics). Moreover, these
pollutants mix in the atmosphere, moving with the winds subject to
local topography and climate but paying no heed to state and
county lines.

If one thinks back to 1970, then, the architects of the CAA
faced a formidable challenge. In place of the available common law
nuisance actions, which necessarily provided only retrospective
remedies and required proof of causation and harm, in place of a
patchwork of state laws with poor effectiveness, the drafters of the
CAA needed to create an overarching national law for an entire
class of pollutants from disparate sources. Indeed this would be the
first truly comprehensive national pollution law. Congress needed
to decide not only how clean we want our air to be, but how much
we are willing to pay for clean air and who should pay for it. To
clarify this challenge, consider how the law needed to address the
policy questions posed by *what, how much, where,* and *how* to
regulate.

What to Regulate

As a threshold matter, the CAA needed not only to identify which particular air pollutants to regulate (and therefore which not to regulate) but whether the pollutants should be prioritized, regulating some of the more common pollutants differently, perhaps, than others.

How Much to Regulate

Once the pollutants were identified, the next obvious question was at what levels they should be regulated. Assuming we would not simply ban all air pollutants, which would play havoc with the economy, how much pollution should be allowed? Most people might say, "at a level that protects the public's health," but this begs the question of who "the public" is. Is the public's health represented best by the average person, a John or Mary Doe, or by more sensitive populations, perhaps their asthmatic children? Protecting the former is surely less costly, but to what extent should we take costs into account when setting national standards to protect the public health? Is clean air an issue of individual rights? Should people have to move because the government in their region chose a lower level of air pollution control?

Where to Regulate

Assuming we have decided on a permissible level for an air pollutant (e.g., 5 parts of SO_2 per million parts of air, described as "5 ppm"), we need to decide where we are talking about. In the air pollution context, ideally we want to regulate based on units of risk to individual receptors. That is, we want to regulate the harm to each one of us from the actual air we breathe outside (known as "ambient air"). The problem, though, is that we can't directly regulate the air each one of us breathes. Beyond the nuisance of having an EPA official follow you around with an air quality monitor, how would the regulator know how much pollution you can breathe without harm? Individuals have different sensitivities. And even if this were known, how would the pollution be traced back to specific sources? This would simply recreate the problem with reliance on the common law—the difficulty in proving causation. Because airsheds and wind patterns are not uniform, the same emission in some places causes more damage than in other places. If it's technically too difficult to regulate where the air is breathed, then we have to go upwind.

Put another way, regulators must determine the *optimal point* of regulation. In the pollution context, ideally one wants to regulate emissions from a particular power plant based on the pollution's specific impact on *each* individual. This is technically too difficult and expensive to determine, however. Short of that, we should seek to regulate the level of exposure to classes of people (accepting that individuals have different sensitivities) but this, too, is hard to do. Moving further upstream, the next best site to regulate would be the ambient concentration (realizing that airsheds and wind patterns are not uniform), and finally at the level of particular emission sources (the site we actually do regulate). Recognize that at each step further from the ideal point of regulation, the regulatory target less accurately reflects what we care about as it relies on proxies, moving from the ideal regulation of harm to individual receptors, to populations, to ambient air concentrations, to tons of emissions. Indeed, environmental law relies almost entirely on proxy measures.

In the case of power plant emissions, for example, the ultimate point of regulation is quite far upstream from our ultimate concern (the people and forest harmed by the pollution). Since our concern is ambient air quality, though, we're still faced with the challenge of figuring out how *each* of the many sources' emissions combines and determining the quality of the downwind air when it is breathed. And this requires complex modeling. No matter where the regulator focuses, though, whether at the individual or the airshed, at the end of the day the regulated party needs to know if it is in compliance with the law, and this requires some kind of standard set at each source (e.g., a municipal incinerator needs to know how many tons of SO_2 it may emit per year).

How to Regulate

In part because the CAA was the first modern pollution law and in part because air pollution is such an important problem, the CAA has provided fertile ground for a whole range of policy approaches. Given the many different sources of air pollutants, which mix of regulatory tools will work best? Should mobile sources (e.g., cars and trucks) be regulated differently than stationary sources such as incinerators and power plants? Should new sources be treated differently than sources in operation when the law was passed? Since air pollution pays no heed to state lines, uniform national standards for air pollutants would seem to make a lot of sense, but is treating every location in the country the same economically efficient? In political terms, what role do such national standards leave for the states?

The CAA passed in 1970 and, with its subsequent amendments in 1977 and in 1990, had to address all of these challenges, and more. As a result, it is a massive piece of legislation. Indeed some professors spend almost their entire survey course covering *only* the CAA! Much of the CAA can be understood as the product of what might be called "cooperative federalism," as a dynamic balance between federal standard setting and state implementation. Once you understand which areas were reserved purely for federal regulation, the CAA starts to make more sense.

A.　National Ambient Air Quality Standards (NAAQS)

The keystone of the CAA is its treatment of the most common pollutants of concern in the outside air, and most of the CAA's provisions are driven by its regulation of these so-called *criteria pollutants*. Defined as pollutants that are emitted from numerous or diverse sources and that can endanger public health or welfare, criteria pollutants include many of the pollutants mentioned above—O_3, NO_x, CO, fine particles, SO_2—as well as lead.[2] The CAA requires that these pollutants not exceed uniform levels at *any* outside point to which the public has access. Thus the standards don't apply indoors or in outdoor areas not accessible to the general public.

These National Ambient Air Quality Standards (NAAQS) are set for each criteria pollutant at a level that must "protect the public health" with an "adequate margin of safety."[3] But what constitutes an adequate margin of safety and *whose* health is the public health? These questions were addressed in the case, *Lead Industries Association v. EPA.*[4] Here, in setting the NAAQS for lead, EPA chose a very vulnerable target population—young children. The court held that EPA had discretion in determining an adequate margin of safety. The NAAQS levels must be based solely on health considerations—the agency may not consider economic or technical feasibility. The requirement of basing the NAAQS on health and not cost was reaffirmed in the *EPA v. American Trucking Associations* case two decades later.[5]

There are actually two types of NAAQS. *Primary standards*, described above, protect human health while *secondary standards* protect the public welfare, broadly defined to include effects on animals, wildlife, water, and visibility.[6] EPA is required to consider new NAAQS, review existing NAAQS, and make appropriate revisions at least every five years. In practice, however, EPA has been reticent to add new NAAQS because of the tremendous political and economic costs involved. Indeed there have been only

---

[2]　42 U.S.C. § 7408(a)(1).

[3]　These are known as "primary air quality standards." As noted below, "secondary air quality standards" must be set at levels that protect property and the environment.

[4]　*Lead Industries Association v. EPA*, 647 F.2d 1130 (D.C.Cir.1980), *cert. denied*, 449 U.S. 1042 (1980).

[5]　*EPA v. American Trucking Associations*, 531 U.S. 457 (2001).

[6]　42 U.S.C. §§ 109(b)(1) & (2).

seven NAAQS established since passage of the CAA four decades ago. Revisions have been infrequent and environmental groups have had to sue EPA on a number of occasions to initiate reviews. Despite a lot of political heat, in recent years EPA has moved to tighten the standards for ozone and establish new standards for particulate matter.

LEAD INDUSTRIES ASSOCIATION, INC. V. EPA

647 F.2d 1130 (D.C. Cir.1980).

Exposure to significant amounts of lead can cause anemia, kidney damage, severe brain damage, and even death. In the 1970s, automobile emissions were by far the most significant source of airborne lead, accounting for 88% of total lead emissions. The EPA's first approach to controlling lead in the air was to limit lead emissions from automobiles by restricting the amount of lead in gasoline. These measures proved effective but, in 1975, the Natural Resources Defense Council and other groups brought a suit against the EPA to require the Agency to establish national ambient air quality standards for lead. A District Court agreed, the Second Circuit Court of Appeals affirmed, and the EPA commenced development of the standards.

After a process of scientific and public review, the EPA released its "Air Quality Criteria for Lead" in December 1977, which would serve as the basis for the NAAQS. Central to the document was an analysis of the effects of lead on human health, especially its effects on the blood-forming system and the neurological system. It also identified preschool-age children and pregnant women as sub-groups that were particularly vulnerable to lead. After a public comment period, the Administrator released the final air quality standards in October 1978. The standards relied on 1 to 5 year olds as the target population, and set an adequate margin of safety that protected high risk sub-groups.

The new air quality standards would have significant impacts on the lead industry and, in December, 1978, the Lead Industries Association, Inc., a nonprofit trade association, petitioned the courts to vacate the standards. The case came before the Court of Appeals for the D.C. Circuit in November, 1979. The Lead Industry Association argued that the EPA Administrator had exceeded his statutory authority under the Clean Air Act because the proposed standards were stricter than necessary, e.g., alleging that the standards were improperly set to protect the public against "sub-clinical" health effects, the maximum safe blood lead level that was used was too low, and the margin of safety was incorrect. The suit also disputed certain aspects of how the Administrator had calculated the final standards and the choice of scientific studies.

The Court ruled in favor of the EPA, holding that EPA had complied with the procedural and substantive requirements of the Clean Air Act and that the Administrator's discretion was appropriate. The lead standards were reviewed from 1986 to 1990 and the agency did not propose any revisions. The standards currently remain at the same level at which they were established in 1978.

The uniform application of NAAQS to all regions of the nation and EPA's inability to consider their costs and benefits have been criticized by some as inefficient. The health impacts of dirty air clearly vary from place to place, as do the costs of control. Just think of setting the NAAQS for lead based on the target population of young children. By setting a uniform national standard to protect the most vulnerable population (and assuming the standard is accurately set), this will necessarily lead to "overprotection" of people in much of the country. Inner-city kids, for example, are exposed to far more non-air sources of lead than kids living in rural areas (flakes of peeling lead-based paint, in particular). If the national lead standard for air were set to protect urban kids, this would overprotect rural kids. Given this seeming inefficiency, why would Congress choose a uniform approach over air quality standards that vary from region to region?

The NAAQS approach provides a classic example of inflexible but easily-administered standards. Such "one-size-fits-all" standards make it easier for an agency to establish, monitor, and enforce than the more flexible and tailored local standards that vary from place to place. Local standards are also, one would expect, more susceptible to local political pressure than national standards, and some areas would certainly resent having lower air quality standards than others.

From a health perspective, given our uncertainties in epidemiology and growing understanding of the health effects of air pollutants, a standard that seemed overprotective a decade ago may not seem so today. Moreover, despite the statutory prohibition of cost considerations in setting NAAQS, given the nature of the political process perhaps it is unrealistic to assume that the costs of compliance and its effect on jobs and local economies would not enter into the NAAQS standard setting, even if only indirectly and unofficially.

Another major reason for the uniform NAAQS approach is that it stifles potential interstate competition for industry. A driving force behind the CAA was the historic failure of state programs to control air quality and the consequent fear that, absent national standards, states might be willing to sacrifice air quality for economic growth. In other words, because there existed no national clean air requirements prior to the CAA, each state was free to set standards as it wished. This made it potentially easy for states to become "pollution havens," offering lax environmental standards in exchange for an influx of new industries and jobs. This could encourage an environmental "race-to-the-bottom," much as Delaware has led the race to create a corporate friendly state, sacrificing air quality for economic growth. There has been a vigorous debate over whether environmental races to the bottom actually occur (indeed some have pointed to California, arguing that a "race-to-the-top" and stricter environmental standards is more likely), but national standards made the point moot.

1. State Implementation Plans (SIPs)

In practice, the inflexible and uniform approach of the NAAQS has been tempered in implementation. EPA sets ambient air quality standards nationwide, and each state then has the responsibility of setting emission standards that will result in attainment and maintenance of those standards. Each state is required to submit a State Implementation Plan (SIP) that demonstrates how the NAAQS will be achieved by the deadline dates established in the statute.[7] In principle, the SIP should satisfy the NAAQS while taking into account local conditions, thus allowing a degree of flexible, site-specific standards. In fact, the opportunity for local adaptation is even greater because there are well over 200 areas in which NAAQS are measured, known as air quality control regions. In simple terms, a state creating a SIP must first inventory the current emissions from sources within a region, choose control strategies for reductions, and then demonstrate through computer modeling that the SIP will satisfy the NAAQS levels.

On its face, this is a broad grant of authority, giving the states a great deal of freedom to allocate emissions. In practice, however, exceptions in the CAA serve to take back to the federal government much of what it had seemed to give away. New Source Performance Standards, described later, establish federal standards for new sources and major modifications of existing sources. Existing major sources of ozone must generally employ federally-mandated control technologies if located in areas that have not met the NAAQS. And

---

[7] 42 U.S.C. § 7410.

emission standards for motor vehicles are set by the federal government (with a specific exception for California and states adopting California's standards).

What's left then for the states to do? Primarily tighten the standards on existing sources. Any stationary source emitting 100 tons or more of a pollutant, 10 tons per year or more of a hazardous air pollutant, or 25 tons per year or more of combined hazardous air pollutants must comply with the SIP. In deciding whether to approve a SIP, EPA may only consider the overall question of whether the SIP will satisfy the NAAQS. As the *Union Electric Company v. EPA* case made clear, states' restrictions on *specific facilities*, even if they force certain companies to go bankrupt or greatly increase the emissions for others, may not be considered by EPA so long as the state demonstrates that its SIP is adequate.[8] With few exceptions, EPA can only look at the overall question of whether the NAAQS will be met, not every permit or rule the state issues. Thus states have great discretion to achieve their NAAQS through regulating existing sources. And the differences from state to state can be striking.

If EPA believes the SIP will not achieve the NAAQS, EPA may start a process establishing a Federal Implementation Plan (FIP) that effectively supplants the SIP and imposes its requirements directly on polluters. A FIP was developed for Los Angeles in the 1970s but was extremely controversial, as any proposed curbs on land use or driving naturally would be. Indeed Congress subsequently took away EPA's authority to impose land use or transportation controls in a FIP. Since then EPA has imposed a number of partial FIPs for parts of the CAA program that states do not want to run (such as the PSD program, described below), but the threat of imposing a wholesale FIP has largely been a paper tiger because of EPAs limited authority and budget constraints.

Non-attainment

Unfortunately, for both political and economic reasons many SIPs have been unable to achieve the "clean air" levels required by the NAAQS, and some cities remain out of compliance with the NAAQS. The term for this is *non-attainment* and it has been the most challenging aspect of the CAA's history. Non-attainment has been most serious in Southern California, where smog alerts have become a standard part of the weather forecast. In fact, a number of places have never been in attainment for ozone. Los Angeles is generally held out as the poster child of nonattainment for ozone, though a suburb of Houston has occasionally taken pride of place as the most polluted region in the country. Students often get confused

---

[8] *Union Electric Company v. EPA,* 427 U.S. 246 (1976).

over the concept of non-attainment. When navigating the CAA universe, remember that for *each criteria pollutant* you are either in a non-attainment area or in an attainment area. Where you live, for example, might be in non-attainment for ozone but in attainment for CO.

EPA's quiver to deal with noncompliance has never had many arrows. The threat of a FIP, as discussed above, is available but rarely used. EPA could deny federal highway and sewage treatment funds and, in the past, simply ban new construction in a state that fails to write or implement a SIP. The CAA also requires that new and modified major stationary sources in non-attainment areas employ control technologies with the "lowest achievable emissions rates" and that existing sources use "reasonably available control technologies." In practice, though, forcing compliance in the face of state opposition has proven difficult, and throughout the 1970s and 1980s the EPA and the states basically muddled along in quest of the increasingly frustrating goal of attainment for criteria pollutants such as ozone, CO and NO$_x$. The CAA of 1970 had called for states to meet the NAAQS by 1975 (with the possibility of two years in administrative reprieves) and secondary standards within a "reasonable time." The 1977 Amendments pushed the compliance deadlines into the 1980s, and the 1990 Amendments pushed the deadlines out again.

In retrospect, this recurring postponement was inevitable given the economically disruptive, massive efforts required for some areas to move into attainment. As an example, consider EPA's 1988 study of the steps necessary to bring Los Angeles into attainment. The EPA concluded that in order to achieve the NAAQS, the SIP "would have to prohibit most traffic, shut down major business activity . . . [and] destroy the economy of the South Coast, so that most of the population would be forced to resettle elsewhere."[9] Not a politically likely move.

The ad hoc accommodation with failure changed, however, when the 1990 Clean Air Act Amendments broke down the goal of attainment into achievable, intermediate steps. Non-attainment areas were divided into five categories, from Marginal, Moderate and Serious to Severe and Extreme. As an area's level of non-attainment increases, the requirements become more onerous. Taking the example of ozone non-attainment, those areas in Moderate non-attainment must show 3% emissions reduction per year, establish transport control measures, and institute a clean fuels program to reduce VOCs, among other requirements. Areas that are in Extreme non-attainment (i.e., Los Angeles) must do all

---

[9] 53 FED. REG. 49495 (Dec. 7, 1988).

of this *in addition to* other steps such as offsetting the growth in vehicle emissions by reducing emissions elsewhere.

By breaking down the goal of attainment into discrete, additive requirements, SIPs no longer had to meet (or fail to meet) the NAAQS in one fell swoop. Instead they must demonstrate "reasonable further progress," defined as steady progress toward attaining compliance with the NAAQS by the statutory date.

B.   New Source Performance Standards (NSPS) and Grandfathered Sources

In the earlier discussion over *where* to regulate, we set out the choice of whether to regulate at the source of pollution (the smokestack) or at the point of impact (where the air is breathed). In fact, as we shall soon see, the CAA does both. The NAAQS regulate the ambient air at the point of the air we breathe. But the rest of the CAA regulates the emissions of smokestacks and vehicles as an indirect means of influencing the quality of the ambient air. Presumably the tighter the standards of emission sources, the better the quality of the downwind air we breathe.

As we have seen, the SIP process allows states to impose restrictions on emissions from stationary sources such as incinerators, power plants, and industrial sites. Section 111 of the CAA sets a floor by requiring EPA to set emission standards for pollutants from categories of new or modified stationary sources. These New Source Performance Standards (NSPS) have now been determined for over 70 categories of facilities and apply to "major sources" or major modifications. These emission limits are technology-based, reflecting the best pollution control technologies available in each particular industry. This indirectly ensures costs will be taken into account, since exorbitant control technologies wouldn't be commercially feasible. As the name suggests, all major new stationary sources are subject to NSPS where source category standards have been established.

The pre-construction permitting process covers both new sources and major modifications to existing sources, and is collectively known as New Source Review (NSR). The specifics of the preconstruction review turn on location—whether the source is in an attainment area (and subject to the PSD permit program discussed below) or in a nonattainment area (subject to the nonattainment permit program) for a specific criteria pollutant. Thus an area can be in attainment for particulates but in nonattainment for ozone. In either case, the NSR process is how the EPA and state agencies determine the specific technology requirements for individual sources. It can be an expensive undertaking and important in ensuring air quality, yet it is one that regulated parties are eager to avoid.

One strategy is to ensure that new sources and major modifications of existing sources fall under the emission limits set out in the statute, though this is often not possible. For the PSD permit program in attainment areas, for example, a "major emitting facility" is defined as a source that has the potential to emit at least 250 tons per year of a regulated pollutant or at least 100 tons of a regulated pollutant if the source is within one of 28 listed source categories. The nonattainment permit program defines a "major" source as one with the potential to emit at least 10 to 100 tons per year of the nonattainment pollutant, depending on the pollutant and the seriousness of the nonattainment problem in that area.

A second strategy relies on history, and a curious practice known as grandfathering. By its very name, the NSPS provision assumes that new and existing stationary sources should be treated differently (after all, it is not called *Existing* Source Performance Standards). But why treat existing and new sources differently, given that both cause pollution? One might argue that high standards for new facilities promote technological development, creating a market by forcing new sources to employ the best commercially available technologies. But this would apply equally well if older facilities were also covered. Part of the reason for treating new and existing sources differently was clearly political. By limiting federal performance standards to new sources (and passing on burdens to parties less likely to oppose passage of the CAA), an important exemption was carved out for classes of facilities already operating at the time of the act's passage. These "grandfathered" plants do not have to meet the NSPS requirements unless they undertake major modifications that increase emissions. For utilities, grandfathering has allowed older power plants to emit four to ten times more SO_2 and NO_x per megawatt-hour than new sources. In this way, the CAA shifted some of the pollution control costs from existing businesses onto future market entrants.

To be fair, this grandfather exemption probably seemed quite reasonable in the 1970s, given the high costs of retro-fitting existing plants. And it would likely not be of long-term importance, it was thought, since the grandfathered plants would shut down over time to make way for more modern, efficient, and cleaner facilities. At least that was the plan. Consider, though, whether grandfathering can create an incentive to keep older facilities operating as long as possible. What would you do if you owned a major facility that was grandfathered and wanted to increase its capacity while avoiding the high cost of NSR and its NSPS requirements? Might you try to make use of regular maintenance and repairs as an opportunity to gradually rebuild the plant, classifying these as minor improvements rather than major modifications? In a series of lawsuits, the EPA alleged that this is exactly what a number of utilities had done over the last 30 years, violating the spirit and intent of the CAA.[10]

Even if one chooses to regulate new and existing plants differently, why give the federal government primary responsibility for regulation of major new sources? In pure cost terms, national NSPS standards made sense because it is much more efficient for the EPA than for fifty separate states to understand and stay on top of the technical capability of industries to control pollutants. One might imagine, as well, that powerful local industries would have more influence at the state level to lobby for lax standards than at the national level (though this is debatable, since Washington surely has more than its fair share of lobbyists). Perhaps most important, setting national standards for new sources and major modified sources stifles potential interstate competition for industry. It would seem odd, indeed, to battle the dangers of a race-to-the-bottom by mandating a uniform, national strategy of NAAQS while, at the same time, allowing states eager for economic growth to entice major new facilities with the lure of lax emissions standards for particular industry sectors.

C. Trading

The unceasing pressure over the last four decades to improve our nation's air quality has provided a valuable opportunity for experimentation and fine-tuning the CAA's regulatory approaches. This is most evident in the area of trading, where experiences under the CAA have truly influenced environmental policy around the globe.

Two key challenges to implementation of the CAA have been how to (1) clean up the nation's air at lowest cost while at the same time (2) allowing increased economic growth and the pollution this will create. Put simply, how can the government minimize the cost of meeting a particular pollution goal? And how can the government reduce the pollution in a non-attainment area while permitting the number of sources to increase? The government has achieved these goals by clever use of market instruments to develop trading mechanisms. In principle, these trading systems achieve the goals of the CAA at a lower cost than direct regulation of each source.

---

[10] *See, e.g., United States v. Ohio Edison Co.,* 276 F.Supp.2d 829 (S.D. Ohio 2003); *Wisconsin Electric Power Company v. Reilly,* 893 F.2d 901 (7th Cir.1990) (*en banc*); *United States v. Southern Indiana Gas & Electric Co.,* 245 F.Supp.2d 994 (S.D. Ind. 2003).

Bubbling is the simplest form of trading. As shown in the figure on the next page, imagine that you manage an industrial site with 4 plants, each of which has a smokestack; each smokestack emits 10 tons per year of NO_x, for a total of 40 tons (10+10+10+10). The state SIP requires a 10% reduction in emissions from the site. You clearly could comply by emitting one ton less from each smokestack (9+9+9+9). But if some of the plants are more efficient than others, this uniform approach would be costly. It's expensive to reduce 10% of emissions from a plant that is already efficient. By contrast, it would be less expensive to reduce emissions from the least efficient plant. If one of your plants could more cheaply reduce all 4 tons, should you be allowed to take the reductions from this plant and none from the others (10+10+10+6)? After all, the total emissions from your site have still been reduced by 10%. By drawing an imaginary bubble over your manufacturing site, and regulating only the total emissions from the bubble, EPA says you can.

And it goes farther. In a similar practice known as *netting*, facilities can increase emissions by one source in the facility but avoid permitting requirements for major modifications by reducing a similar amount of emissions from another on-site source. If, in placing a giant bubble over the facility, the regulator does not see a net increase in emissions then the facility has succeeded in avoiding the costs of permitting requirements while maintaining air quality. Through bubbling and netting, multiple emission sources are treated as a single source. By placing the imaginary bubble over a facility, separate smokestacks underneath can trade with one another and take advantage of the different marginal costs of reduction within the site.

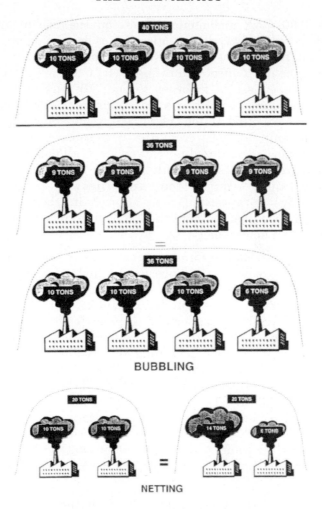

Offsets occur within a non-attainment area and rely on both the idea of bubbling and the trading of pollution rights. In simple terms, offsets create a bubble over an air quality region. A new source (or old source with a major modification) may not pollute *unless* it offsets its emissions by reductions from other existing sources in the region. For example, a new source that will emit 100 tons of NO_x must offset this amount by paying existing sources in the airshed already in compliance to reduce emissions by 100 tons. Thus the reductions from the existing sources are offset against the emissions of the new source, resulting in *no net increase* in total emissions within the region. By forcing the source of the new emissions to buy reductions from current sources, offsets permit economic growth in a non-attainment area while maintaining air quality.

The 1990 CAA amendments built on the use of offsets by requiring increasingly stringent offset ratios depending on the level of non-attainment. Thus new sources in Marginal non-attainment areas for ozone must offset at a ratio of 1.1:1.0 (e.g., offset 11 tons of current ozone emissions in order to emit 10 tons from the new source) while sources in Extreme non-attainment areas must offset at a ratio of 1.5:1 (find 15 tons of current ozone emissions to retire in order to emit 10 tons from the new source). Through this mechanism, new sources end up *reducing* overall emissions in non-attainment areas. States have gotten into the act, as well. Virginia's SIP, for example, required the state Highway Department to decrease usage of a certain type of asphalt, thereby reducing hydrocarbon pollution, by more than enough to offset the expected pollution from a new refinery.[11]

More sophisticated trading systems allow separate facilities to trade rights to pollute. The government first decides how much pollution in total to allow. The government next allocates *pollution allowances* among the regulated facilities. An allowance is effectively the right to undertake a proscribed action, such as emitting one ton of SO_2. To allow trading, the government then establishes a set of rules governing the exchange of allowances among facilities. Facilities that find it relatively expensive to reduce their emissions and need more than their allotted allowances can then purchase additional allowances from facilities that can reduce their emissions more cheaply. In the end, total emissions will be reduced to the level mandated by the government. By allowing firms to trade allowances, the government can reduce the overall cost of achieving the reduction. This is known as a "cap-and-trade" program.

The CAA's first use of trading (indeed the first use in any environmental law) focused on reducing lead in gasoline. EPA began phasing out lead in gasoline in 1982. To try to reduce the cost of the lead phase-out, EPA allocated lead content credits among gasoline refiners and allowed refiners to trade the lead content credits or bank them for later use or trading. Refiners were required to have sufficient credits to cover the lead additives in the gasoline they produced. If they did not have enough credits to cover the lead additives they were using, they needed to go on the market and buy more credits from other refiners. The key to this, and all such trading programs, is that the total number of credits available is capped at the desired regulatory level.

The CAA's treatment of acid rain has resulted in the most comprehensive trading program in the world and provides a nice

---

[11] *Citizens Against Refinery's Effects, Inc. v. EPA*, 643 F.2d 183 (4th Cir.1981).

example of clean air politics. The term, "acid rain," describes the atmospheric transport and deposition of sulfur and nitrous oxides, and the resulting ecological damage to forests, lakes and streams. Acid rain has been the subject of a charged political and scientific debate since the 1970s. The basic premise has been that Midwest power plants, burning high sulfur coal, have been primarily responsible for lake acidification and forest thinning in the conifer forests of the Northeast and Canada, among other environmental and health-related harms. The history of how to deal with the acid rain problem presents a fascinating regional political battle between "dirty coal" Appalachian states, injured upwind states, and "clean coal" Western states. This is one case where a simple clean air regulation mandating strict smokestack emissions would immediately create big winners and big losers. But such a simple result was politically unacceptable.

Early on, it was recognized that Midwestern coal-burning power utilities would have to be regulated. Their heavy reliance on high-sulfur coal, coming from the Midwest and northern Appalachia, was a prime source of SO_2 emissions. Their initial reaction was almost comical—sources built much taller smokestacks. While this eliminated many of the problems for the SIPs of the polluting states by dispersing the pollution, it made the overall problem of acid rain much worse because it increased long-range transport of the pollutants. The 1977 CAA Amendments forced the SIPs to include emissions from tall smokestacks, but this now raised a political problem. After taller smokestacks, the next cheapest way to cut sulfur emissions would be to burn low-sulfur coal plentiful in the western United States. This, however, would be an economic blow to local communities in the Appalachians where high-sulfur coal is mined. Robert Byrd, a senator from West Virginia, was majority leader in the Senate at the time. In a political compromise, rather than imposing a performance-based standard (e.g., X tons of SO_2 emitted per year) the 1977 CAA Amendments mandated a uniform technology-based solution. All new utilities had to employ "scrubbers," expensive pollution control technologies that remove sulfur from smokestack emissions. This uniform requirement of scrubbers seemed overprotective for many plants already using low-sulfur coal. One might argue that it was equivalent to a track coach requiring all runners to use crutches, even though only a few of the runners had injuries.

Fast forward to 1990. George H.W. Bush is now in office, a president who ran on an environmental platform. The majority leader in the Senate, George Mitchell, is from Maine, an upwind state that has suffered from acid rain for decades. Repealing the uniform requirement of scrubbers, the 1990 CAA Amendments instituted performance-based standards and the first national program of tradable emissions allowances.[12] The program was designed to reduce SO_2 emissions by 10 million tons per year beginning in the year 2000, a more than a 50% reduction compared to 1980. It also provided for NO_x reductions of 2 million tons below 1980 levels. Starting in 1995, 110 large plants in 21 states were covered by the SO_2 program. In 2000, all power plants in the country were subject to the program.

How does it work? As we have seen, the CAA already limits the annual emissions from utilities. It also creates a new kind of property right known as an "allowance." One allowance represents an emission of one ton of SO_2 over a year. Thus, for example, if a power plant has 25 allowances, it is allowed to emit 25 tons of SO_2 per year. Note that this is the case even if the plant has an operating permit to emit 50 tons. The permit caps the potential emissions, but the facility still needs an allowance for each ton of SO_2 emitted. The total number of allowances available is set at the total level of desired emissions nationwide. Thus far fewer allowances were available in the year 2000 than had been at the start of the program. This not only results in a gradual lowering of SO_2 emissions, but it allows market mechanisms to allocate the emissions. Anyone who wants to emit more than their allowances has to buy them from someone else, thus re-allocating the cost of control.

There are three sources of allowances. First, under a formula involving past emissions and fuel consumption, allowances are allocated to existing plants. The CAA also awards "bonus" allowances to particular utilities, including those employing "clean coal" technology or investing in conservation and renewable energy. Plants built after 2000 get no allowances. The practice of granting existing (and often dirtier) plants more allowances than newer (and often cleaner) plants is little different than the grandfathering practice we discussed in connection with the NSPS. Second, new plants that need allowances and existing plants that need more allowances can buy them from other plants. They can do so through bilateral exchanges, simply paying another plant for allowances they do not need, or through a spot market run by the Chicago Board of Trade. You know environmental law has come a long way when you see sulfur allowances sold in the pit alongside pork bellies and orange juice futures! Finally, EPA holds auctions in which it sells new allowances.

As a political side payment, the 1990 Amendments also provided a good deal of money to assist unemployed Appalachian

---

[12] 42 U.S.C. § 7651.

coal miners. This is noteworthy because it is so rare in environmental statutes to compensate the losers.

The acid rain program is far more complex than these simple paragraphs have described, and its proponents had high hopes that creating a market for sulfur dioxide emissions would spur technological developments and efficient operations. The incentive for technological development would depend on how much allowances sold for and the cost of non-technological means of complying (i.e., switching from high to low-sulfur coal). Industry had warned in 1989 that an allowance would cost at least $1,500. EPA responded that this was a gross exaggeration, and that $750 per allowance was more likely. In early trades, though, allowances cost only $250 and have gone much lower than that.

Why so much lower than the industry and EPA estimates? In part, no doubt, industry exaggerated the costs of compliance for advocacy reasons. The low cost is due in part to the unrelated drop in rail freight rates from deregulation of the rail industry, making it cheaper to transport low-sulfur coal. But the low cost is also due to an efficient market that ensured low transaction and information costs for exchanges to take place. Moreover, there is strong empirical support that technology has improved. Scrubber technology was estimated to have reached 90% to 95% efficiency by 1990. And one reason for this improvement was the seemingly nonsensical requirement of scrubbers in the 1977 CAA Amendments, since it gave utilities and scrubber manufacturers an incentive to get the scrubbers to work better. Reductions in SO_2 have also, in the process, reduced other power plant pollutants, resulting in improved visibility and public health protection.

In theory, trading is preferable to source-specific regulation because it increases efficiencies. In the case of air pollutant markets, for example, imagine a source that can reduce more emissions than needed to comply with its permit limits at a relatively low cost. It now faces a business decision. Will it make more profit by continuing to emit the full 10 tons allowed under its permit, for example, or is it better off by selling its allowances at a profit to higher-cost agents, or perhaps reducing its emissions but banking its allowances for future use? If the market operates efficiently, the greatest share of reductions will come from agents who can do so at the cheapest cost, allowing each polluter to weigh the marginal cost of abatement against the cost of buying credits and make an efficient individual decision. The net result allows the regulated community to select appropriate control strategies and, in so doing, creates a market incentive for innovative practices and technologies.

This is an important point, since technology-based approaches have been criticized by some as stifling innovation—so long as you have a control technology on your smokestack that satisfies the standards, why reduce emissions further? In a trading system, by contrast, any reduced emissions can be sold on the market to other sources who find it expensive to reduce their emissions, or banked for later sale (on the bet that prices will rise). It has been estimated, for example, that the lead trading program saved hundreds of millions of dollars compared to the costs of requiring every refinery to meet the same lead standard. It was expensive for many of the smaller refineries to come into compliance, and they took advantage of the trading system.

Flush with the success of the acid rain program, proponents of trading have been pushing for its adoption in other areas, ranging from wetlands and endangered species habitat to water pollution and greenhouse gases. The Kyoto Protocol to the Framework Convention on Climate Change (described in Chapter 6) has taken trading global. The Protocol allows developed countries to trade greenhouse gas emissions with each other and, in its Clean Development Mechanism, calls for a variant of offsets, with carbon sinks such as forests offsetting emissions of greenhouse gases.

Despite these attractive potential benefits, however, trading can have its drawbacks. Property rights must be secure and costs must be low or few trades will occur. As described in the offsets example, these costs include market information costs (identifying buyers and sellers) as well as transaction costs (the direct costs of doing the deal) and potential indirect costs such as regulators tightening your permit based on knowledge of your willingness to trade.

Most important, however, trading can lead to what are called *hot spots*—areas of concentrated pollution—and environmental justice concerns. Because a trading program relies on the market rather than regulators to allocate emissions (subject, of course, to each source's overall permit level), it is possible that sources in close proximity to one another may purchase most of the allowances. This could result in much higher levels of the air pollutant in some communities than others. Often times, these are poor communities of color. Trading designers can take steps to avoid hot spot problems but these can decrease the number of participants or make participation more expensive, both problematic if the goal is to create a robust trading market.

In 2008, a decision from the D.C. Circuit Court of Appeals placed the future of some trading programs in doubt. Plaintiffs in *North Carolina v. EPA* challenged EPA's proposed Clean Air

Interstate Rule (CAIR).[13] CAIR was designed to address the regional problem of nitrogen oxide and sulfur dioxide emissions. States were given the option of either creating their own SIPs for these criteria pollutants or joining a regional cap and trade program for NO_x and SO_2. The idea was that the regional trading program would result in overall reductions of these pollutants at lower cost than state-specific plans. So far, so good. The CAA, however, prohibits sources within the state from "contribut[ing] significantly to nonattainment in . . . any other state. . . ."[14] The court held that CAIR could violate this requirement. One might imagine, for example, a cluster of sources in one state buying most of the emission credits, leading to significant problems of nonattainment in states immediately downwind, even though overall regional emissions were reduced. In response to the decision, EPA issued a revised rule in 2011 that was also struck down by the D.C. Circuit.[15] As this book was going to press, the Supreme Court had agreed to hear the case in its 2013–2014 term.

PROBLEM EXERCISE: RULE 1610[16]

In part because of local geography and prevailing winds, in part because of the high population density and heavy reliance on cars, the Southern coast of California has long had some of the worst air pollution problems in the country. Under state law, the California Air Resources Board (known as CARB) coordinates statewide efforts to meet the NAAQS. CARB has divided the state into 35 Air Quality Management Districts, each of which has primary authority to control local pollution in meeting the SIP.

In the early 1990s, recognizing that old cars on the road were major sources of air pollutants, the South Coast Air Quality Management District sought to take advantage of market efficiencies and adopted Rule 1610. Rule 1610 established a new trading program to reduce NOx, VOCs, CO, and particulate emissions from motor vehicles in the Los Angeles region.

Large stationary sources (primarily oil refineries) were required to reduce emissions, but they could choose between (1) lowering their *actual* emissions or (2) using Rule 1610 to purchase and retire enough cars to gain sufficient emission reductions. In simple terms, Rule 1610 placed a bubble over the South Coast District and allowed stationary sources to reduce at the facility or, instead, take old polluting cars off the road. The net result, proponents claimed, would be an overall reduction of pollution in the Los Angeles airshed at least cost, since taking old

---

[13] *North Carolina v. EPA*, 531 F.3d 896, 903 (D.C. Cir.2008) (per curiam).

[14] 42 U.S.C. § 7410(a)(2)(d)(i)(I).

[15] Cross-State Air Pollution Rule, 76 Fed. Reg. 48208 (Aug. 8, 2011); *EME Homer City Generation v. EPA*, 696 F.3d 7 (D.C. Cir. 2012).

[16] *Adapted* from Stanford Law School Case Study Number 98–013, written by Mary Decker under the editorial guidance of Barton H. Thompson, Jr.

polluting cars off the road could prove cheaper than pollution control retrofits in some, perhaps many, circumstances.

Under Rule 1610, passenger cars and light-duty trucks in model years 1981 and earlier qualify as "old vehicles." Stationary sources could earn mobile source emission reduction credits ("MERCs") in exchange for taking these older, higher-polluting vehicles off the road. The District estimated that 1.9 million vehicles in their region fit this description. Once acquired, MERCs last up to three years, based on the assumption that the old vehicles could have been driven three more years if they had not been scrapped.

Regulated sources could either generate MERCs for compliance with their emission reduction requirements or choose not to participate in the trading program and, for example, install vapor recovery equipment at their facilities to reduce VOCs rather than purchasing MERCs.

Assume you are a lawyer for the environmental justice organization, Communities for a Better Environment (CBE). Would you support or oppose Rule 1610? Can you think of ways that this program might harm poor communities of color? How might the trading program prove inefficient in reducing absolute levels of pollution in the South Coast District? What specific changes would you recommend to improve the program's effectiveness and fairness?

D.   Interstate Pollution

Air pollution pays no heed to state lines and downwind states are especially vulnerable to polluting upwind states. This was made starkly clear in the early 1970s, when power plants in the Ohio Valley built taller smokestacks so that their emissions would move far beyond their state—especially bad news for states in the Northeast who could hardly erect fences to keep out air pollution carried by the prevailing winds. It is not hard to imagine how a downwind state, despite its best efforts, could fail to meet its SIP through no fault of its own.

Under the original 1970 CAA, states were simply required to exchange information about interstate pollution. The 1977 amendments banned the construction of high smokestacks and mandated that SIPs must control emissions that would "prevent attainment or maintenance" of the NAAQS in neighboring states. A new part of the law, Section 126, permitted states to petition EPA and, if it determined that a major source in another state was preventing attainment or maintenance of the downwind state's SIP, EPA could prohibit the construction of new sources and major modifications of existing sources. In practice, however, these protections were ineffective because it proved too difficult to show that an *individual* emission source would prevent attainment of a state's SIP. The modeling was simply too complex and the impact too attenuated.

As discussed earlier, the 1990 CAA amendments created a separate trading program in a new Title IV for acid rain—one of the major interstate air quality concerns. The Amendment also strengthened the interstate pollution provisions by requiring that SIPs control a source or groups of sources that "contribute significantly" to nonattainment of an NAAQS or that "interfere with maintenance" of NAAQS in another state. As a result, downwind states carry an easier evidentiary burden when petitioning EPA under Section 126.

E.　Prevention of Significant Deterioration (PSD)

New major sources, no matter where they are located, must employ at least NSPS and, as we have seen, in a non-attainment area also purchase offsets and meet lowest achievable emissions rates unless they can net within a larger facility. These requirements are expensive. Wouldn't it make economic sense for a company deciding where to build a plant to set up in a region that is already in attainment? Thanks to the CAA's Prevention of Significant Deterioration (PSD) requirements, not necessarily.[17] One might think that so long as an area is in compliance with the NAAQS there should be no additional requirements to ensure health beyond NSPS. As a result of a court decision in 1973 and following CAA amendments in 1977, the PSD program says otherwise.[18] The CAA requires EPA to "protect and enhance" air quality, and this was interpreted as ensuring that air quality doesn't significantly drop even in areas that meet or are well below the NAAQS levels. New major sources in PSD areas must employ the "best available control technologies," which much be at least as and, in practice, more stringent than the NSPS.

The PSD program is quite complex. In simple terms, it divides the country into three classes of areas with varying degrees of restriction. Class I areas include national parks such as the Grand Canyon while Class II areas cover most of the rest of the country. The class category determines the amount of development allowed through so-called "increments." These increments place an upper limit on the increase in ambient concentration of pollutants in the area and may place the area's ambient air quality well below the NAAQS. The growth increment for sulfur dioxide, for example, is ten-fold smaller in Class I areas than for Class II areas. In other

---

[17] 42 U.S.C. §§ 7470–7492.

[18] *Sierra Club v. Ruckelshaus*, 344 F. Supp. 253 (D.D.C.), aff'd per curiam without opinion, 2 Envtl. L. Rep. 20656 (D.C. Cir.1972), aff'd by an equally divided Court, 412 U.S. 541 (1973).

words, Class II areas can accept greater increases in air pollutant concentrations than Class I areas. When a new source or major modification seeks a permit to pollute, the government must calculate by modeling whether the increased pollution in combination with increases in emissions from other sources will violate the growth increment. Note that, as with non-attainment, PSD is pollutant-specific. An area can be a non-attainment area for ozone but a PSD area for particulates.

At first glance, the PSD program is puzzling. Presumably there are no health issues involved because the NAAQS are met. The public health is already protected by the NAAQS with an adequate margin of safety. One possible explanation is the importance of preserving clean air in undeveloped regions and national parks. Another possible explanation is political—the PSD program restrains the flight of industry from dirty to clean areas and ensures non-attainment regions remain competitive by raising the cost of moving into PSD areas.

F.   Hazardous Air Pollutants

In 1999, EPA reported emissions of over 10 billion pounds of hazardous air pollutants. As their name suggests, hazardous air pollutants (HAPs) are airborne chemicals that can harm human health or the environment. Adverse impacts can include cancer, neurological, respiratory, and reproductive effects. As with other air pollutants, the likelihood of harm depends both on the type and amount of exposure.

Section 112 of the CAA of 1970 called for EPA to control HAPs by developing a list of covered pollutants and setting National Emission Standards for Hazardous Air Pollutants (known as NESHAPs) that, similar to the NAAQS, would provide "an ample margin of safety to protect the public health." The program, however, progressed remarkable slowly. Indeed, over the first twenty years, only seven NESHAPs were established. Some of the delay arose from the difficulty in determining what constituted an ample margin of safety. For a carcinogen with no known safe level, presumably the standard should be an emissions level of zero. But what if there was genuine uncertainty over the effects at very low doses? And would the health and environmental benefits from a zero emissions level for industrial chemicals be worth the economic cost?

In NRDC v. EPA, better known as the "vinyl chloride" case, the D.C. Circuit addressed how EPA should determine an ample margin of safety for HAPs.[19] In a unanimous en banc decision, the Court held that in order to determine the proper margin of safety, EPA also needs to determine what is safe. The Court set out a two-step process. EPA must first determine a safe level based purely on the scientific data, expressly not considering cost or technological feasibility. The Court made clear, though, that a "safe level" is not the same thing as a "risk-free level." EPA was free to set an emissions level that posed an "acceptable" risk to health, not zero risk. In the second step, EPA could then consider costs and technological feasibility in setting a standard stricter than that dictated by purely safety concerns. EPA first applied this procedure in setting emission levels for benzene, discussed in Chapter 8.

Frustrated with the slow progress of the NESHAPs program, Congress revamped the regulation of air toxics in the 1990 CAA Amendments. Most important, Section 112 was changed from a purely health-based risk assessment to a hybrid process, listing 187 HAPs that must be regulated. New and major sources must meet emission limits determined by the Maximum Achievable Control Technology (MACT). Similar to the NSPS standards described earlier, EPA is charged with promulgating technology standards for discrete industry categories that provide the "maximum degree of reduction" that is "achievable." While MACT have not been issued for all the HAPs, it has done so for over half, far more than under the prior NESHAPs program, and it's easy to see why. Determining achievable control technologies for specific HAPs is far more straightforward than the risk analysis necessary to set the emissions level at an ample margin to protect the public health. In an additional creative twist for early movers, the 1990 amendments provide a bonus of an extra six years to comply with the MACT if a source reduced its emissions by 90% or more prior to the proposal of the applicable MACT.

G. Mobile Sources and Technology-Forcing

Mobile sources, including cars, trucks, buses, etc., are major sources of air pollutants. Vehicle emissions currently contribute to roughly three-quarters of CO, over half of NO_x, and almost half of VOC levels. Most of the areas that are currently not in compliance with ozone and CO standards fail primarily because of automobile emissions. This was dramatically demonstrated in 2011 in Los Angeles, when the city closed a 10-mile stretch of the I-405, its busiest highway, over the weekend for repairs. During "Carmageddon," the streets were largely empty as drivers stayed home. Air quality in that part of the city improved by an

---

[19] *Natural Resources Defense Council, Inc. v. EPA*, 824 F.2d 1146 (D.C. Cir.1987).

astonishing 75% compared to other weekends, and by 25% over the entire airshed. Remove cars from Los Angeles and air quality won't be nearly as big a problem, though getting to the beach and Disneyland may.

Title II of the CAA regulates mobile sources, setting standards for tailpipe emissions. Combined with provisions in Title I, for certain areas the CAA mandates cleaner fuels (such as reformulated gasoline) and vapor recovery systems (the accordion-like gas pumps). The net result has been impressive. Despite the fact that the number of automobiles has gone up over the last three decades, lead in the air has decreased by over 90% (primarily by requiring unleaded gas) and VOCs, CO, and NO_x from cars are down, as well, so next time you fill up your tank, you should thank the CAA! At the same time, however, substantial challenges remain. Some predict that many cities in the U.S. will never be able to meet NAAQS for ozone until mobile source emissions are cut drastically.

The CAA could have given states authority to set mobile source standards and therefore more flexibility in meeting the NAAQS. As with the NSPS, though, Congress chose to give this power to EPA. Unlike the NAAQS or NSPS, however, it hardly seems plausible that states would compete for industry through regulating car emissions. Given the weak race-to-the-bottom concerns, why set national standards for mobile sources? One might think it's more economically efficient, since the federal government is better placed to determine the capability of the auto industry to reduce emissions than individual states, but this is hardly an overwhelming argument. The main reason appears to have been that the auto industry *wanted* national standards enacted into law rather than having to meet a patchwork of state requirements. Manufacturing different cars for different states would wreak havoc with the economies of scale possible through large production lines. In recognition of Southern California's ozone problem, though, Title II provides an exemption for California to request a waiver from EPA in order to increase the stringency of its mobile source requirements. In what has become of increasing importance to climate change strategies, any state with an approved nonattainment plan may choose to adopt California's mobile source standards.

The history of mobile sources provides the classic example of "technology-forcing." The 1970 act required a 90% reduction of VOCs and CO emissions in car exhaust by 1975, and a 90% reduction of NO_x by 1976. Strong medicine for Detroit, and stronger still because no technologies were commercially available to achieve these standards. So why did Congress set such tough standards?

Part of it was technological optimism, coming just one year after landing a man on the Moon. Part was corporate cynicism, since the Department of Justice had recently settled an antitrust conspiracy case against the "Big Three" auto-makers for working together to suppress emission control technologies. And part was Congress's judgment of what was needed to protect the public health. Unless the standards were met, the EPA had the awesome authority to shut down the auto industry. EPA actually turned down a one-year extension of the VOC and CO standards, which was overturned by the D.C. Circuit.[20] Taking matters into its own hands, Congress extended the deadlines, but by the early 1980s the standards had been met through industry-wide adoption of the catalytic converter.

This type of approach, called technology-forcing or "aspirational commands," is a regulatory version of high-stakes chicken. Auto-makers surely knew that Congress would never allow EPA to shut down the industry, but were they willing to take that risk? And what kind of treatment would the auto-makers get if Congress did adjust the standards? Technology-forcing approaches provide a powerful means to move beyond incremental technological improvement, but also require strong political support to ensure a credible threat in case the goals are not met. In fact, without credible sanctions there is a perverse incentive in favor of collective non-compliance and *against* reducing emissions, since those that comply and spend money to reduce emissions on time will be at a competitive disadvantage if others who delay do not have to incur the same costs. Of equal concern, in forcing technology the government may actually force the wrong technology. Making use of its Title II exemption, for example, in the 1990s California tried to force the introduction and sale of "zero-emission vehicles" (electric cars). Despite millions of dollars spent by auto-makers to develop these cars, the market seems to be moving instead toward "hybrid" vehicles that rely on gas.[21]

H. The CAA of Tomorrow

The history of the CAA has been much like the Red Queen in the storybook, *Alice in Wonderland*. Huffing and puffing, the Queen complains that she has to run faster and faster to stay in the same place. The evolving CAA has faced the same challenge. Vehicle miles traveled have more than doubled since 1970, for example, requiring ever-tighter standards for vehicle emissions and fuel efficiency to improve air quality. Although our city air is much cleaner than three decades ago, we continue struggling to get our

---

[20] *International Harvester Co. v. Ruckelshaus*, 478 F.2d 615 (D.C. Cir. 1973).

[21] For a provocative argument that the auto industry undermined the zero-emission vehicle initiative, see the documentary, "Who Killed the Electric Car?"

cities out of non-attainment and, with better knowledge, adding to our list of what remains to be done.

We can, no doubt, be even stricter in our regulation of stationary sources and provide carrots and sticks for more efficient mobile sources (such as the hybrid car and fuel cells), but this will only get us so far. At the end of the day, to dramatically improve our air quality we may well need to address basic lifestyle issues— such as our ever-stronger reliance on the car or our aversion to adopt strong energy efficiency measures in our everyday activities and where we live. But changing personal habits and preferences is never a popular option and may, in fact, be beyond the power of the law. If it can be done, however, the CAA will surely be playing a central role.

Indeed the next chapter of the CAA is already unfolding— whether and how to apply the law to greenhouse gases. Climate change poses fundamentally different types of challenges than criteria or hazardous air pollutants and many have wondered aloud whether the CAA should play a role, at all. Until Congress passes climate legislation, however, the CAA is the law of the land and will apply, whether efficiently or not. The issues surrounding the CAA and climate change are addressed in Chapter 6, at page 165.

QUESTIONS AND DISCUSSION

1. As a result of the *Massachusetts v. EPA* decision, discussed in Chapter 4 at page 106, the EPA has begun to regulate carbon dioxide as a pollutant under the Clean Air Act. Representative John Dingell has complained that addressing climate change through the CAA would be "a glorious mess." Why might this be the case? More specifically, what are the potential challenges to creating a NAAQS for carbon dioxide? What about setting NSPS for carbon dioxide?

2. The CAA does not allow EPA to consider cost when establishing NAAQS. Does this make sense to you? Do you think the small number of NAAQS established since the CAA was passed in 1970 suggests that EPA really does take cost and technical feasibility into account?

3. As noted in the text, when EPA set the NAAQS for lead, it did not set a standard that would protect the most vulnerable population—inner-city children who already had high blood levels of lead from paint and other sources. Is this permissible under the CAA? Is it another indication that EPA takes cost and technical feasibility into account in setting NAAQSs?

4. A number of the criteria air pollutants actually contain two primary standards. Sulfur dioxide, for example, has an annual standard of 0.03 ppm and a 24–hour standard of 0.14 ppm. Similarly, particulate matter ($PM_{2.5}$) has an annual standard of 15 micrograms per meter cubed and a 24–hour standard of 35 micrograms. Why do you think EPA promulgated two separate standards, one annual and one over twenty-four hours?

5. In light of the *North Carolina v. EPA* (CAIR) decision, what do designers of air pollutant trading programs need to avoid in the future? Does the decision have any implications for a potential greenhouse gas trading program?

Chapter 6

GLOBAL AIR POLLUTION

I. Ozone Depletion

As of 2013, the Montreal Protocol had been ratified by 197 countries, including all industrialized countries and most developing countries. While the Protocol and its amendments have not eliminated the dangers of ozone depletion, they have established national commitments that will lessen the threat in years to come. The most important precedent in international law for the management of global environmental harms, the Montreal Protocol provides a useful model for other long-term environmental challenges such as climate change. The difficulties diplomats faced during the negotiation of the Protocol are much the same—genuine scientific uncertainty over the scale of harm, a sharply divided international community, potentially high transition costs, and a global problem requiring a global solution.

The problems posed by ozone depletion were unlike anything international environmental law had ever addressed. With traditional air and water pollution, the harms are generally perceived as localized and discrete. Even when pollution crosses national borders as acid rain or oil spills, the harm is still confined at worst to a region. The Protocol was thus the first treaty to address fully the global nature of a set of pollutants. Moreover, during the initial negotiations and ratification, there was genuine doubt whether ozone depletion had even occurred. Thus the Protocol was the first "precautionary treaty," instituting tough technology-forcing controls as a safeguard against uncertain future harms. It has also provided an important model for efforts to reduce greenhouse gas emissions.

A. The Science of Ozone Depletion

Ozone (O_3) is a simple molecule of three oxygen atoms and occurs naturally as a trace element of the atmosphere. The highest concentration of ozone occurs in the middle of the stratosphere, from 6–30 miles above the earth's surface in a region commonly called the "ozone layer." Although a relatively small part of the atmosphere, ozone performs a critical function. It absorbs certain frequencies of harmful ultraviolet (UV–B) radiation emitted by the sun, blanketing the planet in a protective shield that effectively protects life on earth from solar radiation. In the stratosphere, as ozone molecules absorb the incoming UV–B, they are blasted apart. Equilibrium is maintained, however, by a series of chemical reactions that create ozone as a counterbalance to the ozone destroyed through absorption of UV–B.

Fifty years ago, one would never have suspected that the ubiquitous compounds known as chlorofluorocarbons (CFCs) could cause environmental harm. CFCs had been developed in the 1920s by General Motors' chief chemist, Thomas Midgely, as a safe substitute for the ammonia and sulfur dioxide refrigerants then commonly in use. In place of these explosive and poisonous refrigerants, Midgely synthesized a non-flammable, non-toxic substitute. His invention, CFC–12, was first announced at an American Chemical Society meeting. It is reported he demonstrated the compound's beneficial qualities by inhaling the gas and then exhaling over a fire to extinguish the flame. CFC–12 was quickly adapted to the Frigidaire line and soon became the refrigerant of choice. In a clever commercial strategy, General Motors did not patent the compound, thus speeding up its wide adoption throughout the economy, in uses ranging from air conditioning, refrigeration, and foams to aerosol propellants, cleaning of electronics, and degreasing of parts.

The role of chlorine, bromine, and several other chemicals in the destruction of ozone as part of the natural atmospheric balance was relatively well understood by the early 1970s. It was not until 1974, however, that F. Sherwood Rowland and Mario Molina published the first credible explanation of what happens to CFCs and their potential role in destruction of the ozone layer. They argued that the inert CFCs would be relatively stable in the lower atmosphere, in part because the ozone layer blocks UV–B from penetrating through the stratosphere. Even though CFCs are heavier than most atmospheric molecules, CFCs emitted on the earth's surface would eventually migrate to the stratosphere because of the constant mixing of the atmosphere. Once in the stratosphere, Rowland and Molina hypothesized that ultraviolet radiation would blast the CFCs apart, releasing highly reactive chlorine (Cl) and chlorine oxide (ClO) molecules. These molecules would then set off a chain-reaction, in which just one reactive chlorine atom could destroy thousands of stratospheric ozone molecules. Thus CFCs would act as a catalyst, upsetting the natural balance of ozone creation and destruction. There would not literally be a "hole" in the ozone layer, but a reduction in the concentration of ozone, and hence its ability to absorb radiation. Over time, the role of CFCs and other ozone depleting substances (ODS) in reducing the ozone layer has been confirmed.

Increases in UV–B radiation have serious impacts on human health, including greater incidence of skin cancers, cataracts and sunburns. More recently, UV–B has been demonstrated to suppress the immune systems in humans with respect to some diseases. Unlike sunburns and skin cancers, the immunosuppression impacts of UV–B affect humans of all skin color pigmentation. Just as disturbing are the potential impacts on agricultural crops. The growth and photosynthesis of certain plants, including strains of commercially valuable plants such as rice, corn, and soybeans, are reduced by relatively low increases in ultraviolet radiation. Increases in UV–B can also reduce the growth of marine phytoplankton, which is the base of the ocean food chain and produces at least as much biomass as all terrestrial ecosystems combined; and UV–B damages midge larvae, the base of many fresh-water ecosystems.

B.   International Controls

From today's perspective, gaining broad international support for the strict control of ozone depleting substances perhaps seems inevitable, but in the mid-1980s the likelihood of international controls on CFCs, much less on halons or other substances, appeared slim indeed. To make sense of the Protocol's development, one must keep clearly in mind how little was known with certainty at the time. As noted above, it was not until 1974 that Rowland and Molina first raised the potential role of CFCs in ozone depletion. With the advent of national laws in America and Scandinavia banning CFCs in aerosols in the late 1970s, in 1981 the United Nations Environment Program's Governing Council gave approval to develop an international agreement to protect the ozone layer.

Attended by 43 nations (of which 16 were developing countries) and three industry groups, negotiations in Vienna produced the first international agreement to address CFCs. Expectations were low, with minimal public interest and no participation by any environmental organizations. The result of these initial negotiations, the Vienna Convention for the Protection of the Ozone Layer, was signed by 20 countries.[1] Rather than impose controls on CFC consumption or production, the Convention called for countries to take "appropriate measures" to protect the ozone layer and established an international mechanism for research, monitoring, and exchange of information. With very little known about the scale of CFC production in Soviet bloc and developing countries, it was hoped this data would form the basis for establishing a global production and consumption baseline. No chemicals were identified as ozone-depleting substances (ODS). At the end of the meeting, despite objections by the European Community, a non-binding resolution was passed calling for the next meeting to work toward a legally binding protocol addressing controls. Nonetheless, with the

---

[1] UNEP Doc. IG.53/5, *reprinted in* 26 I.L.M. 1529 (1987).

Vienna Convention's failure to establish controls on production or consumption, the future of CFCs still seemed bright. In what might have seemed a minor requirement at the time, the parties agreed to meet again in two years to assess progress.

In 1985, two months after negotiations ended over the Vienna Convention, British scientists announced an "ozone hole" in the Antarctic, triggering enormous public interest in ozone depletion. The scientists' data showed a 50% springtime reduction in the ozone layer compared to levels in the 1960s. Sharp decreases, however, had only begun in 1979, suggesting the reduction was non-linear. Ironically, because the data showed such a dramatic decline the British team had delayed publication of their findings for three years to confirm the accuracy of the data, and U.S. satellites' computers had automatically rejected accurate data of the depletion as clearly erroneous. While the ozone hole findings were startling and focused nations' attention on the negotiations, the discovery was of little help to diplomats because there was no proof of CFCs' role in creating the hole. Were CFCs to blame, or was there another mechanism at work? Despite uncertainty among scientists, though, media attention linked the ozone hole in the public's mind to CFCs.

Industry played a critical role in the development of international controls, as well. While originally providing a unified front against controls on CFCs, responding to the public clamor over the ozone hole, the chemical giant, DuPont, announced in 1986 that it could develop CFC substitutes within five years provided that regulatory requirements justified such a heavy investment in research and development. Without a legally-fixed phase-out goal to spur the market for CFC alternatives, DuPont feared developing more expensive substitutes for CFCs would prove a poor business decision.

The meeting in Montreal in 1987 could not have shown a greater contrast to the small affair two years earlier in Vienna. With representatives from over 60 countries participating (more than half from developing countries), many industrial and environmental groups, and wide media coverage, the world's attention focused on ODS. In response to the public pressure, the Montreal Protocol on Substances That Deplete the Ozone Layer was adopted by consensus.[2]

In the Vienna Convention, no chemicals had been identified or regulated as ODS. The Protocol, however, not only froze production and consumption levels of CFCs upon ratification and of halons three years later, but also set in place a reduction schedule for

---

[2] 26 I.L.M. 1550 (1987).

CFCs. Because monitoring consumption of ODS was thought infeasible, a surrogate formula was adopted defining a country's consumption of CFCs or halons as:

$$consumption = production + imports - exports$$

Thus a major CFC producer could satisfy the reduction requirements by decreasing its domestic use but still continuing to export. An importing country would measure its consumption simply by adding domestic production and imports together.

In order to give countries flexibility in their reduction schedules, the Protocol developed a "basket" strategy. Each chemical's ozone-depleting potential (ODP) was compared to that of CFC 11 (arbitrarily given a value of 1). Since CFC 113 is less destructive of the ozone layer than CFC 11, its ODP is 0.8. Using the basket strategy, a country would achieve the same reduction in consumption levels by using either 8 tons less of CFC 11 or 10 tons less of CFC 113 (8 tons x ODP of 1 = 10 tons x ODP of 0.8). This arithmetic was important because CFC 113 was widely used as a solvent in the electronics industry. Countries like Japan, which had opposed CFC 113's inclusion in the Protocol, could now choose to reduce a greater percentage of other CFCs while conserving CFC 113's use.

The reduction schedules and basket strategy not only avoided chemical-by-chemical negotiations but provided clear signals to industry by removing uncertainty. CFC producers like DuPont and ICI could now justify heavy research and development spending on CFC alternatives. CFC users like IBM and Toshiba could justify investments for in-process recycling and recovery systems to reduce the need for additional, and certainly more expensive, CFC stocks. For companies in ratifying countries, long-term investments in CFC production or CFC consumption technologies suddenly seemed less attractive.

If the Protocol's only teeth were scheduled phase-outs of controlled substances, countries would have had a strong incentive not to sign in order to gain the newly-freed market share for themselves. To avoid this free rider behavior and as an incentive for countries to join, the Protocol provided tough trade measures.

Regarding imports, parties to the Protocol are prohibited from importing from *non-parties* either controlled substances or certain products containing controlled substances. These products include domestic, commercial, and vehicle air conditioners, refrigerators, and portable fire extinguishers. The parties also decided to ban the import of products produced with controlled substances. The country of origin can avoid these onerous restrictions only if it demonstrates full compliance with the Protocol's reduction schedules. Regarding exports, parties must similarly ban the export of controlled substances to *non-parties* unless the country of destination can demonstrate full compliance with the Protocol's reduction schedules. Exports to non-parties that are in compliance are not counted as exports in the country's consumption calculation, so they must be offset by an equal reduction in production or imports.

As an example, if Country P is a party and Country N is a non-party and not in compliance with the Protocol, there can be no trade in controlled substances between the countries, and Country P cannot import products that are controlled substances, contain controlled substances, or (in some instances) were produced with controlled substances from Country N. If Country N remains a non-party but complies with the Protocol, Country P can export controlled substances to Country N but cannot subtract this amount from imports or production in calculating national consumption. Subject to the reduction schedules, parties may freely trade controlled substances amongst themselves.

Article 5 of the Protocol addressed aid to developing countries. While developing countries' per capita consumption of CFCs in 1987 was much lower than in the developed world, their domestic requirements were steadily growing. Since the manufacture of CFCs is a low-cost, low-tech operation, no practical barriers prevented cottage CFC industries from sprouting around the globe. Thus in part to accept the responsibility for having created most of the ozone depleting substances and in part to encourage broad international participation, developed countries supported a ten-year grace period following ratification for developing countries before the control measures would apply. During this period developing countries were permitted to increase their consumption to 0.3 Kg per capita in order to meet basic domestic needs. Following this period, developing countries would have ten more years to reduce their consumption by 50%. While this allowed growth may seem counterproductive, even if all the developing countries had increased their use of ODS to 0.3 Kg per capita the total consumption would still only have been 25–30% of the 1986 U.S. and European Community consumption.

With 24 nations signing in Montreal, the Protocol was universally hailed as a diplomatic triumph. Starting from low or no expectations in Vienna, within eighteen months strict international controls had been negotiated that would be refined and changed over time with the benefit of more knowledge. This flexible, structured evolution marked a new feature of international environmental law and showed great foresight. Because parties were required to assess and review controls periodically, this would ensure that the Protocol's international controls reflected scientists' improved understanding of the mechanisms and causes of ozone depletion. And, in fact, this is exactly what has happened. Not only have the parties met regularly since 1987, but every time parties have sought to tighten reduction schedules and bring new compounds under control.

C.　Developing Countries

While Article 5 provided a grace period for developing countries coming into compliance, Montreal had glossed over the terms of financial assistance to developing countries. Some simple facts, however, illustrated the importance of bringing these countries on board. Industrialized countries, with less than 25% of the world's population, were consuming 88% of the CFCs, over twenty times the per capita consumption of developing countries. Ozone depletion, unlike most international issues that had come before it, clearly could not be solved without the full cooperation of all countries, particularly large developing countries. China and India, representing approximately 37% of the global population, were not parties to the Protocol. These countries' large and growing domestic markets made the Protocol's trade restrictions moot. Huge local CFC industries could develop over time and never sell products outside the Chinese or Indian borders. Moreover, products containing CFCs, like refrigerators and air conditioners, were viewed as necessary to improve the standard of living in those countries and, indeed, essential in a number of applications. These facts gave developing countries additional power in the negotiations, requiring innovative compromises to meet their demands.

Developing countries showed keen interest in the emerging global scientific consensus over ozone layer depletion but rejected as unacceptable the options of either going without these products or paying more because of expensive substitutes and retrofitting existing equipment. Indeed, they charged it would be adding insult to injury to actually increase the profits of the multinational chemical industry that had produced the damaging substances in the first place. If the Protocol would produce winners and losers, developing countries wanted guarantees they would not suffer. They sought assurance that if aid proved insufficient they would be relieved from meeting their treaty obligations. They wanted to avoid writing their own check. The developed countries, however, wanted to avoid writing a blank check—providing financial and technical aid with the amounts determined by the recipient country. As a compromise, the parties approved an interim funding source

that, in 1992, was permanently established as the Multilateral
Fund. By April 2013, contributions made to the Multilateral Fund
by some 45 countries totaled over US$ 3.09 billion. Multilateral
funds pay for so-called "incremental costs"—the additional costs
incurred in a project by not using ODS technologies. Thus, for
example, if it cost more to build a meat-packing plant in India with
refrigeration technology that does not use CFCs than if traditional
refrigeration technologies had been used, the Fund could pay for
this additional, incremental cost of using an "ozone-friendly"
technology.

D.   Lessons Learned

Assuming that all countries meet the Protocol's broad
reductions, scientists predict the ozone layer will stabilize by
around 2050. With nearly universal ratification and coverage of
over 90 ozone depleting compounds, the Protocol must be regarded
as a triumph of international diplomacy. The ozone depletion story
offers three key lessons.

The first is the necessity of international cooperation to deal
with international environmental challenges. In practical terms,
this means creative "North-South deals." Throughout the
negotiations in Montreal and after, developing countries pressed for
explicit linkage between financial assistance provisions and any
developing country obligations. Fulfillment of their commitment
was ultimately made contingent upon the "effective
implementation" by developed country parties of the provisions for
technology transfer and for financial co-operation. The
establishment of the Multilateral Fund to finance the incremental
costs of acquiring substitute technologies helped allay developing
countries' fears that they might be charged exorbitant prices for
new substitute technologies. Without the Fund and technical
assistance, the Protocol would almost certainly have been a failure
because CFC use in developing countries would eventually have
eclipsed use in developed countries.

Second, the participation of non-state actors proved just as
important as the participation of developing countries. Scientists'
study of the ozone layer laid the foundation for all of the
negotiations and persuaded governments of the need for haste.
Despite being the target of much criticism, the chemical industry
played a critical role, as well. Reacting to mounting evidence of the
impacts of ODS, the relative certainty of control measures being
adopted, and pressure from ODS consumers for alternatives, ODS
manufacturers quickly adapted to rapid marketplace and
regulatory changes. For ODS manufacturers, the products under
threat of regulation were highly profitable. Any control measures

reducing the demand for ODS would hurt their bottom line. Thus the earliest press releases and advertisements from ODS manufacturers had argued forcefully for a "go-slow" approach. Later, however, seeking a competitive edge, certain ODS manufacturers actively led the effort to develop alternatives. Indeed, chemical giants like DuPont had a distinct competitive advantage both because the 1978 U.S. aerosol ban had given them a head start in looking for alternatives and because of their expertise in fluorocarbon chemistry. Ironically, DuPont, the leading CFC producer, would come to be seen as a champion of CFC phase-outs and even make a well-publicized promise to halt the production of CFCs ahead of schedule. The Montreal Protocol, for its part, established clear and certain timetables which gave companies confidence to invest in development of new chemicals.

Third, a precautionary approach to treaty making can work. While the Protocol has not proven a total success, its adoption and implementation did represent a diplomatic breakthrough. In no other treaty have so many disparate actors in international society successfully cooperated and compromised to address a global environmental threat. At the heart of this success is the flexible nature of the Vienna Convention. Despite having only minimal substantive standards, the Vienna Convention provided a framework for the international community to respond through an evolving consensus to the urgency of ozone depletion. The Convention specifically helped to organize scientific reviews, to incorporate new scientific and economic developments, and to ensure that international policy makers had a forum for ongoing negotiation. By moving ahead step-wise, acknowledging that more information was needed but not halting action in the meantime, the ozone treaties provide the best examples of international implementation of the Precautionary Principle. As we shall see in the section that follows, the Ozone experience provided a valuable (though incomplete) model for addressing a much harder problem—climate change.

II. Climate Change

Of all the topics in environmental law, climate change is currently the most dynamic, complex, and controversial. Climate change looms as a defining issue of the 21st century, pitting the potential disruption of our global climate system against the future of a fossil fuel-based economy.

A. The Science of Climate Change

The basic mechanism of how carbon dioxide (CO_2) and other greenhouse gases warm the planet has been well known for decades. Indeed, over a century ago, in 1896, the Swedish chemist Arrhenius first advanced the theory that carbon dioxide emissions from combustion of coal would lead to global warming. This process is known as the greenhouse effect because, in some respects like a glass greenhouse, greenhouse gases allow sunlight to pass through the atmosphere; they then absorb heat from the earth's surface and re-radiate heat back, leading to additional warming. Assuming all else is held constant (e.g., cloud cover, capacity of the oceans to absorb carbon dioxide, etc.), the physics is straightforward—increases in greenhouse gases lead to greater energy stored in the atmosphere that results not only in "global warming"—an increase in global average temperatures—but other changes in the earth's climate patterns, as well.[3]

It is important to recognize that the debate regarding the science of climate change has *not* been over the proven warming potential of gases or whether the greenhouse effect is "real." If you have any doubts, look at Mars (where, because there is no atmospheric greenhouse effect, the planet is a frozen block of ice) or Venus (where there is a runaway greenhouse gas effect, making surface temperatures so hot that liquids vaporize and permanently cover the planet in clouds). The real debate concerns how much, at what rate, and where the planet will warm, and how such warming will affect human health and the environment.

The major man-made (or "anthropogenic") greenhouse gases include carbon dioxide (CO_2), methane (CH_4), nitrous oxide (NO_x), and chlorofluorocarbons (CFCs). These gases account for only 3% of the earth's atmosphere, but concentrations have been steadily increasing over the last century (*See* figure below from the U.S. Department of Energy showing the contribution of anthropogenic

---

[3] Often the media and others confuse weather with climate. Weather refers to meteorological conditions at a specific place and time, including temperature, humidity, wind, precipitation, and barometric pressure. Climate refers to weather patterns that prevail over extended periods of time, including both average and extreme weather. Climate change often receives front-page media coverage only during droughts or floods. Unfortunately, this means that as soon as the weather breaks or appears to go back to normal, media coverage wanes and many people are left believing that the climate change stories were a false alarm. One particularly warm winter or cool summer tells us nothing about climate change.

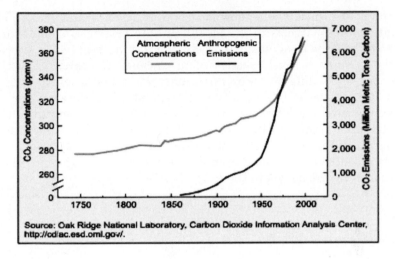

Source: Oak Ridge National Laboratory, Carbon Dioxide Information Analysis Center, http://cdiac.esd.ornl.gov/.

atmospheric concentrations). Ice core samples taken from the Antarctic and Greenland ice caps show that atmospheric concentrations of anthropogenic greenhouse gasses—carbon dioxide, methane, and nitrous oxide—have increased by about 37%, 150%, and 19%, respectively, in the industrial era. The pre-industrial concentration of CO_2 was 280 parts per million. Today's levels have exceeded 400 parts per million and many estimates suggest levels of 450 parts per million or higher by 2050. In short, our fossil fuel-based economy is unlocking and releasing greenhouse gases taken out of the atmosphere in prehistoric times and stored in fossil fuels such as coal, oil, and natural gas. Carbon dioxide and NO_x remain in the atmosphere and contribute to the greenhouse effect for many decades to centuries. This means that we have "banked" substantial amounts of greenhouse gases already, and any reductions taken today will not reduce the overall impact for some time.

Only about half of the carbon dioxide emitted over the past 50 years has remained in the atmosphere. The additional carbon has been assimilated, either through plants and the soil or through increased absorption by the oceans. Thus in addition to emissions of greenhouse gases by burning fossil fuels, many land-use and agricultural practices directly influence climate change. "Carbon sinks" refer to *processes that remove* a net amount of carbon from the atmosphere (e.g. through photosynthesis). Thus, carbon sinks present important opportunities for reducing the overall increase in atmospheric concentrations of greenhouse gases. "Carbon reservoirs" *store* carbon previously removed from the atmosphere. When disturbed, carbon reservoirs release carbon and add to the concentrations of greenhouse gases in the atmosphere. Forests are perhaps the most well known carbon reservoirs and sinks. The relationship of forests to the global climate system is complex and not completely understood. Forests can act as reservoirs (storing carbon), sinks (actively sequestering carbon), or sources (emitting carbon), depending on the relative maturity of the forest as well as the human uses of the land. Over time, changes in forest cover, for example through deforestation and conversion to agriculture, have contributed significantly to the level of carbon in the atmosphere. Indeed, estimates suggest that roughly 20% of anthropogenic carbon contributions come from deforestation. The dynamics of the carbon cycle are shown in the figure below.

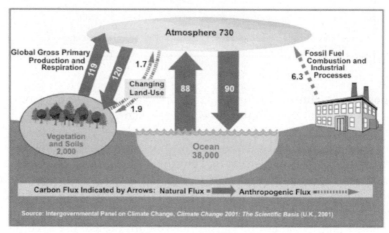

Anticipating the critical role that scientific consensus would play in building the political will to respond to climate change, the United Nations Environment Program (UNEP) and the World Meteorological Organization (WMO) created the Intergovernmental Panel on Climate Change (IPCC) in 1988. Following the example of the Ozone Trends Panel, the IPCC was assembled with over 2,000 accomplished natural and social scientists from around the globe and initially charged with assessing the scientific, technical and economic basis of climate change policy in preparation for the 1992 Earth Summit and the negotiations of the Climate Change Convention. After the Convention entered into force, the IPCC has continued to provide regular technical reports to the Conference of the Parties and its scientific advisory body.

Although legitimate and important areas of uncertainty still exist with respect to the ultimate impacts of climate change, the range of uncertainty is narrowing over time. Perhaps most important, a global consensus now exists among the international scientific community that we are witnessing discernible impacts on our climate and natural systems due to human activities. The IPCC's Second Assessment concluded in 1995 that the observed warming trend was "unlikely to be entirely natural in origin" and that the balance of evidence suggested a "discernible human influence" on the Earth's climate.[4] Given the conservative nature of the IPCC, this conclusion was critical for fueling the 1997 Kyoto negotiations. The IPCC compiled and released its Third Assessment in 2001, which concluded that "most of the warming observed over the last 50 years is likely to have been due to the increase in greenhouse gas concentrations" attributable to human activities.[5] The Fourth Assessment, released in 2007, found that "[t]here is *very high confidence* that the global average net effect of human activities since 1750 has been one of warming. Most of the observed increase in global average temperatures since the mid-20th century is *very likely* due to the observed increase in anthropogenic greenhouse gas (GHG) concentrations."[6] In the 2013 Assessment, the probability was viewed as "extremely likely," over 95%.

Despite variations in weather over the short-term, the long-term climate data suggest that the planet's average surface air temperature has increased by an estimated 1.37° Fahrenheit (0.74° Celsius) since the 1970s, with the most significant warming occurring in Alaska, Siberia, and the Antarctic Peninsula. The year 2010 was the warmest year on record for the Northern Hemisphere, while 2005 was the second warmest year on record. In fact, nine of the last 11 years (2002 through 2012) have been the warmest in recorded history.[7] In 2012, Arctic winter ice reached the lowest coverage since records were first kept. Glacial melting and thermal expansion of water have also resulted in sea level rise. These trends are shown in the IPCC charts on the following page.[8]

---

[4] IPCC, Working Group I, The Science of Climate Change 3–5 (Second Assessment Report, 1995).

[5] IPCC, Working Group I, Summary for Policymakers 10 (Third Assessment Report, 2001).

[6] IPCC, Climate Change 2007 Synthesis Report 39 (Fourth Assessment Report, 2007).

[7] NOAA Global Analysis (2012).

[8] IPCC, supra note 6, at 31.

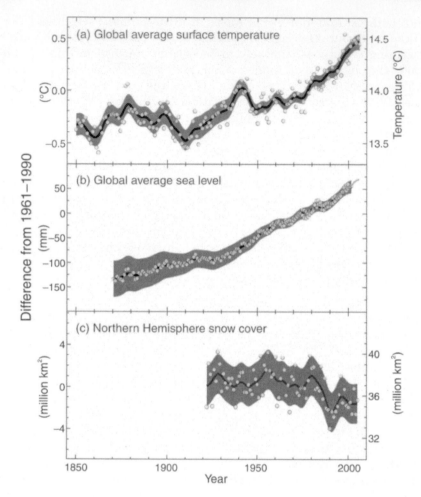

(a) Global average surface temperature

(b) Global average sea level

(c) Northern Hemisphere snow cover

According to the IPCC, failure to mitigate greenhouse gases will result in a further projected increase of between 1.5° to 4.5° Celsius by the year 2100. Such a rate of warming is apparently without precedent for at least the last 10,000 years. The expected impacts of climate change include not only an increase in global temperature but a rise in the energy of storms and weather patterns, sea level rise, water availability, disease, and loss of biodiversity. The range of possible impacts is so broad and severe that many observers believe climate change to be the most significant long-term problem facing the planet.

Who's to Blame?

Not all greenhouse gases are created equally; different gases have different "global warming potentials" (GWPs). Thus, for example, the GWP of methane is 56 times that of CO_2 (which has a

GWP of 1.0) or, put another way, a molecule of methane is 56 times more potent in causing global warming than a molecule of CO_2. The global warming potential for nitrous oxide is 280 and the global warming potential is in the thousands for the major CFC replacements (HFCs and PFCs). Thus emitting one ton of these compounds into the atmosphere has dramatically higher impacts than emitting one ton of CO_2 or even methane.

Most greenhouse gas emissions come from industrial activity and thus, not surprisingly, industrialized countries have been the primary contributors to the increase in atmospheric concentration of greenhouse gases over the past century. With roughly 30% of historic carbon dioxide emissions, the United States has been by far the largest single contributor to atmospheric levels of carbon dioxide, equaling the total emissions by Europe. While historically a small emitter, China recently passed the United States as the largest national emitter of carbon dioxide. National totals, however, represent only part of the picture, because they depend on both population size and the level of industrial activity. Per capita emissions provide a measure for comparing an average individual's contribution to emissions in each country. From this perspective, an American emits four times more CO_2 than a Chinese, and almost eighteen times more than an Indian. As developing countries raise their standard of living and industrial activity, however, absent changes in technology these per capita and absolute levels will surely change, dramatically increasing greenhouse gas emissions. These data are set out in the chart below,[9]

Country	Total CO_2 (mega tons)	Ton CO_2/capita
China	6534	4.9
United States	5833	19.2
Russia	1729	12.3
India	1280	1.1
Japan	1214	9.5
Germany	829	10.0
Canada	574	17.3
Korea	542	11.2
Iran	511	7.7
Saudi Arabia	466	16.5
Australia	437	20.8
Indonesia	434	1.8
Brazil	428	2.2
South Africa	451	9.2

B. Impacts of Climate Change

The impacts from climate are expected to be significantly different across regions, with potentially dramatic environmental

---

[9] Data for 2008. *Adapted* from Global Warming: Each Country's Share of CO_2 Emissions, Union of Concerned Scientists. <www.ucsusa.org>

and social ramifications. For starters, the impacts of climate change are already with us. As the IPCC has described:

> Examples of observed changes include shrinkage of glaciers, thawing of permafrost, later freezing and earlier break-up of ice on rivers and lakes, lengthening of mid- to high-latitude growing seasons, poleward and altitudinal shifts of plant and animal ranges, declines of some plant and animal populations, and earlier flowering of trees, emergence of insects, and egg-laying in birds.[10]

Global sea level has risen over 7 inches since the Industrial Revoluation, and this rise is very likely caused by global warming. The IPCC estimates a sea-level rise of between 10–32 inches during the next century, caused in part by the melting of polar ice and in part by thermal expansion of water. Sea level rise coupled with changes in storms or storm surges could result in the erosion of shores and associated habitat, increased salinity of estuaries and freshwater aquifers, altered tidal ranges in rivers and bays, and increased coastal flooding. Under different estimates of sea-level rise, the impacts on low-lying areas could, of course, be severe. For example, several countries could be entirely submerged, including the Maldives and the Cook Islands.

Warmer global temperatures introduce more energy into the global weather system and are likely to lead to a more vigorous hydrological cycle; this translates into prospects for more extreme and unpredictable weather events, with more severe droughts, floods, and heat waves in some places. According to the IPCC, changes in the occurrence or geographical distribution of hurricanes and other tropical storms are possible. Changes in the total amount and frequency of precipitation directly affect the magnitude and timing of floods and droughts. A warmer climate could decrease the proportion of precipitation falling as snow, leading to reductions in spring runoff and increases in winter runoff.

The increase in global temperatures may also have significant impacts on public health. The World Health Organization has linked warmer temperatures with the spread of insect-borne diseases, such as malaria, increased illnesses and deaths from heat waves and air pollution, and increased cases of diarrhea and other water-borne diseases, particularly in developing countries. The IPCC suggests that under most scenarios both malaria and dengue will expand their geographical and seasonal ranges.

Existing studies suggest that global agricultural production could remain relatively stable in the face of anticipated climate

---

[10] 3rd IPCC assessment, 2001.

change, but crop yields and changes in productivity could vary considerably across regions and among localities. Many of the world's poorest people—particularly those living in subtropical and tropical areas and semi-arid and arid regions—may face the greatest risk of increased hunger.

As suggested by the preceding discussion of impacts, climate change could also cause quite substantial harm to biodiversity, since forests and other ecosystems will not be able to adapt to the rate of change. Indeed there is strong evidence that distributions, population sizes, population density, and behavior of wildlife already have already been affected directly by climate change.[11] And this is not even considering low probability but catastrophic events such as significant slowing of the ocean circulation that transports warm water to the North Atlantic or large reductions in the Greenland and West Antarctic Ice Sheets.

While the concern over climate change stems from the costs described above, it should be kept in mind that there will likely be some beneficial impacts, as well. The IPCC, for example, has identified the prospects of increased crop yields in some regions at mid-latitudes such as Siberia, an increase in global timber supply, increased water availability in some water-scarce regions (e.g., in parts of southeast Asia), reduced cold-weather mortality in mid and high-latitudes, and reduced energy demand due to higher winter temperatures.[12] Nonetheless, the IPCC has firmly concluded that the costs of climate change will clearly and significantly outweigh the benefits.

C. *International Legal Responses*

Concern about climate change and calls for international action began in the 1970s and continued throughout the 1980s. Following the model of the ozone treaties, in 1990 the United Nations authorized an Intergovernmental Negotiating Committee on Climate to begin discussions of a global treaty. These negotiations culminated in the 1992 Framework Convention on Climate Change ("the Climate Change Convention") signed at the Earth Summit.[13] The Climate Change Convention established a general framework, but delineated few specific or substantive obligations to curb climate change. Central to the Convention is the objective found in Article 2, requiring that Parties achieve "stabilization of greenhouse gas concentrations in the atmosphere at a level that would prevent dangerous anthropogenic interference with the climate system."

---

[11] IPCC Working Group II, at 11 (2001).

[12] IPCC Working Group I, at 5–6.

[13] 31 I.L.M. 849 (1992).

The Conference of the Parties is charged with periodically evaluating implementation of the Convention to ensure that commitments are adequate to meet this overall objective.

The most significant provisions of the Climate Change Convention addressed the specific commitments of the Parties. The Parties are essentially divided into three categories: all Parties; "Annex I," which includes all industrialized country Parties; and "Annex II," which includes all industrialized country Parties except those from the former Soviet bloc in a process of economic transition. In order to create a credible baseline, information and data collecting requirements are imposed on all Parties. Annex I countries are subjected to additional requirements, including most notably the obligation to "adopt national polices and take corresponding measures on the mitigation of climate change, by limiting anthropogenic emissions of greenhouse gases and protecting and enhancing greenhouse gas sinks and reservoirs."

In 1995, the IPCC released a report stating for the first time that "the balance of evidence suggests that there is a discernible human influence on global climate."[14] The growing scientific consensus that climate change was not only a serious long-term problem but was actually occurring provided the political leaders with critical support for adopting targets and timetables. At the same time, global emissions of greenhouse gases had increased dramatically in the years since Rio, making efforts based on a 1990 baseline even more difficult for some countries, including the United States.

In December 1997, the Parties responded by negotiating the Kyoto Protocol to the Climate Change Convention, which established binding reduction targets for the United States and other developed countries.[15] The core of the Kyoto Protocol was targets and timetables, or "quantified emissions limitation and reduction objectives" (QELROs), for industrialized (Annex I) Parties to reduce their net emissions of greenhouse gases. Most European countries agreed to lower their emissions 8% or more below 1990 levels, while the United States agreed to a 7% reduction. Countries in economic transition were allowed to select a baseline year other than 1990, and several countries did so. All of the reduction targets had to be met over a five-year commitment period—from 2008 to 2012—which, it was assumed at the time, would be followed by subsequent commitment periods and presumably stricter emission targets.

---

[14] IPCC, Working Group I, The Science of Climate Change 3–5 (Second Assessment Report, 1995).

[15] 37 I.L.M. 22 (1998).

The issue of emission targets for developing countries was hotly contested during negotiations. Based on the reasoning that developed countries have been responsible for the lion's share of emissions to date and are better able to pay for reductions, the Kyoto Protocol did not address emission reductions for developing countries.

In addition to the targets and timetables, the Kyoto Protocol also called for various flexibility mechanisms, including emissions trading, joint implementation, and an initiative called the "Clean Development Mechanism." The Protocol also addressed compliance monitoring and the accounting of certain land-use and forestry activities that could alter carbon reservoirs or sinks. Many of these provisions, though, raised as many questions as they answered, and set the stage for further negotiations after Kyoto.

Indeed, several provisions of the Protocol had been deliberately left ambiguous, allowing countries to make their own interpretations and thus their own calculations of the costs they faced in meeting their emission reduction targets. And no sooner had the ink dried on the Kyoto Protocol then it became clear that significant ambiguities existed in the text of the Protocol that could lead to vastly different reduction requirements for the Annex I countries.

D. Climate Change Policies—No Regrets, Trading, Joint Implementation, and the CDM

A wide range of policy options are available for addressing climate change. These can be grouped into two broad categories. The goal of a *mitigation* approach is to lower the atmospheric concentration of greenhouse gases, whether through reduced emissions at source or creating new sinks, primarily through land use and forestry management. This is a long-term strategy. *Adaptation* strategies, by contrast, address the consequences of climate change and focus on near-term measures that adapt to these changes. In low-lying coastal areas, for example, this might include construction of sea walls to dampen storm surges.

Until recently, the climate change negotiations have primarily focused on mitigation strategies. Some proposals would require significant restructuring of our economies, particularly the energy and transportation sectors, but a large number do not, relying on currently available technologies. The Kyoto Protocol has focused on imposing clear national targets and timetables for overall reduction of greenhouse gases, but ultimately left the policy mix of how to achieve the targets and timetables largely to national governments.

Generally, policymakers have focused on the "no-regrets" approach to climate change policy, undertaking measures such as improvements in energy efficiency, forest management, and air pollution control that provide economic and environmental benefits additional to any climate benefits that may be achieved. Increased energy efficiency technologies often pay for themselves through lower energy costs. Reduced air emissions may improve local public health conditions more than the cost of the technologies. Thus, these "no-regrets" policies make good sense, and can be pursued even while the extent of harm from climate change remains uncertain. One significant problem, however, is that no low-cost reliable technology exists for removing or sequestering CO_2 from fossil-fuel combustion emissions. Once the carbon is released from oil or coal, little can be done to prevent it from ending up in the atmosphere. Thus, the strategies for reducing CO_2 do not typically include end-of-the-pipe or substitution solutions, making this a far more difficult challenge than phasing out ozone depleting substances.

One of the most controversial and complicated issues in the climate change negotiations has been the extent to which industrialized (Annex I) countries will be allowed to meet their own obligations by financing or undertaking activities in other countries. For example, would Canada be allowed to meet its obligations under the Convention by investing in energy efficiency in China? In some respects, climate change is ideal for establishing global trading markets in pollution; the reduction of one ton of carbon dioxide emissions anywhere in the world reduces climate change as much as any other ton of reduction somewhere else.

The Protocol contains four trading mechanisms (collectively known as "flexibility mechanisms") that allow parties greater flexibility in meeting their climate change targets. Emissions trading under Article 17 allows an Annex I party to purchase or otherwise transfer part of its "Assigned Amount Units" to another Annex I party, presumably in exchange for payment. For example, assume Country A has excess reductions to meet its goal under Kyoto (e.g., it has reduced its emissions by 200 tons compared to its 1990 emissions, and this is 40 tons more than required to meet its Kyoto reduction target of 160 tons.). It can sell its remaining emissions (up to 40 tons) to Country B. These can then be subtracted from Country B's total emissions in calculating its emissions under Kyoto.

Like emissions trading, joint implementation (JI) under Article 6 can take place only between Annex I countries. JI involves the sale of "Emissions Reduction Units" from one Annex I party, or private enterprise, to another Annex I party or enterprise.

Reduction units are generated by specific projects that reduce emissions or increase removals in the selling country. JI may be distinguished from emissions trading in that emissions trading is country-based, while JI is project-based. JI reduction units can be transferred only after they had been accrued.

The third approach, joint fulfillment of commitments under Article 4, allows an agreement between two or more parties to meet their combined commitments by reducing their aggregated emissions. Article 4 essentially allows parties to create a bubble around one or more of them to create their own targets and timetables, as long as the aggregate emissions from the parties did not exceed the aggregate allowances under the Protocol. Article 4 allowed the European Union, for example, to operate essentially as one entity within the Protocol.

Indeed, one of the most exciting developments in climate policy has been the creation of a fully operating market for carbon trades. Known as the EU Emission Trading Scheme (EU–ETS), tons of carbon are traded in a spot market. In its first year, 362 million tons of CO_2 were traded on the market for $9.2 billion. One year later in 2006, that amount had more than tripled to 1.1 billion tons of CO_2 totaling $24.9 billion in trades. Following the collapse of allowance prices, the trading program has been significantly modified and is currently in its third trading period, set to extend through 2020.

Finally, the Clean Development Mechanism (CDM) allows developing countries to help developed countries meet their emission reduction commitments. Article 12 provides that Annex I parties, or their private entities, may fund activities in non-Annex I countries that result in emissions reductions and, after they are certified, use those reductions to offset their domestic emissions. Typical CDM projects included destruction of greenhouse gas by-products (such as hydrofluorocarbons (HFCs)) from industrial activities, planting new trees to sequester carbon, replacing an inefficient industrial boiler with a new unit than would have occurred without the outside investment, etc. There is an extensive verification process for CDM projects, involving host and investor country agreement, third party assessment, and registration by the CDM Executive Board. Once verified, the holder of the credits can sell them to Annex I parties who can then subtract this amount from their total emissions.

The flexibility mechanisms have been controversial. A key issue has concerned whether credits from emissions trading should be capped in satisfying emissions targets. In other words, should countries be forced to meet most or at least some of their emission reduction targets by reducing emissions *at home,* or can they simply purchase all of their needed emissions from the emissions credit markets. This is particularly problematic because Russia and other economies in transition have significant emission reduction units to sell as a result of their economies' collapse following 1990 (these credits are called "hot air" by climate connoisseurs).

CDM projects have raised their own concerns. Beyond the technical issues of calculating the amount of carbon sequestered by CDM projects and monitoring to ensure the projects are properly implemented, CDM raised concerns of "carbon leakage." Leakage refers to the displacement of emissions from one source to another source. Since Kyoto capped total emissions of Annex I nations but not developing countries, for example, it was possible emissions could be reduced in an Annex I nation simply by moving an emissions-intensive activity to a developing nation.

The combination of hot air, large number of credits from projects involving the destruction of HFC compounds in China (HFC's are ozone-friendly refrigerants and very powerful greenhouse gases) and other factors have led to a glut of CDM credits and the collapse of their prices.

The flexibility mechanism with the greatest potential going forward will likely focus on explicit land use incentives. Deforestation through slash-and-burn agriculture, development, and clearing for grazing poses a huge threat to forests around the globe, but particularly in the tropics, where it accounts for up to 20% of global carbon dioxide emissions. Many environmentalists criticized Kyoto because it provided no incentive for keeping current forests intact. Because the CDM only granted credit for reforestation or afforestation, public and private landowners that kept their forests (and their carbon sequestration) intact received no credit for doing so. The basic approach for a new flexibility mechanism has centered on granting carbon credits for reduced emissions from deforestation and forest degradation (known as REDD).

In a simple example, if a country has had an annual deforestation loss of 3% over the last ten years, it would gain credits or be paid for reducing this rate of loss (e.g., down to a 1% annual loss or even an increase in forest cover). There is strong support for variants of this approach and it seems likely that REDD will be an integral part of any future climate treaty. The challenges to operating this program, though, are significant—establishing an accurate baseline to measure against, comprehensive monitoring of land use changes, determining how credits should be awarded (for percentage of deforestation, total amount of deforestation avoided?), etc.

E.   *Beyond Kyoto*

In December 2009, the Framework Convention's Conference of the Parties met in Copenhagen. This had been held out as the point of final negotiations and approval of the post-Kyoto treaty regime. With diplomats and heads of states from 192 nations, hopes were high. Deep disagreements over the level of reductions, monitoring mechanisms, and financial assistance, however, prevented widespread agreement. Following a day of hectic negotiations among heads of state, an informal agreement was reached between the United States, China, India, South Africa, and Brazil. When brought to the plenary floor for adoption, however, consensus could not be reached. In the end, the plenary agreed merely to "take note of the Copenhagen Accord."

Under the key terms of the Accord, $30 billion was pledged to the developing world for adaptation projects from 2010–2012, rising to $100 billion annually to 2020. The parties also agreed to submit economy-wide emissions targets for 2020 as well as a list of specific mitigation actions. Progress against these commitments will be assessed domestically. Given the high hopes prior to Copenhagen for countries to adopt tighter reduction targets and timetables, the summit was widely viewed as a failure.

Kyoto has now entered its second commitment period (through 2020) but the only developed countries subject to binding reductions are those in the European Union. International negotiations continue toward a new climate agreement, with a current goal of completing negotiations by 2016 for a new treaty to enter into force by 2020. Given the failure of Copenhagen, however, there is a great deal of skepticism. Needless to say, Beyond Kyoto remains a high-stakes work in progress.

F.   *The Clean Air Act*

During the Bush Administration, the EPA argued that the CAA did not apply to greenhouse gases; hence the Clean Air Act was not used to address climate change. This position was challenged in *Massachusetts v. EPA,*[16] when a group of states, cities, and environmental groups sued over EPA's decision not to regulate GHG emissions from mobile sources. Among its justifications, EPA claimed that carbon dioxide was not a "pollutant" under the Act.[17]

---

[16] 549 U.S. 497 (2007).

[17] The EPA also refused to certify the waiver that California and other states sought from the CAA for greenhouse gas emission standards for mobile sources. Industry challenges to these waiver requests were rejected by the courts in *Green*

The Supreme Court agreed to hear the case and issued its opinion in 2007 (described in the box below). The Court made three significant findings. First, it held that greenhouse gases are air pollutants under the CAA. Second, EPA must either issue an endangerment finding under Section 202—a finding that mobile source pollutants "may reasonably be anticipated to endanger public health or welfare"—or provide a valid reason to decline to do so. Finally, and of potential significance for future tort litigation, the Court held that, at least in the climate context, sovereign states are owed a "special solicitude" and have a lower threshold for standing than private parties.

MASSACHUSETTS V. EPA

549 U.S. 497 (2007)

In 1999, nineteen private organizations filed a petition, asking the EPA to regulate greenhouse gas emissions from new motor vehicles under Section 202 of the CAA. To do so, EPA would have to find that vehicle emissions contributed to air pollution "which may reasonably be anticipated to endanger public health or welfare." EPA denied the petition in 2003, providing two reasons—it did not have authority to issue regulations to issue mandatory regulations addressing climate change and, even if it did, it would be unwise to do so because of the broad policy implications.

EPA claimed Congress had declined to enact amendments specifically designed to force the EPA to regulate carbon dioxide emissions from motor vehicle and that the Clean Air Act was only designed to regulate local air pollutants. As a result of this legislative history and because of the major economic and political repercussions that would occur from regulation, EPA concluded that greenhouse gases should only be regulated if Congress "spoke with exacting specificity" on the issue. Further even, if EPA had authority to regulate greenhouse gases, the agency did not find an unequivocal link between carbon dioxide emissions and climate change. Any action taken by EPA would be "piecemeal" and might interfere with a comprehensive approach to climate change.

Following EPA's denial of the petition, a coalition consisting of Massachusetts and eleven other states, the District of Columbia, American Samoa, New York City and Baltimore, along with a number of leading environmental NGOs sought review of the EPA's decision in the D.C. Circuit Court. Massachusetts cited a number of harms that would result from climate change,

---

Mountain Chrysler v. Crombie, 508 F. Supp. 2d 295 (D. Vt. 2007), The Obama administration incorporated the California standard into federal standards in 2009.

particularly rising sea levels, which would cause a significant proportion of the state's coastal land to be temporarily or permanently flooded and result in hundreds of millions of dollars of harm.

The D.C. Circuit found for EPA. The majority held that the scientific uncertainty behind climate change as well as the policy concerns about the impact of unilateral U.S. action made it reasonable for the EPA to decline to regulate. The concurring opinion also argued that the plaintiffs could not prove the "particularized injuries" necessary for standing. Massachusetts and the other plaintiffs then appealed to the Supreme Court.

The Supreme Court ruled in favor of Massachusetts and the other plaintiffs in a 5–4 decision, holding that EPA had authority to regulate greenhouse gas emissions under the Clean Air Act as an air pollutant. Because greenhouse gas emissions were air pollutants, EPA must offer a reasoned explanation for refusing to make an endangerment finding. While the Court acknowledged that EPA regulation alone could not reverse global warming, it would help mitigate the damage and that agencies must whittle away in the face of such massive problems. The Court also found that Massachusetts had standing, given the special solicitude of states to act on behalf of their citizens.

Soon after commencement of the Obama administration, in April 2009, EPA issued a proposed endangerment finding under Section 202, the first step toward regulating greenhouse gas emissions from mobile sources.

Wasting little time, soon into the Obama administration the EPA issued a proposed endangerment finding under Section 202, a precondition to regulating automobile emissions. Similarly structured endangerment finding requirements are found in other sections of the CAA, in particular under Section 108 (the first step to triggering a greenhouse gas National Ambient Air Quality Standards—NAAQS) and Section 111 (triggering New Source Performance Standards—NSPS). Does a finding that mobile source emissions of GHGs likely endanger public health or welfare imply that emissions from stationary sources must do the same? If so, then three CAA programs are directly implicated—NAAQS/SIPs, NSPS, and the Prevention of Significant Deterioration (PSD) preconstruction permits. These are addressed below in turn.

Section 108 states that EPA shall issue NAAQS for any air pollutant not regulated by the CAA for which the EPA "plans" to issue air quality criteria. In the 1970s, *Natural Resources Defense Council, Inc. v. Train* had held that EPA has no discretion to opt

against issuing NAAQS in the face of an endangerment finding.[18]
How to do so, though, poses a real challenge. A moment's reflection
makes clear that the scale of the greenhouse gas problem and the
scale of the NAAQS/SIP structure provide a poor fit. Greenhouse
gases are a global pollutant. In terms of the net effect on the
environment, it makes little difference whether an emission comes
from Durham, North Carolina, from Palo Alto, California, or from
Kathmandu. Yet the whole structure of the CAA assumes both that
it makes sense for the nation to set national air quality standard
(through NAAQS) *and* that states have the ability to improve the
air quality within their airsheds (through SIPs). How, then, to deal
with the problem that greenhouse gas levels are virtually the same
worldwide and, therefore, a single state has little or no power to
reduce greenhouse gases in the state's airshed no matter how
draconian the regulation? Does the SIP strategy even make sense
with global pollutants?

Nor is this the only pressing question. In setting NAAQS, both
Lead Industries and *American Trucking* made clear that the EPA is
explicitly forbidden from considering costs. What, then, is the
limiting factor on setting the NAAQS for GHG levels? Rather than
a national standard, could EPA allocate GHG reduction
requirements according to each state's ability to reduce emissions,
with the greatest burden falling on the states that can most quickly
or cheaply achieve reductions? Could EPA acknowledge the global
nature of greenhouse gases, declare all state SIPs inadequate (or
advise states not to issue SIPs), and then create a federal
implementation program along the lines of a mandatory cap-and-
trade program?

Section 111 provides the means to reduce air pollutants
through New Source Performance Standards. This program is much
more flexible than NAAQS, since it potentially allows the EPA to
craft greenhouse gas regulation with particular sectors in mind,
deciding not only which subsectors of the economy to tackle first but
also how stringently to regulate them. In theory, this would allow
EPA to go slowly and methodically. Another advantage of the NSPS
program is that, unlike the NAAQS program, it would allow EPA to
consider costs and take into account the potential drag of
regulations on the economy. The EPA has focused its initial efforts
creating NSPS for electricity generating power plants (likely
focusing on carbon capture and storage) and petroleum refineries.

The PSD program requires pre-construction permits for any
new or modified "major" stationary sources. Such a permit must
contain emissions limitations based on a technology standard
referred to as the Best Available Control Technology (BACT) for

---

[18] 421 U.S. 60 (1975).

each pollutant subject to regulation. The thresholds for the pre-construction permit are clearly set out in the statute. A source is defined as a "major" stationary source if: (i) it is one of the sources explicitly listed in the statute and it emits more than 100 tons of any pollutant regulated under the CAA; or (ii) it emits more than 250 tons of any pollutant regulated under the CAA. Given that some greenhouse gases (especially carbon dioxide) are frequently emitted in much larger amounts than traditional pollutants, the 100 and 250 ton thresholds would be easily crossed, pushing many thousands of emitters into the category of "major stationary sources" for the first time. In practice, this could dramatically extend the PSD program, the expense of permitting, and BACT requirements far deeper into the economy, potentially from fast food restaurants to apartment buildings.

Seeking to limit the coverage of greenhouse gas regulation under the CAA, EPA proposed its "Tailoring Rule" in 2009. Existing industrial facilities that emit at least 25,000 tons per year of carbon dioxide must obtain construction and operating permits under Title V. Pre-construction permitting under the PSD program would be required for new sources and existing sources making major modifications that result in emissions of 25,000 tons per year of carbon dioxide.[19] The agency estimated that this would affect about 14,000 large sources of carbon dioxide, exempting millions of smaller sources of carbon dioxide emissions such as bakeries, soft drink bottlers, dry cleaners and hospitals that would have been covered by a lower threshold.

One potential problem with this approach was the statutory language requiring PSD permitting for emissions of more than 250 tons. The agency justified its 100-fold increase from the statutory levels (i.e., setting the threshold at 25,000 tons) by claiming the defense of "administrative feasibility"—relying on the emissions thresholds in the statute would be unworkable because it would cover too many sources. The regulations stayed in place following a challenge before the D.C. Circuit in 2012, which ruled that the industry challengers had not satisfied the requirements for standing.[20] As this book was going to press, the Supreme Court had agreed to hear the case in its 2013/14 term.

While the House of Representatives passed a climate bill in 2010, a companion bill died in the Senate and the current prospect

---

[19] The threshold is set at 25,000 tons of carbon dioxide equivalent, measured by assessing whether the combined emissions of carbon dioxide, methane, nitrous oxide, hydrofluorocarbons, perfluorocarbons and sulfur hexafluoride are equivalent to the global warming caused by 25,000 tons of carbon dioxide. The Environmental Defense Fund calculated that 25,000 tons of carbon dioxide is comparable to the emissions from burning 131 rail cars of coal or the annual energy use of about 2,200 homes.

[20] *Coalition for Responsible Regulation v. EPA,* 684 F.3d 102 (D.C. Cir. 2012).

for national climate legislation seems remote. As a result, the CAA remains critical to national efforts reducing greenhouse gases. Through one perspective, this is what makes environmental law such an exciting subject. The EPA is making climate law through the CAA in real time. Through another view, though, this is more than a bit unsettling. Congress crafted the Clean Air Act back in 1970 as a response to local and regional air pollution, not a global threat such as climate change. As a result, crafting a sensible climate policy for the CAA can feel a bit like jamming a square peg into a round hole, with potentially similar results. Until Congress or the courts say otherwise, however, the CAA will remain in the center of the national action on climate change.

G.   Sub-National Activity

Despite voicing support during the 2000 presidential campaign for regulating GHGs, shortly after taking office President Bush declared that the Kyoto Protocol was unacceptable and would not be submitted to the Senate for ratification. As a result, the Bush administration's approach to climate change largely focused on voluntary initiatives. Seeking to fill what they regarded as a void in leadership on this issue, dozens of states, hundreds of local governments, environmental groups, and corporations stepped in with actions of their own. The range and dynamism of these activities is striking.

Litigation

- For example, several U.S. municipalities, including Boulder and Oakland, and several NGOs brought suit in August 2002 under NEPA against U.S. export credit agencies for funding fossil fuel projects. The Export–Import Bank (ExIm) and the Overseas Private Investment Corporation (OPIC) provided over $32 billion in financing and insurance for oil fields, pipelines, and coal-fired power plants over the past 10 years without assessing their contribution to global warming or their impact on the U.S. environment as required under NEPA. After six years, the parties agreed to a broad-ranging settlement. OPIC, for example, agreed to conduct environmental impact assessments of projects that emit more than 100,000 tons and a policy goal of reducing greenhouse gas emissions from these projects by 20 percent over the next 10 years.[21]

- In 2004, eight States, New York City and environmental groups filed a nuisance claim against the five largest power companies. The suit claimed that the power plants'

---

[21] *Friends of the Earth, Inc. v. Watson*, 2005 WL 2035596 (N.D. Cal. 2005).

emissions contributed to climate change and constituted a public nuisance. The case was dismissed on the basis of the political question doctrine—that legislatures rather than courts should decide such a significant and complex policy issue. In 2011, the Supreme Court held that polluters could not be sued for greenhouse gas emissions under federal common law.[22]

While unsuccessful to date, there have many other cases underway around the country. These are examples of creative lawyering, testing new legal theories before the courts. The website, <http://www.climatelaw.org>, provide a comprehensive list of lawsuits and recent developments.

State Initiatives

State efforts to reduce greenhouse gas emissions within their borders have been particularly important. They provide models and case studies for potential national regulation. And by generating a patchwork of state-level regulations, they create an incentive for multistate businesses to seek uniform national legislation (just as early efforts by the states to regulate motor-vehicle emissions led the automobile industry to lobby for national standards in the 1970 Clean Air Act).

- Almost half the states, along with the District of Columbia, have adopted targets for reducing their greenhouse gas emissions.

- To try to achieve these targets, virtually all of these states have adopted laws designed to reduce emissions from electricity generation, which accounts for roughly 30% of U.S. greenhouse gas emissions. The most common approach has been the adoption of "Renewable Portfolio Standards" that require electric utilities within their borders to generate a set percentage of electricity from renewable sources. A handful of states also directly regulate CO_2 emissions from electric generation. Washington and Oregon require new utilities to offset their carbon dioxide emissions through mitigation projects or payments. New Hampshire and Massachusetts have ordered reductions from existing utilities.

- Automobiles and other vehicles account for almost the same level of greenhouse gases in the U.S. as electricity generation. Taking advantage of its ability to set motor vehicle standards under the Clean Air Act that are more stringent than federal standards, California in 2002 passed

---

[22] *American Electric Power v. Connecticut*, 131 S. Ct. 2527 (2011).

the Clean Cars Law that required new motor vehicles to significantly reduce their greenhouse gas emissions by 2020 (with further reductions mandated by 2030). Over a dozen states and the District of Columbia subsequently announced that they would adopt California's standard. Although EPA refused to approve the California standard under the Clean Air Act during the Bush Administration, President Obama in 2009 announced new federal standards that effectively incorporate the California standard—demonstrating again how state action can help drive federal environmental policy.

- California has also enacted AB 32, a cap-and-trade system designed to reduce California greenhouse gas emissions to 1990 levels by 2020 (a 25% reduction) and then to reduce them by another 80 percent by 2050. This is the most aggressive state action currently underway and is garnering a great deal of attention from around the country over implementation strategies, the effect on California's economic competitiveness, and the success of legal challenges. California held its first auction of carbon allowances in late 2012.

Regional Trading Schemes

- States in many regions of the country have also agreed to create regional trading schemes to reduce greenhouse gases. Most states in the northeast, for example, have joined to form the Regional Greenhouse Gas Initiative (RGGI). Participating states commit to a 10% reduction in carbon dioxide from electricity utilities by 2019, relying on a cap-and-trade system. Seven western states, including California, and four western Canadian provinces have created the Western Climate Initiative to design a regional trading system that would permit emission reductions at a lower cost than any state by itself could achieve. Six midwestern governors, along with the premier of the Manitoba province in Canada, have similarly signed a Midwestern Greenhouse Gas Accord.

Corporate Initiatives

- A wide range of corporations have established corporate greenhouse gas reduction targets, including Alcoa, British Petroleum, Cinergy, Deutsche Telekom, Dupont, Intel, Rio Tinto, Shell Oil, and many others. Companies see multiple benefits from voluntary action, including reduced energy costs, improved corporate reputation, and the generation of credits that might be usable under future climate legislation.

- Through the Carbon Disclosure Project, a coalition of institutional investors are asking the world's largest companies to report voluntarily annual greenhouse gas emissions information. The 2009 information request was signed by 475 institutional investors with assets of $55 trillion and asked questions about whether the companies had climate change policies, emissions reduction strategies, emissions data, etc. The initiative has been quite effective. Eighty-one percent of Global 500 companies completed the annual questionnaire in 2012, covering over 10 percent of the world's total greenhouse emissions.

QUESTIONS AND DISCUSSION

1. What were the crucial factors underpinning the ozone regime's effectiveness? How many of these does the climate regime share? Which differences between ozone and climate explain why addressing climate change remains so challenging? To make this clear, create a chart with two columns. In the first column, list at least six factors that were critical to the success of the ozone legal regime (e.g., availability of an affordable technological substitute, etc.). In the next column, place a check (✓) or an X next to each factor, assessing whether this factor is also true for climate change.

2. As law students all dutifully learn in their first year Torts class, a prima facie negligence claim must satisfy four elements—duty, breach, causation, and injury. None of these elements is easy to establish in a climate lawsuit. In terms of causation, for example, how can plaintiffs persuasively link the particular emissions of cars driven in California with reduced snow pack in the Sierra Nevada? And even if a causal link can be established between the offending action and the harm, what is the proper measure of the car companies' liability in the face of multiple sources of greenhouse gases over an extended time period?

3. Injured plaintiffs have successfully brought tort suits against cigarette manufacturers and asbestos producers. Are these useful models for climate change lawsuits? Assume that you have been hired by the inhabitants of a small island off the coast of South Carolina. Recent storm damage has been eroding the island and, if this trend continues, the island will cease to exist in another thirty years (if sea level rises 10 inches, what's left of the island will be submerged). Can you link the harm and predicted future harms to climate change? If so, whom should you sue? What duty of care did these defendants owe the island's inhabitants? Do you have standing to sue? What should you propose for a remedy?

4. Much of the debate over the successor to the Kyoto Protocol has centered on the appropriate measure for assessing national reduction targets. What are the arguments in favor and against the following goals?

- Percent reduction of national emissions (e.g., 10% reduction of Japan's total GHG emissions, measured against a 2012 baseline)

- Reductions calibrated against historic emissions (e.g., United States and Europe have more stringent reduction targets than India or China because of their total GHG emissions over the last century)

- Per capita target (e.g., national goal set at 8 tons per capita by 2020—China emits 4.7, Japan 9.6, and the United States 19.2 tons per capita)

- Energy intensity target (goal based on percent improvement of GHG emissions divided by gross national product)

5.   The Bush Administration consistently called for voluntary rather than regulatory approaches to climate change. In which sectors do you think voluntary reduction of greenhouse gases would be an effective approach? Do you think voluntary approaches can work without the threat of possible regulations behind them?

6.   California signed an agreement with the United Kingdom in 2006 committing to urgent GHG emissions reductions and the promotion of low carbon technologies. As part of the pact, Prime Minister Tony Blair and Governor Arnold Schwarzenegger agreed to collaborate on market-based mechanisms to spur innovation and on the linkages between climate change, energy security, human health, and economic development. In 2013, California signed a two-year Memorandum of Understanding with China to cooperate on lowering carbon dioxide emissions and strengthening emissions standards. Do these types of sub-national/international agreements undercut the federal government's foreign policy authority? How would you argue that these types of arrangements strengthen U.S. foreign policy?

7.   Do you think the UN process of giving a small number of countries the ability to block adoption of an agreement is compatible with negotiations over an issue as complex as climate change? If not, what is a feasible alternative? Does it make better sense for the major economies of the world and the major countries with carbon sequestration potential to negotiate on their own? What might be lost in this transition from global negotiation to negotiation among a much smaller group of "important" nations?

Chapter 7

WATER POLLUTION

A river catches fire, so polluted that its waters have "no visible life, not even low forms such as leeches and sludge worms." This could describe the mythological River Styx from Hades, but it was the federal government's assessment of the Cuyahoga River from Akron to Cleveland in 1969. Discharging raw sewage, industrial sludge, and other pollution into our rivers, lakes, and estuaries was long a common practice—with distressing results. By the late 1960s, *Time* magazine had pronounced Lake Erie to be "dead," and even Dr. Seuss referenced the lake's sad fate in *The Lorax*.[1]

Having tackled air pollution in 1970, Congress turned its attention two years later to the sad state of the nation's waterways in the Clean Water Act (CWA), originally known as the Water Pollution Control Act of 1972.[2] Just as the Clean Air Act has improved air quality, the CWA has reduced significantly the volume of effluents discharged from factories and sewage treatment facilities into our waters. As a result, our nation's waterways are cleaner than when the CWA was passed three decades ago. Unfortunately, though, we still have a long way to go in ensuring good water quality across the nation.

The EPA estimates that about half of our rivers and streams, one-third of lakes and ponds, and two-thirds of bays and estuaries are "impaired waters," in many cases not even clean enough for fishing and swimming. Ninety-eight percent of the Great Lakes shoreline miles are impaired, primarily from PCBs, toxic organics, and dioxins. And this is just the state of the waterways that we have recently monitored. The nation still does not regularly monitor most of its waters.

Environmentalists not surprisingly find much to criticize about the CWA. As discussed in more detail later in this chapter, the CWA focuses primarily on the discharge of pollutants into

---

[1] Dr. Seuss, *The Lorax* (1971):
    You're glumping the pond where the Humming-Fish hummed!
    No more can they hum, for their gills are all gummed.
    So I'm sending them off. Oh, their future is dreary.
    They'll walk on their fins and get woefully weary.
    In search of some water that isn't so smeary.
    I hear things are just as bad up in Lake Erie.
Fourteen years after *The Lorax* was published and significant strides had been made to clean up Lake Erie, the author removed the last line from the book.

[2] 33 U.S.C. §§ 1251 et seq.

waterways, while largely ignoring hydrological changes to waterways, such as dams and water withdrawals, that also can harm water quality. More importantly, while reducing pollution from factories and sewage plants, the CWA has done a poor job of reducing effluent from farms, mines, construction sites, and other "nonpoint" sources of pollution.

Economists, by contrast, object that the CWA requires factories and other "point" sources of pollution to adopt pollution control technologies that are sometimes more expensive than justified by the benefits to water quality. Economists also complain that the CWA does not take a "least cost" approach to improving water quality. Rather than focusing on those effluent discharges that produce the greatest damage or that can be reduced least expensively, the CWA typically imposes uniform effluent limitations on all companies within an industry. A number of studies suggest that Congress could achieve the same level of water quality at a lower cost by adopting a more flexible regulatory approach.

I.   An Overview of Water Pollution

Before examining the CWA's provisions, it is worth getting a better sense of the multiple causes of water pollution. Start with the sources of water pollution, as shown in Figure 6–1. Many factories, commercial facilities, and sewage treatment works discharge sludge and other effluents directly into waterways. These sources are known as *point sources* because they typically dump pollution into the waterway at a particular point along its shore through a pipe or channel. Other industrial and commercial facilities do not discharge their wastes directly into a waterway but instead empty their wastes into the local sewage system. These facilities are frequently labeled *indirect sources* of water pollution.

Thanks to the Clean Water Act, point sources of pollution are no longer the major contributors to water pollution in our nation's rivers and lakes that they were when the Cuyahoga River caught fire in 1969, helping to motivate the CWA's passage. Indeed, industrial facilities are not even among the top ten sources of water pollution in the nation's rivers and lakes; municipal sewage breaks into the list of top ten pollution sources, but not the top five. Sewage and industrial waste, however, are still a major source of estuarine pollution, ranking third (affecting 67 percent of the impaired miles) and fourth (59 percent) respectively.

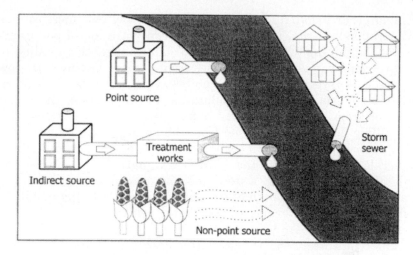

Figure 6–1: Sources of Water Pollution

Much of today's water pollution comes from farms, mines, construction sites, parking lots, and other land uses. When a farmer irrigates her crops, for example, much of the water runs off the land and, laced with various pesticides and other agricultural chemicals, find its way back into a river or other waterway. Rain or snow may pick up oil from parking lots, debris from construction sites, or tailings from mines before flowing into local watercourses. Because such runoff is often diffuse, these sources of pollution generally are called *nonpoint sources*. Storm sewers often collect such runoff from urban land, streets, and parking lots, and then convey the runoff to a waterway. Unfortunately, as we will discuss in a moment, the Clean Water Act has not done much to reduce nonpoint pollution. As a result, agriculture is today the primary source of water pollution in the nation's rivers and streams and the third most important source of lake pollution. Urban runoff is the fifth most important source of river pollution.

Perhaps surprisingly, air pollution is the major source of water impairment in the nation's lakes and estuaries. Pollutants can blow miles away from their source and then settle into local waterways. Moisture in the atmosphere also can pick up or combine with air pollutants and then deposit the pollution as rain or snow into waterways or onto land where it again can run off into waterways. The problem of acid rain, discussed in Chapter 5, occurs when water combines with airborne sulfates (which in turn arise from sulfur dioxide pollution) to form sulfuric acid.

Changes to the hydrology of a waterway also can affect water quality. When water is diverted from a river, for example, there is less water to dilute downstream pollutants. Similarly, the creation of a large artificial reservoir along a waterway can increase the evaporation rate and thus increase the concentration of pollutants in the remaining water. Dams also can change the quality of downstream waters. Water releases from dams sometimes are low in dissolved oxygen, reducing the ability of the water to break down organic materials and other pollutants. In other cases, the water released from dams can become "supersaturated" as it mixes with air, killing fish. Water released from the lower "hypolimnion" layer of a reservoir can contain overly high concentrations of various minerals and nutrients that can again harm fish, reduce the palatability of drinking water, and increase plant growth; this water also can be colder than the natural river, harming or killing fish acclimated to warmer water. Water released from the upper "epilimnion" layer can be warmer than the natural river and injure or kill cold-water fish. Such *hydromodifications* are one of the leading causes of water pollution in rivers and streams, contributing to more than 10 percent of the impaired mileage.

Finally, water pollution can arise naturally. Many rivers and lakes, for example, are naturally salty. The Colorado River gains salinity as it passes over soils and rocks laden with soluble salts; one of its feeder streams, Blue Springs, alone contributes 550,000 tons of salt every year.

II. A Brief History of Water Quality Regulation

As in other environmental areas, courts played the primary role in regulating surface water pollution until well into the twentieth century. By the 1930s, most states had adopted administrative programs to control water pollution, but the regulatory measures were generally quite weak. States were reticent to impose the expense of better sewage treatment on local governments and feared driving industry elsewhere if they clamped down on industrial discharges. Nonpoint pollution was not even on the states' radar screens.

Congress first addressed water pollution in the 1965 Water Quality Act. Like many early laws, the 1965 Act relied almost entirely on the states to improve water quality. This law required the states to designate intended uses for interstate waterways within their jurisdiction: a state, for example, could designate that an interstate waterway should be usable for "drinking water supply," "primary contact," "swimming," "aquatic life support," or a number of other potential uses. The 1965 Act also required the states to adopt water quality standards that would ensure that each stretch of interstate water met its intended use and to formulate plans to implement those standards.

The 1965 Act failed to bring water pollution under control. *was* States did not have the political willpower to meet the water quality *in-* standards that they set. More importantly, the Act's water quality *effective* approach proved technically daunting. States typically did not have the scientific information needed to determine the appropriate water quality standards for any particular use such as aquatic life support. And even if a state could determine the correct standards, the state then faced the more complicated task of trying to set effluent standards for individual sources. The available models for translating the overall water quality standards into individual effluent standards were exceedingly complex but still did not come close to representing the actual processes by which effluents mix and influence water quality. In the face of such scientific uncertainty, polluters often argued that their discharges were not the cause of water quality problems.

As described above, the nation was beset by serious water quality problems by the nation's first Earth Day celebration. About half of the states still had not promulgated water quality standards under the 1965 Act. Less than ten percent of municipal sewage facilities used anything other than filters and settling tanks to treat their sewage before dumping it into the closest waterway. Less than a third of industrial facilities treated their wastes. Although the Cuyahoga River captured the public's attention when it caught fire in 1969, the Cuyahoga had already caught fire at least a dozen times before. A 1952 fire caused over $1 million in damages to boats and a building.

III. The Clean Water Act

Congress responded to these problems in 1972 by passing the Clean Water Act. As with the Clean Air Act, Congress set extremely ambitious goals for its new regulatory regime: the CWA was to "provide for the protection and propagation of fish, shellfish, and wildlife" and for "recreation in and on the water" by July 1, 1983, and to eliminate *all* discharges of pollutants into the nation's waterways by 1985. Although Congress passed the CWA by overwhelming margins, many observers were dumbfounded by Congress' announced goals. Among the critics was the National Water Commission, a bipartisan federal panel of water experts created in the late 1960s by President Lyndon Johnson to study the nation's water problems. The critics argued that the goals were totally infeasible and thus destined to lead to public disappointment. More importantly, the critics observed that the "no discharge" goal implied that clean water was of infinite value and thus worth whatever costs were needed to eliminate all effluent discharges. Or, to quote from the National Water Commission's final report, the "no discharge" goal imputed "an extravagant social value to an abstract concept of water purity."[3]

The CWA in fact has come nowhere close to meeting its goals. No major waterway in the United States is pristine. As noted above, recent state surveys suggest that over half of the nation's river mileage, and about two-thirds of the lake area and estuary mileages, still are not clean enough to fulfill their designated uses. When Congress passed the CWA, most of its members recognized that the zero-discharge goal was "quite possibly 'beyond the ability of the American people to absorb the cost.'"[4] Indeed, the regulatory provisions in the CWA do not proscribe all pollution and often permit EPA to consider cost in setting specific discharge limits.

So why did Congress set unattainably aggressive goals? No matter how much Congress realized that costs and political realities would prevent it from eliminating all pollution, Congress may have wanted to make a moral statement that water pollution is bad. As we discussed in Chapter 2, moral outrage, not pragmatic cost-benefit comparisons, motivated the flood of federal environmental legislation in the early 1970s, including the CWA. Congress also may have believed that ambitious goals were needed to keep the government's feet to the fire. As Senator Edmund Muskie commented, a "national commitment" was needed to ensure that the nation developed the necessary new pollution-control technology. Anticipating that industry and municipalities were likely to fight vigorous implementation of the CWA, Congress may also have felt that the fishable-swimmable and "no discharge" goals would provide a valuable counterweight.

The key water quality provisions of the CWA fall into three main categories. Historically the most important set of provisions regulates point sources of pollution through a diverse array of effluent limitations and technological standards. A second, and to date far less consequential, body of provisions requires states to develop plans for the regulation of nonpoint pollution. As discussed in more detail later, the CWA itself does not regulate nonpoint pollution but leaves it largely to the discretion of the states. A final group of provisions, of growing relevance today, requires states to set water quality standards for the waterways within their borders and to limit discharges as needed to achieve those standards. The CWA also contains a number of other regulatory provisions of less direct relevance to water pollution. The most important of these—

---

[3] National Water Commission, Final Report: Water Policies for the Future 70 (1973).

[4] *National Wildlife Federation v. Gorsuch*, 693 F.2d 156, 181 (D.C. Cir. 1982) (quoting from the legislative history).

section 404 of the CWA—restricts the filling of wetlands and is discussed in Chapter 10.

The CWA applies only to "navigable waters," but defines these expansively as "the waters of the United States, including the navigable seas."[5] As discussed at greater length in the wetlands section of Chapter 10, courts have concluded that Congress did not intend to limit the CWA to waterways that would be considered "navigable" either in the dictionary sense of the term or under traditional legal definitions of navigability. The CWA applies not only to rivers and streams, but also to man-made canals, dry creek beds, and even the waste streams inside an industrial facility. Courts have concluded that the CWA generally does not apply to groundwater. But the CWA might apply even here if the groundwater feeds a spring or otherwise drains into surface waters.

A. Regulation of Point Sources

[Congress' principal goal in passing the CWA was to reduce discharges from point sources.] Congress could have done this in several ways. Congress could have set water quality standards for the entire nation and then left it to the states to develop plans to meet those standards. As Chapter 5 discusses, Congress took this approach in regulating air pollution under the Clean Air Act (through establishment of NAAQSs and the SIP process). But the problems that arose in implementing the 1965 Water Quality Act, discussed earlier, convinced Congress that the states would find it difficult to translate water quality standards into numeric effluent limitations for individual point sources. Congress therefore chose instead to have the United States EPA establish effluent limitations for each type of point source, based on what the available technology could accomplish. Rather than figuring out what levels of pollution are consistent with various uses and then using complex models to translate these standards into individual effluent limits, EPA only needs to evaluate the technological opportunities for effluent reduction. States still play a role in applying the technological limitations to each individual point source, but this role is far more straightforward and involves much less discretion than the states' responsibilities under the 1965 Act. Put another way, the CWA reverses the approach of the CAA. Instead of setting ambient water concentrations and working backwards to determine individual emission levels, the CWA starts with individual effluent levels.

how point sources are regulated

---

[5] CWA § 502(7), 33 U.S.C. § 1362(7).

1. NPDES Permits

The system that Congress chose to implement these technological limitations is the National Pollutant Discharge Elimination System ("NPDES"). Under the CWA, the "discharge of any pollutant by any person" is unlawful without an NPDES permit. The CWA defines "discharge of a pollutant" as "any *addition* of any *pollutant* to *navigable waters* from any *point source*."[6] Thus point sources generally must obtain an NPDES permit before discharging their wastes into a waterway. The permits are generally good for five years, after which they must be renewed, and during their life are subject to modification or revocation for cause. States can qualify to issue the NPDES permits if they can show that they have the needed administrative and engineering capability, and about three quarters of the states currently are qualified to issue them. In the other states, the United States EPA issues the permits.

As discussed in Chapter 4, a regulatory system is only as good as its enforcement mechanisms, and the NPDES approach provides for quite effective enforcement. Each point source must report discharges on a regular, usually monthly, basis to EPA and to any state that has been delegated enforcement authority. Anyone wishing to determine whether a point source is violating the CWA can easily compare the effluent limitations contained in its NPDES permit with the reported discharges. Because the permits and reports are public records, anyone can check for violations. The CWA also includes a citizen-suit provision (see page ___) that permits citizens and environmental organizations to sue to enforce violations. And the discharge reports are admissible as evidence of a violation in court. As a result, citizens or environmental groups interested in enforcing the Clean Water Act have both the information needed to show a violation and the ability to go into court to prove the violation. When the Natural Resources Defense Council feared in the early 1980s that the Reagan Administration would prove reluctant to prosecute CWA violations, it trained a cadre of students and other individuals to compare the permits and discharge reports and began filing citizen suits. Although companies can lie about their actual discharges, any misrepresentation in the discharge reports is subject to severe sanctions.

2. Publicly Owned Treatment Works

The effluent limitations in an NPDES permit depend on whether the permitted facility is a sewage plant, otherwise known

---

[6] CWA §§ 301(a) & 592(12), 33 U.S.C. §§ 1311(a) & 1362(12).

as a publicly owned treatment work or "POTW," or another type of point source. POTWs are passive receivers of pollution, unlike most point sources. While most point sources must comply with numeric limits on their effluent discharges, the CWA requires POTWs to use a specific type of technology. A quick overview of the different types of sewage treatment technology is worthwhile in this regard. Engineers often distinguish between three broad categories of technology. In *primary treatment*, POTWs separate out solid from liquid waste using filters, screens, and settlement tanks. In *secondary treatment*, POTWs use microorganisms to biologically break down organic matter. The microorganisms, which need oxygen to survive, feed on the organic matter. POTWs can speed up this process by blowing air into the sewage in aeration tanks. These are the round tanks you often see from the air when landing at airports. In *tertiary treatment*, POTWs "polish" any remaining contaminants out of the water through physical methods such as sand filters or membrane microfiltration or by using ultra-violet light to kill bacteria.

Originally, the CWA required all POTWs to use secondary treatment by 1977, and by 1983 to use the "best practicable waste treatment technology over the life of the works." Congress assumed that the latter standard would require secondary and often various forms of tertiary treatment. Because Congress recognized that many municipalities did not have the funds needed to upgrade their POTWs, the CWA also provided federal grants to municipalities of up to 85 percent of the cost of installing the needed technology.

Unfortunately, these provisions were singularly unsuccessful. Many cities dragged their feet and were still not using secondary treatment in 1977. The costs of converting to secondary treatment, moreover, were higher than expected. Critics attacked the grants program for undermining the incentive that municipalities might otherwise have had to keep down the costs of facility upgrades. Many cities used the federal funds to expand their sewage systems to meet growing population needs rather than to improve effluent quality. And budgetary constraints made it difficult for Congress to continue to fund the grants program. In light of these problems, Congress amended the CWA to eliminate the stricter 1983 standard and to permit EPA to waive even the secondary treatment standard for POTWs that discharged their sewage sludge into coastal waters. A shrinking number of POTWs still enjoy a waiver from secondary treatment—thirty years after the CWA originally intended that all sewage plants would meet the standard. Congress also phased out its grant program and replaced it with a revolving loan program.

3. *Industrial Point Sources*

Point sources other than POTWs must meet technology-based effluent limits. For these sources, the CWA does not require the point sources to use a particular technology. The government instead decides on an appropriate numeric effluent limitation based on what specific technology can accomplish. Sources are then free to meet the effluent limitation in whatever manner they wish. Most sources are likely to adopt the technology used by EPA to set the limitation because the sources know that this technology will permit them to meet the effluent limitation. But a source is free to use a different technology if it will be at least as effective in reducing the pollution. This flexibility can be valuable to the firm that figures out a cheaper way to meet the effluent limitation.

In drafting the effluent-limitation provisions, one of the first questions that Congress faced was which technology EPA should use in determining the numeric limitations. First, what *types* of technology should be considered? "End-of-pipe" technologies help clean up the harmful byproducts of industrial processes before they are discharged into a waterway. But facilities often can reduce their discharges even more by changing their industrial processes and finding ways of reducing their production of the harmful byproducts in the first place, an approach known as "pollution prevention" and further discussed in Chapter 9. While end-of-pipe technologies merely treat the water pollution, process changes can prevent or reduce all harmful by-products and sometimes even reduce a company's costs by making more efficient use of raw materials and eliminating disposal costs. Most companies, however, oppose efforts to regulate their processes for a number of reasons: (1) process changes can prove more expensive than end-of-pipe technologies, (2) government regulation of processes intrudes more into business decisions, (3) process changes are generally less certain to meet effluent limits than proven end-of-pipe technologies, and (4) because production processes determine the characteristics and quality of a company's product, process changes can negatively affect product quality and hurt a company's sales and reputation. So although environmentalists have consistently pushed the government to consider process changes, most companies have strongly resisted such interventions.

Second, no matter what types of technologies are considered, how should the government choose the particular technology to use in calculating the effluent limitations? An economist would argue that the government should pick the technology based on a cost-benefit comparison: what is the most exacting technology for which benefits outweigh costs? But there are other options. The government, for example, might pick the best technology that companies can afford, without considering whether its benefits outweigh its cost. The government might believe that balancing the benefits and costs is too difficult, or that pollution reduction is a moral rather than economic issue, and that the only relevant question therefore should be economic feasibility. The government might even conclude that the only question should be whether the technology works; if companies cannot afford the technology and must close down, that's the necessary price of having clean rivers and lakes.

Third, should effluent limitations be determined on a facility-by-facility basis or industry by industry? Assume, for example, that the government is setting effluent limitations for pulp and paper mills and has decided to select the best technology that is economically feasible. If 80 percent of the mills in the United States can afford a particular technology, but the other 20 percent would be forced out of business if they had to meet effluent limitations based on the technology, what should the government do? Should the government set a uniformly high effluent limitation for all mills based on the technology, recognizing that some mills will cease operating and throw their employees out of work? Alternatively, should the government set lower standards for those facilities that cannot afford the technology, even though water quality will suffer and some mills will be forced to take on a greater burden than others? Or should the government reject the technology because it is economically infeasible for some mills and use a lower, feasible effluent limitation for all mills, to the detriment of water quality throughout the nation? Administrative costs can play a major role in whether to make determinations facility by facility or industry by industry. While there are tens of thousands of industrial facilities in the United States that discharge effluent into waterways, these facilities can be reduced to just a few score of industry groups. So it's easier to set limitations for each industry rather than for each individual facility.

The CWA unfortunately does not take a consistent approach to these issues. Instead, Congress has chosen to set standards in different ways depending on whether facilities are new or old and depending on the type of pollution being discharged. The approach that Congress has taken to different types of facilities and pollution, moreover, has varied over time. Just as it did in the case of POTWs, Congress started out with more rigorous criteria for setting effluent limitations than are found in the CWA today. As industry balked at the initial criteria for selecting the appropriate technology, Congress backed down. The lawyer trying to understand the CWA therefore must master a number of different technological standards, each with its own acronym. This is where environmental law begins to resemble a child playing with a bowl of alphabet soup. To help you through the morass, Figure 6–2 provides a quick summary of the various standards, all of which are discussed in more detail below. The standards are listed in their general order of stringency, with the standards at the top of the table being less stringent than those at the bottom.

Name of Standard	Possible Technology	Role of Cost
BPT	"End of the pipe"	Cost compared to benefit
BCT	"End of the pipe"	Cost can be considered
BAT	"End of the pipe"	Cost can be considered
BCT	"End of the pipe," process changes, operation changes	No consideration of cost

Figure 6–2: CWA Technological Standards

4.   Existing Point Sources

The CWA originally provided that effluent limitations for existing point sources should generally reflect the "best practicable control technology currently available" ("BPT") by 1977 and the "best available technology economically achievable" ("BAT") by 1983. Although the "best practicable control technology currently available" might sound more stringent than the "best available technology economically achievable," Congress anticipated that BAT would be the more stringent of the two. In choosing BPT, EPA must balance the costs and benefits of alternative technologies. By contrast, EPA can "consider" cost in determining BAT, but is not supposed to directly compare the costs with the benefits. (If you find that difference a bit subtle, you are in good company.) In practice, BAT generally has been the environmentally best technology that is economically feasible. BAT does not require that the technology actually be in use, so long as it can be shown to work. In summary, the 1970 CWA anticipated that the technological standard for existing sources would become more stringent over time, with the cost of the technology playing less of a role.

In drafting the 1970 CWA, Congress also believed that a technological approach was not appropriate where a point source was discharging toxic pollutants. Here, Congress believed that the effluent limitations should be strict enough to protect human health, no matter how difficult or costly point sources would find it to meet the limitations.

Faced by industry objections, however, Congress backed away from applying the BAT standard on a universal basis to all existing point sources and abandoned entirely its health-based approach to toxic pollutants. Under the CWA today, the technological standard that EPA uses to determine the effluent limitations for an existing point source depends on whether the pollution being released by the source is "toxic," "conventional," or "nonconventional."

Toxic Pollutants. Toxic pollutants include a list of 126 chemical substances specified by Congress in the CWA, as well as any other pollutants that EPA determines to be toxic based on the pollutant's toxicity, persistence, degradability, and impact on organisms. Because scientists only recently have begun to understand the health effect of many toxic pollutants in waterways, EPA found it virtually impossible to implement Congress' original health-based approach. As a result, Congress abandoned the health-based approach and now requires EPA to use the BAT standard to calculate effluent limitations for these pollutants.

Conventional Pollutants. The CWA defines "conventional pollutants" as those pollutants that commonly pollute waterways, including biological oxygen demand (BOD), suspended solids, pH, fecal coliform, bacteria, oil, and grease. In place of the BAT standard, the CWA now requires EPA to use the "best conventional pollutant control technology" (BCT) to set effluent limitations for these pollutants. Although Congress anticipated that BCT would lie somewhere between BPT and BAT, EPA in most cases has treated BCT as very similar to the BPT standard.

Nonconventional Pollutants. Any pollutants that do not fit within the definitions of toxic or conventional pollutants, including ammonia, chloride, color, iron, and nitrate, are regulated as "nonconventional pollutants." Such pollutants are generally subject to the BAT standard, although the CWA permits EPA to waive or modify the BAT requirement where justified either by cost or by the quality of the receiving water.

5.   *New Point Sources*

Like the Clean Air Act, the CWA singles out new industrial point sources for tighter effluent limitations. Both policy and politics again help explain why. From a policy perspective, new sources do not need to retrofit their facilities, which can be very expensive. Instead, new sources can build pollution control technology into their design from the outset and achieve low discharge standards at less cost than existing facilities would incur. Over time, moreover, companies will need to replace old plants with new facilities, so that ultimately all companies will be meeting the tighter standards established for new sources. Politically, existing sources usually are a potent lobbying force against stringent discharge standards, while few companies are as worried about hypothetical future plants. In fact, existing companies often favor saddling new facilities with stricter standards because the stricter standards can make it more difficult for competitors to enter the industry; stricter standards, in short, act as economic barriers to entry.

The imposition of tighter effluent standards on new point sources poses potential problems. Because the stricter standards can act as a barrier to entry, for example, they in theory can reduce the number of companies competing in any given industry; the reduced competition, in turn, can lead to higher product prices and other monopoly harms. By making new facilities more expensive, moreover, stricter standards for new sources may encourage companies to keep their existing facilities in operation as long as possible (as EPA charges has happened with coal-fired power plants avoiding New Source Performance Standards under the Clean Air Act). Not only may this be economically inefficient, but old facilities tend to have poorer environmental performance across the board.

Whatever the possible disadvantages of differentiating between existing and new facilities, however, Congress has found such differentiation to be irresistible time and time again. Under the CWA, New Point Sources Standards ("NSPS") for water effluent must reflect the "greatest degree of effluent reduction which the Administrator [of EPA] determines to be achievable through application of the best available control technology, processes, operating methods, or other alternatives, including, where practicable, a standard permitting no discharge of pollutants." Note that in setting NSPS, EPA can consider not only end-of-pipe technology, but also changes to a facility's processes and operations. Also note that cost does not play any explicit role in the selection of NSPS under the CWA.

6. Industry-by-Industry Determination

The CWA unfortunately does not say whether effluent limitations are to be set on a facility-by-facility basis or industry by industry. Although one section of the CWA refers to "effluent limitations for *categories and classes* of point sources,"[7] other sections are more ambiguous. In 1977, the Supreme Court concluded that EPA could set industry-wide guidelines for effluent limitations.[8] Otherwise, as the Court observed, EPA would need to determine technological standards for tens of thousands of individual permits—a result the Court did not believe Congress intended. As a result, EPA now has set technological standards for

---

[7] Clean Water Act § 301(b)(2)(A), 33 U.S.C. § 1311(b)(2)(A) (emphasis added).

[8] *E.I. du Pont de Nemours & Co. v. Train*, 430 U.S. 112 (1977).

more than fifty major categories of industrial facilities. If companies within an industry are dissatisfied with the guidelines, they must challenge the guidelines when issued by EPA, not when the government uses the guidelines to set the effluent limitations in individual NPDES permits.

Industrial plants that feel they are different from the bulk of their industry are not without remedy. First, point sources that can show that key assumptions behind the EPA effluent limitation guidelines are inapplicable to them can apply for a "fundamentally different factor" (or "FDF") variance. A point source cannot ask for a FDF variance because of cost factors. Instead, it must show that the applicable technology will not work or achieve the same results because of unique characteristics of the facility (e.g., a fish cannery is located on a mountainside instead of by the shore). If EPA grants a FDF variance, the permit writer must develop a site-specific standard based on the statutory criteria for the particular type of pollution. Second, an industrial facility can sometimes obtain a variance from the BCT limits for conventional pollutants because the national standard is beyond the facility's economic capability or because less stringent limitations will adequately protect water quality conditions. Although variances could play a major role in shaping water discharges, EPA in practice has issued only a very limited number of variances.

7.   Indirect Sources

Like playing chess, designing an environmental law requires legislators to think one step ahead of regulated companies. Not only must the legislator design an effective regulation, but the legislator must predict how companies might try to get around the regulation. Faced by expensive effluent limitations, for example, what might a company do to avoid the limitations? One option is to discharge the waste into the local sewage system rather than directly into the waterway. This can pose at least two problems. First, the secondary treatment required of (most) POTWs does not adequately treat a number of common industrial pollutants. In fact, at one point, over a third of the toxins that polluted the nation's waterways flowed from industrial facilities through POTWs. Second, pollution from industrial facilities can increase the risk of fire or explosion at a POTW and can interfere with the POTW's treatment of other waste.

To address these problems, the CWA regulates such indirect sources of pollution through both *prohibited discharge standards* and *categorical pretreatment standards*. Under the former, the CWA prohibits indirect sources from discharging wastes into a POTW system that will interfere with the proper operation of the POTW or pass through the POTW untreated. Under the categorical pretreatment standard, the CWA requires indirect sources to meet BAT standards for any discharge of toxic pollutants into a POTW system, unless the POTW has demonstrated that it can treat the pollutant adequately. In addition to these federal standards, most POTWs impose their own restrictions on what forms of industrial wastes can be discharged into the sewer system.

8.　Criticism of the Technological Approach

Many economists have criticized the technology-based standards in the CWA because the standards do not take the most cost-effective route to reducing water pollution. All facilities in the same industry must generally meet the same technological standards, even though the pollution from one facility may not be as harmful as pollution from another facility (because the receiving water is already highly degraded or, alternatively, has a greater assimilative capacity) and even though some facilities may find it more expensive than others to install the technology. Under the CWA's technological standards, moreover, an industry with minimal impact on water quality might be required to install more expensive equipment than an industry with serious pollution problems. From the economist's perspective, the government should focus on those facilities where the *net* benefits of installing pollution-control equipment (i.e., the benefits from reducing pollution minus the cost of the reduction) are greatest. But the CWA instead generally looks only at technological issues and, in some cases, economic feasibility and imposes uniform standards across all facilities in an industry.

Environmentalists also have been critical of the technology-based standards, but for other reasons. Because the standards require complex technical studies and judgments, EPA sometimes takes years to develop and adopt individual standards and has often missed statutory deadlines for the issuance of standards. Moreover, rather than studying the effects of pollution on water quality and human and aquatic health, EPA officials have more often focused their attention on engineering questions.

So why then does the CWA continue to focus on technological standards? The simplest answer is that, by and large, this strategy has worked in reducing water pollution in the United States. Determining practicable technologies is much simpler, less costly for EPA, and far less controversial than weighing the costs and benefits of various control measures. Technological standards, moreover, are relatively easy to enforce. For all practical purposes, government officials need only check to see if a facility has installed and is using the relevant technology.

B.   The Non-Regulation of Nonpoint Sources

The CWA's highly effective regulation of point sources must be balanced against its lackadaisical approach to nonpoint pollution. The CWA effectively leaves the regulation of nonpoint pollution up to the individual states. Section 208 of the CWA was Congress' original effort to control nonpoint pollution. Section 208 requires states to designate lead agencies to head up pollution control efforts for waterways with "substantial water quality problems" and orders these agencies to prepare "areawide waste treatment management plans." Such plans must include procedures and methods to control pollution from agriculture, silviculture, mining, and construction "to the extent feasible." Section 208, however, does not require the states to implement these plans. Even the planning requirements, moreover, are toothless. States must submit their management plans to EPA for approval. But if a state fails to submit a plan or submits an inadequate plan, EPA has no authority to make the state submit an adequate plan or to issue a federal management plan. Left to their own discretion and faced with significant opposition by agricultural, mining, and construction lobbies, most states have chosen not to adopt meaningful management plans under section 208.

By the mid-1980s, nonpoint pollution had eclipsed point discharges as the largest contributor to water pollution in the United States. Given the failure of section 208, numerous members of Congress urged a "renewed commitment to the cleanup of nonpoint sources of pollution."[9] The result was the addition to the CWA in 1987 of section 319 which requires states to implement a "nonpoint source management program." Section 319 instructs each state to prepare a report identifying those categories of nonpoint sources that are preventing the state from attaining its designated water quality standards and describing the measures needed to "reduce, to the maximum extent practicable, the level of pollution" from those sources. States also must require nonpoint sources to use "best management practices ['BMPs'] . . . at the earliest practicable date." According to the Senate Report on section 319, BMPs for agriculture can include soil conservation programs, such as the terracing of agricultural land, or "simple" changes in agricultural practices, such as the careful scheduling and application of fertilizer and pesticides. Section 319 finally instructs each state to prepare a management plan describing how the state will implement its program.

Although section 319 appears on paper to push states toward greater regulation of nonpoint pollution, Congress again failed to

---

[9]   133 Cong. Rec. S744 (Jan. 14, 1987) (comments of Sen. Baucus).

back up its bark with any bite. If a state failed to prepare its first report, which was due in August 1988, section 319 required the United States EPA to prepare a report for the state identifying the categories of nonpoint sources that the state needed to address. But Congress did not authorize EPA to identify control measures or to. impose a management plan on any state. The omission was intentional. According to Senator George Mitchell, who was one of the sponsors of the amendment, section 319 does not require a state to control nonpoint pollution. "If a state decides that it does not want a program to control nonpoint pollution, that is it."[10]

Why has Congress been so reticent to adopt measures that will reduce nonpoint pollution firmly and effectively? Nonpoint sources often are more difficult to regulate than point sources. Nonpoint sources far outnumber point sources. They are more varied, complicating the effort to determine appropriate technological standards. And it is often difficult to monitor their performance. The government can readily measure the pollutants flowing out of a pipe, but how do you evaluate the runoff from a construction site? None of these problems, however, is fatal. Without great difficulty, the government could prescribe best management practices for common land uses that contribute sizable amounts of nonpoint pollution. Under a BMP approach, the government also does not necessarily need to monitor pollution. Instead, the government can monitor whether sources are actually using the mandated BMPs. Another possible hurdle to nonpoint regulation is that land uses have been the traditional province of state and local governments. But the federal government can require states to reduce nonpoint pollution, yet leave the choice of specific BMPs to the states. The problem with the CWA's nonpoint pollution provisions has not been the delegation of authority to the states, but the lack of any effective mechanism to force the states to use that authority to reduce the nonpoint pollution. After analyzing all of the policy considerations, one inevitably is left with the conclusion that politics has driven the CWA's failure to take on nonpoint pollution in any meaningful way. The agricultural lobby, in particular, has been very successful in weakening or killing off proposals to regulate nonpoint pollution more rigorously.

C.   Escaping Regulation as a Point Source of Pollutants

A repeated lesson in environmental regulation is that if the law draws a bright-line distinction between two different types of activities or actions and regulates one far more than the other, the regulated community will fight hard to end up on the less onerous side of the line. Under the CWA, a lot depends on whether a source

---

[10] 133 Cong. Rec. S1968 (Feb. 4, 1987) (comments of Sen. Mitchell).

must apply for an NPDES permit. So not surprisingly, this question has generated a number of hard-fought disputes. As described earlier, the "discharge of any pollutant by any person" is unlawful without an NPDES permit, and the CWA defines "discharge of a pollutant" as "any *addition* of any *pollutant* from any *point source.*" To escape NPDES regulation, therefore, a potential regulatory target must argue that it either is not a "point source" or is not "adding" a "pollutant" to navigable waters. (The definition of navigable waters is discussed at pages 278–280.)

1.   *What Is a Point Source?*

One of the most important questions in the early years of the CWA was whether agricultural runoff could be a point source of pollution. The CWA originally defined a point source as "any discernible, confined and discrete conveyance, including but not limited to any pipe, ditch, channel, tunnel, conduit, well, discrete fissure, container, rolling stock, concentrated animal feeding operation, or vessel or other floating craft, from which pollutants are or may be discharged." Although the runoff from some farms and ranches is diffuse, many farms, ranches, and agricultural districts collect runoff and discharge it into waterways through confined conveyance facilities. In 1973, however, EPA issued a regulation exempting farms of less than 3000 acres, as well as animal feedlots and silviculture, from the NPDES permit requirements, even if a conveyance facility satisfied the statutory definition of a point source. As justification for the exemption, EPA argued that it would be infeasible to apply numeric effluent limitations to agricultural operations. "An effluent limitation must be a precise number in order for it to be an effective regulatory tool; both the discharger and the regulatory agency need to have an identifiable standard upon which to determine whether the facility is in compliance."[11] EPA also argued that the exempted agricultural sources numbered in the hundreds of thousands and, if subject to NPDES requirements, would overwhelm EPA and state permitting agencies.

An environmental organization sued, arguing that EPA did not have the discretion to exempt discharges that met the statutory definition of a point source. In 1977, the D.C. Circuit agreed and invalidated the regulation. In *Natural Resources Defense Council v. Costle*,[12] the court held that Congress had not authorized EPA to grant categorical exemptions from the NPDES requirements. The court, moreover, found EPA's administrative concerns

---

[11] The language is from an EPA memorandum quoted in *Natural Resources Defense Council, Inc. v. Costle*, 568 F.2d 1369, 1378 (D.C. Cir. 1977).

[12] 568 F.2d 1369 (D.C. Cir. 1977).

unconvincing: EPA could adjust the permit terms to fit the unique characteristics of agricultural sources and could reduce the sheer numerical burden by issuing general permits for various classes of agricultural polluters.

The court's decision was short lived. Only a few months after the D.C. Circuit issued its decision, Congress amended the definition of point source to exclude return flows from irrigated agriculture. Congress also banned EPA from requiring an NPDES permit for "discharges composed entirely of return flow from irrigated agriculture" or from, "directly or indirectly, requir[ing] any State to require such a permit." The lobbying power of agriculture had once again prevailed over environmental interests. Although a committee of the National Academy of Sciences has recommended that Congress repeal the agricultural exemption, Congress has indicated no interest in doing so.

In 1987, however, Congress did choose to bring some forms of storm water runoff under the NPDES system. Storm water runoff is rainwater that picks up contaminants as it flows across the land and then into a waterway. Where municipal storm sewer systems or industrial activities, such as pulp mills or chemical plants, discharge the storm water runoff, section 402 of the CWA requires an NPDES permit.

2. When Does a Point Source "Add" "Pollutants"?

As noted above, hydrologic modifications of rivers and other waterways are a major source of water pollution in the United States. Dams can change both the temperature and oxygen content of downstream water, harming local fish populations. Diversions of water from rivers and streams can concentrate downstream pollutants, whether natural pollutants like salt or human-added pollutants.

Given the importance of hydrologic modifications, a recurring question has been whether such modifications require NPDES permits. A number of courts have addressed the question in connection with dams. Dams, unlike agricultural operations, clearly meet the definition of a "point source" since they release water from confined openings. Courts, however, have uniformly held that dams do not "add" "pollutants." The list of "pollutants" contained in the CWA consists primarily of substances; "heat" is the only water condition included. Courts, moreover, have questioned whether, even if conditions such as low dissolved oxygen, cold, and supersaturation are pollutants, dams "add" such pollutants to the water. Although courts could easily go either way on these definitional questions, courts have concluded that Congress in the CWA did not intend to interfere with states' traditional authority over water management. Section 101(g) of the Act, also known as the Wallop Amendment, supports this view by declaring that it "is the policy that the authority of each State to allocate quantities of water within its jurisdiction shall not be superseded, abrogated, or otherwise impaired by this Act."

The question of whether hydrologic modifications require NPDES permits also has come up in connection with water projects designed to move water from one area to another. New York City, for example, takes water from its Schoharie Reservoir, which is high in suspended solids, turbidity, and heat, and discharges the water into the clearer, cooler waters of Esopus Creek. Must the city get an NPDES permit? In 2001, the federal Court of Appeals for the Second Circuit held that an NPDES permit is required.[13] In response to New York's argument that the Wallop Amendment demonstrates that Congress did not intend to interfere with state and local water management, the court noted that the CWA "balances a welter of consistent and inconsistent goals." Although requiring New York to obtain an NPDES permit might interfere with local water management, artificial water transfers can threaten the "chemical, physical, and biological integrity of the Nation's waters," undermining the principal purpose of the CWA.

The United States Supreme Court addressed the same issue several years later in a case arising from the Everglades. Florida and the federal government have vastly reconfigured the Everglades by draining wetlands for farms and other human uses, constructing flood control projects, and developing water supply systems for the burgeoning urban regions of the state. These actions often involve moving water from one part of the Everglades to another. In *South Florida Water Management District v. Miccosukee Tribe*,[14] Native American and environmental groups argued that a state agency needed an NPDES permit to pump water from a canal containing phosphorus-laden storm runoff and groundwater and then dump it sixty feet away into an undeveloped wetland. The federal government argued that this water transfer did not require an NPDES permit because all water bodies in the United States "should be viewed unitarily for purposes of NPDES permitting requirements," even if the water bodies are hydrologically separate. Under the government's theory, water transfers from one waterway to another would never require an NPDES permit, "even if one water body were polluted and the other pristine, and the two would not otherwise mix," because the

---

[13] *Catskill Mountains Chapter of Trout Unlimited v. City of New York,* 273 F.3d 481 (2d Cir. 2001).

[14] 541 U.S. 95 (2004).

transfer would not be "adding" pollutants to the navigable waters of the United States.

The Supreme Court declined to decide whether the United States' interpretation of the CWA was correct, because it was not clear whether the canal and wetlands in *Miccosukee Tribe* were "distinct water bodies" with no hydrologic connections. The Court remanded for further consideration of the case. In 2008, EPA adopted a new regulation formally incorporating the government's unitary-waters argument. According to the new rule, transfers of water from one water body to another do not require NPDES permits if there is no "intervening industrial, municipal, or commercial use."[15] Applying *Chevron* deference, a federal court of appeals subsequently followed EPA's rule and held that such water transfers do not require NPDES permits. Although this "may seem inconsistent with the lofty goals of the Clean Water Act," according to the court, "it is no more so than to leave out all nonpoint sources, allowing agricultural run-offs to create a huge 'dead zone' in the Gulf of Mexico."[16] Legislation involves "compromises cobbled together by competing political interests and compromise is the enemy of single-mindedness."[17]

D.　Water Quality Standards

As discussed earlier, the 1972 CWA took a largely technological approach to water pollution because of the 1965 Water Quality Act's singular failure to regulate water pollution through ambient water quality standards. Given the problems under the 1965 Act, the Senate in 1972 proposed abandoning water quality standards entirely. At the House of Representatives' insistence, however, the 1972 CWA retained water quality standards as a backup or safety net to the technology-based effluent limitations.

Section 303 of the CWA sets out a multi-step process for regulating ambient water quality. First, each state designates specific beneficial uses for each of its waterways. These *designated uses* can include "public water supply," "protection and propagation of fish, shellfish, and wildlife," recreation, agriculture, and industry. Given the CWA's goal of providing fishable-swimmable water by 1983, a waterway at a minimum must typically protect and propagate fish, shellfish, and wildlife and allow recreation in and on the water. However, if a state can demonstrate that the fishable-

---

[15] 73 Fed. Reg. 33397 (2008).

[16] Each year, nutrient-rich runoff from farms in the Mississippi River basin drain into the river system and ultimately the Gulf of Mexico, where the nutrients use up the oxygen in thousands of square miles of the Gulf, suffocating any sea life that cannot swim away.

[17] *Friends of the Everglades v. South Florida Water Management Dist.*, 570 F.3d 1210, 1227 (11th Cir. 2009).

swimmable standard is unattainable for a particular waterway because of naturally occurring pollution, low water flows, or other factors, EPA sometimes can permit the state to "downgrade" the designated use to a lower standard such as agriculture or industry. Once a state has designated the use for a waterway, it must review the designation at least every three years.

Second, states determine the *water quality standards* needed to support the designated uses. The standards are typically quantitative (e.g., no more than 8 milligrams of a particular contaminant per liter of water in a river). Standards for toxic pollutants *must* be quantitative. To help states determine the necessary standards, EPA uses the latest scientific information to prepare *water quality criteria* that show the minimum physical, chemical, and biological parameters required to support the various designated uses of a waterway. If a state fails to establish adequate quality standards for a waterway, the United States EPA can set standards for the state.

Third, the states must identify *quality-limited waterways*—those waterways where the technology-based effluent limitations imposed under NPDES permits are insufficient to attain the water quality standards. For each quality-limited waterway, a state must determined the *total maximum daily load* (or *"TMDL"*) of pollutants that can be discharged into the waterway and still achieve "the applicable water quality standards with seasonal variations and a margin of safety which takes into account any lack of knowledge concerning the relationship between effluent limitations and water quality." The states must submit a list of both the quality-impaired waterways and associated TMDLs to EPA for approval.

What happens after a state establishes the TMDLs is not entirely clear. If the technology-based effluent limitations for point sources are not sufficient to achieve the water quality standards, section 301 of the CWA requires that the effluent limitations be lowered to the degree needed to meet the standards. But must a state reduce nonpoint pollution if needed to achieve the water quality standards? In many cases, because of significant nonpoint source pollution a waterway will not meet water quality standards even if point sources discharge no waste whatsoever. The CWA is silent on this question. The Act does not explicitly require states to regulate nonpoint pollution if needed to achieve water quality standards and does not say what happens if states do not. Section 303 of the Act requires states to engage in a "continuing planning process" ("CPP") to achieve water quality standards. But section 303 does not give EPA the authority to implement a CPP if the state fails to do so.

For the first twenty-five years of the CWA, states generally did not even prepare TMDLs for their quality-limited waterways. And EPA made no effort to force the states to do so; instead, EPA focused on the Act's technology-based effluent limitations. Congress, moreover, encouraged this neglect. According to Senator Edmund Muskie, who was the principal Senate sponsor of the 1972 CWA, EPA should assign "secondary importance" to the water quality standards. Given the problems implementing the 1965 Water Quality Act, Congress wanted EPA to focus on the provisions of the CWA that appeared to have the greatest chance of success— the technology-based effluent limitations—not the water quality standards. Even if EPA had wanted to implement the water quality standards, EPA's authority to force states to act is unclear. If EPA concludes that a state's list of quality-impaired waterways and TMDLs are inadequate, the CWA authorizes EPA to prepare its own list. But the Act does not explicitly say what, if anything, EPA can do if a state fails to submit a list at all. As noted already, the CWA also does not grant EPA explicit authority to implement TMDLs.

A series of judicial decisions starting in the mid-1980s, however, has put pressure on EPA and states to take TMDLs more seriously. In 1984, a federal court of appeals held that the "prolonged failure" of a state to file a list of quality-impaired waterways could constitute a "constructive submission" of no TMDLs, triggering EPA's duty to prepare its own TMDLs.[18] A decade later, a federal district court found that EPA had acted arbitrarily and capriciously in approving a list of quality-impaired waterways that omitted, without explanation, waterways that the state previously had identified as impaired. In 2002, a court of appeals held that states must set TMDLs for a waterway that does not meet water quality standards even if only nonpoint sources pollute the waterway (and EPA can impose a TMDL for the waterway if the state fails to act).[19] States in short can no longer ignore their obligation to prepare lists of quality-impaired waterways and TMDLs, and EPA must analyze the lists carefully before approving them. The ultimate question nonetheless remains: what happens after an adequate list is prepared? Does the CWA require process but no substance?

Notice also that the concentration of pollutants in a waterway can be reduced either by reducing the pollution entering the waterway or by increasing the amount of water (thus diluting the pollution). In a controversial move, point sources and states

---

[18] See Scott v. City of Hammond, 741 F.2d 992 (7th Cir. 1984).

[19] See Pronsolino v. Nastri, 291 F.3d 1123 (9th Cir. 2002).

occasionally have proposed meeting water quality standards by augmenting the flow of quality-impaired waterways. To some environmentalists, "flow augmentation" merely masks pollution and encourages risky "engineering" of rivers and streams. Section 102(b)(1) of the CWA forbids the federal government from releasing water from federal water projects "as a substitute for adequate treatment or other methods of controlling waste at the source." EPA regulations, however, authorize flow augmentation in other settings where point sources are meeting the technology-based effluent limitations and flow augmentation is "the preferred environmental and economic method to achieve the [water quality] standards."[20]

E. Always Cleaner, Never Dirtier

Most federal environmental laws assume that regulations should act like a ratchet: environmental standards should continually be tightened, and they never should be loosened. In line with this theme, the CWA suggests that technology-based limitations should become progressively more stringent over time. The CWA, moreover, generally forbids a state from modifying an NPDES permit to permit an increase in pollution. There are only a few exceptions to this "anti-backsliding" policy. If new information becomes available demonstrating a lower technology-based standard is appropriate, a more lenient permit can be issued. Similarly, if a point source is unable to meet its NPDES requirements despite the installation and operation of appropriate pollution-control equipment, a state can reconsider the standards that it originally set.

The water quality provisions of the CWA also include an "antidegradation" policy. Where waterways are meeting their existing designated uses, states must protect that water quality. States, moreover, cannot permit the degradation of "high quality waters," defined as waterways that meet the fishable-swimmable standards, unless they can demonstrate an economic or social justification for the decline in water quality.

F. Water Quality Trading

Chapter 5 discussed the role of pollution trading under the Clean Air Act, particularly its SO_2 provisions. Although the CWA does not explicitly provide for similar trading, EPA over the last decade has encouraged states to adopt and implement water quality trading programs.[21] In the simplest form of trading program, a point source that "over controls" its discharge of a particular pollutant (e.g., nutrients) receives a credit that it can sell to another

---

[20] 40 C.F.R. § 125.3(f).
[21] EPA, Water Quality Trading (2003).

point source that is not able to reduce its pollution as cost-effectively. Such a water quality trading program can have advantages similar to air quality trading. First, it can reduce the overall societal cost of meeting particular pollution standards by allowing companies that find it less expensive to reduce their pollution to generate credits that enable other companies facing higher discharge-control costs to avoid or reduce those costs. According to EPA, the annual savings from water quality trading in the United States could exceed $900 million.[22] Second, economists believe that water quality trading programs can encourage the development and use of new and better control technologies. Companies that are selling pollution credits have an incentive to find and employ new technologies that permit them to generate even more credits that they can sell, while companies that are buying credits want new technologies that reduce their need to purchase those credits.

Some trading schemes also permit trades between point sources and nonpoint sources. Recall that point sources must reduce their pollution discharges beyond their applicable technology-based effluent standards if needed to meet TMDL requirements. In many cases, it might be easier for the point source to pay a nonpoint source to reduce its emissions than to further reduce its own discharges. Rather than reducing its nutrient discharges, for example, a point source might pay farms in the region to change their irrigation or fertilizer practices. Point-nonpoint trading schemes promise the same advantages as point-point trading systems. Because most nonpoint sources have not been regulated in the past, they often can reduce their discharges at significantly less cost than point sources that have already made the least expensive reductions. One study in 2000 found that point-nonpoint trading could be eight-times more cost effective in achieving water quality goals.[23] In addition, to the degree that nonpoint sources reduce their discharges of particular pollutants by reducing their overall discharges into waterways, point-nonpoint trading systems might enjoy the "co-benefit" of reducing multiple types of pollution at the same time.

Water quality trading programs raise complex scientific and administrative issues and are better suited to some situations than others. A reduction in discharges at one point on a waterway, for example, is not necessarily equivalent to a reduction somewhere else on the same waterway. Determining equivalency often requires

---

[22] EPA, Water Quality Trading Assessment Handbook: Can Water Quality Trading Advance Your Watershed Goals? (2004).

[23] See Paul Faeth, Fertile Ground: Nutrient Trading's Potential to Cost-Effectively Improve Water Quality (World Resources Inst. 2000).

complex scientific analyses. The complexity is particularly high in the case of point-nonpoint trades. Where a particular pollutant (e.g., toxins) has a high local impact, moreover, trades can lead to localized concentrations of pollutants with attendant health risks—the "hot spots" problem discussed in Chapter 5.

Because of these and other limitations, water quality trading is still largely in an experimental stage. In 2009, there were 26 active trading systems, and another 21 were under development or consideration. Most of the trading programs have been pilot projects and often have involved trades among a circumscribed set of facilities.

PROBLEM EXERCISE: WATER-QUALITY TRADING IN THE MINNESOTA RIVER BASIN[24]

In the late 1990s, two companies in the Minnesota River Basin (Minnesota Malting Company and the Minnesota Sugar Beet Processing Company) wished to expand their operations. The problem was that they and other companies along the Minnesota River already were discharging as much pollution as the TMDLs for the river allowed.

The Minnesota Pollution Control Agency, however, had been studying the possibility of starting a point-nonpoint trading program for the Minnesota River. The study concluded that a trading program had the "potential to promote efficiency, equity and effectiveness." Any trading system, however, needed to meet four criteria. First, the trading system needed to be "efficient": it had to reduce the overall cost of meeting the river's water quality standards. Second, the trading system needed to provide for "equivalency." Any decrease in nonpoint pollution had to at least offset any increase in point pollution. Third, any trade had to ensure "additionality"—i.e., the parties to the trade had to show that the reduction in nonpoint pollution would not have occurred if it had not been for the trade. Finally, the trading scheme had to provide for accountability, to ensure that nonpoint pollution was indeed reduced and that the equivalency and additionality criteria were met. Both Minnesota Malting and Sugar Beet Processing saw the opportunity to offset their increased waste-water discharges with reductions in nonpoint pollution as the only way to pursue their expansion plans.

Sugar Beet Processing planned to build a new waste-water treatment plant to allow expanded operations, which would increase phosphorous discharges. To offset this increase, the company proposed to pay sugar-beet growers to take various steps to reduce erosion and thus phosphorus runoff into the river. Scientific models would be used to determine how much

---

[24] This problem exercise is based on Feng Fang, K. William Easter, & Patrick L. Brezonik, Point-Nonpoint Source Water Quality Trading: A Case Study in the Minnesota River Basin, 41 J. Am. Water Res. Ass'n 645 (2005). Although the problem exercise is based on actual water-quality trades, the facts have been modified to highlight key questions in water-quality trading and the names of the companies therefore fictionalized.

phosphorus pollution would be reduced from the farms. Growers had long wanted to reduce erosion because of its impact on their lands (the erosion was sometimes so severe that it threatened nearby homes), but lacked the funding to pay for the erosion control. Because of the difficulty of determining exactly how much phosphorus pollution would be reduced, the company proposed a 1.6:1 trading ratio (i.e., the company would reduce emissions from local farms by 1.6 units in order to increase its own discharges of phosphorus by one unit).

Minnesota Malting proposed a more complex offset that would not involve a direct offset of a specific pollutant. Minnesota Malting planned to expand its facility, which would increase the amount of carbonaceous biochemical oxygen demand ($CBOD_5$). Minnesota Malting proposed to offset this increase by paying local farmers to reduce their discharges of nitrogen and phosphorus, two nutrients that also increase $CBOD_5$. Scientific models indicated that a one-unit reduction of nitrogen or phosphorus runoff would decrease $CBOD_5$ by four and eight units respectively. Recognizing again the scientific uncertainty in determining the equivalency of the proposed trades, Minnesota Malting proposed a 2:1 trading ratio. In two of the proposed trades, farmland would be converted back into floodplains with native grasses and trees, providing valuable habitat for local species.

Trying to directly measure and monitor the actual reduction of nonpoint pollution from these actions would have been prohibitively expensive, if possible at all. The companies, however, agreed to provide detailed technical and management reports before and after each trade. And government inspectors would periodically visit the participating farms to ensure that landowners were carrying out the agreed steps and to engage in limited site sampling.

If you were the regional director for EPA, would you approve the proposed offset transactions under the criteria established by the point-nonpoint trading study? An economic analysis indicates that the nonpoint offsets proposed by the two companies would be significantly less expensive than any potential reductions in point pollution (if that even were possible). Would you propose any changes in the proposed offsets? What, if any, additional information would you want before making a decision? Given the uncertainties involved in point-nonpoint trades, should EPA ever permit them?

G.   Interstate Water Pollution

As the Supreme Court has observed, "Interstate waters have been a font of controversy since the founding of the Nation."[25] Interstate pollution, moreover, presents the strongest case for federal intervention because downstream states have limited options, at best, for protecting themselves from the effluent discharges of upstream states. Yet the CWA pays surprisingly

---

[25] *Arkansas v. Oklahoma*, 503 U.S. 91, 98 (1992).

meager attention to the problem of interstate pollution. Section 103 of the CWA requires the EPA Administrator to encourage "cooperative activities by the States . . . and so far as practicable, uniform State laws relating to the prevention, reduction, and elimination of pollution." The same section authorizes states to regulate interstate pollution through interstate agreements (or "compacts," to use the constitutional terminology).

The CWA's ambient water quality provisions may offer downstream states the most protection. Recall that point sources cannot discharge effluents in concentrations that would violate water quality standards. EPA has decided by regulation that a state cannot issue an NPDES permit if the effluent discharges would violate the water quality standards of any downstream states. Sections 401 and 402 of the CWA also require that a state give notice and an opportunity to be heard to downstream states before issuing an NPDES permit. If a downstream state believes that the proposed discharge would interfere with its water quality standards, it may ask the EPA Administrator to disapprove the permit.

EPA is unlikely to intervene unless the discharge would cause a clear deterioration in water quality in the downstream state. In *Arkansas v. Oklahoma*,[26] Oklahoma objected to EPA's issuance of an NPDES permit to a POTW in Arkansas that planned to discharge sewage effluent into the Illinois River only 39 miles upstream from the Oklahoma border. Noting that the Illinois River already was out of compliance with Oklahoma's water quality standards, Oklahoma argued that the Clean Water Act prohibited any additional discharge that would reach Oklahoma waters. EPA disagreed and looked instead to see if the proposed discharge would cause an "actual detectable or measurable" impairment of Oklahoma's water quality standards. The Supreme Court upheld EPA's approach. The Court concluded that EPA has the authority to consider downstream states' water quality standards in issuing NPDES permits but does not have to ban all discharges where downstream water quality standards are not being met.

The CWA has reduced states' ability to deal with water pollution from other states in at least one way. In 1972, immediately before Congress enacted the CWA, the Supreme Court had held that a state could sue under the "federal common law" of nuisance to abate pollution resulting from operations in another state. However, almost a decade later in what has become known as the *Milwaukee II* decision, the Court held that the CWA preempts

---

[26] 503 U.S. 91 (1992).

such federal common law actions.[27] A few years after *Milwaukee II*, the Court further held that a Vermont resident could not invoke Vermont nuisance law to enjoin discharges that occurred in New York.[28] "The inevitable result of such suits would be that Vermont and other States could do indirectly what they could not do directly—regulate the conduct of out-of-state sources." A Vermont resident still presumably can go to a New York court and try to block the discharge under New York nuisance law. But New York courts may be unsympathetic to out-of-state plaintiffs, particularly where an injunction might harm New York economic interests.

QUESTIONS AND DISCUSSION

1. What should be the goal of the CWA? Should the goal be to eliminate all discharge of pollutants into the nation's waterways, no matter what the cost? To ensure that all waterways are fishable and swimmable? To limit water pollution to an "efficient level"? How much should Congress worry whether its goal is achievable?

2. While the Clean Air Act takes a largely health-based approach to regulating pollution (see Chapter 5), the CWA primarily takes a technology-based approach. Is one approach better than the other? If so, which approach, and why? Are there differences between air pollution and water pollution that you believe calls for taking different approaches in the two statutes?

3. One potential goal of pollution regulation is to encourage the development of new technologies and approaches that can further reduce pollution, reduce pollution at a lower cost, or (ideally) both. How effective do you believe the regulatory approaches in the Clean Air Act and CWA are at promoting the development of new pollution-reducing technologies and approaches? What other steps might the federal government take to promote technological innovation?

4. Should the CWA subject nonpoint pollution to stronger regulation? If so, how? Should the federal government set technological standards (perhaps in the form of "best management practices" or BMPs) for farms, construction sites, parking lots, and other typical sources of nonpoint pollution? How might the government determine BMPs? Alternatively, should the government require the states to manage nonpoint pollution by developing plans that will ensure that neither point nor nonpoint pollution exceeds TMDLs? Are there even better approaches to regulating nonpoint pollution?

5. The increased use of personal care products and medications poses special challenges to water quality. Recent studies have identified more than 50 pharmaceuticals or their by-products in the drinking water of major metropolitan areas. Some of the contaminants include antibiotics, anti-anxiety drugs, and hormonal medications such as birth-control pills.

---

[27] *City of Milwaukee v. Illinois*, 451 U.S. 304 (1981).

[28] *International Paper Co. v. Ouellette*, 479 U.S. 481 (1987).

The U.S. Geological Survey found 82 contaminants, most of them personal-care products and drugs, in 80 percent of the streams sampled in 30 states. The concentrations of these "emerging contaminants" is very low, in most cases on the order of parts per billion. With few exceptions, POTW's do not remove emerging contaminants from waste water, primarily for cost reasons. What information would you need in order to decide whether the government should invest in special treatment technologies to remove this type of water pollution?

6. How should the CWA deal with hydrologic modifications? Should either of the following actions require an NPDES permit? If so, what type of regulatory requirements should be included in the permit? If the action should not require an NPDES permit, should the CWA deal with the environmental consequences of the hydrologic modification in some other fashion?

    a.   The City of Coastal California collects crystal-clean local water in the Grand Reservoir and distributes the water to its residents. Running short of water, Coastal decides to import water from the Colorado River, which is naturally high in salt. Coastal will store the water in the Grand Reservoir and then distribute the mix of local water and water from the Colorado River to its customers.

    b.   The City of Sandy withdraws relatively pure water from the Blue River. The Blue River feeds the Salty River and helps dilute the salt concentration of the Salty River. Because of Sandy's withdrawals, the salt concentration of the Salty River significantly increases downstream of its confluence with the Blue River, threatening fish species and the drinking water supplies of several cities that use water from the Salty River.

7. Many economists have argued that the federal government should impose a tax on water pollution, equivalent to the cost that the pollution imposes on the environment. Do you agree? Would this be a good approach to nonpoint pollution? To hydrologic modifications? Would it be a better approach to point pollution than the current system of effluent limitations?

Chapter 8

REGULATING TOXIC SUBSTANCES

The Clean Air Act and the Clean Water Act both focus on "conventional" pollutants—industrial and other by-products that are discharged in large quantities and pose known health problems. But from the earliest days of the modern environmental movement, "toxic" substances—products and by-products presenting a potential risk of serious harm at even low levels of exposure—have often generated greater attention and concern. Rachel Carson's famous best seller, *Silent Spring*, which helped launch the modern environmental era, dealt not with particulate air pollution or with fecal coliform in the nation's water but with the grave dangers that pesticides such as DDT present to humans and other animals. Most people today are worried far more about the potential risks from toxic substances such as lead and asbestos than they are about the chronic side effects of carbon monoxide or particulates.

Toxic substances differ in a number of key ways from conventional pollutants. First, many toxins are valuable agricultural, industrial, or consumer products. While the Clean Air Act and the Clean Water Act deal primarily with by-products that businesses and individuals happily would do without, farmers, businesses, and consumers each year buy millions of dollars of pesticides and other toxic chemicals. Second, we often are not sure what degree of risk, if any, a suspected toxic actually poses. Third, the probability that a toxin will injure any one individual is typically quite small. Finally, because even low levels of exposure to a toxic substance frequently present a risk, safe levels of human exposure often do not exist. As this chapter will discuss, the unique characteristics of toxins make regulation particularly difficult and controversial.

An eclectic collection of federal environmental statutes addresses toxic substances. As discussed in the last two chapters, the Clean Air Act and the Clean Water Act include special provisions regulating toxic and other "hazardous" pollutants. The Resource Conservation and Recovery Act ("RCRA") and the Comprehensive Environmental Response, Compensation, and Liability Act ("CERCLA"), which are the subjects of the next chapter, focus on the proper disposal of hazardous waste in land-based facilities and the clean-up of land contaminated by hazardous substances. A number of statutes regulate particular categories of substances. For example, the Federal Insecticide, Fungicide, and Rodenticide Act ("FIFRA") governs agricultural chemicals, while the federal Food, Drug, and Cosmetic Act regulates food additives and drugs, and the Atomic Energy Act and related statutes manage radioactive substances. Several statutes also regulate specific routes of exposure. The Occupational Safety and Health Act ("OSHA"), for example, limits worker exposure to unhealthy levels of toxins and other dangerous substances, while the Safe Drinking Water Act limits the amount of toxic substances permitted in drinking water. Finally, the Toxic Substances Control Act ("TSCA") serves as a "catch all" statute that regulates the production, sale, and use of toxic substances not regulated otherwise by federal law.

I.　The Difficulties of Regulating Toxic Substances

The regulation of toxic substances has generated tremendous controversy, in large part because it poses some of the most difficult policy questions to be found in the environmental field, or in any regulatory field for that matter. Given that life is not risk free, should the government be concerned about the extremely low levels of risk posed by some toxic substances? If some risks are too small to regulate, what should be the trigger point for regulation? How should the law deal with scientific uncertainty? How much money should society invest to get a better sense of the risks posed by particular substances? And if significant uncertainty remains after all the scientific studies have been conducted, should the government err in favor of the economy or of protecting human health?

If toxic substances were of little or no value to society, these questions would be easy to answer. The government would ban any and all substances that posed a potential health risk. Unfortunately, businesses and consumers view many suspected or known toxins as all but "indispensable." Consider, for example, pesticides and other synthetic organic chemicals. These chemicals have improved many people's lives by boosting agricultural yields, increasing the durability of consumer products, producing life-saving drugs, and decreasing product prices. The chemical industry, moreover, is one of the largest manufacturing sectors in the United States, employing almost a million people and supporting about 25 percent of the nation's gross domestic product. The chemical industry is also one of the largest exporters in the United States economy, exporting over $180 billion worth of chemical products in 2012.

A.　Is "Tolerable Risk" an Oxymoron?

Most toxic substances present only a *risk* of injury. For example, of every million people exposed to a hypothetical *carcinogen* (or cancer-causing substance) only two ultimately may contract cancer as a result of that exposure. Is that a sufficiently large risk to justify regulating the substance, particularly if the substance is economically valuable? It may be tempting to respond that we should not add any substance to the environment that increases the overall risk of cancer or other serious health injury. The natural world, however, is replete with health risks, and people often voluntarily assume additional risks in return for varied benefits. Bruce Ames, a retired professor of biochemistry and molecular biology at the University of California, has observed that the food we eat contains far more naturally occurring carcinogens than synthetic carcinogens in the form of pesticides and other farm chemicals.[1] The average person voluntarily increases their risk of serious injury by driving in cars, flying in airplanes, playing sports, and even traveling to or living at high altitudes. The strength of the ultraviolet rays in Denver, Colorado, the "mile high" city, is 25 times stronger than at sea level, so residents of Denver sustain a higher risk of skin cancer. Should the government regulate chemicals that pose lower risks than these every-day activities?

Some people say "no—the government should outlaw only those substances that pose greater risks of injury than those risks voluntarily assumed by people in their regular lives." Risks, however, vary in a number of important aspects in addition to their probability of occurring. First, different risks pose different types of threats, some worse than others. Cancer risks obviously are of greater societal concern than risks of eye irritation. Even risks of death can differ because people dread some forms of death (e.g., death from cancer) more than others (e.g., death from a heart attack). The acceptability of a risk involves a balancing of probability and severity (including dread): the more severe the potential injury, the lower the probability of injury that society will accept, and the less severe the injury, the higher the acceptable probability.

Second, people view voluntary risks very differently than risks that are imposed on them. Although people willingly put their lives at risk when they drive a car, most people would be upset to learn that the fumes from a nearby factory present them with an equivalent risk of dying from cancer. Third, some risks may seem less equitable than others. Public surveys, for example, reveal that people are less willing to accept the risk of an accident that could kill 1,000 people in a concentrated geographic area (e.g., a nuclear accident) than a risk that could kill 1,000 people spread out over the

---

[1] *See, e.g.*, Lois Gold et al., *Rodent Carcinogens: Setting Priorities*, 258 Science 261 (1992); Bruce Ames, *Ranking Possible Carcinogenic Hazards*, 236 Science 271 (1987).

entire nation (e.g., asthma-related deaths from factory fumes around the Unites States). Deciding whether a risk is acceptable, in summary, can be a complex determination that depends on a wide variety of factors. In regulating risks in a manner acceptable to society, it is not enough to know only the probability of harm.

Congress, as the nation's popularly elected legislature, seems best suited to determine acceptable risk levels, either by regulating substances directly or by setting out clear instructions to regulatory agencies. As discussed below, Congress sometimes has faced up to that challenge. In many cases, however, Congress has ducked the issue and either delegated broad discretion to a regulatory agency or, even worse, provided conflicting cues on how the agency should manage potential toxins. Faced with serious health concerns on the one side and important economic interests on the other, Congress often has proven unable or unwilling to resolve the competing interests and left the ultimate decision to the regulatory agencies and courts.

The Supreme Court addressed the question of "acceptable" risk in *Industrial Union Department, AFL–CIO v. American Petroleum Institute* (commonly known as the *"Benzene Case"*).[2] Under the Occupational Safety and Health Act ("OSHA"), the Secretary of Labor regulates workplace exposure to toxic materials. Section 6(b)(5) of OSHA specifies that, for each toxic substance, the Secretary shall set an exposure standard "which *most adequately assures*, to the extent feasible, on the basis of best available evidence, that *no* employee will suffer material impairment of health or functional capacity" even if exposed to the substance for his or her entire working life (emphasis added). Section 3(8) of OSHA, by contrast, says that the Secretary is to set standards that are *"reasonably* necessary or appropriate to provide *safe* or healthful employment and places of employment" (emphasis added again). In the late 1970s, the Department of Labor decided to lower the exposure standard for benzene, a liquid chemical frequently used in manufacturing processes and known to cause leukemia. Concluding that no known level of benzene exposure was safe, the Secretary decided to reduce air exposure in factories from 10 parts per million (ppm) to the lowest level that the Secretary believed was feasible, 1 ppm. The petroleum industry challenged the legality of the new standard.

The Supreme Court agreed with the industry and reversed. Justice Stevens, joined by three other justices, concluded that OSHA authorizes the Department of Labor to ban only those levels of exposure that present a "significant risk of material health

---

[2] 448 U.S. 607 (1980).

impairment." Pointing to the language of section 3(8), Justice Stevens reasoned that OSHA requires only a "safe" work place, not a work place that is "risk free." According to Stevens, people consider many activities, like driving a car, to be "safe" even though they entail some risk.

> Some risks are plainly acceptable while others are plainly unacceptable. If, for example, the odds are one in a billion that a person will die from cancer by taking a drink of chlorinated water, the risk clearly could not be considered significant. On the other hand, if the odds are one in a thousand that regular inhalation of gasoline vapors that are 2% benzene will be fatal, a reasonable person might well consider the risk significant and take appropriate steps to decrease or eliminate it.

Justice Marshall's dissenting opinion fired back that Justice Stevens was ignoring the broad discretion given the Secretary of Labor to protect workers' health and instead imposing his own "personal views . . . as to the proper allocation of resources for safety in the American workplace."

Justice Rehnquist in a concurring opinion concluded that OSHA was unconstitutional because it improperly delegated to an administrative agency the important legislative decision as to the appropriate level of protection. As discussed in Chapter 3, the Supreme Court has not used the "unconstitutional delegation" doctrine to invalidate a Congressional delegation since early in the 1940s. Rehnquist, however, argued that the doctrine cried out for application here. In Rehnquist's view, "one of the most difficult issues that could confront a decisionmaker" is the acceptability of a risk of future deaths. This is exactly the type of decision that Congress should make. Reading OSHA, it "is difficult to imagine a more obvious example of Congress simply avoiding a choice which was both fundamental for purposes of the statute and yet politically so divisive that the necessary decision or compromise was difficult, if not impossible, to hammer out in the legislative forge."

B.   The Problem of Uncertainty

Scientific uncertainty also plagues efforts to regulate toxic materials. Note that *risk* and *uncertainty* are not the same thing and that they need not be present simultaneously. Scientists might know with a high degree of certainty that exposure to a certain chemical will lead to cancer in two out of every thousand people. If so, there would be risk but little uncertainty. Alternatively, scientists might suspect that *everyone* who consumes 10 milligrams of a particular substance will contract cancer, but not have enough information to be sure. In that case, there would be scientific uncertainty, but if studies confirmed that the substance was carcinogenic, exposure would pose a certitude rather than a mere risk of injury. In the real world, most toxic substances pose only a risk of injury (and typically a very small risk). Scientists, moreover, often are uncertain whether a substance really poses a risk and, if so, about the size of that risk. Both risk and uncertainty thus combine to make the life of the regulator very tough indeed.

1.   A Paucity of Information

Part of the problem is that we have not studied carefully many of the chemicals in regular use. In 1984, a panel of the National Academy of Sciences concluded that toxicity information for most chemicals was "scanty."[3] Indeed, for the "great majority of [toxic] substances, data considered to be essential for conducting a health-hazard assessment [was] lacking." Although we have more information today, we still lack data on a large percentage of chemicals.

Businesses worldwide currently manufacture over ten million chemicals. Researchers, moreover, discover thousands of useful new chemical formulations every year, so that the universe of potential toxins continues to expand. Performing comprehensive safety tests on all of these chemicals would be extremely time consuming and exceptionally expensive. Information comes at a cost, and so the government must decide how much testing is worthwhile. Additional testing and analysis always will provide greater insight into the safety of a product, but at some point the cost of that testing may outweigh the marginal value that society gets from the additional information.

Rather than require manufacturers to engage in extensive safety testing of all new chemicals, the federal government generally settles for requiring manufacturers to test only those categories of chemicals that are of high concern because of their general characteristics or their proposed use. Pesticides and other agricultural chemicals, for example, are designed to kill living organisms and thus raise automatic toxicity concerns; moreover, farm workers, rural residents, and consumers are all likely to come into frequent contact with these chemicals. As a result, the Federal Insecticide, Fungicide, and Rodenticide Act ("FIFRA") requires producers to conduct extensive toxicology tests in the laboratory and the field before applying to produce and sell new agricultural chemicals. These toxicology tests can easily take over five years to complete and cost $5 million or more. The Federal Food Drug & Cosmetic Act also requires comprehensive testing of chemicals that will be added to food or included in cosmetics.

---

[3] National Academy of Sciences, Toxicity Testing: Strategies to Determine Needs and Priorities (1984).

By contrast, the Toxic Substances Control Act ("TSCA"), which regulates chemicals not covered by other more specific statutes like FIFRA, does not automatically require producers to conduct any specific tests. Before manufacturing a new chemical, a producer must file with EPA a pre-manufacture notification (PMN), along with whatever data the producer believes shows that the chemical "will not present an unreasonable risk."[4] But TSCA does not mandate any particular testing. Because tests can cost thousands of dollars and take a year or more to conduct, companies generally do not perform comprehensive tests if not required. As a result, most TSCA chemicals have not undergone broad testing. Only about 15 percent of manufacturers submit data on health and safety risks of new chemicals. Most submit no information whatsoever.

Section 4 of TSCA authorizes EPA to require more tests if the agency concludes (1) that it does not have sufficient information with which to determine a chemical's toxicity *and* (2) that the chemical "may present an unreasonable risk of injury to health or the environment," will be produced in substantial quantities, or may result in substantial human exposure.[5] EPA, however, normally does not exercise this authority unless the chemical is similar in structural makeup to a substance already known to be toxic or unless EPA has other good reason to suspect its toxicity. In an effort to expand the number of chemicals tested, EPA over the last five years proposed or issued rules requiring tests for almost 60 chemicals. Yet even when EPA requires tests, years can pass between when EPA decides to seek the tests and completion of the tests, and many of the rules call only for "screening tests" that will help indicate whether there is reason to be concerned—not whether a chemical should be banned or limited.

The tests required under statutes such as FIFRA often also leave significant gaps in the government's knowledge of the toxicity risks presented by a chemical. FIFRA, for example, requires extensive testing of the carcinogenic risks of individual chemicals. But FIFRA currently does not mandate that a chemical be tested for some other significant risks, nor does FIFRA require tests of the potential synergistic effects of exposure to multiple chemicals.[6] Once EPA licenses an agricultural chemical, moreover, FIFRA generally does not require regular retesting of the chemical as testing processes improve. Concerned that early testing of agricultural chemicals might have been inadequate, Congress

---

[4] TSCA § 5(b)(2)(B)(ii), 15 U.S.C. § 2604(b)(2)(B)(ii).

[5] TSCA § 4, 15 U.S.C. § 2603.

[6] In a synergistic effect, the sum of contributors is greater than their individual contributions. Thus two mildly toxic compounds might, when combined, produce a highly toxic effect. In these situations, 2+2 can equal 8, or even 80.

amended FIFRA in 1988 to require reregistration, and thus additional testing, of the tens of thousands of pesticides registered prior to 1984. EPA finally completed this reregistration process two decades later in 2008.

2.   The Difficulty of Determining Cancer Risks

Even if the government required exhaustive tests of every chemical, the exact health risks of many chemicals would remain uncertain. This is true particularly of cancer risks. Historically, the two principal methods of determining the cancer risk of a chemical have been epidemiological studies and animal bioassays. In epidemiological studies, scientists look to see if populations of humans who have been exposed to a substance suffer greater incidences of cancer or other illnesses than the general population does. Because humans must have been exposed to a substance in order to conduct an epidemiological study, this approach obviously does not work well where the government is trying to determine whether to permit a new substance to be produced and sold. Before an epidemiological study can determine the risks of a carcinogen, the substance already must have harmed real people—the very danger that regulation is trying to avoid. Even if a carcinogen has been on the market for several years, epidemiological studies may not provide an accurate assessment of the risk. Virtually all carcinogens present long-term risks; someone exposed in 2010 may not manifest any cancer symptoms, for example, until 2030 or 2040. Early epidemiological studies thus may not indicate any risk. In addition, because people are exposed to a variety of different health risks over time, the data in most epidemiological studies are extremely "noisy." An increase in a given form of cancer among the exposed population may be the consequence of exposure to the studied material or, alternatively, of totally different causes.

Given the obstacles to effective epidemiological studies, regulators have relied primarily on animal bioassays to determine cancer risks. In an animal bioassay, researchers expose laboratory animals to a substance and then observe whether the exposed animals suffer a higher incidence of cancer than that of a control group of animals that have not been exposed. Rats and mice are two of the more common animals used in cancer studies.

Although animal bioassays can help identify potential carcinogens, a number of limitations undercut the ability to use bioassays to predict the probability of a risk accurately. First is the problem of determining whether a substance that is carcinogenic for rats, mice, and other laboratory animals is also carcinogenic for humans, and vice-versa. Every animal species has a different predisposition or susceptibility to various forms of cancer. Just because a chemical produces cancer in mice does not mean that it will cause cancer in humans. Similarly, a chemical might be a human carcinogen even though animal bioassays come up negative. There generally is enough correlation between what's carcinogenic to humans and carcinogenic to lab animals that scientists feel comfortable extrapolating from animals to humans, but uncertainty remains and conclusions need to be carefully couched.

A second limitation of animal bioassays is the problem of translating animal exposure into human exposure. A basic rule of pharmacology is that "the dose determines the poison." A small amount of chlorine in a cup of water will kill dangerous bacteria, making the water safe to drink. Drink a cup of chlorine, though, and it will kill you. Because of the differences in the sizes of rats and humans, exposing a rat to 2 milligrams of benzene per day is not equivalent to exposing humans to the same amount. Scientists unfortunately disagree on the best way of translating exposure of laboratory animals to exposure of humans. Some scientists, for example, believe that relative exposure levels are proportionate to weight; if the average person weighs 120 times the average laboratory rat, exposure of a rat to 2 milligrams is equivalent to exposing a human to 240 milligrams. Other scientists, however, believe that the ratio of surface exposure is more appropriate. Yet other scientists argue for other metrics.

Because researchers cannot wait years to see if the animals contract cancer and must study a limited population of laboratory animals, researchers also must expose the animals to large "mega doses" of the substance under study. No matter how the laboratory exposure is translated into human exposure, humans typically will *never* be exposed to the substance at the levels that the laboratory animals suffer. In predicting human risk, scientists therefore must extrapolate from high levels of exposure to much lower levels of exposure. The resulting risk prediction depends on the assumed relationship between exposure dosage and risk. Under some dose-response models, a chemical might pose no risk of cancer at typical exposure levels even if the risk is significant at higher levels.

Scientists more recently have turned to *in vitro* cell and tissue cultures to examine the potential risks of chemicals. In these tests, scientists look to see the effect of chemical agents on cells and tissues in the laboratory. Such tests are far cheaper and faster than are animal bioassays or epidemiological studies. Scientists, however, disagree on the accuracy of such tests.

Even if scientists feel somewhat confident that they understand the risk of a substance at various levels of exposure, the government must still determine exposure levels in order to determine the projected risk. Although this might sound easy, it often is not. Risk analysts largely must guess, for example, the level at which farm workers and their families are exposed to various toxic pesticides. In one study, scientists asked rural families to estimate their children's exposure to potential toxic pathways and then videotaped the children's actual exposure. There was virtually no correspondence between the two.

3.   Regulating Under Uncertainty

The high degree of uncertainty involved in estimating toxicity risks makes burden of proof particularly important. The government is likely to regulate fewer substances if it must prove that a substance is "unsafe," however that might be defined, than if producers must prove that the substance is "safe." This is particularly true because producers are likely to have much better information than the government concerning the risks posed by their products.

The standard of proof also is important. Scientists often demand a high degree of certainty, e.g., a 90 or 95 percent probability, before concluding that a particular substance is carcinogenic or poses some other serious health risk. The law generally is willing to act with far less certainty. In *Reserve Mining Co. v. EPA*,[7] the federal government sought to enjoin the Reserve Mining Company from discharging taconite tailings into Lake Superior, using a provision of the Clean Water Act that authorizes the government to sue to stop discharges that "endanger" public health.[8] Although taconite tailings contain asbestos fibers, which were suspected at the time to cause cancer and other serious health harms, health studies of the risk of ingesting taconite tailings in drinking water were inconclusive. A panel of the Eighth Circuit Court of Appeals ruled that the government had not met its burden of showing endangerment and, given the existing scientific uncertainty, probably could never meet its burden. According to the panel, a mere "medical hypothesis" was insufficient to justify abatement.[9] Rehearing the case en banc, the Eighth Circuit disagreed with the panel and held that the government need show only a "reasonable medical concern for the public health." Given the serious consequences if the medical hypothesis should prove true, courts should not be powerless to act in the face of uncertainty. In the court's view, Congress had "used the term 'endangering' in a precautionary or preventative sense and, therefore, evidence of

---

[7]   514 F.2d 492 (8th Cir.1975).

[8]   33 U.S.C. § 1160(g)(1).

[9]   *See Reserve Mining Co. v. United States*, 498 F.2d 1073 (8th Cir. 1974).

potential harm as well as actual harm comes within the purview of that term."

A year later, the D.C. Circuit also emphasized the importance of precautionary measures in *Ethyl Corp. v. EPA*.[10] The Clean Air Act authorizes EPA to regulate gasoline additives that "will endanger" public health. The question in *Ethyl Corp.* was whether EPA could use this authority to reduce lead in gasoline. A number of studies suggested that lead presented serious health risks, particularly to children, but the studies were far from conclusive at the time. The D.C. Circuit nonetheless upheld EPA's authority, again emphasizing the precautionary nature of the environmental legislation. The court stressed that administrative agencies need not meet scientific standards of proof before regulating potentially harmful substances. The court also suggested that the appropriate standard of proof might depend on the potential severity of harm. Very serious harms might call for a lower standard of proof, and vice-versa.

Politically, however, truly precautionary regulation can be difficult to sustain in the long run. Under precautionary regulation, the government will regulate some substances that later, on further study, turn out to be safe. Greater levels of precaution lead to an increasing number of safe (as well as unsafe) substances being regulated. Producers and consumers of regulated materials are likely to cite such "false positives" as evidence that the government is over-regulating. In hindsight, the government will appear to have interfered unnecessarily with the market, even though ex ante its decisions were sound. Over time, the accumulation of these "errors" may undermine support for a precautionary approach. In practice, however, the federal government has seldom taken as precautionary an approach as environmentalists have urged.

II. Major Regulatory Options

The government has used a wide variety of approaches in regulating toxic substances. In deciding how to regulate a potential toxin, the government must choose among a number of options. First, the government must decide whether to ban or limit the production of the toxic substance or to permit production but attempt to control exposure. The government, for example, could ban pesticides that present a significant risk of cancer or instead require farm workers to wear protective clothing and to take other precautions against exposure.

Second, the government must decide the appropriate regulatory standard. The government, for example, could choose a

---

[10] 541 F.2d 1 (D.C. Cir. 1976).

health based approach and proscribe all risks or all significant risks. The government could take a *feasibility* approach and reduce risks, or significant risks, only to the degree technologically and economically feasible. The government also could engage in *risk-benefit* balancing and regulate substances only when their risks outweigh their societal benefits. Although a zero-risk approach is clearly the toughest possible standard, the other standards cannot be ranked neatly by regulatory rigor. In most cases, risk-benefit analysis will be more lenient than a "significant-risk" or "feasibility" standard because it permits risks to be balanced against benefits. In some cases, however, risk-benefit analysis might be stricter. Imagine, for example, a chemical that presents a relatively insignificant risk but that also has little economic value. The government might choose not to regulate the chemical under a significant-risk standard because the risk is so small. Under a risk-benefit analysis, by contrast, the government might decide to regulate the chemical because the benefit is even smaller than the risk. If banning a pesticide would cause a large number of farms to close down, a feasibility approach might not ban the pesticide, while a risk-benefit analysis would call for banning the pesticide if the health risk is large enough to justify the cost.

A. Pure Health-Based Statutes

Congress has chosen only occasionally to ban all risks in a class of substances. The most famous examples of a zero-risk approach are the so-called Delaney Clauses in the federal Food, Drug, and Cosmetic Act. The Act prohibits the use of unsafe additives in food, drugs, and cosmetics. The Delaney Clauses, one of which deals with food additives and the other with color additives, require the government to treat additives as unsafe if they are "found . . . to induce cancer in man or animal."[11] If an animal bioassay finds that an additive causes cancer in laboratory animals, the Delaney Clauses prohibit the additive's use, whether or not there is any direct evidence that the additive causes cancer in humans and no matter how minuscule the risk at actual levels of human exposure.[12]

Given Congress' clear and unyielding intent to eliminate all risks, courts have refused to let administrative agencies create a "de minimis" exception to the Delaney Clauses. In *Public Citizen v. Young*,[13] the Food and Drug Administration (FDA) refused to ban the use of two color additives in cosmetics even though studies

---

[11] Food Drug & Cosmetic Act §§ 409 & 706, 21 U.S.C. §§ 348(c)(3)(A) & 379e(b)(5)(B).

[12] The Delaney Clauses focus only on additives. Thus, they do not ban naturally occurring carcinogens, no matter what the human risk.

[13] 831 F.2d 1108 (D.C. Cir. 1987).

showed that they caused cancer in laboratory animals. Noting that the color additives presented lifetime cancer risks of only one in nine million for one of the additives and one in 19 billion for the other, the FDA concluded that the risks were "so trivial as to be effectively no risk." The D.C. Circuit Court of Appeals disagreed, concluding that Congress clearly intended to ban such additives. In *Les v. Reilly*,[14] the Ninth Circuit Court of Appeals rejected a similar effort by EPA to affix a de minimis exception to the food-additive Delaney Clause. According to the court, "Congress intended to ban all carcinogenic food additives, regardless of amount or significance of risk, as the only safe alternative."

Many people find the Delaney Clauses mulish and irrational. Echoing Justice Steven's observation in the *Benzene Case* that "safe" is not the same thing as "risk free," critics see no reason to ban substances that present only trivial risks. Critics, moreover, fear that, by imposing such an extreme regulatory requirement, Congress may drive federal agencies to ignore or avoid the statute and thus pervert the regulatory process. Critics also argue that the Delaney Clauses could backfire by regulating rigidly some but not all risks. Unable to use a color additive that presents a one in 19 billion cancer risk, for example, cosmetic manufacturers might turn to an alternative color additive that presents no known cancer risk but a very high risk of other injury. According to critics, the government should engage in a risk-risk comparison of additives and their alternatives rather than simply banning substances that present a cancer risk.

So was Congress insane when it passed the Delaney Clauses? And why has Congress never chosen to repeal the Delaney Clauses in the face of these criticisms? Defenders of the Delaney Clauses make a number of arguments in response to the critics. Defenders first argue that the scientific uncertainty surrounding cancer risks calls for a precautionary approach. Although scientists currently might believe that a color additive presents only a one in 19 billion risk, additional studies might find that the risk is far greater. Indeed, defenders of the Delaney Clauses charge that most risks have turned out worse than scientists originally thought.[15] Defenders also argue that few, if any, additives are of significant economic or societal value, so banning those that pose a cancer risk is typically costless. Although this is not always true, most

---

[14] 968 F.2d 985 (9th Cir. 1992).

[15] We are unaware of any convincing empirical evidence one way or the other as to this assertion. Although scientists have conducted occasional retrospective studies on the risks of particular substances, the jury is still out on whether scientists tend on the whole to underestimate or overestimate risks at early stages of study. Of course, one might conclude that only the underestimates are troublesome, but this ignores the economic and social costs of "overregulation."

consumers can get along fine without most color or food additives. Finally, defenders of the Delaney Clauses note that the public places a high value on eliminating even small risks of cancer.

By singling out additives for special regulatory treatment, the Delaney Clauses, like all bright-line rules, can lead to illogical distinctions. Until 1996, for example, the food-additive Delaney Clause applied to pesticide residues in processed foods (e.g., canned corn) but not in raw foods (e.g., fresh corn). Thus people who bought fresh fruits and vegetables believing the fresh foods were better and healthier actually enjoyed less protection than people getting their essential food groups out of cans. In 1996, Congress finally extended protection to raw foods as part of a political compromise that also lowered the standard of protection for pesticide residues in processed foods. The Food Quality Protection Act of 1996 (FQPA), rather than the food-additive Delaney Clause, now regulates pesticide residues in foods, whether processed or raw. Unlike the Delaney Clause, the FQPA does not ban all pesticide residues that cause cancer. Instead, it requires only that there be a "reasonable certainty that no harm will result from aggregate exposure to the pesticide chemical residue."[16] The legislative history of the FQPA indicates that extremely low lifetime cancer risks of less than one in a million may be acceptable under this standard.

B.   Feasibility Statutes

In other statutes, Congress requires regulatory agencies to reduce toxic health risks, but only to the degree "feasible." The federal Occupational Health and Safety Act ("OSHA") takes this approach in regulating work place exposures. As noted earlier in connection with the *Benzene Case*, OSHA requires the Secretary of Labor to ensure a "safe" work place but only "to the extent feasible."[17] A major question under such feasibility statutes is the meaning of the term "feasible," which Congress often does not define. In the case of OSHA, courts have concluded that exposure standards must be both technologically and economically feasible. The Secretary of Labor thus cannot set an exposure standard that engineers have no idea how to meet. Nor can the Secretary set an exposure standard that would destroy an entire industry or undermine the industry's competitive structure, although a standard that bankrupts a few marginal firms would be okay.

The Safe Drinking Water Act ("SDWA") also takes a feasibility approach toward reducing toxins in the nation's drinking water. EPA starts by identifying contaminants that, in its judgment, "may

---

[16] 21 U.S.C. § 346a(b)(2)(A)(ii).

[17] OSHA §§ 3(8) & 6(b)(5), 29 U.S.C. §§ 652(8) & 655(b)(5).

have [an] adverse effect on the health of persons and which is known or anticipated to occur in public water systems."[18] Next, EPA sets "maximum contaminant level goals" or "MCLGs" for each contaminant that it has identified. The MCLGs are purely health based. Under the SDWA, EPA must set MCLGs "at the level at which no known or anticipated adverse effects on the health of persons occur and which allows an adequate margin of safety."[19] Because scientists do not know whether there is a safe threshold of ingestion for most carcinogens, EPA often sets MCLGs of zero. Rather than force water suppliers to meet such "goals," however, OSHA requires EPA to establish "maximum contaminant levels" or "MCLs" that are "as close to the maximum contaminant level goal as is feasible."[20] It is these MCLs, rather than the MCLGs, that water suppliers must meet. A standard is "feasible" under the SDWA if EPA, after seeing if the necessary technology works "under field conditions," concludes that the technology is "available (taking cost into consideration)."[21]

Although Congress understandably does not want to impose regulations that would put an industry out of business, feasibility standards can sometimes lead to disturbingly arbitrary distinctions. Under OSHA, for example, workers in economically strapped industries could be subjected to relatively high risks because the industries cannot afford to reduce the risks, while workers in economically flush industries might enjoy freedom from even relatively minor risks. If wages are proportional to industry profitability, moreover, a feasibility approach can expose the poorest employees to the greatest risks.

Feasibility standards also create implementation problems. Regulatory agencies must spend valuable time determining whether each individual standard is technologically and economically feasible. Reviews can take a year or longer and cost hundreds of thousands of dollars. Much of the information needed to determine feasibility, moreover, is in the hands of the regulated industry, which has every reason to overstate the costs and problems of implementing stricter standards.

Economists remain troubled that feasibility requirements do not ensure that the benefits from regulation are "worth" the costs. Assuming that it is "feasible" to rid drinking water of a contaminant that poses a very low risk, but the cost of the needed filtering technology would raise national water bills by 20 percent

---

[18] 42 U.S.C. § 300g–1(b)(3)(A).

[19] 42 U.S.C. § 300g–1(b)(4).

[20] 42 U.S.C. §§ 300g–1(b)(4)–(5).

[21] 42 U.S.C. § 300g–1(5).

or more, is it sensible to ban the contaminant? "Feasible" does not mean "optimal" or "ideal." Faced with growing concerns over the costs of reducing lead and other contaminants in drinking water, Congress chose to amend the SDWA in 1996 to permit EPA to relax MCLs if it believes that the risks of a contaminant do not justify the costs of regulation. If EPA concludes that the benefits of a MCL "would not justify the costs of complying," EPA now may set a MCL that "maximizes health risk reduction benefits at a cost that is justified by the benefits."[22]

C.   Risk-Benefit Statutes

1.   Federal Insecticide, Fungicide, and Rodenticide Act

A number of statutes require EPA to balance the risks and benefits of a product in determining the appropriate level of regulation. Under the Federal Insecticide, Fungicide, and Rodenticide Act ("FIFRA"), the manufacturer of a new pesticide or agricultural chemical must register it with EPA before producing and selling it. Before registering the pesticide EPA must determine (1) that the pesticide will do what the manufacturer says (truth in advertising) and (2) that the pesticide "when used in accordance with widespread and commonly recognized practice" will not pose an "unreasonable risk to man or the environment, taking into account the economic, social, and environmental costs and benefits of the pesticide."[23] EPA thus must balance risks and benefits in determining whether a pesticide presents an "unreasonable risk." If the pesticide presents an unreasonable risk, EPA can address the problem either by refusing to register the pesticide or by imposing conditions on how the pesticide is used. To date, the federal government has registered over 50,000 agricultural chemicals.

Over time, scientists learn more and more about toxic risks and how to measure them. As a result, pesticides that originally looked safe may become suspect later. FIFRA therefore requires EPA periodically to reevaluate and reregister existing pesticides. FIFRA also authorizes EPA to cancel a registration or to change a pesticide's use conditions if EPA determines that the pesticide presents an unreasonable risk—although EPA must jump through significant administrative hoops, including scientific reviews and a full adjudicatory hearing, before taking action. Congress originally required EPA to reimburse both the manufacturer and users of a pesticide for the costs of canceling the pesticide, perhaps intentionally deterring EPA from taking such actions. In 1988, however, Congress amended FIFRA to eliminate the requirement

---

[22] 42 U.S.C. § 300g–1(b)(6).

[23] FIFRA §§ 2(bb) & 3(c)(5), 7 U.S.C. §§ 136(bb) & 136a(c)(5).

that manufacturers be indemnified. Consumers of a cancelled pesticide, however, are still entitled to compensation.

2.   *Toxic Substances Control Act*

The Toxic Substances Control Act ("TSCA") also requires EPA to balance the risks and benefits of chemical products. The manufacturer of a chemical substance that is not regulated under another federal law such as FIFRA must file a Pre–Manufacturing Notice ("PPM") before producing and selling the chemical. Because TSCA chemicals generally are less suspect than pesticides, TSCA does not require EPA to evaluate the risks of every chemical for which a PPM is filed. EPA, however, can ban or restrict the use of a chemical if there is a "reasonable basis to conclude" that the chemical "presents or will present an unreasonable risk of injury to health or the environment."[24] Like FIFRA, TSCA requires EPA to balance the risks of a substance against its benefits in determining whether the risks are "unreasonable." According to a 2005 study by the U.S. Government Accountability Office, EPA review has led to the withdrawal or restriction of about 10 percent of the chemicals submitted under TSCA.

3.   *"Paralysis by Analysis"*

Many environmentalists worry that statutes like FIFRA and TSCA, by requiring EPA to balance risks and benefits, may lead to "paralysis by analysis." Once EPA starts down the road of trying to evaluate and compare risks and benefits, EPA might find that it never gets to its destination but instead gets bogged down in the details of the analysis or has an inadequate budget to carry out the analysis. Perhaps recognizing this danger, Congress occasionally has emphasized that it does not expect EPA to complete formal, quantified risk-benefit analyses in all cases. A rough, qualitative comparison often should be enough. But FIFRA and TSCA inevitably have drawn EPA into quantitative comparisons.

The Fifth Circuit Court of Appeal's decision in *Corrosion Proof Fittings v. Environmental Protection Agency*[25] demonstrates the dangers of paralysis by analysis. The case dealt with EPA's efforts under TSCA in the late 1980s to regulate the use of asbestos in a variety of products such as pipes, shingles, and brake pads. Scientists know perhaps more about asbestos than any other toxic substance, and everything they know about asbestos is bad. Asbestos is one of the most dangerous substances around. Exposure, sometimes at very low levels, can lead to asbestosis, lung cancer, and mesothelioma (a particularly deadly cancer of the chest

---

[24] TSCA § 6(a), 15 U.S.C. § 2605(a).

[25] 947 F.2d 1201 (5th Cir. 1991).

cavity). Despite the serious health risks, EPA decided to be deliberate and thorough in its evaluation of the asbestos products. At the time, TSCA was a relatively untried weapon in EPA's arsenal, so EPA wanted to get things right. As a result, EPA spent almost ten years reviewing the asbestos products and building the case for banning them. By the time EPA was finished, it had amassed a 45,000-page administrative record.

Based on this record, EPA decided that only a total ban could avoid the known health risks of asbestos. Attempts to limit exposure of particular groups, such as workers or consumers, would leave other persons unprotected. In EPA's view, moreover, the risks justified a total ban. When it reached its decision in the late 1980s, EPA conservatively estimated that, from 1988 to 2000, a ban would save the lives of 202 people who otherwise would die from lung cancer or mesothelioma. EPA calculated that, assuming the price of asbestos substitutes declined over time, the cost of the ban would be $459 million—or $3.1 million per death avoided. (If both the costs and the lives saved were "discounted" to the present, EPA estimated that the cost per death avoided would be only $2.4 million.) In EPA's view, this cost was more than acceptable.

The Fifth Circuit reversed. The Fifth Circuit began by criticizing the methodology that EPA used as incomplete and inadequate. First, EPA had compared the risks and benefits of only two options: no regulation, and a complete ban on using asbestos in the products. The Fifth Circuit held that EPA should have performed a marginal analysis in which it compared the reduced risks and benefits of successively tighter restrictions. As the Fifth Circuit noted, a restriction somewhere in the middle might provide a better balance of risks and benefits. Second, the Fifth Circuit criticized EPA's failure to quantify risks and benefits beyond the year 2000, despite EPA's belief that uncertainty would plague any effort to quantify the risks and benefits that far into the future. Although the court recognized that EPA must use some finite time frame, the court believed that 13 years was "unreasonably" short. Third, the court decided that EPA should have weighed the potential harms from any substitutes that manufacturers might use in place of asbestos. Finally, the court ruled that EPA should have performed separate risk-benefit comparisons for each product, rather than for all the products in aggregate.

The Fifth Circuit's opinion assumes that EPA should and can perform a perfect risk-benefit analysis. The Fifth Circuit may be correct that a risk-benefit analysis in theory should examine the marginal benefit and cost of each incremental regulatory step, quantify all the possible risks and benefits far into the future, and make decisions for each product individually. But these "improvements" increase geometrically the difficulty of implementing TSCA and immerse EPA in a sea of scientific and economic uncertainty. As noted, EPA spent ten years completing the relatively complex analysis that the Fifth Circuit found wanting. At some point, the cost of additional analysis and quantification is not worth the increased understanding and analysis.

Corrosion Proof Fittings also raises the question of the appropriate role of courts and administrative agencies in determining the appropriate level of risk. Looked at product by product, EPA's ban on asbestos would have cost as much as $76 million per life saved: banning asbestos pipe would have saved only about three lives at a cost as high as $227 million. The Fifth Circuit concluded that this was unreasonably high. The court was unclear whether it believed that the acceptability of the cost was a legal issue or a factual question. Nor did the court discuss whether it should defer to EPA's "expertise" in risk analysis. EPA, however, would seem the better body to make such judgments for reasons of both uniformity and democratic accountability. Different courts are likely to have different views about what is an acceptable risk, creating considerable regulatory confusion if courts generally impose their view. EPA, moreover, is more directly responsible to the public for its actions.

4. Criticisms

Risk-benefit analysis has many critics. One concern, illustrated by *Corrosion Proof Fittings*, is that risk-benefit analysis slows down government regulation and, by making regulation more difficult, reduces the likelihood that the government will restrict harmful toxins. Under FIFRA, it took EPA 17 years to conduct a special review of Alar, 9 years to review Captan, and 12 years to review EBCD. Critics also worry that risk-benefit analyses imply greater certainty than actually exists. As highlighted earlier, considerable uncertainty plagues virtually all elements of risk-benefit analysis, in particular the risk calculations. By quantifying the risk and developing an estimate of the "cost per life saved," EPA suggests that it can compare the risks and costs with a high degree of precision, disguising the need for a precautionary approach. In a similar vein, critics sometimes worry that the government can too easily cook the books under the guise of scientific risk assessment. Given the many judgments that go into a risk-benefit analysis and the underlying uncertainty, an agency can reach a wide range of conclusions based on any given data. Underlying EPA's "scientific" analysis may be a number of important policy decisions.

Critics also raise the traditional concerns with using economic efficiency to guide environmental policy that Chapter 2 discussed. Is the appropriate level of toxic exposure an economic question or a moral one? As a society, are we willing (and do we have the right) to expose people to harmful substances if it means more jobs, more consumer products, and a higher gross domestic product? Even if we believe that the goal of environmental policy should be to maximize utility, can society impose a health risk on one individual in order to make others better off? Although each of us trades off risk and wealth every day (e.g., by buying a cheaper car that is not as safe), that is a very different decision than choosing as a society to accept interpersonal tradeoffs. How, moreover, can the government determine the overall utility of permitting farmers to use a pesticide that can cause cancer in humans? To many people, health risks are incommensurate with economic benefits; there is no common metric with which to compare costs and benefits.

Despite all of these concerns, risk-benefit analysis still tempts. As emphasized earlier, the modern industrial world is not risk free and never will be. Reducing risks, moreover, can be economically costly. So long as that's the case, the government inevitably will ask itself whether various regulations are "worth" the cost—the inquiry that is at the heart of risk-benefit statutes.

D. *Informational Approaches*

A final approach to toxins is to provide the public with information regarding toxic exposure and let public pressure and market choices address the problem. Few companies want to be known as the toxic leader of their community or industry. Armed with information about a company's toxic releases, members of the public may be able to pressure a company to reduce its emissions. Similarly, few people want to buy products that include toxic ingredients. If the government requires companies to reveal toxic substances in their products, producers may remove the offending ingredients to retain their customers.

1. *The Toxic Release Inventory*

The Emergency Planning and Community Right-to-Know Act of 1986 ("EPCRA") takes such an informational approach to toxic releases. Under EPCRA, EPA maintains a list of approximately 650 hazardous substances. Any company that releases more than a specified threshold amount of each substance in any calendar year must report the releases to both EPA and the state. EPA then compiles this data into a national toxic release inventory ("TRI"), which it posts on its public website. The TRI data is picked up and reported by journalists and by other popular websites, such as

Scorecard, which combines the data with information about the potential health risks of each of the substances.[26]

The TRI has become an important weapon in reducing toxic releases. Numerous companies have worked to reduce their releases rather than place high on the TRI rankings—and for good reason. Bad publicity can hurt sales and poison local community relations. Studies even show that companies with high toxic releases, as reported in the TRI, have poorer stock market performances.

The TRI, however, is not perfect. Some evidence suggests that companies occasionally reduce their reported emissions not by improving their actual environmental performance but by changing their reporting standards or analytical methods. Because material sent for recycling is not counted as a TRI release, moreover, there has been far less pollution prevention (i.e., reduction of waste at the source) than one might expect. EPCRA similarly does not require companies to report on the amount of toxins that they use or that are in their products; companies must report only releases of toxins into the environment. As a result, EPCRA does little to reduce consumer or worker exposure to toxins. Environmental groups have lobbied (unsuccessfully to date) to broaden the TRI either to cover all waste (including waste destined for recycling) or to focus on the amount of toxic substances going into the manufacturing process rather than only the amount coming out as waste. Finally, the TRI covers only a fraction of all toxic chemicals and does not address releases by some significant sources, such as farms.

2   California's Proposition 65

In the same year that Congress passed EPCRA, California voters passed Proposition 65, a voter initiative that requires public disclosure of both toxic releases and toxic ingredients in consumer products. Under Proposition 65, the Governor of California publishes a list of those chemicals known to cause cancer or reproductive toxicity; this list currently contains over 900 chemicals. Businesses cannot knowingly discharge or release a listed chemical into water or onto or into land if the chemical probably would travel into a source of drinking water. More importantly, businesses cannot knowingly and intentionally expose someone to a listed chemical without first providing a "clear and reasonable" warning. Thus, if a consumer product contains a listed chemical, the seller must post a notice either on the product or in a location that purchasers will see. Factories emitting toxic air pollutants must warn neighboring residents.

---

[26] The *Scorecard* website http://www.scorecard.org provides one of the best examples of how information about environmental releases and performance can be used to try to influence improved corporate behavior.

Businesses are exempt from these rules if the amount of chemical at issue is "insignificant." Recognizing that whether a level of exposure is significant or not can be the source of considerable scientific debate, Proposition 65 reverses the normal burden of proof. In order to qualify for the exemption, the business has the burden to show that the exposure amount is insignificant. This led businesses to press California in the early days of Proposition 65 to quickly issue regulations specifying what would constitute an insignificant amount. The resulting regulations define an insignificant amount for carcinogens as an amount that presents a risk, assuming lifetime exposure, of less than one in 100,000. For reproductive toxins, a quantity is insignificant if the toxin would have no observable effect on people who are exposed over their lifetime to 1000 times that quantity.

Proposition 65 also was one of the first environmental statutes in the United States to include a "bounty" provision. Whoever brings a lawsuit for a violation of Proposition 65 receives 25 percent of any penalty imposed by the court. Courts can assess penalties of up to $2500 per day for each violation. Fearful that the bounty provision might be encouraging frivolous lawsuits, California in 2002 added a requirement that plaintiffs file a "certificate of merit" certifying that the plaintiff believes that there is good cause for the lawsuit. Plaintiffs also must give the California Attorney General 90-days notice of their intent to file a lawsuit, and the Attorney General can block the lawsuit by filing a governmental action at any point within that 90-day period.

When Proposition 65 originally passed, some people questioned whether consumers really would pay attention to warning labels and signs. Concern mounted when Proposition 65 warnings began to sprout up virtually everywhere—in liquor stores (potential for birth defects), bars and restaurants (alcohol and, before cigarettes were banned in California bars and restaurants, second-hand smoke), and gasoline stations (toxic fumes)—making them commonplace. Under Proposition 65, moreover, warning signs typically are quite generic. A typical warning reads "Warning: This product contains a chemical known to the State of California to cause cancer." The warnings virtually never provide detailed information about the exact nature and size of the potential risk.

Proposition 65, however, has resulted in significant reductions in toxic exposures. Producers have responded to Proposition 65 by reformulating their products. Producers simply do not want to take a chance on how consumers will respond to warning labels. Wine makers therefore no longer use lead foil for the tops of their bottles, and the maker of Progresso tomatoes stopped using lead solder in its cans. Because most manufacturers do not want to manufacture one version of a product for California and another version for the rest of the nation, moreover, these changes generally have benefited consumers nationwide.

PROBLEM EXERCISE: CALCIUM SUPPLEMENTS & ANTACIDS[27]

More than a third of American households regularly consume dietary calcium supplements or antacids, such as Tums or Mylanta. Manufacturers obtain the calcium from naturally-occurring sources, including fossilized oyster shells dredged from the ocean floor. In the late 1980s, scientists discovered that many natural sources of calcium contain high levels of lead. Lead is a known human reproductive toxin. Pregnant women face particularly serious health hazards from lead exposure because they absorb lead more readily than most people from the gastrointestinal tract. And unfortunately lead can easily cross the placenta. As a result, high exposures among pregnant women can lead to impairment of fetal development (including damage to the brain, major organs, nervous system, and blood cells of the fetus), slower sensory-motor development, delayed early cognitive development, and slower growth.

Calcium, however, also can provide important health benefits to pregnant women and the population as a whole. Researchers, for example, have found that calcium can prevent osteoporosis, pregnancy-induced hypertension, and premature delivery; calcium also can decrease the risk of colon cancer. As a result, the National Institute of Health recommends that women from the age of 19 to 50 take 1000 milligrams of calcium daily.

The Food and Drug Administration historically did not regulate the amount of lead found in calcium supplements and antacids. In the mid-1990s, the Natural Resources Defense Council (NRDC) tested various calcium supplements and antacids and found that they contained widely varying amounts of lead, ranging from 0.2 to 20.75 micrograms of lead per maximum daily dose. Under Proposition 65, NRDC threatened to sue those manufacturers of calcium supplements and antacids that contained more than 0.5 micrograms of lead per 1000 milligrams of calcium—a virtually "lead free" level. The largest manufacturer of calcium supplements quickly agreed to meet this standard. When other manufacturers balked, NRDC in early 1997 sued them for failing to provide a Proposition 65 warning that their products contained lead. The California Attorney General, however, took over the Proposition 65 action by filing his own action several days later and within 90 days of NRDC's original notice letter.

The manufacturers and the Attorney General soon began settlement discussions. According to the manufacturers, there was no

---

[27] This Problem Exercise is based on a case study written by Mary Decker for the Stanford Law School Environmental and Natural Resources Law and Policy Program under the editorial guidance of Professor Thompson.

evidence that the levels of lead found in their products were dangerous. They also argued that lowering lead levels would require reformulating the products without understanding the performance characteristics of the new calcium sources. The Attorney General ultimately agreed to a settlement involving a phased reduction in lead levels. Before April 1, 1999, the manufacturers would need to provide a Proposition 65 notice only for calcium products that contained over 4.0 micrograms of lead per thousand milligrams of elemental calcium. Starting April 1, 1999, the acceptable level would drop to 1.5 micrograms. The settling manufacturers also would pay the Attorney General's costs (approximately $120,000) and pay $458,000 into a trust fund for lead-related research and public education.

Although NRDC was no longer an official party to the lawsuit, it could still oppose the settlement in court. If you had been an attorney for NRDC at the time, would you have chosen to oppose the settlement? If so, is there any settlement that you would have supported (short of your original demand)? What information would you want to know in making your decision? What factors would you take into account? Note that a company called Specialty Minerals informed NRDC in 1997 that it could supply the entire California market with low-lead calcium carbonate "virtually immediately," but that there was no way to confirm or disprove this claim.

QUESTIONS AND DISCUSSION

1. Do you believe that there is an "acceptable" level of risk for toxic substances? If so, how should the government determine that level of risk?

2. Ideally the government would like to have as much information as possible about the potential risks of a product before permitting companies to manufacture and sell the product. But toxicity studies cost money. How should the government decide how much information to require for any particular product? Who should pay for the toxicity studies—the manufacturer (which means that the cost will probably be passed on to consumers) or the government (which means it is borne by taxpayers)?

3. How should the government deal with uncertainty in regulating toxic substances? Assume that there is a new pesticide that is carcinogenic to rats. Despite years of testing, however, scientists have no idea how risky the pesticide is to humans. Scientists expect that it is probably a human carcinogen, but they are not sure. The pesticide could kill no one or thousands of people. To make matters difficult, the pesticide would be extremely valuable to farmers. The Department of Agriculture estimates that the pesticide could save the farming industry over a billion dollars per year. Should EPA allow sales of the pesticide, or ban it?

4. Of the various regulatory approaches to toxic substances described in this Chapter (health-based, feasibility, and risk-benefit), which approach is best? Why? Is there any reason why the government should take different approaches in different statutes?

5.   If the government requires the seller of a potentially toxic product to put a label on the product warning of the product's risks, is there any reason for the government to directly regulate the product? If Mrs. Jones wants to purchase the product despite its health risks, shouldn't Mrs. Jones have the right to do so? So long as consumers have the risk information, why not let the market deal with the risks?

6.   Can a price be placed on human life? Risk-benefit statutes frequently require the government to put a value on human life in order to determine whether banning or regulating a substance is worth the economic cost. Do you believe that it is appropriate for the government to be making such decisions?

7.   The European Union has adopted a chemicals law, known as REACH, that takes a very different approach. Companies manufacturing or importing chemicals into the EU in quantities greater than one ton must register them with a specialized agency. Companies bear the burden of identifying and managing the risks posed by their substances. Chemicals of high concern (such as carcinogens, toxins, and bioaccumulative compounds) require specific authorization, and companies must demonstrate to the agency how the substances can be safely used, communicate this information to users, and make efforts to find safer substitutes. The agency can ban substances if the risks are deemed unmanageable. How would you compare this approach to the statutes you have read in this Chapter?

Chapter 9

WASTE MANAGEMENT

I. The Resource Conservation Recovery Act

Americans have a remarkable quality of life, enjoying a range of goods and services that kings and queens in past centuries could only have dreamed of. This material wealth comes at a cost, though, for it also generates a remarkable amount of waste. As with air and water pollutants, wastes come in all shapes and sizes. While some wastes are toxic and highly hazardous, others can be treated to become non-hazardous or are easily assimilated by the environment. To get a sense of the enormous volumes involved in waste management, consider that we generate the equivalent of 4.5 pounds of municipal solid waste daily for every American man, woman, and child, an almost 70% increase since 1960. This comprises a wide range of different waste streams—from household garbage (55–65% of all waste by weight) and industrial waste to construction and biomedical waste. Of all this household waste generated, only about 1% of it is considered hazardous to health.[1] Most hazardous waste is generated by industrial facilities (over 16,000 facilities produced over 34 million tons of hazardous waste in 2011).[2]

Why is waste a problem? One concern has been the so-called "landfill crisis," the concern that we're running out of places to dispose of our waste. From 1988 to 1999, almost 70% of the nation's municipal landfills closed. While the closure of these sites was largely in response to stricter regulations, the lack of *new* landfills is not due to lack of space. Rather, NIMBY (Not In my Back Yard) pressures from communities that do not want to live near a dump have resulted in a lack of landfill permits. Another concern is that waste means inefficiency. By throwing away or burning so much waste, we create the need to extract more virgin materials from the earth. The concerns here are both depletion of natural resources and harmful environmental impacts caused by extraction and synthesis of these materials that are then transformed into wastes. By reducing waste through better product and process design, increased re-use of materials, and greater recycling, we can reduce life-cycle impacts.

---

[1] Municipal Solid Waste In The United States, 2007 Facts and Figures, EPA530–R–08–010 (EPA, Nov. 2008) at 4, 5, 28,

[2] *See* EPA, THE NATIONAL BIENNIAL RCRA HAZARDOUS WASTE REPORT (2011).

The single biggest environmental problem posed by waste (and certainly the biggest public concern), though, is its health effects. Drinking water, for example, can be contaminated by waste "leachate." This is easy to understand if one thinks of a landfill as a giant "Mr. Coffee" filter. As water percolates through the landfill it becomes contaminated with hazardous constituents. This leachate can then mix with groundwater and surface water that may be consumed by humans. Incinerators burning waste are a major source of dioxins, mercury and other hazardous air pollutants. Incinerators, for example, are the primary source of mercury in the Chesapeake Bay.

Prior to the 1970s there were poor and, in some cases, no requirements for waste disposal. The precursor to the Resource Conservation and Recovery Act, the 1965 Solid Waste Disposal Act, merely encouraged states to develop waste management programs. The tougher Clean Air Act and Clean Water Act in 1970 and 1972 had required installation of pollution control devices on smokestacks and pipes throughout the nation, but where was the *waste* collected in these end of pipe controls supposed to go? Many landfills were simply holes in the ground that were compacted by bulldozers until full, and then covered over by topsoil and turned into golf courses or commercial developments. Nor were there stringent record keeping requirements to identify where the waste had come from (a failure that would curse the Superfund program, described later in this chapter). The Resource Conservation and Recovery Act (RCRA)[3] was drafted in this regulatory void.

RCRA is an amendment to the earlier Solid Waste Disposal Act and accomplishes four basic goals. It (1) creates definitions to determine the classes of wastes coming under its authority; (2) creates a tracking system for hazardous waste from its creation to its disposal (the first environmental law to take such a life-cycle approach); (3) establishes handling standards for the waste from its generation to its disposal; and (4) provides authority for mandatory clean-up of polluted treatment, storage, and disposal facilities.

The key provisions in RCRA deal with the disposal of solid waste (regulated in Subtitle D of the act) and the treatment and disposal of hazardous waste (regulated in Subtitle C). Because Subtitle C makes it much more expensive to dispose of hazardous waste, much of RCRA's legal history can be read as a "Great Escape" story of industry attempts to avoid having its waste considered hazardous waste and, once within the grips of Subtitle C's coverage, to avoid being classified as a treatment, storage, or disposal facility. As with every other federal environmental law, it

---

[3] 42 U.S.C. § 6901–6992k.

goes without saying, at the time of RCRA's passage Congress greatly underestimated the size and complexity of the problem.

For many students, studying RCRA quickly becomes a voyage into Alice's Wonderland, a statutory dreamscape where "solid" includes liquid and gas, where "hazardous" may not look hazardous, and where the King Midas fable is reversed with certain wastes turning everything they touch into even more waste. To understand RCRA, then, one must accept at the outset that it is internally consistent and relies on bright-line distinctions, but many of the critical terms have specific, often counterintuitive meanings within the statutory structure. To wind one's way through RCRA, there are three existential questions to keep in mind—"what is it?", "where is it?", and "who am I?".

A.   What is It?

Because RCRA's requirements for handling solid hazardous waste are very expensive, companies want to avoid their waste being characterized as either solid or hazardous waste. RCRA is an all-or-nothing proposition. Either your waste is in, and covered by the statute, or it's out. It is no exaggeration to say that the classification of waste is the key concern of regulated parties, for everything else flows from this. Thus the first practical questions in any RCRA analysis are (1) is it "solid" waste, and, if so, (2) is it solid "hazardous" waste?

1.   Solid Waste and Strategic Behavior

RCRA regulates only the disposal of "solid waste." If your waste is not considered solid waste under RCRA's regulatory definitions, you can laugh at the statute with impunity. The term "solid," however, is far broader than everyday usage, and covers virtually every form of matter except uncontained gases.[4] This broad definition was necessary to prevent parties from converting their wastes to avoid coverage. Add enough water and mix, and most solid wastes become liquid.

The coverage of solid waste is not as extensive as the overbroad definition might suggest, though, because there are a number of important, large exemptions. Some wastes are exempt because they are regulated by other statutes. Thus RCRA does not cover waste in sewage that passes through a public water treatment plant, wastewater discharges regulated by a Clean Water Act permit, mining wastes or nuclear wastes, just to name some of the largest exceptions. Municipal garbage, a very large waste stream that may contain small amounts of hazardous materials, such as batteries

---

[4]   42 U.S.C. § 6903(27).

and insecticide aerosols, is exempt from treatment as hazardous waste for practical reasons because of its sheer size. And other wastes, such as irrigation return flows, are exempt for political reasons because of the farm lobby's clout (recall that Congress exempted these from the Clean Water Act's coverage, as well).

While a case can be made to justify every one of these exemptions, the net result encourages strategic behavior by the regulated community. The more onerous and expensive RCRA regulation of waste becomes, the stronger the incentive to move out of its coverage entirely and into another statute. And rest assured that there are often significant differences over how statutes treat the same wastes. Some laws are far more rigorous than others, depending on the politics of the area and the time when the statutes were passed. The less demanding treatment of waste water under the Clean Water Act, for example, explains the large amount of hazardous waste that is disposed through either the public sewage system or direct emissions into a waterway.

While it may seem a stupid point to make, RCRA only covers solid wastes that are waste products. This seemingly redundant statement becomes important because waste can also resemble products and raw materials. Imagine, for example, that you run a farm and mix large vats of pesticides for application on crops. Under FIFRA, these pesticides can legally be sprayed onto fields, only to wash off into streams and drinking water supplies. But, under RCRA, the same pesticides that remain as residue in the barrel cannot be disposed of in landfills without extensive and expensive pre-treatment. They have now become RCRA waste.

Consider, too, the challenge posed by recycling. One of RCRA's goals is to encourage recycling. This not only reduces the amount of waste destined for disposal but the amount of raw materials needed for production, as well. Because recycling turns waste into a raw material for the manufacturing process, this avoids the environmental impacts from synthesis and production of virgin materials. Set against this, though, are the legislative goals of protecting the environment from hazardous substances and not interfering with the production process. While often held out as a wonderful and blessedly green activity, recycling can be a dirty business, creating significant wastes itself. Indeed a number of recycling sites later transformed into Superfund sites. How, then, to create regulations that define solid waste in a manner that can be meaningfully applied and enforced, that encourage recycling, and that prevent dangerous or sham recycling? The two mining cases, *American Mining Congress v. EPA I* and *II,* addressed this very challenge.

RCRA's definition of solid waste includes a number of waste streams, such as garbage, liquid material, solid material, "and other discarded material" resulting from certain activities. In *American Mining Congress v. EPA* (known as *AMC I*), the American Mining Congress argued that wastes produced in its manufacturing processes should not be considered solid waste if they would later be used again in the process. The statutory definition of waste includes the catch-all phrase, "and other discarded material." Plaintiffs argued that the materials were not being "discarded" but, rather, recycled, instead.[5] To make this clearer, consider the diagram below of a hypothetical production process. The process turns squares into circles, and in so doing produces a by-product of triangles. If the triangles can be re-inserted back into the manufacturing process, are they discarded wastes (and therefore subject to RCRA) or raw materials?

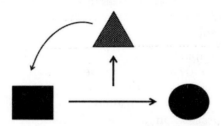

The D.C. Circuit agreed with the American Mining Congress that waste should not be considered discarded if it would later be used in an ongoing manufacturing process. The court held that the materials had "not yet become part of the waste disposal problem; rather, they are destined for beneficial reuse or recycling in a continuous process by the generating industry itself." The dissent took a more functional view. Promoting recycling is surely a goal of RCRA, but its overarching goal is environmental protection. Thus the main issue is whether the waste material creates the opportunity to cause environmental harm by spilling or leaking, even if it eventually will be recycled. If so, then EPA should be able to regulate it as a solid waste. After this decision, RCRA's definition of solid waste seemed to depend as much on the owner's plans for the materials as on the nature of the materials. Did the owner plan to dispose of the materials (in which case they were covered by RCRA) or re-use them in the process? As you might expect, this created an incentive not only for real recycling, but for "sham recycling," as well, stating you would re-use the materials in the manufacturing process but really just storing them on-site indefinitely to avoid the cost of disposal.

---

[5] *American Mining Congress v. United States EPA*, 824 F.2d 1177 (D.C.Cir.1987).

These problems were addressed in a subsequent case with the same parties, *American Mining Congress v. EPA* (known as *AMC II*).[6] Here, plaintiffs argued that sludge stored in a surface impoundment (a holding pond) should not be considered RCRA solid waste because it was being held for potential re-use (despite the fact that in the meantime the wastes might overflow or leak into other bodies of water). Cutting back on its earlier holding, the court stated that the recycling exemption only applies to wastes that are safely stored for *immediate re-use* in an *on-going process*. Otherwise, the materials become part of the waste disposal problem and must be regulated as solid waste. In practice, "immediate" has been interpreted to mean use within 90 days and "on-going process" to mean the same process. As a result of these cases and subsequent decisions, the by-products of a production process destined for recycling are not considered solid wastes if stored safely and used within 90 days in the same process (a practice known as closed-loop recycling). If any of these conditions are not met, these materials are regulated as solid waste.

A final example of how the same materials can receive different regulatory treatment may be found in *American Petroleum Institute v. EPA*.[7] Building off the logic of the *American Mining Congress* cases, plaintiffs argued that the by-products of a manufacturing process should not be considered solid waste once they arrive at a reclamation facility for recycling. Further distancing itself from the *AMC I* holding, however, the court declared that once waste arrives at a reclamation facility it remains solid waste because it has already become part of the waste disposal problem, even if it undergoes the *exact same process* it would have undergone at the original facility. In other words, the materials cannot shed their label of solid waste once they enter the waste stream, even if they clearly will be recycled. Unlike the children's game of Tag, RCRA doesn't provide a safe "base."

Taken together, these cases provide stark examples of the difficulties in drafting regulations. By-products processed on-site at a plant for re-use within 90 days are unregulated by RCRA, yet the identical treatment at an off-site reclamation facility is highly regulated. This different treatment of the same activities is perhaps an inevitable result of trying to develop regulations that encourage recycling while, at the same time, closing loopholes. Indeed, the greatest challenge in drafting regulations can lie in trying to fulfill the statute's intent while knowing full well that the regulated community will act strategically to take advantage of any

---

[6] 907 F.2d 1179 (D.C.Cir.1990).
[7] 906 F.2d 729 (D.C.Cir.1990).

possibility of favorable treatment. In this regard, it's instructive to note that EPA convened a task force in the early 1990s to create a better definition of "solid waste," one that promoted genuine rather than sham recycling. In its 1994 report, the task force proposed a comprehensive four–part classification for regulating different types of recycling. Due to its complexity, the proposal was never adopted. EPA revised its recycling exemptions for hazardous waste in 2008 and proposed further revisions in 2011.

2. *Solid Hazardous Waste and Closing Loopholes*

For any regulatory scheme to work, the regulated business has to know clearly what is required of it and the regulator needs to know how to verify this. Imagine, for a moment, that you were the EPA official in charge of identifying and defining the wastes that will be covered by RCRA. Intuitively, given the range of toxicity among various wastes it might seem most effective to distinguish among separate categories of waste, subjecting the most hazardous wastes to the most stringent controls. But this is easier said than done. Should the mere presence of a hazardous substance in a waste stream make the entire stream hazardous, or should there be some kind of assessment to determine the overall hazard it poses? Realize, as well, that there are tens of thousands of types of waste streams. Precision has a cost.

RCRA distinguishes between two broad categories of covered wastes. If a material is considered a solid waste, it is covered by Subtitle D. If it a solid waste *and* hazardous it falls under the more onerous coverage of Subtitle C. There is a much greater cost difference between treating Subtitle C and Subtitle D waste than treating Subtitle D waste and no treatment at all, so the regulated community cares a great deal about the definition of "hazardous waste."

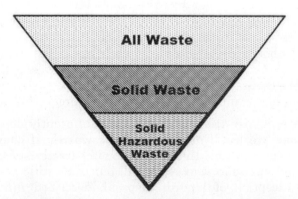

In contrast to determining whether or not materials are "solid waste" under RCRA or fall under the various exemptions, however, defining a material as a solid "hazardous waste" is relatively straightforward.

RCRA identifies two categories of hazardous waste—"listed wastes" and "characteristic wastes."[8] Listed wastes are, as the name suggests, substances that EPA has determined routinely contain hazardous constituents or exhibit hazardous qualities. These are listed in the Code of Federal Regulations. If a company produces a listed waste but believes that it should not be treated as hazardous waste, it may petition EPA to delist the waste but this can be an expensive and lengthy process.

It would be nice, of course, if EPA produced a comprehensive list of all hazardous wastes, but given the fact that over 50,000 chemicals are now used in commerce EPA is lucky to list even a fraction of the possible waste streams. Thus the second category identifies hazardous wastes by their characteristics. If a waste is not a listed waste but has the characteristics of being ignitable (i.e., products that are capable of causing fire during routine transportation, storage, or disposal), corrosive, reactive, or toxic then it is treated as a hazardous waste. While the burden of identifying listed wastes falls on EPA (since, after all, it creates the list), the burden of identifying characteristic wastes falls on the waste generators who must determine through standard tests whether their waste is ignitable, corrosive, reactive, or toxic. Hence the need for rigorous compliance monitoring by EPA.

Recall the previous discussion of how companies producing solid waste could avoid RCRA coverage if they satisfied the recycling exemption. Companies producing hazardous waste would clearly like to avoid Subtitle C coverage, as well. But how? As described above, they could petition for delisting of specific waste but this is an expensive process. They could also try to modify their waste so that it no longer has the characteristics of a hazardous waste. What happens when waste is transformed, either through mixing with other wastes, dilution, or synthesis into another compound? Should EPA regulate it as a hazardous waste (once a waste, always a waste), or has it escaped the coverage of Subtitle C? And with the thousands of sites using hazardous wastes in all kinds of processes, how can EPA ensure credible enforcement?

RCRA regulates treated wastes very differently depending on whether they are listed or characteristic wastes. If characteristic wastes no longer exhibit their hazardous characteristics, they are treated simply as solid waste and fall out of Subtitle C's coverage (with the exception of landfill disposal, described *infra*). Listed wastes, though, are subject to two rules. The *mixture rule* states

---

[8] 40 C.F.R. § 261.

that any mixture of a listed waste with another solid waste is *still* considered a hazardous waste (with an exemption for municipal solid waste).[9] The *derived from rule* requires that wastes derived from the treatment of a hazardous waste also be treated as hazardous wastes, such as sewage sludge or incinerator ash.[10] As a consequence, EPA has created a perverse variation on King Midas' tragic gift. Whereas everything Midas touched turned to gold, everything listed hazardous waste touches turns to more listed waste. The related *contained-in policy* holds that contaminated media (generally soil) becomes a hazardous waste. This has important consequences for CERCLA (discussed below), since contaminated soil at Superfund sites must often be treated as hazardous waste.

In combination with RCRA's broad exemptions, the mixture and derived from rules have created a bizarre situation. The rules require strict treatment of many wastes that are significantly less hazardous than wastes that are not covered *at all* because of the broad exemptions for wastewater discharges, mining wastes, etc. The increasingly quixotic dilemma of creating precise, clear, and fair definitions of solid and hazardous waste remains unresolved after more than four decades, frustrated by strategic behavior of firms seeking to avoid having their waste fall under these definitions.

B.　Who am I?

1.　Generators, Transporters and TSDs

Just as RCRA divides the waste world into solid waste and solid hazardous waste (listed and characteristic) with very different requirements for each, RCRA divides the world of actors into three categories—generators, transporters, and "treatment, storage, and disposal facilities" (TSDs). While each class of actor faces differing responsibilities, all must comply with the tracking requirements. RCRA follows the disposal of waste by establishing a "cradle-to-grave" tracking scheme from the generators of waste to transporters through to disposal facilities. In principle, if we know where the waste is at all times and ensure that people handling the waste at each stage act responsibly, then no worries. To this end, when a generator produces a threshold amount of hazardous waste it must obtain an identification number for the waste from EPA and fill out a "manifest." This sheet accompanies the waste shipment to its final disposal and, at each stage it changes hands, the manifest stays with the shipment while a copy is sent back to the generator.

---

[9]　40 C.F.R. § 261.3(a)(2).

[10]　40 C.F.R. § 261.3(c).

When the TSD finally receives the waste, it must inspect it to check that the contents match the manifest. This cradle-to-grave tracking ensures that the problem of unidentified wastes at contaminated sites, regulated by CERCLA and described later in this chapter, is not repeated.

In addition to the manifest requirements, generators are subject to a variety of requirements. Generators must determine if their waste is a listed or characteristic hazardous waste. They must also ensure proper storage and labeling of wastes, keep records of waste generation and test results, and submit periodic reports. For small companies, these requirements can prove quite resource intensive. Indeed, RCRA was drafted primarily to regulate facilities routinely generating large amounts of the same small number of waste streams. In some relatively new sectors such as the biomedical industry, however, scores of different waste streams are infrequently produced. RCRA's requirements have come to be seen as so ill-fitting that the state of California created a special task force to reform its regulation of laboratory wastes. As the economy continues its trend toward custom manufacturing and biotech, the regulatory fit of RCRA will continue to be challenged.

Transporters face fewer requirements, but must comply with EPA and Department of Transportation requirements for the transportation of hazardous materials (identified as "hazmat" on highway signs), including proper packaging and labeling, reporting, record keeping, and the manifest. These requirements take on added significance when one realizes that more than 3 billion tons of hazardous materials are transported each year, with over 800,000 shipments of these materials every day.

RCRA's requirements are *much* more onerous on TSDs than on generators or transporters. Many Superfund sites were formerly TSDs, and RCRA seeks to ensure not only clean operation but clean shut down at the end of the TSD's life. To operate, a TSD must obtain a permit from EPA or an authorized state agency. The permit process often lasts from two to four years and the permit is good for ten years. TSDs must satisfy a range of operating requirements that include personnel training, record keeping, groundwater monitoring, security, and technical standards. The technical standards are rigorous and require, for example, that landfills have two or more impermeable liners and a leachate collection system. With the problem of contaminated sites in mind, TSDs must also create comprehensive plans for closure. These address not only the closing of the facility but maintaining and monitoring the facility for a period of 30 years after closure. In addition, TSDs must provide financial assurance (through insurance, bonds, or other means) that they will have enough money to pay for closure as well as any consequent liability. While seemingly onerous, in light of the many TSDs that shut down with no resources, leaving only contaminated land beneath them, these requirements are important in ensuring companies do not strategically plan bankruptcy.

Amendments to RCRA in 1984 by the Hazardous and Solid Waste Amendments (HSWA)[11] provided another important tool to ensure that TSDs did not become Superfund sites. EPA was given authority to require that TSDs clean up present or past contamination on their sites following the release of a hazardous waste or constituent of a hazardous waste. Known as "corrective actions," these clean-ups may be enforced through a civil action or by suspending operating permits, and represent a clear example of CERCLA and RCRA moving closer together. Unlike CERCLA, however, corrective actions can include clean ups of petroleum and petroleum products (both of which are exempted from CERCLA's coverage), liability rests solely with the TSD owner or operator, and there have been over 5,000 corrective actions, far exceeding the number of CERCLA cleanups, though far smaller, as well.

2. The Land Ban and Regulatory Hammers

HSWA also took aim at landfills. By the mid-1980s, Subtitle C's requirements for generators, transporters, and TSDs had clearly succeeded in at least one area—raising the cost of waste disposal. By making waste disposal more expensive, one would expect waste production to go down. And if waste was produced then EPA had clear preferences for its disposal. This was reflected in the so-called "waste hierarchy," the accepted rule of thumb in managing waste.

---

first **reduce**

     then **re-use**

          then **recycle**

               then **landfill**

Raising the cost of waste disposal would certainly promote waste reduction, re-use, and recycling, but how to minimize landfill and the fear of groundwater contamination? HSWA greatly restricted the land disposal of wastes, requiring EPA to prohibit disposal of waste in landfills unless there will be "no migration" of hazardous constituents from the landfill. Although Congress could have stopped here, essentially banning the disposal of hazardous waste in landfills, it created an exception for wastes that had been

---

[11] Pub. L. No. 98–616 (1984).

treated to "substantially diminish the toxicity of the waste" or the migration of hazardous constituents. RCRA's "land ban," then, effectively prohibits the disposal only of *untreated* hazardous wastes. Fearful of the Reagan administration delaying implementation, Congress also included a unique "hammer" provision. It shifted the burden of regulatory delay from the agency to industry by providing that if pretreatment regulations were not issued for a particular waste by a particular date, there would be no land-based disposal of that waste *at all*. Needless to say, spurred on by industry interests EPA moved on the issue quickly.

The interesting question that Congress did not clearly answer, though, was how to determine the pre-treatment standards for hazardous waste. RCRA provides that pre-treatment standards must "substantially diminish the toxicity of the waste or substantially reduce the likelihood of migration of hazardous constituents from the waste so that short-term and long-term threats to human health and the environment are minimized." Does this mean that the standards should try to minimize the chances that any waste will ever migrate from landfills, pushing EPA to require the maximum treatment technologically possible? Or should the standards require pre-treatment only to the degree deemed sufficient to ensure that the waste is no longer hazardous to human health and the environment, even if greater treatment is feasible?

Put in simple terms, EPA was faced with two different approaches to protecting groundwater from landfilled waste. One approach would require pre-treatment based on *best available technology*—perhaps overtreating the waste to levels far below any proven health risk. The other would rely on *risk assessment*—treating the waste to a level with acceptable risks to health. This choice of regulatory strategies poses unavoidable trade-offs—technology-based regulations that are inflexible but relatively easy to administer versus more flexible (and arguably economically efficient) but more complex risk-based standards. We saw this very same conflict between technology-based and risk-based standards in our discussion of NAAQS in the Clean Air Act and technological standards in the Clean Water Act. In fact, it occurs throughout environmental law. At the end of the day, the "correct" implementation strategy depends on the regulator's priority, whether it be low cost of administration, impetus to force technological development, desire for potential over-treatment to reflect scientific uncertainty over health effects, or high cost of compliance to drive out marginal TSDs and create barriers to entry for new participants. EPA's final decision to go with a technology-based standard was largely upheld in the case, *Hazardous Waste Treatment Council v. EPA*.[12]

In navigating this regulatory shoal, EPA commenced with a hybrid approach, requiring pre-treatment by the best demonstrated available technology, but only to the degree necessary to move below the maximum concentration of a hazardous constituent that posed health concerns. In response to outrage by environmentalists and Congress (who basically argued that "no migration" means just that, and that a risk approach was inappropriate), EPA later moved to a pure technological approach. In so doing, however, it incurred the wrath of economists at the Office of Management and Budget (OMB), who estimated that the cost of the land ban exceeded $4 billion for each life saved.

While making good copy for columnists to decry yet another boneheaded decision by EPA, such monetary estimates warrant careful consideration. How did OMB treat uncertainties? Did they only consider lives saved through reduced cancer deaths? Did they value the benefit of avoided Superfund clean-ups in the future? What about the general impacts on waste reduction? Did they consider the possibility that treatment costs might drop in the future? While it's easy to pick apart the OMB estimate, it's equally worth noting that EPA's scientists have stated that groundwater contamination poses a relatively low health risk compared to other environmental hazards. Public polls, however, consistently rate groundwater contamination quite high on their list of environmental concerns. RCRA reflects the public perception but not, perhaps, the scientific community's. In a democracy, is this the appropriate result?

A final consequence of the land ban worth noting is the problem of media shifting. EPA's pre-treatment requirements increased the cost of landfill disposal of hazardous waste. Because waste disposal is a market, generators sought the cheapest disposal option and many settled on incineration. Following the land ban, there was a decline in waste sent to landfills and a significant increase in the amount of waste incinerated. Did the waste disappear? Of course not. It simply shifted form, from solid and liquid wastes to gaseous waste. It may be that environmentally this was a good thing, but only if incinerators release fewer contaminants than landfills. And that's far from clear, given that incinerators are major sources of heavy metals, dioxins, and furans in the environment.

---

[12] *Hazardous Waste Treatment Council v. EPA*, 886 F.2d 355 (D.C.Cir.1989); *Chemical Waste Management, Inc. v. EPA*, 976 F.2d 2 (D.C.Cir.1992).

RCRA Cheat Sheet Questions

Does my activity make me a: Generator
                                       Transporter
                                       TSD

Is the waste I am dealing with: exempted by statute
                                       municipal waste
                                       domestic sewage
                                       etc.

Is the waste "hazardous":   listed waste
                                       characteristic waste

Does the recycling exemption apply: ongoing process
                                       Immediate re-use

If a characteristic waste: can the character change
                                       by mixing
                                       by synthesis

If a listed waste, am I producing more waste by:
                                       the mixture rule
                                       the derived-from rule

If I am a TSD, must I take corrective action

C.   Subtitle D

Despite the importance of RCRA in regulating solid hazardous waste, the regulation of solid non-hazardous waste has largely remained the responsibility of state and local governments. And it's a *lot* of waste. In 2011, municipal solid waste accounted for 250 million tons of waste. As might be expected, although exempted from Subtitle C, municipal waste still contains some hazardous waste (e.g., from nickel-cadmium batteries). Subtitle D requires states to create plans that ensure responsible management of these wastes, from collection to disposal. EPA has also created regulations for the design and operation of landfills, ensuring for example that landfills not discharge pollutants into surface waters or engage in open burning. In a clear example of cooperative federalism, these regulations set minimum standards (e.g., no pretreatment requirements), and states are free to regulate landfills more strictly as, indeed, Pennsylvania, New York, and several other states have (Subtitle C delegates permitting authority to states, as well, so long as their programs are "equivalent" to and "consistent" with the federal program and provide for "adequate enforcement").

D.   The Challenge of Pollution Prevention

Despite its broad scope, it is important to note what RCRA does not cover. Consider the solid wastes involved in a typical manufacturing operation. The environmental impacts of the raw material inputs and product outputs are regulated, if at all, by other statutes such as TSCA and FIFRA (discussed in Chapter 8). The Occupational Safety and Health Administration regulates occupational exposure to contaminants during the process. RCRA, then, covers only the waste stream, a narrow subset of the total environmental impacts from manufacturing operations. And, as we have seen, not all wastes fall under RCRA. Congress intentionally chose not to regulate the manufacturing process, effectively treating the facility as a black box. Indeed, environmental law as a whole treats factories as giant black boxes, refusing to look at what happens inside. With rare exception, our pollution statutes only kick in when the waste leaves the facility, whether as air and water pollution or as solid waste.

This "end-of-pipe" approach has certainly been successful, given the improvements in air and water quality over the last three decades. Recycling has clearly increased as a result of RCRA. In 1960 only 6.4% of municipal solid waste was recycled. By 2011 it was approaching 35%. Even with recycling, though waste is still being produced that has to be managed. Wouldn't it be preferable not to produce the waste in the first place?

Indeed, it is not clear at all that this approach has been efficient, for in treating facilities as black boxes, our laws intentionally favor a business-as-usual attitude known as "pollution control." In a pollution control strategy, the company collects the waste from its processes and then ships them off in compliance with RCRA and other environmental laws. Waste disposal becomes a cost of doing business and the pollution control technologies—the filters, scrubbers and settling ponds—are nonproductive assets (insofar as they don't contribute to the bottom line). To be sure, RCRA has greatly increased the cost of waste disposal and this has provided an incentive for companies to reduce their waste generation. Because of the many exemptions, RCRA has provided an even greater incentive to manage the waste so that the waste falls out of RCRA's coverage, either through the recycling exemption, discharge to sewers, or some other exempted route. Recycling and composting, for example, diverted 87 million tons of material from landfills and incinerators in 2011, more than double the amount in 1990.

Instead of disposing of waste trapped at the end of the pipe, though, why not simply produce less waste in the first place? This strategy is known as "pollution prevention" (and in Europe as "cleaner production"). Indeed in many cases manufacturing waste is simply valuable raw material down the drain. Pollution prevention focuses on good housekeeping, waste audits, and closing production loops rather than more efficient waste treatment technologies at the end of the pipe. Why pay to dispose of waste when you can avoid producing it in the first place? Such strategies have allowed companies such as 3M, Dow, and S.C. Johnson to reduce their waste by over 50%, saving money in the process both through less loss of raw materials and avoided costs of waste disposal. RCRA, though, does little directly to promote a pollution prevention approach. Beyond the recycling exemption, RCRA doesn't care how the waste gets produced. Indeed one might argue that, by failing to go to the heart of the production process, RCRA misses the most important waste disposal issue of all—waste reduction at source. Put simply, RCRA is limited in its ability to solve the hazardous waste problem by the fact that it only deals with the results of the production process. It can only encourage reduction or recycling by making disposal less attractive.

PROBLEM EXERCISE: RECLAIMING LEAD FROM VEHICLE BATTERIES[13]

The year is 1986. There are approximately 70,000,000 vehicle batteries ready for disposal because they no longer work. Spent batteries can cause serious harm to people and animals living in the area where the battery may be discarded. Even a small number of batteries thrown into the woods, discarded along roadways or in government designated garbage areas represent a significant threat to the water we drink, the food we eat and under limited circumstances, the air we breathe. The source of this trouble in a battery is lead.

Because lead is an expensive commodity, an industry has developed over the years to reclaim the lead from spent batteries. The smelters themselves pose major environmental threats through their surface water run-off and discharged effluent, on-site and off-site storage, and air pollution. In 1986, 55,000,000 of the available 70,000,000 batteries were reclaimed, the source for 60% of all lead used in the United States. But this left 15,000,000 unreclaimed spent batteries, potentially endangering the health of people and the environment near the site of their disposal.

In sum, secondary lead smelting of batteries is both a dirty and vital industry. Without the industry, over 70,000,000 contaminated batteries would be scattered throughout the country annually.

The Interstate Lead Company, Inc. (ILCO) owned and operated a secondary lead smelting facility in Leeds, Alabama. In 1986, ILCO reclaimed over 2,500,000 batteries, or about 5% of those reclaimed in the

---

[13] Adapted from *United States v. Interstate Lead Company, Inc.*, 996 F.2d 1126 (11th Cir. 1993).

United States.

ILCO purchased batteries from various suppliers and placed them in a reclamation process. Incoming batteries were cracked open and drained of sulfuric acid. The rubber or black plastic battery boxes were chipped and washed to remove lead particles. The lead battery components known as "plates and groups" were then removed from the broken batteries and run through ILCO's smelting process to produce lead ingots for sale.

EPA has commenced a RCRA enforcement action against ILCO, arguing that the reclaimed lead plates and groups are waste products. Once the spent batteries were placed in the waste stream they were discarded and subject to RCRA. Somebody has discarded the battery in which these components are found. This fact does not change just because a reclaimer has purchased or finds value in the components.

ILCO counters that the lead plates and groups should be viewedas reclaimed material from spent car and truck batteries for recycling purposes, exempt from regulation under RCRA. ILCO never "discarded" the plates and groups and, therefore, the material it recycles is not RCRA "solid waste." Indeed, the lead plates and groups are valuable feedstock for a smelting process with a clear commercial value.

Assume you are the law clerk for the judge hearing this case.

- As a legal matter, should ILCO's reclamation of lead from the batteries be regulated as RCRA solid waste?

- As a policy matter, do you think RCRA should cover this type of activity?

II. The Comprehensive Environmental Response, Compensation and Liability Act

Arguably the most contentious and, certainly for lawyers and consultants, the most profitable environmental law has been the Comprehensive Environmental Response, Compensation and Liability Act (CERCLA, known popularly as "Superfund").[14] While RCRA addresses the issue of *current* waste disposal through a command-and-control approach, CERCLA responds to problems from *prior* waste disposal practices and imposes liability to ensure the cleanup of contaminated sites. It is this imposition of liability, however, that has sparked harsh criticism over CERCLA's fairness and cost effectiveness.

To understand the drama surrounding CERCLA, one must go back in time to upstate New York and the amorously named town of Love Canal, near Niagara Falls. In the 1960s and 1970s, a number of Love Canal residents began complaining of a series of medical problems, ranging from chronic headaches and skin rashes to

---

[14] 42 U.S.C. §§ 9601–9675.

seemingly high incidences of cancer, birth defects, and miscarriages. Soil samples in 1978 revealed high levels of chemical contaminants in the soil and air. Further study uncovered that much of Love Canal had been built on top of a landfill containing over 21,000 tons of chemical wastes. Covered with a layer of clay in 1952, the site had been sold by the Hooker Chemical Company to the Niagara Falls Board of Education for $1 and subsequently developed into houses and schools. The buried wastes, though, had broken through the clay liner and were seeping into the soil and basements. As news of the health threat became a national story, President Jimmy Carter declared a State of Emergency, permanently relocating 239 families in the houses that encircled the landfill area. The toxics had migrated, however, and the next year federal funding was provided for the permanent relocation of all 900 residents of Love Canal.

The tragedy of Love Canal had exposed a gap in the nation's hazardous waste regulation. While FIFRA and TSCA (described in Chapter 8) regulated the manufacture, distribution, and use of commercial chemicals, and RCRA regulated the disposal of hazardous wastes, no law effectively addressed hazardous wastes that had been buried years earlier and mostly forgotten. Responding to public cries for immediate action, Congress moved to pass a law but faced significant uncertainties.

How many potential Love Canals were out there? There was an unknown number of sites leaking toxics into the soil. Some of these likely posed serious threats to drinking water supplies. At some sites, it was possible to identify the waste and where it had come from, but in many cases the nature and origin of the wastes were unknown. Because RCRA had been passed just three years earlier, recordkeeping was spotty. Indeed some sites were likely still buried beneath prime real estate; others were abandoned sites cluttered with rusting barrels, their owners bankrupt or out of business. In the face of such vexing unknowns, to meaningfully address the problem of contaminated sites the draft legislation had to deal with four basic challenges.

The first was how to *identify and prioritize* the problem sites. Clearly the sites posing the greatest risks should be remediated first, but where were these? How could EPA find out about them? The second basic challenge was to decide *who should perform the cleanup.* If government took charge, presumably the cleanups would occur more quickly, though industry claimed that it could manage cleanups more efficiently. Of all the potential parties with responsibility for contamination of the site, which should be responsible for cleaning it up? The landowners, waste generators, transporters, past owners of the site? Third, and related, *who should pay for the cleanup?* One could imagine public funding through general tax revenues or a special tax on hazardous chemicals. If it is desirable to implement the "polluter pays" principle, though, the cost should fall on the potentially responsible parties listed above. But do they all share the same culpability? Finally, EPA needed to decide the question of *how clean is clean*. At what point can the cleanup stop? Should there be national standards or site-by-site determinations? Should the dirt be clean enough to eat?

To place Congress' dilemma in a more domestic setting, imagine you held a big party last night while your parents were out of town. You've just woken up, seen that the house is a mess, and realized your parents return in 45 minutes. You don't have time to clean up everything, but where do you start? The living room, the bathroom, or the kitchen? Is your strategy one of permanent cleanup (mops and bucket) or containment (shove everything in the closet)? Do you clean up yourself or wake up the other potentially responsible partygoers and have them work, as well? And finally, how clean does the house have to be to avoid being grounded?

The sections that follow explain the structure of CERCLA, but as you read them it is important to keep in mind the challenges described above. In understanding CERCLA, one needs to consider not only the problems Congress was trying to address but the options they didn't choose, for the law could have looked very different and, in fact, has been evolving since its passage. In this regard, it is interesting to note that, while U.S. environmental laws such as the Clean Air Act and the National Environmental Policy Act have served as admirable models for laws in many other countries, *no* country has followed the approach set out in CERCLA.

A final insight into CERCLA lies in the nature of its passage. While various contaminated land bills had been considered prior to 1979, CERCLA was passed by Congress and signed into law in a remarkably fast period, during the "lame duck" Congressional session between President Carter's electoral defeat and President Reagan's taking office. As a result, not only is there scant legislative history, but the law itself is not well drafted. And resentful at having a law forced down its throat just prior to taking office, the Reagan administration was both ideologically and politically opposed to CERCLA, obstructing its implementation so aggressively that EPA's reputation was damaged, with high-profile resignations and even a jail term for an EPA official.

A.   *The Cleanup Process*

In many respects, CERCLA is a simple statute. Unlike RCRA or other major environmental laws, CERCLA itself doesn't require anyone to do anything beyond one requirement. Any person who knows of a release of a reportable quantity of hazardous waste must notify EPA. That's it. So much for the command-and-control approach. The rest of the statute creates a process for cleaning up contaminated sites through two basic grants of power. First, it gives the government the power to compel parties to clean up releases of hazardous substances from a facility. Second, it gives government and private parties the authority to recover the costs of cleanup. These simple powers allow parties both to force cleanups and to allocate their costs, with enormous indirect effects on the treatment and disposal of waste.

1. Listing and Prioritization of Sites

To determine which sites should be cleaned up first, EPA created a National Priority List (NPL) of the most seriously contaminated sites.[15] Those sites presenting the greatest danger to public health, welfare, or the environment are ranked higher, according to their score based on the Hazard Ranking System, a formula that takes into account a site's toxicity, proximity to local population, potential to contaminate drinking water, etc. The NPL has grown substantially every year since 1985 and, as of May 2013, over 1320 sites were listed. It is important to note, of course, that many more sites are proposed for listing than actually are placed on the NPL. Since the program's creation in 1980, EPA has completed over 91,000 remedial assessments.

2. Responses

CERCLA kicks in whenever there has been a "release" or a "substantial threat" of a release of a "hazardous substance" into the environment from a "facility."[16] As with all of CERCLA's provisions, these terms have been broadly defined and interpreted. "Release," for example, has been defined to include "any spilling, leaking, pumping, pouring, emitting, emptying, discharging, injecting, escaping, leaching, dumping, or disposing into the environment"[17]— in sum, virtually any event where a hazardous substance could be released from its container (indeed, the definition calls to mind a young Capitol Hill staffer eagerly copying from a thesaurus). A "substantial threat of release" is even broader, covering hazardous substances still contained in corroding tanks or abandoned drums. While there are exemptions from this definition, including workplace releases and emissions from autos and other vehicles, they have been narrowly interpreted. Consider, for example, the

---

[15] 42 U.S.C. § 9605(1)(8)(A).

[16] 42 U.S.C. § 9607(1).

[17] 42 U.S.C. § 9601(22).

case of *State of Vermont v. Staco*,[18] where workers in a thermometer factory were found to have released hazardous substances by wearing clothes with mercury residue (washing their clothes had contaminated the public sewage system and septic tanks).

The definition of "hazardous substance" is likewise very broad. Going beyond RCRA, it includes almost any substance considered hazardous under another pollution statute as well as substances that EPA determines "may present an imminent and substantial danger to the public health or environment."[19] Of special significance to leaking underground storage tanks, petroleum and natural gas are specifically exempted from coverage.

While a "facility" would obviously include a chemical plant or landfill, its definition under CERCLA is broad, as well, extending to virtually any type of place or structure, including "any building, structure, installation, equipment, pipe or pipeline, well, pit, pond, lagoon, impoundment, ditch, landfill, storage container, motor vehicle, rolling stock, or aircraft" as well as any place where a hazardous substance "has been deposited, stored, disposed of, or placed, or otherwise come to be located."[20] In fact, except for consumer products in their containers (which are specifically exempted), it's hard to think of much that wouldn't be considered a facility. The term has even been held to include a North Carolina roadside that had been sprayed with PCB-contaminated oil.[21]

Once the threat of release of a hazardous substance from a facility has been established (which, as noted above, is generally easy to do), CERCLA authorizes two types of cleanups. A "removal" action is short term, intended to alleviate immediate dangers to the public health or environment.[22] These are the emergency actions you see on the evening news with folks walking around in moon suits working behind chain link fences. EPA generally carries out these actions quickly to reduce the most significant hazards, in the expectation that longer-term actions will be necessary.

The second, and more common, type of response is known as "remediation." This is a longer-term action, seeking to provide a permanent remedy to the maximum extent practicable.[23] Clean-up approaches can range from the blunt approach of digging up all the contaminated soil and disposing of it as RCRA hazardous waste to pumping clean water into the site through wells and then pumping

---

[18] 684 F. Supp. 822, 832 (D.Vt.1988).

[19] 42 U.S.C. § 9601(14).

[20] 42 U.S.C. § 9601(9).

[21] *United States v. Ward*, 618 F. Supp. 884 (E.D.N.C.1985).

[22] 42 U.S.C. § 9601(23).

[23] 42 U.S.C. § 9601(24).

out now contaminated water (i.e., effectively diluting the waste). There are other common technologies, but all are expensive; indeed cleanups can easily run into the millions of dollars. All cleanups must follow the requirements set out in the National Contingency Plan (NCP), including provisions for extensive remedial investigations and feasibility studies (known as RI/FS), public consultation requirements, etc. If the NCP "recipe" of mandatory procedures is not followed, then CERCLA's grant of authority to recover costs will not apply.

B. Compensation for Response Actions

There are three types of response actions allowed under CERCLA, all driven by the central premise that the taxpayer should not foot the bill for cleanup costs. First, EPA can carry out the cleanup itself and sue the potentially responsible parties (known as PRPs) later in a cost recovery action. For initial funds to pay for the cleanup, EPA was supposed to draw from the "Superfund," a big pot funded primarily by chemical and petroleum taxes. CERCLA originally authorized a Superfund of $1.6 billion and the 1986 amendments increased this to $8.5 billion (the tax expired in 1995). At the time, this was viewed as a great innovation because the cleanup could go ahead quickly without having to wait for liability to be assessed in the courts. The idea was that the fund would be drawn down from time to time, but would replenish itself from private party contributions. Reimbursement, though, has proven more troublesome than anticipated. While cleanups went ahead, the Superfund was quickly drawn down because PRPs more often sued EPA than paid up.

To avoid drawing down the Superfund, EPA's other option is to order PRPs to perform the cleanup. This avoids the problem of delay because CERCLA does not allow any pre-enforcement review of such orders.[24] Thus if EPA orders you to conduct a remediation, you have only two choices. You can disobey and challenge the order in court, but you had better win because you risk fines adding up to $37,500 per day plus treble final cleanup costs. More likely, you can comply and then sue to recover costs either from the Superfund, on the ground that you are not a PRP or that the cleanup order was arbitrary or capricious, or from other PRPs to share the costs in what are known as contribution actions.

A third form of compensation applies to private parties that have cleaned up a site. Recall that a site need not be on the NPL for CERCLA to apply. So long as there has been a release or threatened release of a hazardous substance from a facility, a private party can

---

[24] 42 U.S.C. § 9613(h).

clean up the site (in a manner consistent with the NCP) and sue other PRPs to recover costs. Through this route there is no need for prior EPA approval or, for that matter, any government supervision at all.

CERCLA also authorizes the federal and state governments and Indian tribes to sue for "natural resource damages" to pay for both the restoration and cost of damaged resources.[25] Estimating such costs requires, in most cases, use of shadow pricing methodologies such as contingent valuation because there are no commercial markets for natural resources such as threatened species or the ecosystem service of nutrient filtering. There is no private right of action to recover natural resource damages.

1. Potentially Responsible Parties (PRPs)

As should be clear from the discussion above, under CERCLA the bill ultimately ends up in the hands of PRPs. CERCLA establishes four broad classes of PRPs: (1) current owners and operators of a facility (even if they were not owners when disposal occurred); (2) prior owners or operators at the time of disposal; (3) arrangers of disposal or treatment (often called "generators"); and (4) transporters (*if* they played a substantial role in selecting the facility).[26] As with the rest of the statute, the definitions of PRPs are exceedingly broad. Thus, for example, the category of prior owners and operators could include someone who bought the property *after* the waste had been buried and *before* it was discovered so long as releases occurred (e.g., underground barrels continued to leak).[27] The key question for anyone involved with CERCLA, then, quickly dissolves into who's a PRP. For those caught up in Superfund liability, the experience can descend into a tragi-comedy entitled, "why PRPs pay," or, more accurately, "why it pays not to be a PRP."

2. Liability Standards

While the categories of PRPs set out who *potentially* might pay, CERCLA's kicker and most controversial provision concerns liability—who actually *does* pay. CERCLA does not explicitly refer to a standard of liability. In an awkward form of legislative drafting, the statute refers to Section 311 of the Clean Water Act's oil spill response program. This, in turn, refers to common law principles which, in turn, courts have interpreted to be the standard

---

[25] 42 U.S.C. § 9607(f)(1).

[26] 42 U.S.C. § 9607(a).

[27] *Nurad, Inc. v. William E. Hooper and Sons*, 966 F.2d 837 (4th Cir.1992). *But see Carson Harbor Village v. Unocal Corp.*, 270 F.3d 863 (9th Cir.2001) (holding that passive migration of wastes is not disposal).

of strict, joint, and several liability. The strict liability provision does away with the need for proof of negligence, intent, or harm. So long as there was a release or threatened release of a hazardous substance from a facility, response costs were incurred consistent with the NCP, and the party is a PRP, it's on the hook. The thinking behind relaxing the causation requirement was, ironically, that it would avoid disputes over apportionment. By moving away from the need to show proximate responsibility (or, indeed, that a PRP's actions actually caused any harm), the liability net could be cast far wider than under a common law standard of negligence. Effectively the burden of proof has been shifted from the government to PRPs.

The joint and several provision means that, in theory, a single party could be liable for all the costs even if 20 other parties were also PRPs. While helping ensure cleanup costs can be collected, a strict, joint and several liability standard creates significant fairness concerns. A PRP who pays for the government's cleanup costs can bring a contribution action against other PRPs, and courts can, at their discretion, rely on equitable factors to allocate the costs among the PRPs who are parties to the contribution action. But not all PRPs may be available to contribute toward the cleanup costs. Some contributors to the harm, for example, may be bankrupt. Others may be unknown. As a result, current PRPs must shoulder the burden of paying for these "orphan shares." Moreover, by making all PRPs potentially responsible for the cleanup, there is an incentive for PRPs to implicate as many other PRPs as possible. Thus CERCLA's retroactive joint and several liability has unexpectedly hit a wide range of actors, including federal, state, and city governments, manufacturers, financial institutions, charities, and small businesses. While a bonanza for lawyers and engineers, the high transaction costs in locating and negotiating with PRPs have diverted a great deal of money away from actual cleanups. Moreover, a strict, joint and several liability standard can easily lead to a search for "deep pockets," those PRPs who may not bear much responsibility but have the resources to pay for the cleanup.

The biggest concern raised by the retroactive liability standards and broad categories of PRPs, though, is that of fairness. While such general categories of PRPs help ensure that the taxpayer will not end up paying for the cleanup, it is worth considering whether there is a principled reason to hold many of the PRPs liable. Can they all fairly be thought of as polluters? And is it fair to hold them liable for actions taken years ago that were completely legal at the time? Where is the fairness, for example, in holding a chemical company liable today for shipping its waste back in 1950, in full compliance with the law, to an operating landfill facility that was improperly shut down in 1970? Despite such examples, and there are many others, the SARA amendments to Superfund in 1986 left the liability provisions intact.[28] The traditional explanation for these liability provisions has been that owners, operators, generators, and transporters benefited from the low costs associated with waste disposal practices in the past and should bear the cleanup costs when they arise. You reap what you sow.

C. Defenses

Because CERCLA's liability net has been cast extremely wide, there has been an enormous amount of litigation to find defenses for PRPs. Subsequent amendments to CERCLA have also created a few opportunities to reduce, though usually not escape, liability. These are addressed below.

1. Acts of God, War, or a Third Party

CERCLA exempts releases caused by an "act of God," an "act of war," or an act of a third party.[29] Defenses based on the act of God and war exemptions, though, have met with little success since courts have held that so long as unexpected natural events such as heavy rains, floods, earthquakes, pestilence, raining frogs, or other disasters could be anticipated, the exemption only applies to exceedingly rare and unforeseeable circumstances. CERCLA also provides an escape from liability for PRPs who can establish that the release was caused by the act or omission of a third party (other than an employee or agent of the defendant or someone in a contractual relationship with the defendant) and the PRP exercised due care. Soon after CERCLA's passage, this was held out as a significant defense, but note that the defense does not apply where there is any direct or indirect relationship between the defendant and the person or organization responsible for the release. If a company sends its product to X for fabrication and X disposes of wastes improperly, the company can be liable under CERCLA.[30] However, a selling party is not liable as an arranger for incidental spills during movement and transfer resulting from the "legitimate sale of unused, useful product" unless some portion of the product is intended for disposal during the transfer process. Parent companies also can be held liable for their subsidiaries' past activities.

---

[28] Pub. L. No. 99–499, 100 Stat. 1613 (1986).

[29] 42 U.S.C. § 9607(b)(1).

[30] *See United States v. Aceto Agric. Chems. Corp.*, 872 F.2d 1373 (8th Cir.1989).

2. Divisibility

Joint and several liability can be avoided if a PRP can show its waste is divisible. One might think this would be easy to show. Imagine, for example, that you have records showing you sent 100 barrels of waste to a Superfund site of 1,000 barrels. Yes, you contributed and are willing to help fund the cleanup, but shouldn't you be potentially liable for only 10% of the response costs? After all, you can show that you only contributed one in ten barrels. This might make sense in the abstract, but only if the waste had not leaked from the barrels. If the waste has escaped (which is likely since it's a Superfund site), then it has also mixed with the *other* waste in the site. Thus, because of diffusion in the soil, to remove your waste from the site you would need to remove *all* of the waste from the site because it has all commingled.[31] Note that EPA does not have to show that a particular PRP's waste leaked (or even that waste like it has leaked). It is sufficient that the PRP's waste was simply present and that response costs were incurred. The burden falls squarely on the PRP to demonstrate that its harm is divisible and capable of apportionment.

In the past, most courts and the EPA have as a matter of course imposed joint and several liability on PRPs, with divisibility defenses having little success. The Supreme Court in 2009, however, held in *Burlington Northern* that, in spite of the fact that a contamination event may cause a single harm, such harm may still be divisible if the defendant demonstrates a rational basis for apportionment.[32] Looking to the Restatement (Second) of Torts § 433A(1)(b), the Supreme Court held that apportionment is proper when "there is a reasonable basis for determining the contribution of each cause to a single harm" and that CERCLA defendants bear the burden of proving that a rational basis for apportionment exists. Thus when the government brings a cost recovery suit, the defendants can present volumetric, geographic, and chronological evidence of their specific contribution and the court can apportion the costs among the named defendants based on the sufficiency of evidence.

BURLINGTON NORTHERN & SANTA FE RAILWAY
v. UNITED STATES
556 U.S. 599 (2009)

Shell Oil Co. sold and shipped chemicals to Brown & Bryant, Inc. (B&B), an agricultural chemical distributor. Part of B&B's

---

[31] *See, O'Neil v. Picillo*, 883 F.2d 176, 178 (1st Cir.1989).

[32] *Burlington Northern & Santa Fe Railway v. United States*, 556 U.S. 599 (2009).

facility was located on land leased from the Burlington Northern & Santa Fe Railway Company and Union Pacific Railroad Company. Shell was aware that when the chemical was transferred from tanker trucks to bulk storage tanks some spills were occurring. Shell required all purchasing distributors to implement a program to control the spills. Nevertheless, spills continued to occur on the railroad property and the distributor's property. After undertaking some remediation efforts required by the EPA, B&B went bankrupt and the site was listed on the NPL. EPA spent $8 million in cleanup and brought suit against Shell and the railroad companies for reimbursement of costs.

The district court determined that Shell was liable as an arranger and the Railroads as an owner of the land upon which the facility operated. Unexpectedly, the court then determined to apportion the costs 9% to the Railroads and 6% to Shell, rather than imposing joint and several liability. The Court of Appeals reversed the apportionment and imposed joint and several liability for the entire costs. In a surprising decision, the Supreme Court reversed the Appeal Court on the matter of joint and several liability and the District Court on the matter of arranger liability.

The Court found that sufficient geographic, volumetric, and chronological evidence existed to uphold the district court's 9% allocation to the Railroads—consideration of the smaller size of the Railroad parcel in relation to the facility (19%), the shorter length of time the Railroad parcel was used by the facility in relation to the spills (45%), and the lesser volume of injurious spills occurring on the Railroad property (66%). The district court's apportionment based on multiplication of these geographic, chronological, and volumetric measures (and addition of a 50% margin of error) was sufficiently based in fact.

Concerning the question of whether Shell was an arranger, the Court first acknowledged that an arranger is typically a person who enters a contract for disposal of a no longer useful product and is not a person who merely sells to another party that later improperly disposes. The grey area between "sale" and "disposal", such as arrangements when one party is aware that disposal is occurring or when motivations for the sale are unclear, is a fact intensive inquiry. The Court held, however, that an entity qualifies as an arranger when it takes intentional steps to dispose of a hazardous substance, i.e., there must be the requisite intent to dispose. Awareness of spills does not implicate a planned disposal, especially when occurring incidentally in the sale of a useful, un-used product. Shell's effort to reduce the spills demonstrated it lacked intent to dispose.

3.   Small Contributors

The real tear jerker in any CERCLA Congressional hearing often used to come from the testimony from the owners of Ma and Pa Store, who relate how they spent their life savings in legal fees because they were sued as PRPs for a few barrels they sent to a landfill years ago. To address this possibility, if EPA determines that a PRP contributed a minimal amount of hazardous waste compared to other wastes at the site or, as the property owner, the PRP did not permit the hazardous waste to be stored or have reason to know of its prior storage, EPA can reach an early "de minimis" settlement with the PRP. This settlement includes complete absolution from additional or future liability, in return for the payment of a premium over what would otherwise be a fair share.[33] For even smaller contributors, if PRPs of an NPL site can show they contributed less than 110 gallons of liquid or less than 200 pounds of solid material prior to April, 2001, then they can qualify for a "de micromis" exemption,[34] meaning EPA will not pursue any contribution, but will enter a zero dollar settlement to protect them from other PRPs seeking contribution. These two exemptions do not apply if the waste has or could contribute significantly to the response action. In a fee-shifting arrangement to cut down on litigation, if exempt parties are sued by other PRPs, they are entitled to recover costs and attorney fees.[35] A similar exemption has been created for small businesses, residential property owners and operators, and nonprofits who sent municipal solid waste (i.e., household garbage) to NPL sites.[36]

4.   Municipalities

Municipalities are an equally good poster child for CERCLA's unfairness. Entirely passive in the reception of waste, towns' and cities' landfills often turn out to have received hazardous wastes, thus potentially qualifying them as CERCLA sites. EPA has long had a policy of not going after municipalities for cost recovery actions. Nothing in the statute, however, prevents PRPs from suing municipalities for private contribution. Indeed, more than 650 municipalities and counties in 12 states have been sued as PRPs for contribution claims.

5.   Lenders

CERCLA excludes owners and operators from liability if they hold an "indicia of ownership" in the property primarily as a

---

[33] 42 U.S.C. § 9622(g).

[34] 42 U.S.C. § 9607(o)(1).

[35] 42 U.S.C. § 9607(o)(4).

[36] 42 U.S.C. § 9607(p).

security interest. The narrow scope of this exemption has proven controversial in the context of banks that foreclose on real estate. In the case of *United States v. Fleet Factors Corp.*, for example, the court sent shivers down the spines of bankers by holding that the bank's foreclosure on a future CERCLA site qualified it as a PRP because it had been actively involved in the property's management.[37] Banks that took over outright ownership would become PRPs, as well. Courts took divergent positions on lender liability, with the 11th Circuit assigning broad liability and the 9th Circuit much narrower. Which position makes for better policy? In favor of making banks liable, recognize that lenders can act as effective gatekeepers (or even surrogate regulators), ensuring that borrowers are environmentally responsible with their waste disposal. Lenders are very careful about the financial solvency of those to whom they lend money; why not make them scrutinize environmental records, as well? This approach leverages the influence of financial institutions over the behavior of their debtors. And if banks are protected after property foreclosures, where is the incentive for them to ensure the waste on the property is properly taken care of? Finally, to be blunt, banks have deep pockets (or at least used to) and should be able to fund cleanups.

Nonetheless, it's not clear that these arguments favor unlimited liability. After all, unlike insurance companies, lenders never have served as effective gatekeepers for environmental harms. It's simply not in their area of expertise. Moreover, because of the potential risk involved, making banks liable could dry up credit (or make it exceptionally expensive) for companies handling waste. Indeed, after the decision in *Fleet Factors*, Fleet announced that it would not lend money unless a borrower had environmental liability insurance. And if companies who handle hazardous waste cannot get financing, they will be more likely to do things on the cheap or won't be able to remedy problems.

In 1996, Congress resolved this debate by passing the Asset Conservation, Lender Liability, and Deposit Insurance Protection Act, adding a new section to CERCLA.[38] Banks can foreclose on property "if the person seeks to sell . . . or otherwise divest . . . the vessel or facility . . . at the earliest practicable, commercially reasonable time, on commercially reasonable terms, taking into account market conditions and legal and regulatory requirements." To lose the exemption, a bank must (1) exercise decisionmaking over environmental compliance, or (2) exercise overall management

---

[37] *United States v. Fleet Factors Corp.*, 901 F.2d 1550, 1557–58 (11th Cir.1990).
[38] 42 U.S.C. § 9601(20)(E).

control. As we shall see in the case of brownfields, below, even this level of protection has left banks fearful.

6. Innocent Landowners

As originally drafted, CERCLA imposed liability on all current owners of contaminated property. Responding to complaints over unjust results, in the SARA amendments in 1986 Congress extended the third party defense to "innocent landowners."[39] To qualify, the property owner must have undertaken "all appropriate inquiry" before purchasing the property and have no "actual or constructive knowledge" of the hazardous substances. In principle, this should ensure that prospective purchasers fully inspect the land and history prior to purchase. The "all appropriate inquiry" requirement has been elevated to a high standard in order to ensure that new owners cannot avoid liability simply by sniffing the air or kicking up some dirt prior to purchase. Amendments in 2002 covered not only innocent landowners but also a bona fide prospective purchaser or a contiguous property owner. To undertake "all appropriate inquiries," a prospective purchaser must employ an environmental specialist to conduct interviews with previous owners, review historical data and government records, visually inspect the site and adjoining property, document environmental conditions, and determine the degree of obviousness of the presence of contamination and whether detectible. The prospective purchaser must also inquire into environmental liens, whether the purchase price is close to fair market value, and any other commonly known information.[40]

In an innovative policy, New Jersey imposed greater responsibilities on current landowners in its 1983 law, the Environmental Cleanup Responsibility Act (ECRA).[41] ECRA required an owner to demonstrate, before selling, transferring, or closing industrial and commercial property, that the property was not contaminated by hazardous substances. Failure to comply with ECRA entitled the buyer to recover damages from the previous owner. This law thus sought to ensure that sites were remediated *before* sale by creating a disincentive for sellers to play dumb. By 1991, ECRA had resulted in more than 1,700 clean-up actions. Concerned over ECRA's effect on the real estate market, however, the cleanup standards were relaxed in a 1993 amendment re-naming the law as the Industrial Site Recovery Act.

---

[39] 42 U.S.C. § 9601(35).

[40] Codified at 42 U.S.C. §§ 9601(40), 9607(r).

[41] N.J. Stat. Ann. 13:1K–6 to K–14.

7. Settlement Strategies

As these brief descriptions make clear, PRPs have had few viable defenses when faced with cost recovery or contribution actions, though the *Burlington Northern* case may shift this balance. PRPs who have strong evidence demonstrating divisibility based on geography, chronology, or volume may face less pressure to enter into early settlements in order to avoid paying the majority of the costs under joint and several liability. Going forward, it remains to be seen not only how EPA settlement practice evolves but whether courts will interpret the *Burlington Northern* decision broadly or narrowly.

Nevertheless, the strict liability imposed on PRPs still forces potential PRPs to become their brother's keeper. In other words, once a bank or real estate developer or chemical company realizes that the actions of parties it lends to, buys property from, or sends products to for fabrication can result in their becoming a PRP, they take a really close look. By driving liability *deep* into the transaction, formerly remote players are forced to act as surrogate regulators. This way, it becomes in everyone's interest to ensure that waste is disposed of properly so that new Superfund sites do not arise, sucking every related party into a vortex of liability and recrimination. As the next section explains, however, forcing banks and real estate developers to act as gatekeepers comes at a cost and can have impacts in unexpected places.

D. Brownfields

In many cities today, large tracts of downtown real estate sit idle and derelict because no one will develop them. CERCLA unintentionally plays a role in this. Since many of these sites were former industrial areas, developers have often been wary of purchasing them because they do not want to become PRPs if the sites are discovered to be contaminated. And even if they do want to develop them, financing from banks may be hard to come by. State law plays a role, as well. In New Jersey, as noted above, the ECRA law effectively restricted the sale of contaminated property. If a current owner was unwilling to fund a clean-up (and unable to obtain the funds from the prospective buyer), she couldn't sell the parcel. Such unwanted parcels are known as "brownfields," defined by EPA as "abandoned, idle, or under-used industrial and commercial facilities where expansion or redevelopment is complicated by real or perceived environmental contamination."

In simple terms, then, the "brownfields problem" is that lenders and developers are wary of associating with abandoned sites once used for industrial and commercial purposes. These properties can range from NPL sites to simply dirty areas with no serious contaminants. Investors, however, fear they may find themselves liable for the cleanup of contamination they did not create. As a result, brownfields sit vacant while developers seek clean sites outside the city. These suburban sites are, appropriately enough, known as "greenfields." This trend increases sprawl, takes potential economic development opportunities away from the city, and leaves the inner city sites derelict

The brownfields problem has proven divisive, with community groups battling each other over the proper approach. Leaving urban sites undeveloped, some argue, benefits no one. By working to develop such sites, local jobs are created, the urban tax base is restored, and communities are strengthened. Others, however, contend that this is a case of environmental injustice since, they charge, EPA has been willing to adjust cleanup standards depending on what the site will be used for, with less protection for commercial developments than residential properties. Development on contaminated land is worse than no development at all.

Both federal and state governments have actively been seeking to reduce brownfield problems. Grants have been offered by the Department of Housing and Urban Development and the EPA, and tax breaks are available that allow developers of brownfields to write off their cleanup costs in the year they are incurred rather than over several years. EPA also actively pruned the NPL list of potential sites, hoping to remove the taint associated with potential listing. And even for sites on the NPL, EPA has offered "prospective purchaser agreements" where it pledges not to bring a CERCLA action if the prospective purchaser can (1) demonstrate it is not linked to the site's contamination, and (2) show the agreement would produce environmental benefits. Forty-seven states plus D.C. and Puerto Rico also provide for voluntary cleanup programs that act as a shield from enforcement actions. Despite these programs and others, brownfields remain a concern in large part because of the commercial community's desire to stay clear of the long shadow cast by "CERCLA horror stories," whether true or not. As noted above, the government has attempted to address these concerns by providing greater protections for innocent landowners and bona fide purchasers. In addition, significant funding has been provided for brownfields development. In 2012 alone, over $65 million in grants were approved by the EPA.

E.   How Clean Is Clean?

Environmental justice issues have also arisen over the proper level of remediation at a contaminated site. Imagine, for example, that you are the EPA official in charge of three Superfund sites: one beside an inner city nursery school, one in a cornfield 40 miles from the nearest town, and one in a national wildlife refuge in northern Alaska. Should they be equally clean after remediation? Should the goal even be to make all the sites "clean"? What role should cost play in your decision? And how would your views differ if your child went to that school, the cornfield was on your land, you hiked every summer in the refuge, or, conversely, you were the PRP footing the bill for the cleanup?

The issue of "how clean is clean" was never resolved in CERCLA, with Congress leaving much discretion to EPA. The 1986 SARA amendments require EPA to take into account a variety of factors, including, among others, a preference for permanent on-site solutions that significantly reduce hazards (over offsite transport and disposal), remediation that assures the protection of human health and the environment, and the often conflicting standard of a solution that is cost effective.[42] Making EPA's task even more difficult, if there are legally relevant and appropriate standards covering the site's hazardous substance, the level of cleanup must satisfy their requirements. In plain English, these so-called ARARs (Applicable, Relevant and Appropriate Requirements) are intended to harmonize the requirements of CERCLA with those of other environmental laws, allowing their standards to function as CERCLA cleanup standards. But it is not at all clear, critics contend, why a standard from the Safe Drinking Water Act for, say, benzene, should be used as the remediation target in a CERCLA cleanup unless the soil is likely to filter groundwater for drinking. The net effect of these various factors and ARARs is that EPA exercises great discretion in every cleanup. Environmental justice advocates, for example, have argued that cleanups in poor areas often use less stringent ARARs and less permanent solutions.

What arrangement, though, would provide a better solution? One could rely on uniform national goals for residual contamination. This would ensure equitable cleanups among rich and poor areas, but could be economically inefficient since site context factors such as the exposed population and proximity to water supplies would be ignored. One might try to tailor the cleanup standards to local conditions by requiring cleanup to background levels. This, though, takes no consideration of risk or cost. Alternatively, one could take a more complex approach, setting a uniform level of risk. Thus each site might seek to reduce the risk from contamination to, say, one death in 1,000,000. This approach would take into account site-specific conditions and future health consequences, though how accurately is another matter. Or one

---

[42] 42 U.S.C. § 9621.

could rely on a site classification approach, assuming that standards should differ from site-to-site. Commercial sites need less cleanup, one could argue, than school playgrounds because there will be less exposure to contaminated soil. This might well be the most nationally cost-effective approach, but there would be strong pressure from PRPs at each site for the future use to be an asphalt parking lot.

Closely linked to the issue of "how clean is clean" is the procedural issue of who should decide this. As economist Bob Hahn has observed, everyone wants a Cadillac if someone else is paying for it. Local residents will always want the cleanups to be as rigorous as possible, and for good reason since they live there and are not paying for the cleanup. Similarly, PRPs will seek to keep down costs.

Consider the Superfund site in the small town of Holden, Missouri, for example, where it would cost $71,000 to effectively isolate an abandoned factory and its hazardous chemicals, but another $3.6 million to clean up the residues and bury them under a layer of clay.[43] In this context, recall the Guns and Butter discussion in Chapter 3 and the problem of finite resources. In practical terms, can it ever be a proper goal to make a site "free of risk"? When is it worth spending more than $1 million per acre in an area where real estate costs closer to $10,000 an acre? There is no single right answer to the how "clean is clean" debate because it is, fundamentally, a political decision that pits the goals of efficiency and equity against one another. People surely should not involuntarily be exposed to cancer risks, but there is not enough money to make all NPL sites risk free.

F.   Superfund Reform

In many respects, Superfund has been the victim of high expectations and low performance. Living near contaminated sites is a very emotive issue and public interest in CERCLA has remained high. By any measure, CERCLA has proven an expensive program. For example, the expenditures by just the Department of Defense for environmental restoration on its land in FY 2007 was more than $1.9 billion. In comparison, the EPA's restoration budget was only $7.7 million for the same period. Moreover, for much of the law's early history, a disturbing amount of money was spent on lawsuits and studies rather than cleanups. A Rand study in 1988 found that of the $2.6 billion paid out by EPA, almost 40% had been spent on litigation and administration, with an eight year delay

---

[43] Peter Passell, Experts Question Staggering Costs of Toxic Cleanups, N.Y. Times, Sept. 1, 1991, at 1.

between investigation of a site and commencement of remedial work. Other studies have found higher costs.

To be fair, administration of the program has become much more efficient in recent years, with less litigation over contribution costs and more pre-settlement negotiation. And the total numbers reported on the EPA website look good. Over 6,400 removal actions have taken place at hazardous waste sites. By 2012, exposure had been controlled at 1,361 NPL sites with 46 new projects started. PRPs have paid for about 70% of the cleanup costs, amounting to over $16 billion. And EPA has looked after the little folk, reaching over 430 de minimis settlements with more than 21,000 small waste contributors. Approximately $8 of private response costs have been spent for every $1 of public funds spent on enforcement. All good cause for optimism, except for the fact that it is estimated EPA will need to spend about $1.4 billion every year for the rest of the decade to clean up the remaining NPL sites, and arguments continue over how best to finance the Superfund.

It is hard to find anyone who doesn't think Superfund could be improved, either in terms of fairness or cost-effectiveness. Indeed every legislative session over the last decade has included Superfund reform bills in the House and Senate. Since allowing the special tax funding Superfund to expire in 1995, Congress has not reauthorized the tax and, in 2003, the Superfund ran out of tax revenue. Since then, its funding has come from general revenues appropriated by Congress and litigation awards from PRPs (amounting to $600 million in 2009), leading to lower total funding than in the past.

Other funding reforms have ranged from eliminating liability-based funding for disposal prior to 1986 and more generous de minimis provisions, to greater protection of municipalities and subsequent land purchasers. One consequence of all of these proposals, however, is that they would let some parties off the hook. And that, in turn, is why, despite widespread criticism, CERCLA has remained largely unchanged. The Small Business Liability Relief and Brownfields Revitalization Act in 2002 provided the largest reforms since the SARA amendments 16 years earlier.[44] The most significant changes, though, consisted of codifying prior EPA practices for small contributors, clarifying the innocent landowner defense, and increasing brownfields funding.

Why has political reform proven so difficult? Once the decision has been made that taxpayers will not foot the bill for cleanups, then CERCLA reform becomes a zero sum game. Any reform that lessens the potential liability of some PRPs will increase the

---

[44] Pub. L. No. 107–118.

liability for others. Thus, absent large scale reform, the political dynamic has been one of pushing for reduction of your group's liability while at the same time opposing reforms that would lessen any other group's. You win, I lose, and vice versa, with the result that CERCLA remains much criticized but largely unchanged.

As with the Clean Water and Clean Air Acts, "solving the problem" of contaminated sites has proven far more difficult than Congress anticipated over three decades ago. Despite its flaws, though, CERCLA was, and remains, a groundbreaking law. While the target of constant criticism over its costs and retroactive liability provisions, the assignment of responsibility to virtually all actors associated with the disposal of waste has played a critical role in ensuring that waste is disposed of properly. When tallying the costs of CERCLA, it is important to keep in mind the benefits of avoided future Love Canals, as well.

QUESTIONS AND DISCUSSION

1. Assume that Acme Industries produces a waste stream that qualifies as characteristic hazardous waste. By coincidence, Widget Industries uses this particular waste stream as part of its manufacturing process. If Widget offers to buy the waste from Acme, should it be regarded as Subtitle C waste, potentially making Widget a TSD? If waste that is sold for a profit (i.e., commercially valuable waste) were exempted from RCRA, would this create harmful loopholes for companies seeking to avoid regulation or encourage an important stream of commerce?

2. As the text described, a review by EPA's scientists in the late 1990s found that groundwater contamination poses a relatively low health risk compared to other environmental hazards. Despite this expert opinion, public opinion polls consistently rate groundwater contamination as near the top of environmental concerns. As a result, a great deal of money and effort flows toward cleaning up contaminated soil instead of other threats that may pose greater risks, such as radon exposure. The money dedicated to addressing environmental threats often reflects the public's (inaccurate) perception of risk far more than the scientific community's. In a democracy, is this the appropriate result, even if it places the public at greater risk?

3. Electronic waste (sometimes called "e-waste") represents one of the largest growing streams of waste shipped across national borders. The waste from electronic products such as computers, for example, often contains lead, mercury, cadmium, and other toxic metals. The Basel Action Network estimates that up to 80% of e-waste collected in the United States for recycling is shipped overseas to developing countries and has called for a ban on this trade. They argue that many of these countries lack the capacity to properly reclaim and then dispose of these hazardous materials. What do you think are the strongest arguments in favor of this trade? Under what circumstances do you think it should be allowed?

4. Why do you think CERCLA extends liability to current owners and operators of facilities that were contaminated prior to their purchase? Does this create an incentive to dispose of waste safely? After all, the current owners cannot magically go back in time and ensure the waste is properly disposed. The harm has already occurred and the current owners and operators may well bear no blame; indeed they may not have had anything to do with the improper disposal. Given that, does it make sense to have a different standard of liability for current owners and operators, or no liability at all?

5. As the text describes, the determination of how clean a site needs to be depends on a range of factors. Would it be better policy to establish national, uniform cleanup standards instead of the current site-by-site approach?

6. If you were amending CERCLA, Which funding approach would you support for NPL sites? What are the benefits of purely public funding? If you were relying on private funding, which classes of parties would you make liable?

Part 3
NATURAL RESOURCES

Chapter 10

WETLANDS, ENDANGERED SPECIES, & THE PUBLIC TRUST

I. The Nation's Diminishing Resources

Much of America's history has been shaped by the nation's abundant natural resources and wildlife, from coastal fisheries and forested valleys to powerful rivers and deep aquifers. Yet our nation is losing many of its natural resources. As a result of land development and the introduction of exotic species, nearly 60 percent of the nation outside Alaska has lost its native vegetation. At the same time, more than half of the nation's wetlands have disappeared. Seven states have lost eighty percent or more of their wetlands. With growing water consumption, literally thousands of the county's waterways are totally drained of water at various points of the year. Other waterways turn into mere trickles. To store water for later use, the United States has dammed and flooded natural wonderlands like Glen Canyon and the Hetch Hetchy Valley. Loss of habitat, in turn, has led to a decline in species. One percent of United States species are presumed extinct, and about one-third are at risk of becoming extinct.

The nation also faces the depletion of resources that have been essential to its economic growth and well-being. The country's farm and range soil, for example, has lost some fifteen percent of its natural mineral content through erosion and poor agricultural management. In approximately half of the states, water users are pumping more groundwater from wells than nature is replenishing. Such groundwater mining ultimately can deprive regions of necessary irrigation water. The United States Geological Survey, for example, estimates that groundwater shortages will reduce irrigated acreage on the high plains of Texas by over 50 percent by the middle of this century. The National Marine Fisheries Service has classified about 20 percent of the nation's marine fisheries that it has assessed as overfished. So-called "table fish," such as Atlantic cod and halibut, which historically have provided the bulk of fish for restaurants and stores, are under the heaviest threat.

Hundreds of laws manage and protect the United States' natural resources—though not always effectively, as these statistics testify. While federal laws such as the Clean Air Act play the dominant role in regulating pollution, state governments provide the principal protection for many natural resources. State, not federal, law primarily controls how land is developed and used, how much water is withdrawn from rivers and underground aquifers, the pace of petroleum extraction, and the taking of wildlife and fresh water fish. The federal role in natural resource policy historically was limited to management of national forests, national parks, and the remainder of the federal public domain. In recent decades, however, the federal role has grown. The Magnuson–Stevens Act manages marine fisheries, including salmon fishing. The Coastal Zone Management Act provides for state-federal coordination in the conservation of coastal regions. As discussed below, the Endangered Species Act and section 404 of the Clean Water Act limit how various environmentally sensitive lands are used. The Endangered Species Act also restricts how much water can be taken from many of the country's rivers, streams, and aquifers.

In one short chapter, we cannot even begin to summarize all of the laws governing the nation's resources. This Chapter therefore focuses on three of the most important state and federal means of protecting environmentally sensitive land and water—the public trust doctrine, section 404 of the Clean Water Act, and the Endangered Species Act. The public trust doctrine provides that state governments own navigable waterways and tidelands in trust for the common use of the public. Beginning in the 1970s, environmental advocates turned to the public trust doctrine as one means of forcing the government to protect these and other resources against development threats. Section 404 of the Clean Water Act and the Endangered Species Act, in turn, are perhaps the most powerful federal laws in the nation's current arsenal of natural resource protections.

II. The Public Trust Doctrine

Throughout history, the law has treated some resources as public commons that belong to all and are irreducible to private ownership. This concept forms the core of the traditional public trust doctrine, which provides special protection to tidelands and other navigable waterways. Under the Roman Institutes of Justinian, the ocean and its shores, as well as running water and air, were by the "law of nature" *res communes*, incapable of exclusive private ownership.[1] The codes or customs of most European countries subsequently reaffirmed this principle. In the United States, the Northwest Ordinance of 1787 incorporated the axiom, declaring that the navigable waters of the Mississippi River "shall be common highways and forever free . . . to the citizens of the United States."[2]

---

[1] J. Inst. 2.1.1.

[2] Northwest Ordinance of 1787, 1 Stat. 50 (1789).

The most famous public trust case in the United States is *Illinois Central Railroad Company v. Illinois*.[3] In 1869, Illinois granted over 1,000 acres underlying Lake Michigan along the Chicago shore to the Illinois Central Railroad for harbor and commercial development. Four years later, Illinois changed its mind. The State sued to invalidate the original grant, and the Supreme Court ruled in its favor, holding that the grant was either voidable or void *ab initio*. The reason, according to the Court, is that lands underlying navigable waterways are "different in character" from other governmentally owned lands. Navigable waterways are of special importance to the public, and the State holds title to the underlying lands "in trust for the people" so that "they may enjoy the navigation of the waters, carry on commerce over them, and have liberty of fishing therein freed from the obstruction or interference of private parties." Although the government might convey small parcels of submerged land to private parties where it would not injure the purposes of the trust, the government cannot convey an entire harbor without violating the trust.

The public trust doctrine has evolved today in several states to protect environmental and recreational interests (as well as the traditional public trust purposes of navigation, commerce, and fishing) and to cover a broader set of resources. California law illustrates the expansion. In *Marks v. Whitney*,[4] Marks owned tidelands bordering Tomales Bay in Northern California. When Marks threatened to fill and develop the tidelands, a neighboring property owner who would have lost access to the bay sued. The California Supreme Court held that, except in limited situations, the private owner of tidelands holds title subject to the state's public trust. Any member of the public, moreover, can bring a lawsuit to enforce the public trust and enjoin actions that would violate the trust. Most importantly, the purposes of the public trust "are sufficiently flexible to encompass changing public needs." According to the court, one of the most important purposes of the public trust today is to preserve tidelands "in their natural state, so that they may serve as ecological units for scientific study, as open space, and as environments which provide food and habitat for birds and marine life, and which favorably affect the scenery and climate of the area." Marks therefore could not fill or develop the tidelands on his property.

A decade later, the California Supreme Court held that the public trust doctrine also restricts the amount of water that can be withdrawn from navigable waterways.[5] For years, Los Angeles had

---

[3] 146 U.S. 387 (1892).

[4] 491 P.2d 374 (Cal. 1971).

[5] *National Audubon Soc. v. Superior Ct.*, 658 P.2d 709 (Cal. 1983).

diverted water from streams feeding Mono Lake, a large salt water lake in eastern California that Mark Twain once described as a "solemn, silent, sailless sea," and exported the water over 200 miles to the city's residents. Because of the diversions, Mono Lake shrank by a third, and dropping water levels exposed seagull rookeries to coyotes and other predators. The court concluded that the public trust doctrine applies as much to the waters in a navigable waterway as to the lands underlying the waterway. It would do little good to prohibit landowners from filling in a waterway if water users simply could suck the waterway dry. The state has a "duty" to protect the public's "common heritage of streams, lakes, marshlands and tidelands." Although the state can authorize people to divert water for domestic or economic use, it must "preserve, so far as consistent with the public interest, the uses protected by the trust." In subsequent proceedings, the California courts ordered Los Angeles to reduce its diversions by about two thirds until the lake level rises to a more acceptable level (a goal that scientists expected would take several decades). The Hawaii Supreme Court has since held that the public trust doctrine extends also to groundwater and protects the interests not only of current generations but of future generations as well.[6]

Not every state, however, has followed California's lead. Maine, for example, has decided that the public trust doctrine in that state protects only fishing, fowling, and navigation.[7] Efforts to expand the public trust doctrine, moreover, have often been controversial. When the Idaho Supreme Court tried to apply the public trust doctrine to water diversions, the Idaho legislature passed a law prohibiting the courts from applying the public trust doctrine to water rights or withdrawals.[8] An interesting (and unanswered) question is whether such legislation itself violates the public trust doctrine.

Some commentators have urged courts to use the public trust doctrine even more aggressively to protect environmental resources. Fearing that developers, timber companies, mining companies, and other commercial interests enjoy undue influence in many state legislatures (a fear supported by political science studies), these commentators have argued that the public trust doctrine is essential to safeguard the public's interest in preservation. Although *Illinois Central Railroad* dealt with navigable waterways, the Supreme Court in that case described the public trust doctrine as applying more expansively to "property in which the whole

---

[6] *In re Water Use Permit Applications for the Waiahole Ditch*, 9 P.3d 409 (Haw. 2000).

[7] *See Bell v. Town of Wells*, 557 A.2d 168 (Me. 1989).

[8] Idaho Code §§ 58–1201 to 59–1203.

people are interested, like navigable waters and soils underneath them." Shouldn't the public trust doctrine therefore also apply today as a shield against threats to national parks, forests, wetlands, wildlife, and other environmental resources? Courts, however, have shown little interest in extending the public trust doctrine beyond its traditional amphibious setting, although one federal district court in the early 1970s suggested in dictum that national parks are subject to a common-law public trust.[9]

Critics of the public trust doctrine have argued that the courts are in effect legislating. The legal basis for the public trust has never been clear. If a legislature authorizes water diversions or sells environmentally valuable public lands, what gives the courts the authority to override the legislative judgment? Only constitutions generally trump legislative decisions, yet the few courts to have speculated on the genesis of the public trust doctrine have held that the trust flows from common law, not from state or federal constitutions.

III. Protecting Wetlands

Many people might find it odd that the government protects "swamps" and "bogs," but wetlands such as these are crucial natural resources. Wetlands, which are typically defined as surface areas that are saturated or inundated with water long enough each year to support hydrophilic ("water-loving") vegetation, provide a variety of valuable services. To start, wetlands help protect waterways, and thus drinking water, from a variety of contaminants. Wetlands, for example, filter out nutrients and other contaminants from water running off neighboring lands into a waterway. Studies indicate that wetlands retain about 80 percent of the phosphorous and 90 percent of the nitrogen found in runoff. Forested wetlands also lower water temperature in hot summer months, reducing harmful algal blooms. In addition, wetlands reduce the risk of floods (which in an average year cause over $4 billion in damages and dozens of deaths). Wetlands act as natural sponges, soaking up water during peak runoffs and then releasing the water slowly over time. A study by the Illinois State Water Survey estimated that every one percent increase in wetlands along a stream corridor decreases peak stream flows by an average of almost four percent. A Wisconsin study found that watersheds consisting of 30 percent or more wetlands enjoy 60 to 80 percent lower flood-water levels compared to watersheds with no wetlands.

---

[9] *See Sierra Club v. Department of Interior,* 398 F. Supp. 284 (N.D. Cal. 1975). The Supreme Court has subsequently made clear its view that the public trust doctrine "remains a matter of state law" (*PPL Montana, LLC v. Montana,* 132 S. Ct. 1215, 1235 (2012)), leading some lower federal courts to conclude that there is no public trust doctrine relevant to purely federal decisions.

By storing water during periods of high precipitation and then releasing the water during the dry season, wetlands also serve as natural reservoirs.

Wetlands also provide crucial habitat for migrating birds and other species. Approximately a third of the domestic species listed as endangered or threatened under the federal Endangered Species Act use wetlands as habitat. Half of the nation's migratory bird species use wetlands as nesting, migratory, or wintering areas. Wetlands also provide nursery or spawning habitat for 60 to 90 percent of the nation's commercial fish species. Because wetlands attract so much wildlife, they serve as an important source of recreation. Each year millions of people use wetlands for nature watching, hunting, hiking, and canoeing. Each year, over 50 million Americans spend over $10 billion observing and photographing waterfowl and other wetlands species.

Wetlands, however, have been under threat for centuries. Hydrologic alterations such as dams and water diversions, urban development, new marinas and harbors, mosquito control programs, peat mining, and agriculture all have contributed over the last several centuries to a dramatic decline in wetlands acreage. In the 1600s, the lower 48 states enjoyed over 220 million acres of wetlands; today, fewer than 110 million acres remain. Both California and Iowa have lost about 90 percent of their wetlands. During the peak wetland loss during the 1950s and 1960s, the United States was losing approximately 500,000 acres of wetlands per year. The wetlands that still remain, moreover, are often degraded, reducing their ability to provide the valuable services described above.

A majority of states now safeguard their wetlands. The federal government, however, provides the principal protection. Since 1988, the United States has pursued a policy of "no net loss" of wetlands (and was actually gaining about 30,000 acres of freshwater wetlands per year by the early 2000s). For historical reasons, the Army Corps of Engineers, which is the engineering wing of the Department of Defense, serves as the key regulatory agency. Federal wetlands regulation grew out of efforts to protect the navigability of the nation's waterways, and navigability was the bailiwick of the Corps. Although the federal EPA today plays an important supporting role (and even has the power to veto some Corps actions), the Corps still takes the lead.

A. Rivers & Harbors Act of 1899

The oldest federal regulatory authority over wetlands is section 10 of the Rivers & Harbors Act of 1899.[10] The principal purpose of the Act is to protect navigation. Section 10 prohibits anyone from dredging, filling, or otherwise altering or modifying "navigable waters" without obtaining a permit from the United States Army Corps of Engineers. To qualify for protection under this provision, a wetland must be truly navigable (either now or in the past) or be susceptible of navigation with reasonable improvements. The Act's protection also applies only up to the ordinary high water mark of a waterway. If a wetland qualifies for protection, the Act provides quite broad protections against virtually any form of destruction or modification. Because most wetlands do not qualify for protection, however, section 10 generally serves only a secondary role in federal regulation of wetlands.

B. Section 404 of the Clean Water Act

Section 404 of the Clean Water Act provides the principal protection for wetlands.[11] Under section 404, no one can discharge dredged or fill materials into a wetland without obtaining a permit from the Army Corps of Engineers. Section 404 enjoys much broader jurisdictional reach than the Rivers & Harbors Act of 1899. Although section 404 applies only to "navigable waters," the Clean Water Act defines this term as all "waters of the United States including the territorial seas."[12] As described below, courts have interpreted this definition to encompass wetlands that historically would not have been considered navigable. On the downside, however, section 404 regulates only a limited set of activities and contains a number of broad exemptions. While section 10 of the Rivers & Harbors Act restricts both dredging and filling of wetlands, for example, section 404 extends only to discharges of materials into the wetlands. As discussed in more detail below, section 404 also exempts various activities, including normal farming, ranching, and silviculture activities, from its requirements.

Over the past several decades, section 404 has become a legal battlefield as landowners have tried to limit its scope and environmentalists and governmental regulators have tried to stretch its reach as far as possible. Landowners have focused on the term "navigable waters" and argued that, as a matter of both constitutional power and statutory interpretation, section 404 does

---

[10] 33 U.S.C. § 403.

[11] 33 U.S.C. § 1344.

[12] CWA § 502(7), 33 U.S.C. § 1362(7).

not apply to nonnavigable wetlands. Environmentalists and governmental regulators, by contrast, have argued that a large number of activities, including dredging, result in illegal "discharges" and thus require permits under section 404. Environmentalists and regulators also have urged courts to interpret the principal exemptions narrowly.

1. What Are "Navigable Waters"?

The constitutional basis for Congress' regulation of wetlands is the Commerce Clause. For most of the nation's history, Congress believed that its commerce power extended only to navigable waterways. For this reason, section 10 of the Rivers & Harbors Act and most other Congressional water legislation assert authority only over "navigable waters." When Congress drafted section 404 of the Clean Water Act, it used the same terminology. But in an effort to broaden the stretch of the Clean Water Act, Congress defined the term "navigable waters" to mean the "waters of the United States." The result has been judicial confusion. If Congress meant to regulate all wetlands, why did it use the term "navigable" in section 404? But if Congress did not mean to regulate all wetlands, what is the relevant test for jurisdiction? As is often the case in environmental law, Congress was maddeningly obscure, leaving it to the courts and administrative agencies to make the jurisdictional decisions over section 404's coverage.

The Corps initially took the position that, despite the broad definition of "navigable waters" in the Clean Water Act, its jurisdiction under section 404 extended only to actually, potentially, or historically navigable waterways, which include few wetlands and virtually no freshwater wetlands. Environmental groups successfully challenged this narrow view of the Corps' jurisdiction in *Natural Resources Defense Council, Inc. v. Callaway*.[13] After reviewing the legislative history of the Clean Water Act, the district court concluded that Congress intended to claim as much jurisdiction as its commerce powers permitted. Rather than appealing the decision, the Corps issued new regulations asserting jurisdiction over not only actually navigable waters, but also adjacent wetlands, interstate wetlands, and intrastate "wetlands, sloughs, prairie potholes, wet meadows, playa lakes, or natural ponds, the use of which could affect interstate or foreign commerce."[14]

The first jurisdictional question to reach the Supreme Court was whether section 404 applies to wetlands that are adjacent to

---

[13] 392 F. Supp. 685 (D.D.C. 1975).

[14] 33 C.F.R. § 328.3(a); 40 C.F.R. § 2303(s).

navigable waterways but not themselves navigable. In *United States v. Riverside Bayview Homes, Inc.*,[15] the United States Supreme Court unanimously agreed that the Corps could regulate such wetlands. The Court's logic was simple. Given the broad statutory definition of "navigable waters," the Corps' assertion of authority over wetlands that are integrally connected to actually navigable waters is reasonable. The physical dividing line between navigable waterways and adjoining wetlands is often amorphous, and the federal government could not protect the quality of navigable waterways if it did not enjoy authority over adjacent wetlands.

In the 1990's, the question shifted to whether the Corps possesses authority over isolated wetlands that sit apart from any navigable waters. In its post-*Callaway* regulations, the Corps claimed that section 404's prohibitions extend to isolated wetlands that are the actual or potential habitat for migratory birds. Because over half of all migratory bird species use wetlands as habitat, the preservation of such wetlands is important to the protection of these birds.

The Supreme Court granted review in *Solid Waste Agency of Northern Cook County v. United States Army Corps of Engineers*[16] *("SWANCC")* to decide whether the Clean Water Act extends this far and, if so, whether the act exceeds Congress' commerce power. The Court did not reach the constitutional question because it concluded, by a close 5–4 vote, that the Corps' Migratory Bird Rule exceeded the Corps' statutory authority. But constitutional concerns played a role in the Court's interpretation of the statute. "Where an administrative interpretation of a statute invokes the outer limits of Congress' power" or "push[es] the limit of congressional authority," there must be clear evidence that Congress intended to assert that authority. This is particularly true, according to the Court, where the interpretation would encroach on a "traditional state power," such as land use regulation. Given these constitutional concerns and Congress' express use of the term "navigable," the Court concluded that section 404 does not extend to wetlands with no connection at all to navigable waters.

The Supreme Court addressed the Corps' jurisdiction once again in *Rapanos v. United States*,[17] where the question was whether the Corps could regulate wetlands that were hydrologically linked to navigable waterways but only through miles of ditches, drains, and creeks. Lower courts had upheld the Corps' jurisdiction,

---

[15] 474 U.S. 121 (1985).

[16] 531 U.S. 159 (2001).

[17] 547 U.S. 715 (2006).

but the Supreme Court narrowly reversed. Four justices concluded that "'the waters of the United States' include only relatively permanent, standing or flowing bodies of water," not "transitory puddles or ephemeral flows of water." Although they decided the case on statutory grounds, they again warned of the constitutional implications of a broader interpretation. Upholding the Corps' jurisdiction would "authorize the Corps to function as a *de facto* regulator of immense stretches of intrastate land. . . . We ordinarily expect a 'clear and manifest' statement from Congress to authorize an unprecedented intrusion into traditional state authority. The phrase 'waters of the United States' hardly qualifies." The fifth justice voting to reverse, Justice Kennedy, held that the Corps needed to show a "significant nexus" between a wetland and a traditionally navigable waterway, measured by the wetland's contribution to the waterway's chemical, physical, or biological integrity, to establish jurisdiction.

A few cases also have dealt with the Corps' jurisdiction over artificially created wetlands. Although regulating artificial wetlands might seem odd or even counterproductive (since it might discourage landowners from creating new wetlands), artificial wetlands can serve the same important functions as natural wetlands, and their destruction can be equally problematic. At least one court has held that the Corps does not have jurisdiction over artificial wetlands that it has helped create through its own engineering work (since otherwise the Corps could create jurisdiction for itself by steering water onto private lands) or that are not environmentally beneficial (since there is no evidence that Congress intended to regulate such wetlands).[18] Except in these limited situations, however, courts consistently have held that artificial wetlands are subject to section 404.[19]

2.   What is a "Discharge" of Material?

Section 404 regulates only "discharges" of materials into wetlands. On the surface, this would suggest that section 404 regulates the filling of wetlands but not other significant threats to wetlands such as draining or dredging. The Corps, however, has tried to assert authority over many of these other threats by adopting a broad interpretation of the term "discharge." Under what was called the "Tulloch rule," for example, the Corps asserted jurisdiction over excavation and dredging operations if they led to "*any* redeposit of dredged material."[20] If someone scooped a bucket of a mud out of a wetland and even a drop of mud fell back into the

---

[18] *See United States v. Fort Pierre*, 747 F.2d 464 (8th Cir. 1984).

[19] *See, e.g., Leslie Salt Co. v. United States*, 896 F.2d 354 (9th Cir. 1990).

[20] 58 Fed. Reg. 45,008 (Aug. 25, 1993) (emphasis added).

wetland, the Corps claimed jurisdiction. In practice, this required virtually anyone planning to excavate or dredge a wetland to obtain a permit under section 404.

In *National Mining Association v. United States Army Corps of Engineers*,[21] the D.C. Circuit held that the Tulloch rule exceeded the Corps' statutory authority. To the court, it was absurd to imagine that Congress had intended the term "discharge" to extend to such activities. "Congress could not have contemplated that the attempted removal of 100 tons of [dredged material] could constitute an addition simply because only 99 tons of it were actually taken away." The Corps, however, has continued to push for broad jurisdiction. In response to the D.C. Circuit's decision, the Corps merely changed the words "*any* redeposit of dredged material" in its regulatory definition of "discharge" to the words "any redeposit of dredged material *other than incidental fallback*."[22] The regulations, moreover, provide that the Corps and EPA "regard the use of mechanized earth-moving equipment to conduct landclearing, ditching, channelization, in-stream mining or other earth-moving activity in waters of the United States as resulting in a discharge of dredged material *unless project-specific evidence shows that the activity results in only incidental fallback*."[23]

Not all courts have been as unreceptive as the D.C. Circuit to the Corps' jurisdictional claims. In *Borden Ranch Partnership v. United States Army Corps of Engineers*,[24] a California real estate developer purchased a large ranch with the intent to convert the ranch into vineyards and orchards and then subdivide it into upscale residential parcels. During rainy periods of the year, a shallow layer of impermeable clay formed vernal pools, swales, and other intermittent wetlands on portions of the ranch. Problems arose when the developer started to "deep rip" these areas to accommodate the deep roots of the vineyards and orchards. Deep ripping, in which tractors drag lengthy metal prongs through the soil, tears the clay layer and thus can destroy the wetlands. By a 2–1 vote, a three–judge panel of the Ninth Circuit Court of Appeals ignored the D.C. Circuit's *Tulloch* decision and held that deep ripping moves and redeposits soil and thus constitutes a "discharge." The Supreme Court granted review, but then affirmed by an equally divided vote without opinions.[25]

---

[21] 145 F.3d 1399 (D.C. Cir. 1998).

[22] 33 C.F.R. § 323.2 (emphasis added).

[23] *Id.* (emphasis added).

[24] 261 F.3d 810 (9th Cir. 2001).

[25] *Borden Ranch Partnership v. United States Army Corps of Engineers*, 537 U.S. 99 (2002). Justice Kennedy did not participate, setting the stage for a 4–4 tie.

The legal dilemma in these cases is that, while section 404 applies literally only to "discharges," a variety of other activities can be equally if not more destructive of wetland services. Courts that apply section 404 broadly, like the Ninth Circuit in *Borden Ranch*, focus on the environmental purposes of section 404 and try their best to manipulate the language of the Clean Water Act to accomplish those purposes. Courts like the D.C. Circuit in the *National Mining Association* case take the language more literally.

Why did Congress not use more sweeping language like that found in the Rivers and Harbors Act? The reason may be simply historical: the Clean Water Act was concerned with pollution—and thus "discharges"—rather than with broader environmental problems. Whatever the reason, courts must continue to struggle with the inherent tension in section 404 between purpose and language.

3. Special Exceptions

Section 404 exempts a variety of activities from its permit requirements. Perhaps most important are the farming exceptions, which exempt "normal farming, silviculture, and ranching activities such as plowing, seeding, cultivating, minor drainage, harvesting for the production of food, fiber, and forest products, or upland soil and water conservation practices."[26] Also exempt is the "construction of farm or stock ponds or irrigation ditches."[27] These exceptions again demonstrate the political power of the agricultural community. The exempt activities are generally no less harmful to wetland services than other forms of discharges, so the only justification is that farming is important enough to justify the loss of wetlands. Congress, however, placed a limit on the exemptions. Under what is known as the "recapture provision," even an otherwise exempt activity needs a permit if the activity would change the use of the land and either impair the "flow or circulation of navigable waters" or reduce the "reach of such waters."[28]

Whenever environmental regulations contain a "loophole," of course, members of the regulated community will try to squeeze through it. In the *Borden Ranch* case, for example, the developer argued that the deep ripping was exempt from section 404 because it was a "normal farming" activity like plowing. The majority in *Borden Ranch* held that the exemption did not apply because the developer was converting the land from wetlands to vineyards, triggering the recapture provision. Courts in general have been

---

[26] CWA § 404(f)(1)(A), 33 U.S.C. § 1344(f)(1)(A).

[27] CWA § 404(f)(1)(C), 33 U.S.C. § 1344(f)(1)(C).

[28] CWA § 404(f)(2), 33 U.S.C. § 1344(f)(2).

unsympathetic to farmers seeking to change wetlands into farmland. The legislative history of section 404 makes clear that, while Congress was willing to tolerate some harm to wetlands from farming activities, it did not intend to allow wholesale conversion of sizable amounts of wetlands into dry land.

4. The Permitting Process

The Clean Water Act provides little guidance regarding the appropriate standards for issuing a permit. Instead, section 404(b) instructs EPA to develop appropriate guidelines in consultation with the Corps. Under these guidelines, anyone seeking a permit must show that

(1) there is no practicable alternative to the proposed activity that would have less impact on the aquatic ecosystem,

(2) the proposed activity will not have significant adverse impacts on aquatic resources,

(3) all "appropriate and practicable" mitigation will be employed, and

(4) the proposed activity will not violate other state or federal laws (such as the Endangered Species Act).[29]

Even if an activity meets these specific requirements, the Corps also will scrutinize the activity to see if it would be "contrary to the public interest." In making this determination, the Corps considers a broad range of factors, including the effect of the activity on fish, wildlife, water quality, flood control, recreation, and aesthetics.[30]

The "no practicable alternative" standard has generated significant legal controversy. Although the presence or absence of practicable alternatives might seem a straightforward inquiry, whether something is a practicable alternative can depend on both *how* you define the purpose of the proposed activity and *when* you look to see if there is an alternative. Imagine, for example, that a developer plans to build condominiums along the waterfront of Rivertown. There might be many alternative sites if the purpose is simply to build condominiums, but no alternative site if the purpose is to build waterfront condominiums complete with a boat dock. Indeed, EPA's guidelines presume that there is a practicable alternative where a proposed land use "does not require access or proximity" to a waterway.[31] Similarly, a waterfront parcel down the road that does not involve wetlands might be a practicable

---

[29] 40 C.F.R. § 230.10.

[30] 40 C.F.R. § 320.4.

[31] 40 C.F.R. § 230.10(a).

alternative in 2002 when it is vacant and on the market, but not five years later when someone has bought the land and built a restaurant on it.

Courts have been somewhat inconsistent in how they have determined the purpose of a proposed activity. According to the courts, the Corps must take into account how the *applicant* defines the purpose. If a resort developer sets out to build a resort with a golf course, for example, a resort without a golf course generally would not be a practicable alternative.[32] But the applicant cannot "define a project in order to preclude the existence of any alternative sites and thus make what is practicable appear impracticable."[33] Nor does an alternative "have to accommodate components of a project that are merely incidental to the applicant's basic purpose."[34] Courts unfortunately have been less than clear about how the Corps should determine whether a project component, like a golf course, is or is not "merely incidental." As to timing, the one published opinion to consider the issue held that the Corps should determine whether alternatives were available at the time of "market entry." If alternative land sites were available when the applicant first started looking for a parcel to develop, the Corps should deny the permit even if the parcel is no longer available today.[35]

Another critical question is the adequacy of proposed mitigation. The Corps' first preference is to avoid *any* negative impact on the wetland. If this is not possible, the Corps will look to see if the direct impact can be reduced. If the impact cannot be avoided or sufficiently minimized, the Corps will require the applicant to restore, enhance, or create other wetlands. This is known as "compensatory mitigation." The Corps prefers on-site mitigation to off-site mitigation and prefers that the applicant restore, enhance, or create the same general type of wetland as the wetland that is harmed. In evaluating such mitigation, the Corps favors restoration of prior wetlands over enhancement of low-quality wetlands and favors enhancement over the creation of new wetlands. In rare cases, the Corps even may accept protection of other existing wetlands as adequate mitigation, but this is the Corps' least favored option.

Determining compensatory mitigation on a permit-by-permit basis is not ideal. The resulting restoration and preservation efforts are often piecemeal and uncoordinated, and the costs of monitoring

---

[32] *Sylvester v. U.S. Army Corps of Engineers*, 882 F.2d 407 (9th Cir. 1989).

[33] *Id.*

[34] *Id.*

[35] *See Bersani v. U.S. EPA*, 850 F.2d 36 (2d Cir. 1988).

and enforcing the mitigation are high. For these reasons, the Corps has encouraged *mitigation banking* in which private or public organizations restore, enhance, or create wetlands on a coordinated basis in a region and use the mitigation "credits" to satisfy the 404 mitigation requirements for individual development projects. In private mitigation banks, developers themselves create and operate banks in order to generate credits for their future development plans. In commercial or public mitigation banks, third parties develop the bank and then sell or transfer the resulting credits to developers wishing to meet their 404 mitigation requirements. Today wetlands mitigation banking resembles a commodity market, with freewheeling, entrepreneurial wetlands banks offering for sale (and often profit) finished off-site wetlands as credits to anyone in need of mitigation for their 404 permits. In 2008, there were over 24,000 acres of mitigated wetlands and 312 miles of mitigated stream banks, with over $1 billion changing hands in this fast-growing market.

Despite its potential advantages, wetlands mitigation banking also poses several possible problems. First, unless the mitigation wetlands are of similar composition to the destroyed wetlands, the mitigation wetlands may not provide the same level and type of ecosystem services (such as nutrient retention, habitat, or flood control) as the destroyed wetlands furnished. Indeed an alarmingly high percentage of mitigation wetlands fail to function effectively at all. More subtly, because the wetlands banks are rarely adjacent to the wetlands that are being destroyed, the ecosystem services provided by the mitigation wetlands will often be of lower value. Mitigation banks tend to be where land is cheap and, therefore, far from towns. The ecosystem services, however, tend to be most valuable where the wetlands are near people. The service of flood control, for example, is worth very little if the floods are not diverted from where people live.

5.   *General Permits*

Of the approximately 100,000 activities each year that fall within the Corps' section 404 jurisdiction, only about 15 percent go through the full regulatory review process. The vast majority of the activities are covered by generic nationwide, regional, or programmatic permits known as "general permits." People seeking to engage in an activity covered by a general permit do not need to file individual applications and often do not even need to notify the Corps beforehand, so long as they comply with the conditions set out in the general permit.

To date, the Corps has issued about 50 nationwide general permits. Under section 404(e) of the Clean Water Act, the Corps is to issue general permits only if it determines that the authorized activities "are similar in nature, will cause only minimal adverse environmental effects when performed separately, and will have only minimal cumulative adverse effect on the environment." But in an effort to reduce administrative burdens on both it and applicants, the Corps often has pushed the limits of its authority to avoid full permitting review by issuing general permits. The most controversial general permit for many years was Nationwide Permit 26, which authorized the filling of up to three acres of isolated wetlands for commercial or residential purposes. Faced by mounting criticism that Nationwide Permit 26 was leading to significant cumulative reductions in wetland acreage, the Corps allowed the permit to expire in 2000, replacing it with Nationwide Permit 39, which authorizes the filling of only half an acre or less subject to significant restrictions and mitigation measures, including the maintenance of a vegetation buffer.

6.   EPA Vetoes

Congress did not entirely trust the Corps, which historically has not enjoyed a good environmental record, to police the nation's wetlands. While awarding the Corps the principal permitting authority, Congress therefore asked EPA to develop the permitting guidelines. Congress also awarded EPA veto power over the Corps' decisions. Under section 404(c), EPA can veto a permit if it determines, after public comment and notice, that the proposed discharge "will have an unacceptable adverse effect on municipal water supplies, shellfish beds and fishery areas (including spawning and breeding areas), wildlife, or recreational areas." For years, EPA used its veto authority only sparingly; from 1979 through 2012, for example, EPA vetoed less than 20 permits (even though the Corps issued about 80,000 permits on average each year). EPA has used its veto power somewhat more actively during the Obama Administration—vetoing a permit in one case that had been issued several years earlier in connection with a mountaintop-removal mining project in West Virginia—but vetoes are still quite rare. The ever-present threat of a veto, however, almost certainly encourages the Corps to be more vigilant in its protection of wetlands.

7.   Constitutional Takings Challenges

Section 404 has probably generated more takings challenges in the last two decades than any other federal regulatory scheme. Many property owners who have been denied permits have sued, arguing that section 404 has taken their property by depriving them of all use of the protected wetlands in violation of *Lucas v.*

South Carolina Coastal Council.[36] As discussed in Chapter 3, one major issue in applying the *Lucas* test to these cases is whether the wetlands can be viewed in isolation from any other land owned by the plaintiff. If the wetlands are part of a larger parcel of land owned by the plaintiff, courts have generally held that there is no taking because the plaintiff can still use the remaining land. However, where the remaining land is physically separate or if the plaintiff purchases the wetlands separately, courts sometimes have found takings.[37] Another frequent question is whether the protected wetlands are truly worthless simply because the property owner cannot develop the wetlands under section 404. The wetlands often retain some modicum of value for recreational use or as open space or even as a speculative investment.

C. Incentive Programs

Just as in the pollution field, incentives often can be a more effective means than command and control regulations of protecting natural resources. The federal government has created a number of important incentives for wetlands protection, all of which play a crucial role in helping the nation meet its goal of no net loss. The federal Swampbuster program, for example, denies specified agricultural benefits to farmers who convert non-exempt wetlands into farmland without complying with an approved wetlands conservation plan. Wetlands are exempt if they were previously converted or artificially created or can be farmed with minimal environmental impact. Studies estimate that the Swampbuster program is protecting at least six million acres of wetlands.

In the Swampbuster program, Congress is leveraging its existing farm subsidies to protect wetlands; the program costs the federal government nothing additional. In other cases, Congress uses tax dollars to encourage wetlands restoration and conservation. Under the Wetland Reserve Program (WRP), for example, the Department of Agriculture pays farmers to restore and protect wetlands on their property.[38] In most cases, the farmers provide the federal government with a permanent easement encumbering their wetlands. WRP currently protects approximately two million acres of wetlands throughout the United States.

IV. The Endangered Species Act

Most scientists agree that the world is experiencing the highest rate of species extinction since dinosaurs died out 65 million years ago, although the exact size of the current extinction "crisis" is

---

[36] 505 U.S. 1003 (1992). See pages 81–83 supra.

[37] *See, e.g., Loveladies Harbor v. United States*, 28 F.3d 1171 (Fed. Cir. 1994).

[38] 16 U.S.C. § 3837.

uncertain. Some scientists estimate that, at the current rate of extinction, only half of the world's existing species will survive to the end of this century. Even conservative estimates peg current species loss to be three or four orders of magnitude greater than the historical average. In the United States alone over the last century some sixty species of mammals and forty species of freshwater fish have died out.

Humans are the major cause of the current wave of extinctions. Through habitat degradation, introduction of exotic species, and overhunting, humans threaten the continued existence of a growing number of species. Habitat destruction and modification are the major threats in the United States. Urban sprawl and such commercial land uses as farming, ranching, and silviculture reduce the amount of habitat usable by endangered species and fragment what habitat remains. Competition from exotic species for food and habitat is a growing threat. Some exotic species purposefully have been introduced into the United States, while others have smuggled in as uninvited guests on cargo ships, airplanes, and other objects. Overhunting and overfishing of species are of less importance than habitat destruction and exotics, but still threaten a significant number of species ranging from various runs of salmon to assorted species of freshwater mussels. Species also face a variety of other threats, including climate change, pollution, automobiles, and natural disturbances.

The Endangered Species Act ("ESA") provides the strongest federal protection against species loss. As described in more detail below, the ESA flatly bans the hunting or killing of endangered species and protects against significant habitat loss. But the ESA is not a complete or perfect solution. The ESA does not effectively address the problem of exotic species. Indeed, no federal or state law currently provides a comprehensive and workable solution to this problem. More importantly, the ESA provides no protection to a species until that species is in serious danger of extinction. The ESA thus takes an "emergency room" approach to biodiversity. Rather than protecting species or ecosystems when they are healthy, the ESA waits until a species is on the brink of extinction. At that stage, saving the species is often very difficult. If a species already has lost virtually all its habitat, for example, preserving the remaining habitat may not be sufficient to restore the species to its prior health. The remaining habitat, moreover, is often subject to strong development pressure.

Despite the ESA's limits, many policy makers attack the ESA for going too far. In many regions of the nation, the ESA restricts new land development, angering property owners and local governments. In the western United States, the ESA has reduced the amount of water that farmers and cities can divert from rivers and other waterways. The ESA also constrains the federal government's freedom to build dams and freeways, to develop timber, petroleum, and other natural resources, and to take a variety of other actions of importance to various political constituencies.

The Congress that passed the ESA in 1973 had no idea how controversial the law would become. No Senator and only four members of the House voted against the ESA. Most legislators thought that the ESA simply protected charismatic birds and megafauna, such as grizzly bears, bald eagles, and alligators, against hunters and poachers. Few newspapers thought that the ESA's passage was important enough even to report. But as discussed below, they were wrong. For all its failings, the ESA today is perhaps the most powerful natural resources law in the nation or, for that matter, in the world.

A major controversy is whether the ESA should balance the benefits of preserving a species against the economic costs of preservation. As you will see, cost plays only a marginal role in the direct implementation of the ESA's regulatory restrictions. Federal agencies, for example, cannot take any action that would jeopardize the continued existence of an endangered species or materially alter the species' "critical habitat," no matter how valuable the action would be to society. Where the habitat is located on private land, property owners cannot use their land in a way that would appreciably reduce the likelihood that the species will survive and recover, no matter how valuable the land use. This does not mean that cost is irrelevant. Congress has never provided the funds needed to ensure full recovery of endangered species under the ESA—reflecting an implicit judgment that other budgetary items are more important. Faced with significant regulatory costs, property owners and other interest groups have also tried, sometimes successfully, to undermine or weaken ESA regulation through lawsuits, Congressional legislation, and political pressure. But the ESA's prohibitions do not provide for any explicit balancing of costs and benefits.

How much should society be willing to spend to protect and restore endangered species? To many people, the answer is "however much it takes!" Under some biocentric views of nature, species have an intrinsic right to exist and thrive, and humans have an obligation to respect that right. Many religions, moreover, believe that humans have an ethical obligation to be careful stewards of nature. When Congress threatened to weaken the ESA in the mid-1990s, then Secretary of the Interior Bruce Babbitt turned to the Bible, and particularly the story of Noah, for defense.[39] From these various perspectives, species have an infinite or incalculable value.

To many other people, however, the question is more utilitarian: how much are the endangered species worth to humans? Answering this question is difficult because many of the values are not readily measurable. Some endangered species, such as salmon, have an easily quantified value to humans as food or other commercially traded goods. Others, like whales, might have an indirect commercial value as the focus of ecotourism. Most endangered species, however, do not have any significant commercial value, which is the principal reason they are endangered. Property owners and the government, seeing little direct market value from the species, prefer to devote the species' habitat to "more valuable" economic uses that are often incompatible with the species' continued existence.

When Congress passed the ESA in 1973, some members of Congress believed that we should preserve species for their potential genetic value in the development of pharmaceutical, industrial, or agricultural products. Indeed, one frequently cited House report concluded that the "value of this genetic heritage is, quite literally, incalculable. . . . Who knows, or can say, what potential cures for cancer or other scourges, present or future, may lie locked up in the structures of plants which may yet be undiscovered, much less analyzed?"[40] Species do sometimes provide valuable drugs or genetic information. The oft-cited rosy periwinkle of Madagascar, for example, yielded cures for both lymphocytic leukemia and Hodgkin's disease. Economic studies, however, suggest that the expected value from saving any particular species is quite small, in part because the same genetic information or chemical compounds often will be found in multiple species. According to one study of the value for pharmaceuticals, only ten in 250,000 species, at best, are likely to produce commercially valuable discoveries, yielding an expected value per individual species of less than $10,000.

Turning to potentially greater values, biodiversity (which constitutes the overall community of organisms within a habitat and the physical conditions under which they live) provides a wide range of ecosystem services of immense importance to humans. These services include detoxification and decomposition of wastes, purification of air and water, generation and renewal of soil and soil fertility, pollination of crops and natural vegetation, control of

---

[39] The Bible unfortunately is a two-edged sword on this issue. For every passage that emphasizes the importance of stewardship, there are other passages that emphasize humans' dominion over non-human species.

[40] H.R. Rep. No. 93–412, 93d Cong., 1st Sess. 4–5 (1973).

harmful agricultural pests, support of cultural activities, and the provision of aesthetic beauty and pleasure. Economists estimate that the overall value of these services is immense, totaling in the trillions of dollars. The contribution of any individual species to ecosystem service values, however, is typically uncertain and, in many cases, may be insignificant.

Many people, of course, value the preservation of even commercially worthless species—and this value must go into any utilitarian calculation of the overall value of protecting endangered species. Using "contingent valuation methodology" or CVM (see page 41), some economists have tried to estimate such *nonuse values* by asking people in surveys how much they would be willing to pay to save a species. Most people report that they are willing to pay significant sums, even to save those species with little known commercial value. American residents have reported a "willingness to pay" ranging from $5–10 per household for some little known fish such as the striped shiner to $95 per household for more infamous and charismatic species such as the northern spotted owl. Many economists have questioned the accuracy of these numbers. As explained in Chapter 2, the survey results often appear to be inconsistent with basic economic principles and vary considerably with the exact questions asked. Some critics, moreover, suspect that people report high values not because they would be willing to pay that much but because they want the surveyor to think that they are moral and environmentally beneficent. No matter what the deficiencies of CVM, however, it is probably the best means currently available to estimate nonuse values.

Two federal agencies split administrative responsibilities under the ESA. The Fish & Wildlife Service (FWS) within the Department of the Interior is responsible for protecting terrestrial and avian species and freshwater fish. The National Marine Fisheries Service (NMFS) within the Department of Commerce takes responsibility for marine species, including anadromous fish such as salmon. Interestingly, the only major debate within the Congressional conference committee that put the finishing touches on the ESA was how to allocate responsibility between these two agencies. Most observers believe that the FWS is more protective and proactive than NMFS, and occasionally policymakers propose returning NMFS to the Department of the Interior, where NMFS was part of the FWS prior to 1970. The odds on such a move, however, are currently slim to none. For convenience, the remainder of this chapter will refer to the FWS alone as the ESA implementing agency. Far more species fall within the FWS's jurisdiction, so it is the principal agency. When you read "FWS," however, keep in mind that it can be either the FWS or NMFS depending on the species under protection.

A. Listing Species

The ESA protects only those species that the FWS lists as either *endangered* or *threatened*.[41] A species is endangered if the FWS finds that it is "in danger of extinction throughout all or a significant portion of its range."[42] A species is threatened if it is "likely to become an endangered species in the foreseeable future."[43] Congress created the "threatened" category both to provide some protection to species before they are on the very edge of extinction and as a "halfway house" for species on the road to recovery. For most purposes, the ESA provides the same protections to endangered and threatened species, although there are some differences under section 9 as discussed below.

Under section 4 of the ESA, the FWS can decide to list a species on its own initiative, or an individual or organization can petition to list the species. When Congress passed the current ESA in 1973, the government already had listed 392 species under a prior version of the Act. Over thirty years later, the federal government has listed over 2100 species, of which almost 1500 are found in the United States. Of the listed domestic species, over 600 are animals and over 850 are plants. About 80 percent of the U.S. species are listed as endangered, with the remainder categorized as threatened. All states, as well as the District of Columbia and Puerto Rico, host at least a handful of listed species. Listed species, however, tend to be found more often in those areas naturally high in biodiversity and threatened by significant habitat modification. Thus Hawaii has the most listed species (423 in July 2013), with California the runner up (317). The other states rounding out the "top five" are Alabama (133), Florida (124), and Tennessee (101).

In deciding whether to list a species, the FWS sometimes must decide what a species is. If a flower is very similar to a known species but the flower appears to have slightly smaller petals, for example, is the flower a separate species? If two separate plant species combine to reproduce, is the resulting plant a new and distinct species or merely a hybrid? Unfortunately, the ESA does not define the term "species" or address these issues. In light of the ESA's silence and the FWS's expertise, courts have been very

---

[41] There is one exception to this rule. If a species so closely resembles a listed species that it requires protection from people who might mistakenly take it, section 4(e) of the ESA authorizes the FWS to list the species even if it is not endangered or threatened.

[42] ESA § 3(6), 16 U.S.C. § 1532(6).

[43] ESA § 3(20), 16 U.S.C. § 1532(20).

deferential to the FWS's judgment as to what constitutes a species. The issue is further complicated, however, by the fact that the ESA authorizes the FWS to list not only individual species but also *subspecies* and, in the case of vertebrates, *distinct population segments* that interbreed when mature. Because of their role as reservoirs of genetic diversity, the loss of some subspecies and local populations ultimately can endanger the species as a whole even if other populations currently are numerous; individual populations and subspecies, moreover, can be of ecological or aesthetic importance to a local region. The ESA, however, once again fails to define subspecies and distinct population segments, making the listing of subspecies and distinct populations ripe for controversy.

The ESA tries to keep economic and political considerations out of listing decisions. Under the ESA, the FWS must determine within 90 days of receiving a listing petition whether the petition presents sufficient evidence to pursue a full review of the species' status and must decide within a year of that determination whether to list the species. The FWS must list a species if it finds that "natural or manmade factors" make the species endangered or threatened. The FWS must use the "best scientific and commercial data available" and cannot consider the potential economic consequences of listing the species. In an effort to support the scientific basis for its decisions, the FWS also has adopted a peer review policy of seeking the expert opinions of outside specialists before making a listing determination.

Because listings require the application of scientific expertise, courts have been reticent to overturn the FWS's determinations. Courts review the substance of the determinations under the liberal "arbitrary and capricious" standard and overturn the decisions only where the agency has "failed to articulate a satisfactory explanation for its actions."[44] Courts also have generally resisted ordering the FWS to engage in additional scientific research before deciding whether to list a species, noting that the ESA requires the FWS to consider only the best scientific information "available."

The FWS, nonetheless, often faces significant pressure not to list a species. Where listings are likely to limit local development or other economic activity, property owners and other affected interests frequently threaten lawsuits or seek Congressional or White House intervention. Despite its strict deadlines and requirements, the ESA provides the FWS with a variety of ways to avoid listing a controversial species. The FWS, for example, can conclude that it needs additional information to decide whether the species should be listed (although courts have warned that the ESA

---

[44] *Northern Spotted Owl v. Hodel*, 716 F. Supp. 479 (W.D. Wash. 1988).

does not require "conclusive evidence" before a species should be listed[45]). Under the ESA, the FWS also can conclude that listing is "warranted," but that immediate listing of the species is "precluded" by higher listing priorities (i.e., the agency is too busy at the moment to get around to the listing).[46] As of late 2012, approximately 200 species languished in this purgatory status of *candidate species*. (This number is down from 250 species just a few years ago. In settlement of a lawsuit, the FWS has agreed to continue to whittle away at the list of candidate species through 2018.) At times Congress itself directly intervenes in the listing process. In 1995, for example, Congress imposed a moratorium on new listings for approximately a year.

The FWS also sometimes avoids listings by finding that other efforts to preserve a species provide adequate protection. The ESA explicitly permits the FWS, in deciding whether to list a species, to consider "efforts, if any, being made by any State . . . or any political subdivision of a State . . . to protect" the species.[47] Courts, however, have been skeptical of the FWS's reliance on state and local efforts unless those efforts are in place, enforceable, and comparable to protections provided under the ESA. The FWS also argues that it has the authority to consider all conservation efforts, including efforts being made by private entities.[48] This argument, which relies in part on a general provision of the ESA requiring the FWS to consider "other natural or manmade factors affecting [a species'] continued existence,"[49] remains untested in the courts. To help guide determinations of when local conservation efforts eliminate the need to list a species, the FWS has developed a Policy for Evaluation of Conservation Efforts when Making Listing Decisions—or what the FWS calls its "PECE" policy. The FWS also has developed a program of Candidate Conservation Agreements in which local landowners agree to take specific actions to protect a species in an effort to avoid federal listing. In some cases, the landowners also receive government assurances that, if a species is listed, the FWS will not require additional actions of the landowners. As of late 2012, the FWS had approved over 125 candidate conservation agreements (of which about 25 included assurances).

---

[45] *E.g., Defenders of Wildlife v. Babbitt*, 958 F. Supp. 670 (D.D.C. 1997).

[46] ESA § 4(b)(3)(B)(iii), 16 U.S.C. § 1533(b)(3)(B)(iii).

[47] ESA § 4(b)(1)(A), 16 U.S.C. § 1533(b)(1)(A).

[48] *See* Announcement of Draft Policy for Evaluation of Conservation Efforts When Making Listing Decisions, 65 Fed. Reg. 37102 (June 13, 2000).

[49] ESA § 4(a)(1)(E), 16 U.S.C. § 1533(a)(1)(E).

B. Limits on Federal Agency Actions

Under section 7(a)(2) of the ESA, all federal agencies must consult with the FWS before taking any action that might affect an endangered or threatened species and must insure that the action is not "likely" to either (1) "jeopardize the continued existence" of the species or (2) "result in the destruction or adverse modification of [the critical] habitat of such species." As the Supreme Court has emphasized, this mandate permits no consideration of cost. "The plain intent of Congress in enacting [the ESA] was to halt and reverse the trend towards species extinction, whatever the cost."[50] According to the Court, "Congress intended endangered species to be afforded the highest priorities," adopting a policy which the House Report on the ESA described as the "institutionalization of . . . caution."[51] If written today, the House Report almost certainly would have spoken in terms of the precautionary principle.

TVA v. Hill[52] is one of the most famous environmental cases of the twentieth century and offers a number of useful lessons. Environmentalists for years had been trying to block the Tennessee Valley Authority (TVA) from building the Tellico Dam. The dam promised little hydroelectricity or other benefits, yet would destroy the last free flowing stretch of the Little Tennessee River and flood a beautiful valley rich in farmland and sacred Indian sites. No law, however, proscribed a dam because its environmental and social costs outweighed its economic benefits. The National Environmental Policy Act, described in Chapter 12, required TVA to examine the environmental costs but imposed no substantive mandates. Stopping the dam seemed a lost cause until an ichthyologist discovered snail darters, a previously unknown species of perch about three inches long, just downstream from the dam site. After the FWS listed the species as endangered, several individuals (including University of Tennessee law student, Hiram Hill, whose name was listed as the lead plaintiff) and a local environmental group sued under the ESA's citizen suit provision to enjoin the dam as a violation of section 7(a)(2).

The major issue in *TVA v. Hill* was whether the ESA required courts to enjoin a dam that was essentially complete and had cost almost $80 million. A majority of the Court concluded that Congress meant to forbid agency actions that jeopardized the continued existence of endangered species, no matter what the economic costs. Justices Powell and Blackmun dissented, arguing that the ESA did not apply to projects that already were underway when the Act was

---

50 *TVA v. Hill*, 437 U.S. 153, 184 (1978).

51 H.R. Rep. No. 93–412, supra note 40, at 4–5 (1973).

52 437 U.S. 153 (1978).

passed. Justice Rehnquist also dissented, contending that, absent clear Congressional directives to the contrary, courts retain the equitable discretion to deny injunctions where the costs of the injunction would far outweigh the benefits.[53]

Congress responded to *TVA v. Hill* by creating an Endangered Species Committee, colloquially known as the God Squad because of its power to determine the fate of a species.[54] The God Squad is a cabinet-level committee, comprised of the Secretaries of Agriculture, the Army, and Interior; the Administrators of EPA and the National Oceanic and Atmospheric Administration (NMFS's mother agency); the Chairman of the Council of Economic Advisors; and a state representative appointed by the President. At the request of any federal agency, state governor, or permit applicant, the God Squad can vote to exempt a federal action from section 7(a)(2) if it determines that there are no "reasonable and prudent alternatives," the benefits of the action "clearly outweigh" the environmental costs, and the action is of "regional or national significance."[55] In granting an exemption, the God Squad also can require "reasonable mitigation and enhancement measures."[56]

Congress expected that the God Squad would exempt the Tellico Dam, overturning the Supreme Court's decision. But the God Squad unanimously denied an exemption, finding that the dam was not worth completing even if one ignored the snail darter. Secretary of the Interior Cecil Andrus bemoaned that he hated "to see the snail darter get the credit for stopping a project that was ill-conceived and uneconomical in the first place." In 1980, Congress nonetheless exempted the Tellico Dam from the ESA in a rider to a military appropriations bill. Although TVA completed the dam and thus destroyed the snail darter's principal known habitat, scientists later found other populations of snail darters in the main stretch of the Tennessee River and a number of its tributaries. In 1984, the FWS upgraded the snail darter's status from endangered to threatened.

What are the lessons of *TVA v. Hill*? From a legal perspective, the main lesson is that agencies cannot use cost as an excuse for not complying with the requirements of section 7(a)(2). *TVA v. Hill* also teaches that, if Congress wants to exempt a project from the dictates of the ESA (or any other federal environmental statute for

---

[53] Although Justice Rehnquist failed to convince any other justice that the ESA permits courts to exercise equitable discretion in deciding whether to enjoin agency actions, he later convinced a majority that courts do retain equitable discretion in an injunction action under the Clean Water Act. *See Weinberger v. Romero–Barcelo*, 456 U.S. 305 (1982).

[54] ESA § 7(e), 16 U.S.C. § 1536(e).

[55] ESA § 7(h), 16 U.S.C. § 1536(h).

[56] ESA § 7(h)(1)(B), 16 U.S.C. § 1536(h)(1)(B).

that matter), it better be clear. Subsequent to the discovery and listing of the snail darter, Congress repeatedly appropriated funds to continue constructing the Tellico Dam and, in reports accompanying the appropriation bills, declared that the ESA should not stand in the way of the dam. Noting that courts should be reticent to conclude that Congress has repealed a law by implication, however, the Court held that the appropriation bills did not exempt the Tellico Dam from the ESA. In a subsequent lawsuit, the Ninth Circuit Court of Appeals held that a law explicitly authorizing the University of Arizona to build three telescopes on Mount Graham even if the construction would jeopardize the endangered Mount Graham red squirrel did not exempt construction of one of the telescopes at a slightly different location than specified in the law.[57] On the other hand, the Supreme Court by a 5–4 vote in 2007 decided that the ESA did not override a provision of the Clean Water Act expressly requiring EPA to transfer authority to issue NPDES permits to any state that met nine statutory criteria set out in the Clean Water Act.[58]

TVA v. Hill also demonstrates the immense importance of the ESA in protecting natural resources. The ESA is one of the few federal laws in the natural resources field with real teeth. NEPA, as discussed in Chapter 12, is purely procedural. Environmental groups wishing to derail or modify a proposed federal action thus will typically look to see if the action might menace a listed species. Opponents of the ESA often accuse environmental groups of using the ESA for "ulterior" purposes. The opponents are correct that environmental groups often invoke the ESA to try to kill a project that they oppose primarily for other reasons. Unfortunately, there is no federal law outlawing federal actions that are, to use Cecil Andrus' phrase, "ill-conceived," so environmental groups often are forced to turn to the ESA for help. For better or worse, the ESA remains the strongest tool that environmental groups have to help shape natural resource policy in the United States.[59]

The aftermath of *TVA v. Hill* also illustrates that, no matter what a statute might say, cost and politics are realities of regulation. Given the local political and economic support for the Tellico Dam, completion of the dam may have been inevitable. To date, the God Squad has exempted only two projects (and one of

---

[57] *Mount Graham Coalition v. Thomas*, 53 F.3d 970 (9th Cir. 1995).

[58] *National Assn. of Home Builders v. Defenders of Wildlife*, 551 U.S. 644 (2007).

[59] This is not to say that the ESA is not sometimes abused. Sometimes, for example, local groups opposed to a project because they simply don't want it "in their backyard" will use the ESA to try to kill the project, even though they have no interest in the environment at all.

those exemptions was reversed by the courts).[60] But few agencies have requested exemptions, in large part because the FWS often finds ways to allow federal actions to proceed forward at only slight cost and inconvenience to the agencies and their constituents. Professor Oliver Houck of Tulane Law School studied 186,000 federal projects that the FWS and NMFS reviewed under the consultation provision of section 7(a)(2) from 1987 through 1995. The consultations led to alterations or delays in less than three percent of the projects and blocked less than 0.05 percent. Most of the alterations, moreover, were minor and undemanding.[61]

Recall that an agency violates section 7(a)(2) if its action will either "jeopardize the continued existence" of a listed species *or* destroy or adversely modify a species' "critical habitat." While it seems obvious today, the dual-pronged strategy of protecting both a species *and* its habitat was an important innovation at the time of the ESA's passage. The ESA requires the FWS to designate a species' critical habitat at the same time that it lists the species, so long as the designation is "prudent and determinable."[62] However, because determining a species' critical habitat can cost as much as $500,000 and uses scarce agency resources, the FWS often chooses to postpone designating critical habitat. Because cost is not a legitimate factor in deciding *whether* to designate critical habitat, the FWS generally argues that it does not have sufficient information to determine the critical habitat or that designation would be imprudent (e.g., because the designation would alert poachers and collectors where to find the endangered species and thus increase the risk to the species). This practice has put the FWS on a collision course with environmental groups, which believe that the designation of critical habitat is important in enforcing section 7(a)(2). Environmental groups have brought and won a number of important lawsuits to force the FWS to designate critical habitat.

In contrast to the decision of *whether* to designate critical habitat, the decision of *how much* and *which* habitat to designate as "critical" is one of the few situations where the ESA permits the FWS to consider cost. In deciding what critical habitat is, the FWS must take "into consideration the economic impact, and any other relevant impact, of specifying any particular area as critical habitat." The FWS can exclude an area from the critical habitat if the benefits of excluding the area outweigh the benefits of including

---

[60] *See Portland Audubon Soc'y v. Endangered Species Comm.*, 984 F.2d 1534 (9th Cir. 1993) (reversing an exemption for thirteen timber sales that would have jeopardized the endangered northern spotted owl). The only lasting exemption was for the Gray Rocks Dam, which jeopardized the endangered whooping crane.

[61] Oliver A. Houck, *The Endangered Species Act and Its Implementation by the U.S. Departments of Interior and Commerce*, 64 U. Colo. L. Rev. 277 (1993).

[62] ESA § 4(a)(3), 16 U.S.C. § 1533(a)(3).

it, unless the exclusion "will result in the extinction of the species concerned."[63] Forced by lawsuit to designate critical habitat but lacking the resources to make a detailed delineation, the FWS has sometimes responded by designating broad swaths of land. Property owners and local governments have responded by suing to exclude land on economic grounds. Until Congress gives the FWS sufficient funding to conduct full evaluations of critical habitat, the FWS is between a rock and a hard place. Try to put off the designations, and environmental groups will sue. Try to err in favor of designating all potential habitat, and property owners will sue.

Should section 7(a)(2) apply where Congressional legislation *requires* an agency to take particular actions or where an agency jeopardizes a listed species by *failing* to act? In *National Association of Home Builders v. Defenders of Wildlife,*[64] the Supreme Court held that section 7 does not apply to non-discretionary actions because, in such cases, Congress has told the agency what to do. As Justice Stevens noted in dissent, however, the issue actually raises a question of "conflicting 'shalls'" because the ESA also tells agencies what they can and cannot do. In Stevens' view, there is no reason to prefer one "shall" over another. Noting that section 7(a)(2) applies only to an "action authorized, funded, or carried out" by an agency, most courts also have concluded that the section does not apply to mere failures to act.

Another important but open issue under section 7(a)(2) is the degree, if any, to which it applies to actions that jeopardize the continued existence of species outside the United States. The FWS originally issued a regulation providing that section 7(a)(2) applies to federal actions both inside and outside the United States. Under that regulation, if the U.S. Agency for International Development (AID) had loaned money to construct an overseas dam that would flood the habitat of a listed species, AID would have had to consult with the FWS under section 7. In 1986, however, the FWS changed its mind and issued a revised regulation requiring agencies to consult only with regard to actions taken in the United States or on the high seas.[65] Several environmental organizations sued to invalidate the revised regulation in *Lujan v. Defenders of Wildlife,*[66] but the Supreme Court found that the organizations did not have standing (see pages 103–105). The validity of the regulation still remains untested, although lower federal courts have suggested in dictum that section 7(a)(2) has an extraterritorial reach. On its surface, section 7(a)(2) would appear to apply to all actions that

---

[63] ESA § 4(b)(2), 16 U.S.C. § 1533(b)(2).

[64] 551 U.S. 644 (2007).

[65] 50 C.F.R. § 402.1(a).

[66] 504 U.S. 555 (1992).

jeopardize the continued existence of endangered species, no matter where the actions occur or the species live.

C. Private Violations

1. The Prohibition on "Takings"

Under section 9(a)(1) of the ESA, no one, public or private, can *take* an endangered species of fish or wildlife. The ESA defines "take" to include actions that "harass, harm, pursue, hunt, shoot, wound, kill, trap, capture, or collect" an endangered species. In many cases, this prohibition is easy to apply. If a poacher kills or traps an endangered grizzly bear, for example, he clearly violates section 9. But does a landowner violate section 9 if she cuts down trees that are potential habitat for the endangered red cockaded woodpecker or paves over a sand dune that is the habitat of the endangered Delhi sands flower-loving fly? Does a farmer violate section 9 if he withdraws water from a river in which endangered salmon spawn? In 1981, the FWS issued a regulation providing that "significant habitat modification or degradation" that "actually kills or injures wildlife by significantly impairing essential behavioral patterns, including breeding, feeding, or sheltering," constitutes unlawful "harm" under section 9.[67] This regulation has generated more controversy than any other aspect of the ESA.

It is questionable whether most of the members of Congress who passed the ESA fully understood that section 9 might limit how private landowners use their property and how much water farmers and cities can withdraw from domestic waterways. No one mentioned the possibility during debate on the ESA. Indeed the House floor manager said that the ESA would address the problem of habitat destruction "by providing funds for acquisition of critical habitat" and by enabling the "Department of Agriculture to cooperate with willing landowners who desire to assist in the protection of endangered species, but who are understandably unwilling to do so at excessive cost to themselves."[68]

In *Babbitt v. Sweet Home Chapter of Communities for a Great Oregon*,[69] however, the Supreme Court upheld the FWS regulation by a six to three margin. As the Court explained, the term "harm" normally means to cause hurt or damage and "naturally encompasses habitat modification that results in actual injury or death." Congress, moreover, intended to provide expansive protection for listed species and to define "take" in the "broadest possible terms." Congress also amended the ESA in 1982 to

---

[67] 50 C.F.R. § 17.3.

[68] 119 Cong. Rec. 30162 (1973).

[69] 515 U.S. 687 (1995).

authorize "incidental take permits," described in more detail below, that allow property owners to develop their property without violating section 9. Congress thus implicitly recognized that, absent such a permit, destruction or modification of habitat could violate section 9.

Although *Sweet Home* settled the validity of the FWS regulation, it left open numerous questions regarding the applicability of the FWS regulation. For example, does the regulation apply if timber companies cut down an old growth forest in which spotted owls live, but the owls fly away before the trees fall and thus are not killed? Would it matter if the owls have no place left to breed? Because the plaintiffs in *Sweet Home* had challenged the FWS regulation on its face rather than as applied to particular facts, the justices did not need to decide what actions would actually violate the regulation or what proof is necessary. All the justices in *Sweet Home*, however, agreed that habitat destruction or modification violates section 9 only when it "actually kills or injures wildlife." Everyone also appeared to agree that the injury or death must be "foreseeable" and not merely "accidental." Justice O'Connor, in a concurring opinion, further argued that traditional principles of "proximate causation," including "considerations of the fairness of imposing liability for remote consequences," should apply.

In discussing foreseeability, Justice O'Connor suggested that one of the first cases to interpret section 9, *Palila v. Hawaii Dept. of Land and Natural Resources (Palila II),*[70] was wrongly decided. In the *Palila* case, the State of Hawaii had permitted mouflon sheep to graze on state land that also was habitat for the endangered palila bird. The sheep prevented regeneration of mamane trees, upon which palilas depend for food, by eating the tree's seedlings. In *Palila II*, the federal courts found that this violated section 9 by impeding recovery of the palila population and ordered the State to remove the sheep. Justice O'Connor disagreed with the Ninth Circuit's conclusion. "Destruction of the seedlings did not proximately cause actual death or injury to identifiable birds; it merely prevented the regeneration of forest land not currently inhabited by actual birds."

Justice Scalia, in a dissenting opinion in *Sweet Home*, and Justice O'Connor, in her concurrence, also briefly sparred over the issue of whether habitat destruction that prevents wildlife from breeding violates the ESA. Both agreed that the ESA requires injury or death to *individual animals,* and not simply injury to the species. Justice Scalia argued that breeding interference does not

---

[70] 852 F.2d 1106 (9th Cir. 1988).

injure any animal (but merely keeps some animals from being born) and thus does not violate section 9. Justice O'Connor disagreed. Destroying an animal's breeding habitat, O'Connor urged, injures a living animal much like sterilizing it and also makes it more vulnerable to predators and pollutants.

A question that has arisen on several occasions since *Sweet Home* is whether a court can enjoin the destruction or modification of habitat prior to an actual injury or death. In *Sweet Home*, the Court stated that "the Government cannot enforce the § 9 prohibition until an animal has actually been killed or injured." Subsequent courts, however, have ignored this language as dictum and held that an injunction is appropriate where there is a "reasonable certainty" of "imminent" injury or death.[71]

Where a large number of people are taking an endangered species, environmental groups have sometimes looked for a way of reducing litigation costs by suing just one individual or entity with authority over all the others. Where fishermen in New England were using gear that harmed northern Right Whales, for example, an environmental group decided to sue the Massachusetts fishing regulators who allowed the practice rather than the fishermen themselves. A federal court of appeals validated this "vicarious liability" approach, holding that section 9 "not only prohibits the acts of those parties that directly exact the taking, but also bans those acts of a third party that brings about the acts exacting a taking."[72]

The "takings" prohibition of section 9(a)(1) applies only to endangered species of fish or wildlife. Plants are protected by section 9(a)(2), which bans the removal, digging up, or destruction of endangered plants on federal land or "in knowing violation of any law or regulation of any State or in the course of any violation of a State criminal trespass law."

Neither section 9(a)(1) nor section 9(a)(2), moreover, directly applies to threatened species. Section 4(d) of the ESA authorizes the FWS to issue regulations for the protection of threatened species, and the FWS has used this authority to extend the protections of section 9(a)(1) to threatened species. In a few instances, however, the FWS has used its discretion under section 4(d) to exempt certain species, such as threatened salmon and steelhead, from some or all of the provisions of section 9(a)(1). Although the FWS has argued that other programs adequately protect these species, politics almost certainly has played a role here as it has in listing decisions and implementation of section 7. In listing the polar bear

---

71 E.g., *Marbled Murrelet v. Babbitt*, 83 F.3d 1060 (9th Cir. 1996).

72 *Strahan v. Coxe*, 127 F.3d 155, 163 (1st Cir. 1997).

as a threatened species, for example, the FWS used section 4(d) to avoid the risk that the listing might enable environmental groups to use the ESA to argue that emissions of greenhouse gases are an unlawful taking.

2. *Incidental Take Permits*

To mitigate section 9's potential restrictions on the use of private property, Congress in 1982 authorized the issuance of *incidental take permits*. Under section 10(a) of the ESA, the FWS can permit an otherwise unlawful taking of a species if (1) the taking is merely incidental to an otherwise lawful activity (such as property development), and (2) the permit applicant has devised an acceptable *habitat conservation plan*, or *HCP*. The HCP must minimize the impact of the taking "to the maximum extent practicable," ensure that the taking will not "appreciably reduce the likelihood of the survival and recovery of the species in the wild," and be adequately funded.

As of 2012, the FWS had approved over 1000 HCPs (of which some 850 were still in effect) and issued accompanying incidental take permits covering tens of millions of acres and hundreds of listed species. The FWS has issued most of the permits to individual property owners wishing to develop or otherwise use their land in a manner that might be construed to be a violation of section 9. Many communities, however, have developed *regional HCPs* encompassing multiple property owners and, where relevant, multiple species. Such regional HCPs reduce the burden on individual property owners, who no longer need to apply to the FWS for individual permits, and also enable regions to take a more comprehensive, coherent, and proactive approach to species preservation. In most cases, federal, state, and local governmental officials, property owners, and environmental representatives meet over a lengthy period of time to try to hammer out acceptable terms for regional HCPs.

Many environmental groups are skeptical of incidental take permits and HCPs. In their view, the FWS often does not know enough about the listed species to ensure that the HCPs will adequately protect the species. They also worry that political pressures, and the desire to show that the ESA can "work" without causing economic disruption, encourage the FWS to agree to weak HCPs. Although environmental groups have challenged a number of incidental take permits in court, judges generally defer to the expert judgment of the FWS. This does not mean, however, that the FWS always wins. In *Sierra Club v. Babbitt*,[73] a district court

---

[73] 15 F. Supp. 2d 1274 (S.D. Ala. 1998).

rejected incidental take permits that the FWS had issued for two high density housing developments in the habitat of the endangered Alabama Beach Mouse. In the court's view, the FWS had failed to show that the offsite mitigation funding proposed in the HCPs would reduce the impact on the mouse to the "maximum extent practicable."

3. Administrative Reform Efforts

Faced with increasing Congressional hostility to the ESA, the Clinton Administration in the mid-1990s adopted a number of administrative reforms designed to ease the impact of section 9 on private landowners. First, the FWS announced a new policy of identifying, at the time it lists a species, those activities considered likely or unlikely to violate section 9. This policy has helped reduce the uncertainties that landowners and water users face in deciding whether their actions might violate section 9.

More important, and contentious, was the FWS's announcement of a *no surprises policy*.[74] Many landowners are willing to agree to land use restrictions so long as the agreement buys them certainty. Landowners, however, often fear that, even if the FWS grants them an incidental take permit, the government might later try to limit their land use even further if the government discovers that additional habitat or actions are necessary to preserve a species. The no surprises policy tries to provide landowners with greater certainty by promising landowners who receive incidental take permits that the government will pay for any new habitat or actions that might be needed to meet unforeseen circumstances. At the time the policy was adopted, several environmental groups argued that it exceeded the FWS's authority by tying the government's hands in the event that additional actions are needed to protect a species. Partly in response, the FWS adopted a Permit Revocation Rule, which permits the FWS to revoke an incidental take permit with a no-surprises provision if unforeseen circumstances would "appreciably reduce the likelihood of the survival and recovery of the species in the wild" and the FWS cannot otherwise avert the jeopardy.

The FWS also decided to use *safe harbor agreements* to encourage landowners to enhance, restore, or create habitat on their property. The ESA can actually discourage private landowners from making their land more attractive to species. If a landowner tries to help a species by creating habitat on his property, the land can become subject to section 9's restrictions, and the landowner might never be able to develop the land or change his use of the

---

[74] Habitat Conservation Plan Assurances ("No Surprises") Rule, 63 Fed. Reg. 8859 (1998).

land if endangered species populations become established. Under safe harbor agreements, the FWS agrees that, if a landowner voluntary enhances, restores, or creates habitat, the landowner is free to return the land to its initial condition at a later time without running into problems under section 9. The safe harbor program has been quite successful. In South Carolina, for example, landowners have enrolled over 450,000 acres of land in a program designed to protect the red-cockaded woodpecker.

4. Criticisms of Section 9

Many property rights advocates strongly criticize section 9 for restricting the use of land and water without compensation. The criticisms fall into three general categories. First, critics argue that section 9 encourages landowners to destroy valuable habitat, harming rather than helping listed species. Because section 9 restricts the use of land only if it is habitat, landowners can avoid section 9 by making sure their land is not viable habitat. Nothing prevents a landowner from destroying habitat prior to the listing of a species. And although it is illegal, landowners sometimes can escape section 9's grasp after a listing by surreptitiously destroying habitat on their property. Stories abound of property owners trying to escape section 9 by cutting down trees, plowing their fields, or otherwise altering their land to make it unappealing to listed species.[75] The phenomenon is problematic enough to have its own acronym: "shoot, shovel, and shut up," or the Three–S Syndrome.

Second, critics argue that it is unfair to force a limited group of landowners to "bear the burden" of protecting listed species. To property owners whose land use is restricted under section 9, the fact that their land is habitat for a listed species seems like blind bad luck. A farmer whose land is habitat for an endangered burrowing rodent may have to stop plowing her fields, while a farmer five miles away is unaffected. A property owner may not be able to develop her land because an endangered butterfly lives there, while new residential subdivisions rise up just over the hill. The butterfly may be endangered, moreover, because neighboring landowners previously developed their land, drastically reducing the available habitat. Section 9, however, forces only the current landowner to help in preserving the species. Critics argue that everyone should contribute toward the preservation of the species. If habitat needs to be preserved, the public should purchase it. After all, critics argue, preservation efforts benefit all members of the public.

---

[75] For an interesting empirical study of the phenomenon, see Dean Lueck & Jeffrey A. Michael, *Preemptive Habitat Destruction under the Endangered Species Act*, 46 J. L. & Econ. 46 (2003).

Finally, some critics urge that the costs to society of section 9 outweigh the value of the protected species. To these critics, stopping new development to save a sand fly or a fairy shrimp is absurd. This critique, of course, returns us to the debate over the value of endangered species, with which we began our discussion of the ESA.

5. Constitutional Takings Challenges to Section 9

Only a few property owners have brought constitutional "takings" challenges to section 9 or to equivalent state habitat protections. Section 9 has seldom prevented property owners from making *any* use of their land, so *Lucas v. South Carolina Coastal Council*[76] is generally not relevant. In *Tulare Lake Basin Water Storage District v. United States*,[77] however, the Federal Claims Court held that the ESA had physically "taken" the water rights of an irrigation district in violation of the Fifth Amendment by reducing the amount of water that could be delivered to the district in an effort to protect two listed fish species—winter-run Chinook salmon and delta smelt. The Court of Appeals for the Federal Circuit subsequently found a physical "taking" of water rights in a similar ESA case where the government required a water district to return water to the river for the benefit of the endangered steelhead trout.[78]

Many landowners who have challenged habitat preservation measures as takings have argued that the government is authorizing "permanent physical occupations" of their land by the protected species and thus interfering with a core property interest. In *Nollan v. California Coastal Commission*,[79] the Supreme Court held that states cannot authorize the public to cross someone's land without compensation, so shouldn't compensation be required if the ESA forbids a landowner from excluding endangered species? Courts have rejected the argument, responding in part that the two types of "occupations" are quite different. While *Nolan* involved an intrusion by strangers and thus was especially offensive, endangered species are not "strangers to their . . . habitat."[80]

---

[76] 505 U.S. 1003 (1992). See pages 81–83 supra.

[77] 49 Fed. Cl. 313 (2001).

[78] *Casitas Mun. Water Dist. v. United States*, 543 F.3d 1276 (Fed. Cir. 2008).

[79] 483 U.S. 825 (1987).

[80] *Southview Assocs. v. Bongartz*, 980 F.2d 84, 95 n. 5 (2d Cir. 1992).

PROBLEM EXERCISE: THE EDWARDS AQUIFER[81]

The Edwards Aquifer is a large body of groundwater in central Texas that provides water for over a million people, primary in the City of San Antonio, and over a hundred thousand acres of farmland. Many of the farms receive federal agricultural subsidies, which are critical to the farms' financial viability. In the late 20th century, agricultural and urban users extracted approximately 800,000 acre-feet of water each year from the aquifer, with most of the water going to agriculture. (An acre-foot is the amount of water that would cover an acre of land up to one foot in depth—or 325,851 gallons. The typical rule of thumb is that an acre-foot is enough water to meet the demands of two homes each year.) The region is highly arid, and farmers and cities have few sources of water other than the aquifer. Historically, both farmers and cities, but particularly farmers, were relatively inefficient in their water use.

The Edwards Aquifer also supplies water to several springs, which in turn feed the Guadalupe River. The aquifer, springs, and river are home to seven aquatic species that have been listed as endangered or threatened under the ESA, including the Texas blind salamander, the fountain darter, the San Marcos gambusia, and Texas wild rice. If water users pump too much water from the aquifer, spring flows, river flows, and water levels in the aquifer all drop, to the detriment of the endangered and threatened species that rely on them. Droughts are a particular problem. The aquifer is highly dependent on surface precipitation for "recharge" (the amount of water added to the aquifer during a year), so droughts mean that less water can be pumped without harming listed species. Unfortunately, withdrawals also increase during droughts, because the few surface sources of water in the region dry up.

The exact amount of water that can be withdrawn each year from the Edwards Aquifer without harming endangered and threatened species is uncertain and varies from year to year depending on local precipitation and thus recharge. Scientists, however, estimate that the amount of water that can be withdrawn year in and year out over a lengthy period of time without harming the species is about 400,000 acre-feet—only half of the average yearly withdrawals. During droughts, even less water can be safely pumped.

Assume that you are an attorney for the local Texas chapter of the Sierra Club and that you are interested in trying to use the ESA to protect the seven listed species from excessive water withdrawals. Whom would you sue, and what are your strongest ESA arguments? What counter-arguments would you expect the defendants to make in response? Assuming you win your lawsuit, what type of relief would you seek?

---

[81] For background on the Edwards Aquifer and the ESA, see Todd H. Votteler, *Raiders of the Lost Aquifer? Or, the Beginning of the End to Fifty Years of Conflict Over the Texas Edwards Aquifer*, 15 Tulane Envtl. L.J. 257 (2002); Todd H. Votteler, *The Little Fish that Roared: The Endangered Species Act, Groundwater Law, and Private Property Rights Collide*, 28 Envtl. L. 845 (1998).

Assume next that you are a member of the Texas legislature and that you want to regulate the Edwards Aquifer in order to protect the species and, even more importantly, avoid "federal interference" under the ESA with local water policy. What limits would you put on pumping from the aquifer? And how would you allocate any cutbacks among the water users? In thinking through the last question, you should know that farmers historically did not monitor how much water they pumped from the aquifer (although San Antonio did). Most local farmers, however, use about two acre-feet for every acre that they farm. If you restrict pumping, can local water users challenge the regulation as an unconstitutional taking of their water rights (see pages 79–84)?

D.   *Recovery Plans & Other Provisions*

Once a species is listed as endangered or threatened, the FWS also typically prepares a recovery plan for the species. The ESA does not set any deadline for the preparation of a recovery plan and indeed contemplates that the FWS will prepare a plan more expeditiously for some species than for others. Section 4(f) of the ESA provides that the FWS, in developing and implementing recovery plans, will give priority to those species that are "most likely to benefit" from a recovery plan, "particularly those species that are, or may be, in conflict with construction or other development projects or other forms of economic activity." The FWS does not need to prepare a recovery plan at all for a species if the FWS concludes "such a plan will not promote the conservation of the species."

The FWS has a variety of tools with which it can implement recovery plans. As already discussed, sections 7(a)(2) and 9 furnish valuable protections. Section 7(a)(1) also provides that all federal agencies shall, in consultation with the FWS, "utilize their authorities in furtherance of the purposes" of the ESA by "carrying out programs for the conservation" of listed species. Under section 5, the FWS has the authority to acquire needed land and water "by purchase, donation, or otherwise."

Recovery plans unfortunately typically need funding, and Congress has never provided full funding. Each year, hundreds of species receive no funding. In deciding where to spend federal dollars, moreover, Congress appears to care more about a species' poster quality than about its relative uniqueness or ecological importance. Mammals, birds, and fish, for example, receive significantly more funding than reptiles, amphibians, invertebrates, and plants.

E.   Does the ESA Work?

The ultimate question, of course, is does the ESA work? Does the ESA help to protect species from extinction? The point of the ESA, after all, is not to list endangered species but to restore endangered populations so they can be taken off the list. As of late 2012, only 56 species had been "delisted" (and some of those delistings were under challenge). Ten of these species, moreover, were delisted because they are now extinct. Another 18 were delisted because of taxonomic revisions, new information, errors in the initial listing, or changes in the ESA. The FWS and NMFS had delisted only 28 species because the species had sufficiently recovered to be removed from protection. Among these "success stories" are the American alligator, bald eagle, gray wolf, peregrine falcon, brown pelican, and gray whale.

Delistings, however, may not be a useful indication of success. Given the severe threats that species face when they are listed, one should not be surprised to find few species being taken off the list. Indeed, the fact that so few species have gone extinct after being listed may be the best indication of success. A number of empirical studies have shown that the status of a species improves the longer the species is listed as endangered or threatened.[82] One set of experts also estimates that the ESA prevented 2,227 species from going extinct during the Act's first thirty years.[83]

No matter how effective the current ESA, most policy analysts believe that the ESA could be improved. One major reform would be to protect species at an earlier stage—before a species finds itself on the brink of extinction and before the regulatory options become limited. Another reform would be to refocus the ESA on the general protection of biodiversity, perhaps through the protection of different types of ecosystems, rather than on the protection of individual species.

Proposals to amend the ESA in Congress unfortunately remain mired in controversy. Thankfully, the FWS has been able to implement important reforms at the administrative level. Agency reforms, such as the no surprises and safe harbor policies and the development of regional HCPs, have fundamentally changed the ESA, in many people's view for the better. By easing the burden on property owners, these reforms also have acted as a political steam valve that has deflated calls to weaken the ESA.

---

[82] *See, e.g.,* Jeffrey J. Rachlinski, *Noah by the Numbers: An Empirical Evaluation of the Endangered Species Act,* 82 Cornell L. Rev. 356 (1997).

[83] *See* J. Michael Scott, Dale D. Goble, Leona K. Svancara, & Anna Pidgorna, *By the Numbers,* in The Endangered Species Act at Thirty 16, 31 (Dale D. Goble, J. Michael Scott, & Frank Davis eds., 2006).

QUESTIONS AND DISCUSSION

1.   Some environmental scholars have argued that courts should extend the public trust doctrine to protect environmental resources other than tidelands and navigable waterways. Do you agree? If courts were to expand the reach of the doctrine, how should they decide what additional resources to protect? Should the public trust doctrine apply to (a) Yosemite National Park, (b) the Gettysburg National Military Park, or (c) the last remaining habitat of an endangered woodpecker?

2.   What are the policy justifications for regulating all wetlands and endangered species at the federal level? If an endangered frog species is found only in the middle of Nebraska, why should the federal government decide whether and how to protect the frog? Similarly, if there is an isolated wetland in the middle of a large ranch in Wyoming, does the federal government have an interest in regulating it? Even if the federal government has an interest in the protection of such species and wetlands, do states have a greater interest in being able to decide how land within their borders should be utilized? Should these be matters for the states to decide without interference by the federal government?

3.   Should the federal government permit a landowner to destroy a valuable wetland in return for restoring, creating, or protecting wetlands elsewhere? If so, how should the government decide whether the mitigation is adequate?

4.   Should the ESA permit the FWS to consider economic costs in deciding whether to prohibit the development of a piece of land or to block a proposed federal project? Are endangered species, to use the words of the House report on the ESA, of "incalculable" value? If tearing down a subdivision and restoring the habitat on which the subdivision sits would improve the recovery chances of an endangered species, should the ESA require it? If not, does that mean that species are not of incalculable value?

5.   Should the federal government compensate property owners whose land declines in value as a result of regulation under the ESA? In answering this question, should it matter if Congress is unlikely to appropriate the money needed to regulate large quantities of land? If Congress is unlikely to appropriate the funds, is that an indication that endangered species are not really worth the economic cost of protecting them?

6.   Should Congress pass a new law that would give the Department of the Interior the authority to regulate land use to protect the health and function of ecosystems? Would this make more sense than regulating land use to protect individual species on the brink of extinction?

7.   Does the ESA protect individual members of an endangered species or populations of endangered species? Does this reflect an environmental ethic of animal rights?

Chapter 11

ENERGY

Energy poses one of the major domestic and global policy issues today. You cannot pick up a newspaper without reading about some aspect of the energy challenges facing the nation and the world. Not surprisingly, energy constitutes one of the major priorities for the Obama Administration, Congress, and many states. Although the United States has passed three energy-policy acts over the past 25 years (in 1992, 2005, and 2007), it has not had a coherent energy policy for decades. Instead, the nation has bounced from policy prescription to policy prescription in response to particular events and threats. Public attention to energy has also fluctuated over time. Periodic energy "crises," generally related to oil shortages or increasing oil prices, have generated calls for major policy responses, but as soon as each crisis has abated, the interest of the public and politicians in energy has quickly waned.

I.   Today's Energy Concerns

Three separate concerns have spawned the current interest in energy. All of the concerns stem from the United States' dependence on fossil fuels (coal, natural gas, and petroleum)—and its dependence on petroleum in particular. As Figure 11–1 shows, fossil fuels furnish over 80 percent of the energy consumed in the United States, and petroleum is the most important of these fuels (providing over a third of all the energy). Petroleum is the predominant fuel in the transportation sector, where it constitutes almost 95% of the energy used to power our cars and trucks. Petroleum, however, is of only marginal importance in the generation of electricity. Coal provides slightly less than half of the nation's electrical power, with natural gas furnishing about 20% and petroleum generating less than one percent.

The large environmental impact of fossil fuels presents the first major energy concern. As discussed in earlier chapters, the burning of fossil fuels produces a number of environmental problems, including global climate change and local air pollution. Fossil fuels currently produce about three quarters of the CO_2 emissions in the United States, making it the largest single contributor to climate change. Fossil fuels are also the major source of local and regional air pollution, including CO (motor vehicle emissions), NO_x (vehicle emissions and fossil-fuel power plants), SO_2 (coal-burning power plants), and VOCs (vehicle emissions). The development and extraction of fossil fuels in the United State also has long raised a wide variety of environmental concerns. As discussed earlier, for example, states have recently worried about the risks of fracking in connection with natural-gas development, including groundwater contamination, proper disposal of waste water, and promotion of seismic activity. See pages 46–47.

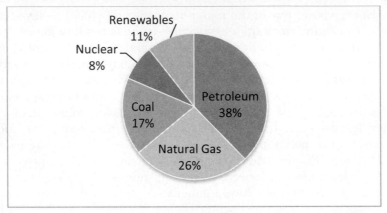

Figure 11–1: Sources of U.S. Energy Consumption (April 2013)[1]

In the case of petroleum, policy makers worry about not only environmental harms but also the potential security risks that high dependence on petroleum poses. This security concern has a number of elements. Some policy makers, for example, worry that the nation's heavy reliance on oil makes us vulnerable to terrorists and unfriendly governments who can disrupt the international flow of petroleum. Three out of every five barrels of oil sold today in the global market originate in insecure or sometimes unfriendly regions and nations, including the Persian Gulf, North Africa, Nigeria, Angola, Venezuela, Russia, and the Caspian states. Other policy makers worry that our need to ensure a steady supply of petroleum forces us to support and defend oil-producing states that are authoritarian or hostile to our national values. Finally, oil profits often find their way into the hands of rogue states and terrorist organizations, which can then use the money to undermine our interests.

A final energy concern is the impact of increasing oil prices, and large swings in the prices, on the nation's economy. From the mid-1980s until the first several years of this century, oil generally sold on the world market for less than $25 per barrel, and average gasoline prices in the United States were less than $1.50 per gallon. Oil prices broke through $30 per barrel in 2003, however, and

---

[1] U.S. Department of Energy, U.S. Energy Information Administration, Monthly Energy Review (July 2013).

ultimately rose to almost $150 per barrel in July 2008 (with average gasoline prices climbing over $4 per gallon). The economic recession of late 2008 and 2009 helped bring the price back down. Oil prices, however, are still far higher than historic levels. Since early 2011, the price of oil has hovered over $100 per barrel, and gasoline has been selling on average for more than $3.50 per gallon. Analysts have blamed today's higher price on multiple factors, including rapidly rising world demand for petroleum (as economic growth has mushroomed in developing nations such as China and India) and a slowdown in the growth of global oil production.

Energy experts, moreover, predict that there is a very high likelihood (80 percent according to one group) that the world will see a major disruption in its oil supplies over the next ten years—leading to a significant spike in world oil prices. Such spikes can have serious economic repercussions in the United States. Virtually every major oil price increase since 1970, for example, has been followed by a recession.

These various concerns do not always point to the same solutions. The federal government and a number of states, for example, currently subsidize U.S. production and sales of biofuels, including corn-based ethanol. This policy reduces, at the margin, our reliance on foreign oil and thus may help address national security concerns. Because fossil fuels are used to grow and process corn, however, greenhouse gas emissions from corn-based ethanol are at best only slightly lower than from gasoline, and some studies suggest that greenhouse gas emissions are actually higher for corn-based ethanol when measured over its entire lifecycle. Because biofuel prices are linked to oil prices in the global market, greater reliance on biofuels also fails to insulate the United States from economic disruptions.

II. Conservation

Energy conservation offers one of the cheapest and fastest ways of reducing the nation's use of petroleum and other fossil fuels. In many cases, energy conservation pays for itself in reduced energy costs. Energy conservation, moreover, addresses all three of the concerns outlined in the last section. Conservation reduces greenhouse gas emissions, lowers our reliance on foreign oil, and softens the impact of increased oil prices. Energy conservation is thus a win-win-win solution.

Given that energy conservation often pays for itself, does the government even need to intervene to promote conservation? The answer is "yes," for several reasons. First, consumers and businesses often do not know the energy savings from different products that they are considering purchasing or from different actions they could take at home or work. To address this problem, the government often provides the public with information regarding the energy-saving potential of appliances and practices. The federal government's *Energy Star* program, jointly created by EPA and the U.S. Department of Energy in 1992, illustrates this approach. Manufacturers whose electronic products meet energy standards established by the federal government can place Energy Star labels on the products. The label promotes sales of these products and places pressure on other manufacturers to improve the energy efficiency of their products. Energy Star has been extremely successful, with a high percentage of major appliances, computer products, and office equipment now enrolled in the program. Studies indicate that Energy Star has reduced energy consumption in the United States by about five percent, saving consumers almost $25 billion per year and producing greenhouse gas emissions equivalent to taking 43 million vehicles off the road. Because of the success of Energy Star's product certification, the program has been extended to residential and conservation buildings.

Information, however, is often not enough by itself to encourage consumers and businesses to engage in a socially optimum amount of energy conservation. Although consumers and businesses may consider the direct savings to themselves of reduced energy costs when choosing a new product or deciding whether to engage in an energy-saving practice, they generally do not take into account the broader benefits to society from reduced pollution or greater energy security. Moreover, as discussed in Chapter 2 at page 28, consumers are often not good at comparing current price differentials among competing products with the long-run savings from energy efficiency. Faced by a choice between a low-priced "energy hog" and a higher priced energy-conserving appliance, consumers often focus on the immediate hit to their pocket books rather than on the longer term energy savings.

Policy makers therefore have turned to a variety of other tools to further encourage energy conservation. Both federal and state governments, for example, have often required that products achieve a minimum level of energy efficiency. Perhaps the best example is the *corporate average fuel economy ("CAFE") standards* for motor vehicles set by the federal government under the Energy Policy and Conservation Act.[2] Fuel efficiency is particularly important in efforts to reduce U.S. oil consumption because transportation accounts for two-thirds of that consumption. Since 1978, the CAFE standards have mandated a fuel economy standard

---

[2] 42 U.S.C. § 6201 et seq.

for new passenger cars (set at 34.4 miles per gallon for 2013) and for light-duty trucks (which include minivans and sport utility vehicles—set at 25.6 mpg). The Obama Administration had adopted two new rules that will dramatically increase the fuel economy standards over time. By 2025, the rules call for a 55.3 mpg standard for passenger cars and 39.3 mpg for light trucks.

The federal government has supplemented the CAFE standards with cash incentives designed to encourage drivers to purchase vehicles with high driving mileage. Purchasers of plug-in hybrids, for example, currently receive federal tax credits ranging from $2500 to $7500 per vehicle. Electric vehicles enjoy tax credits of $7500. A number of states, including California, provide similar incentives. As part of the 2009 Economic Recovery Act, Congress also created a temporary "cash-for-clunkers program" that gave a $4000 rebate to drivers who traded in older, fuel-inefficient vehicles for new cars with high gas mileage.

Beginning in the 1970s and 1980s, several states, including California and New York, established minimum energy efficiency standards for a range of appliances. Manufacturers, concerned that states might set a variety of inconsistent standards, lobbied in turn for national standards that would supersede the state standards. Today the national government has established energy-efficiency standards for many major household appliances, including refrigerators, air conditioners, washers, dryers, and dishwashers. Congress has also banned some high-energy products, such as the traditional incandescent light bulb, which is currently being phased out.

Studies indicate that these product standards have not only reduced energy use but also been cost effective. Studies estimate that the CAFE standards, along with higher gasoline prices, led to more than a 50 percent improvement in fuel economy between 1978 and 1985. As Americans switched to larger and more powerful vehicles over the following two decades, average fuel economy unfortunately worsened, but fuel economy remained better than it would have been without the CAFE standards. Studies estimate that, by the year 2000, CAFE standards combined with higher prices had reduced domestic oil consumption by about 14 percent and reduced carbon emissions by about 100 million metric tons per year (6 percent of total carbon emissions) from what they otherwise would have been. National appliance standards annually save about 1.2 quads of energy (more than the current U.S. production of wind and solar power combined) at a net cost savings of almost $1 billion per year.

State officials have also increasingly encouraged electric utilities to adopt *demand-side management* (DSM) programs. In these programs, electricity producers seek to reduce demand to better match their available supplies. Suppliers use a variety of techniques to reduce demand. Many electricity suppliers subsidize energy-saving products, such as fluorescent light bulbs or better housing insulation. Suppliers also work with commercial and industrial users to find and demonstrate new ways of reducing energy use. DSM programs currently cover millions of residential, commercial, and industrial customers throughout the United States. Amory Lovins has described this strategy as producing "Negawatts."

Although all of these measures have cost-effectively reduced energy use, some economists worry that they also suffer from unnecessary drawbacks and are not as effective as other possible policies. Consider three potential drawbacks to CAFE standards. First, the least expensive way for car manufacturers to improve a car's fuel efficiency is to make the car lighter, so that less fuel is needed to move it. But this also can reduce the crashworthiness of the cars. One study by the National Academy of Sciences estimated that CAFE standards resulted in about 2,000 more fatalities per year in 2003. Second, by improving fuel mileage and thus reducing the cost of driving a car, CAFE standards actually can encourage some drivers to drive more, offsetting some of the conservation benefits that would otherwise result. Finally, if the CAFE standards result in a significant increase in the purchase price of a new automobile and if consumers are sensitive to upfront costs, CAFE standards may encourage people to keep driving their older vehicles, which have low gas mileage and produce high levels of pollution. (This problem is analogous to the problem with strict new source performance standards under the Clean Air Act, which can encourage companies to keep old facilities in operation as long as possible. See pages 122–123.)

Economists would prefer to encourage conservation by raising the price of energy to reflect its true cost to society. Economists argue that the federal government should impose a tax on gasoline and other fossil fuels equal to the impact that fossil fuels have on local air pollution and the global climate. A tax on gasoline, according to economists, would encourage automobile drivers to buy smaller cars *and* to drive less and keep their cars better tuned. A tax on the use of fossil fuels to produce electricity, by raising the price of such electricity, would encourage home owners and companies to reduce their energy consumption both through the products they buy and in the energy practices they follow. Taxes, moreover, would bring new revenue into the federal treasury and help reduce the national deficit. A \$25-per-barrel oil tax would bring in about \$125 billion per year in revenue. To date, however, such taxes have faced fierce political resistance.

A federal cap-and-trade system for carbon could have a similar effect as a tax on fossil fuels (depending on how allowances were allocated). Industries, including electric utilities, that used less fossil fuels would emit less carbon, allowing them either to sell emission credits (if they were at or below their cap) or to purchase fewer credits (if they were above their cap). By effectively creating a price for carbon emissions, a cap-and-trade system would thus encourage energy conservation.

III. Renewable Energy

The environmental, security, and economic drawbacks of fossil fuels have generated significant interest since the 1970s in renewable energy. As shown in Figure 11–1, the vast majority of the energy used in the United States today comes from fossil fuels or nuclear energy. Renewable energy constitutes only about 10 percent of total energy use. Approximately a third of the renewable energy production in the United States, moreover, comes from hydropower, which has very limited opportunity for growth. See Figure 11–2. Even existing hydroelectric dams face significant political opposition because of their impact on fish and the environment. Policy makers therefore have focused their attention on wind, biofuels, geothermal, and solar.

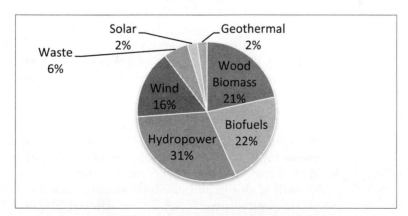

Figure 11–2: Relative Shares of Major Sources of Renewable Energy Consumption (April 2013)[3]

In the electricity sector, the principal interest is in wind and solar. Although wind generates only about two percent of total U.S.

---

[3]   U.S. Department of Energy, U.S. Energy Information Administration, *Monthly Energy Review* (July 2013).

electric power consumption, that's up over 1000% in the last decade, and wind is currently the least expensive renewable, with further cost savings expected in the future. The major obstacles to wind are its intermittency (requiring new energy storage technology if wind is to provide a sizable portion of U.S. demand), the long distances between the best wind resources and population centers (requiring extensive new transmission systems), and opposition from local communities concerned by wind energy's impact on birds and landscapes.

Although solar power currently generates even less electricity in the United States than wind power contributes, solar power is our largest potential energy resource, and its energy contribution is expected to grow with the development of more efficient energy technologies—particularly in the Southwest and Southeast where available sunlight is greatest. Like wind, solar power is intermittent (varying by the time of day and cloud cover). Large-scale solar generation facilities can also impact local land uses and water resources, and photovoltaic panels sometimes contain toxic substances.

In the case of motor vehicles, the major renewable options are liquid biofuels (ethanol and biodiesel), electricity (if generated from renewable fuels), and hydrogen. The most competitive option in the short run is biofuel, which can be used by internal combustion engines and thus does not require a major transformation in the automotive industry. Domestic car manufacturers are already producing millions of "flex-fuel vehicles" that can run on fuels that contain as much as 85 percent ethanol. The use of biodiesel (made from either raw vegetable oils or recycled cooking oil) actually dates back to the invention of the diesel engine in 1878. Plug-in hybrids, which combine sizable on-board battery storage with internal combustion engines that can recharge the batteries and supply independent power when needed, are also likely to play a major role in the short run in weaning drivers from a dependence on petroleum. In the longer run, both electricity and hydrogen are likely to play a greater role. Pure electric vehicles need a significant breakthrough in battery technology to be competitive in the marketplace (although high-priced prototype vehicles, such as the Tesla, are already in limited production in the United States and elsewhere). Hydrogen will require both a major vehicle redesign and a radical new infrastructure for delivering hydrogen to consumers. With new technological breakthroughs, however, both electricity and hydrogen are likely to help motor vehicles break free of fossil fuels in the long term.

The major problem today is that renewable sources of energy generally cost consumers five to ten percent more than fossil fuels.

Some households are willing to pay the premium. About a quarter of all the utilities provide "green power" options to consumers, and "green power" companies in a number of states have marketed the environmental benefits of their product and tried to attract households willing to pay the cost premium. The cost of renewable energy, moreover, has been falling over time as new technologies come on line and power companies gain greater experience with their use. Solar costs, for example, have fallen ten percent just in the last five years.

Renewable energy currently costs more in part because fossil fuels enjoy a variety of governmental subsidies and because consumers do not have to pay the environmental costs of fossil fuels, including climate impacts. The Environmental Law Institute estimates that, from 2002 through 2008, the United States provided $72 billion in subsidies to the fossil fuel industry (in comparison to only $29 billion in subsidies to the renewable sector). In 2007, the House of Representatives voted to eliminate the oil subsidies and use the proceeds to fund work on renewable energy, but the Senate refused to follow suit.

As with transportation, one of the most effective measures that the United States could take to promote renewable energy, according to economists and other policy analysts, would be to impose a tax on the use of fossil fuels that reflects the damages that are likely to result from the carbon emissions associated with fossil use. Such a tax would force utilities to look for ways to reduce their carbon emissions, by switching to less carbon-intensive fossil fuels (e.g., natural gas), using renewable energy sources, or promoting greater conservation (as discussed in the last section).

With no carbon tax or cap-and-trade system to encourage renewable energy production, policy makers in the past have turned to a variety of other mechanisms to help promote the development and use of alternative fuels. One of the principal means that the federal government has used to promote renewable energy has been to fund research and development (R&D) for new energy technologies. In the Renewable Energy and Energy Efficiency Technology Competitiveness Act of 1989, for example, Congress authorized "an aggressive national program of research, development, and demonstration of renewable energy and energy efficiency technologies in order to ensure a stable and secure future energy supply."[4] In the Energy Policy Act of 1992, Congress ordered the Secretary of Energy to solicit competitive proposals for

---

[4] 42 U.S.C. § 12001(b).

demonstration and commercial-application projects for renewable energy.[5]

According to economists, private markets do not provide an optimum level of energy R&D. R&D generally produces benefits not only to the company engaged in the research but also to other companies and to society at large. Yet individual companies decide how much to invest in R&D based purely on the benefits to them. Governmental support of R&D is therefore important.

Studies, however, suggest that both private and public funding for R&D in the energy sector has been inadequate for the past several decades. Federal investments in energy R&D have actually totaled less than one percent of all federal R&D (except for a brief period from 1977–1981 when it rose above 10 percent). R&D by the United States Department of Energy on all energy sources, including not only renewable sources but clean coal technology and conservation, fell over two-thirds in the early 1980s and, since 1986, has remained largely flat in real dollars.

While R&D will hopefully promote long-term advances in renewable energy, it does little to increase the current adoption of renewable technologies. Governments have adopted a variety of other mechanisms to serve this second function. Federal and state governments, for example, have offered financial incentives for the production and use of renewable energy. In the electricity sector, the federal *renewable electricity production credit* (REPC) provides a tax subsidy for the production of electricity from wind, geothermal, landfill gas, and closed-loop biomass equal to about two cents per kilowatt produced. About half the states provide additional subsidies of their own. The federal government also gives a 10 percent tax credit for new investments in geothermal and solar generation facilities. In the case of vehicle fuels, the federal government currently subsidizes the sale of ethanol, making corn-based ethanol competitive with gasoline prices as low as $3 per gallon. The federal government also offers loan guarantees for biofuel refineries.

Nearly 30 states and the District of Columbia have turned to *renewable portfolio standards (RPS)* to promote renewable energy. Under RPS programs, states require utilities within their borders to distribute and, in some cases, generate a minimum percentage of their electricity from qualified renewable systems. Most RPS programs increase the percentage of electricity that utilities must distribute or generate from renewable energy over time. The percentages ultimately required by states with existing RPS programs vary from a high of 40% in Hawaii (which must be

---

[5] 42 U.S.C. § 12005.

achieved by 2030) to a low of 10% in Michigan, South Dakota, Vermont, and Wisconsin (with deadlines in the middle of this decade). Some RPS programs also include trading systems, similar to the SO₂ trading system in the Clean Air Act (discussed in Chapter 5). Utilities that are able to distribute or generate more electricity from renewables than the RPS requires receive credits that they can sell to utilities that fail to meet their renewables quota. Congress has considered, but failed to pass a national RPS on a number of occasions.

RPS programs illustrate the potential conflict among the various goals of reducing reliance on traditional fossil fuels—a cleaner environment, energy independence, and a healthy economy. States differ as to what counts as a renewable energy source for purposes of their RPS programs. All sources exclude traditional fossil fuels. Some states, however, include only those sources that are likely to reduce carbon emissions (e.g., solar and wind power, as well as certain hydroelectric facilities), while other states include a number of other sources that, while reducing reliance on fossil fuels and thus promoting energy independence, could potentially generate significant greenhouse gas emissions (e.g., generators using some types of biomass or biofuels).

To help spur changes in automotive fuels, California has adopted a *low-carbon fuel standard* that requires fuel blenders, refiners, and importers to reduce carbon emissions from their total fuel mix 10 percent by 2020. Regulated companies can meet the standard themselves or buy credits from producers of low-carbon fuels. A major question in the establishment of low-carbon fuel standards is how to measure the carbon emissions of particular fuels. California looks at a fuel's emissions over its entire lifecycle ("well to wheel"), in order to avoid the risk that the mandate will simply shift consumption from fuels with high direct emissions to those that produce lower direct emissions but significant emissions in their production. For example, California's lifecycle emissions score for biofuels includes any emissions from the conversion of forests to farms for the cultivation of a specific biofuel stock. Vehicle manufacturers have strongly opposed California's low-carbon fuel standard, and a federal district court judge in 2011 enjoined the California program on the ground that, because the standard applies to fuels manufactured outside California, it "reaches beyond its boundaries to regulate activities wholly outside of its borders" and "impermissibly treads into the province and powers" of the federal government.[6]

---

[6] *Rocky Mtn. Farmers Union v. Goldstene,* 843 F. Supp. 2d 1071 (E.D. Cal. 2011).

Economists warn that RPS programs and low-carbon fuel standards, depending on how they are designed, can be unnecessarily costly and actually increase carbon emissions. One study of low-carbon fuel standards, for example, found that the cost of reducing carbon emissions from fuels by 10% could cost anywhere from $307 to $2272 per ton of carbon dioxide—much more than the likely cost of CO_2 emission allowances under cap-and-trade systems considered by Congress. The same study concludes that low-carbon fuel standards that place no cap on total fuel consumption could lead drivers to purchase more total fuel, increasing total carbon emissions while decreasing emissions per gallon of fuel.

Some states and localities also promote the development of fuel cells, solar photovoltaic systems, and other on-site sources of renewable energy through *net metering.* If a homeowner or company generates more energy from an on-site solar energy system than the homeowner or company consumes, the homeowner or company normally does not benefit. Under net metering, however, the homeowner or company can run the electricity meter "backwards" and sell the excess energy at retail price to the local energy supplier.

Although these various programs are far from perfect, such governmental efforts, along with the rising price of fossil fuels in recent years, have led to significant increases in renewable energy use. As noted earlier, wind energy increased by an impressive 1000 percent in the last decade. Generation of electricity from fossil fuels unfortunately also increased over this period of time. The open question is how public policy will affect the amount and distribution of electricity generation in the future.

IV. Siting New Energy Facilities and Transmission Lines

An emerging issue in the development of renewable energy is the siting of new renewable energy facilities and the transmission lines needed to carry the electricity from the generation facilities to customers. Wind and solar facilities have to be located in areas where there is adequate wind and sunlight. Unfortunately, many of these areas are located either in regions where transmission infrastructure does not exist or where current transmission capacity is constrained. Tens of thousands of miles of new transmissions lines will be needed in order to make maximum use of these renewable energy sources.

Many communities that have never been home to electric generating plants have suddenly become the subject of proposals to site wind or solar infrastructure. The result has been a new wave of "not in my backyard"—or NIMBYs—that is raising a "green versus green" debate. In one of the most famous examples, the citizens of Cape Cod, Massachusetts, as well as local Indian tribes and the Massachusetts Historical Commission, actively opposed the construction of an offshore wind farm known as Cape Wind, even though the facility could furnish 75 percent of the electricity used on Cape Cod. Opposition delayed the project for years, although Secretary of the Interior Ray Salazar ultimately approved the project in April 2010.

Cape Wind is not an isolated example of controversy. Community and environmental opposition has arisen to renewable energy projects in California's Mojave Desert, Northern Virginia, and many other locations around the nation.[7] Communities oppose the siting of renewable energy facilities in their neighborhoods for multiple reasons, including visual, noise, cultural, and environmental impacts.

One important question is whether the siting of renewable energy facilities should have to comply with the same environmental procedures and standards as conventional energy facilities. Opponents of specific renewable energy projects argue that there is no reason to exempt renewable energy from the same rigorous review and standards as apply to other facilities. Proponents respond that the dangers of climate change call for quick siting and that traditional procedures can take years if not decades to complete. Responding to such concerns, the U.S. Department of Interior has "fast tracked" the environmental review of a number of solar power-plant proposals. Some energy groups have suggested that the government should employ a careful planning process to determine those areas that are best suited for renewable energy and then fast track reviews of individual projects within those areas.

Transmission lines raise similar community and environmental concerns as renewable energy facilities. Where transmission lines cross multiple states in bringing electricity from a generation plant to customers, states in the middle also sometimes object that they are being asked to bear the burden, but enjoy none of the benefits, of the energy transmission. Some states have argued that they should not have to host a transmission line that takes energy to another state if energy facilities can be sited in the other state.

---

[7] The U.S. Chamber of Commerce currently maintains a website, entitled "Project No Project," that lists renewable (and other) energy projects that have been caught up in "green tape." See www.projectnoproject.com.

States historically have enjoyed jurisdiction over the siting of electric transmission lines within their jurisdictions. In response to concerns over the siting of new transmission lines, however, the Energy Policy Act of 2005 (EPAct) authorized the Federal Energy Regulatory Commission (FERC) to issue a permit for the construction of interstate power lines in a "national interest electric transmission corridor" where a state has "withheld approval for more than 1 year."[8] According to then-Energy Secretary Samuel Bodman, "The parochial interests that shaped energy policy in the 20th century will no longer work."

FERC interpreted EPAct as giving them the authority to approve an interstate power line not only where a state fails to act, but also where a state has specifically denied a permit for a new power line. In 2009, a federal court of appeals disagreed by a 2–1 vote and held that FERC cannot override the specific denial of a permit by a state.[9] The majority worried that FERC's broader interpretation would interfere with normal state jurisdiction and a state's ability to "deny a permit based on traditional considerations like cost and benefit, land use and environmental impacts, and health and safety." The dissent, by contrast, argued that FERC's interpretation was supported by the "critical national energy interests that Congress sought to protect." In the view of the dissent, FERC would bring a "broader national perspective to siting proposals . . . than individual states possess."

Since the court of appeals' decision, Congress has considered various options for addressing the issue. Some proposed bills would have given FERC the clear authority to override state decisions in the case of power lines of significant national interest. Other bills would have encouraged the creation of regional siting teams, consisting of representatives of relevant states, national agencies, companies, and environmental organizations, to determine appropriate transmission paths. Most of the bills would have addressed not only the siting issue but also how to determine appropriate cost allocations among affected states. To date, however, Congress has failed to adopt any of the options.

CASE STUDY: THE SPANISH FORK WIND PROJECT[10]

In the early 2000s, Tracy Livingston, an entrepreneur, and his engineering colleague, Christine Mikell, decided to make a "difference in the world" by developing a small 18.9 megawatt wind-energy project near

---

[8] 16 U.S.C. § 824p(b)(1).

[9] *Piedmont Environmental Council v. FERC*, 558 F.3d 304 (4th Cir. 2009).

[10] This Case Study draws its facts from Edwin Stafford & Cathy Hartman, *Wind Development as "Sustainable Entrepreneurship,"* Rural Connections, June 2013, at 23.

the town of Spanish Fork, Utah (population 35,000). Livingston and Mikell began by looking for a good site for their project. They discarded the first site they considered—an abandoned gravel pit away from local housing—when a local official raised water-quality concerns. They then moved their project to another site closer to the homes. The two developers commissioned environmental and noise studies and held a town-hall meeting at which 60 local residents appeared. The residents seemed generally favorable toward the project, and the Spanish Fork city council approved the site in 2005.

Making the project work economically was initially harder. Under the Public Utility Regulatory Policies Act of 1978 (PURPA), utilities must buy sustainable power at the utility's "avoided cost"—i.e., the price that it would cost them to produce the power themselves or buy it from another source. The local electricity utility, Rocky Mountain Power (RMP), was already buying energy from a large wind project in a neighboring state at a price that would have made the Spanish Fork project profitable. However, RMP claimed that its avoided cost was actually the cost of generating power from its own, mostly coal-fired plants. Because the utility had already "depreciated" or written off most of the capital costs of these plants, this "avoided cost" was much less than the price that would permit the Spanish Fork project to break even. Thankfully for their project, Livingston and Mikell were able to convince the Utah Public Service Commission to use the higher price being paid for out-of-state wind as the avoided cost.

The developers also needed other financial help to make the project succeed, including a state tax incentive and a state program that allowed "community re-development areas" to enjoy temporary property-tax reductions. With the tax incentive set to expire, Livingston and Mikell had to rally renewable-energy supporters to push the state legislature for an extension of the incentive. The developers also had to convince local governmental agencies to support the designation of the wind project as a community-redevelopment area. Particularly important was the support of the local school district (which relied heavily on local property tax revenue to support its educational work).

Just when the economics of the project seemed to be coming together, local citizens suddenly raised new objections to the project. Many heard about the project for the first time from a local TV channel several months after the Spanish Fork city council approved the project and claimed that the developers had never consulted them. Local residents worried about the potential impact of the project on noise levels, home values, and the community's character. To quiet concerns, the developers agreed to move the project back to the gravel pit (where an independent engineering study showed that there would not be a water-quality problem after all) and emphasized the benefits of the project to the local community (including $2.4 million in tax revenues over the life of the project and a boost in local employment and spending).

In the end, Livingston and Mikell were successful. In 2008, the developers finished their wind farm, which today provides enough energy to power over 6,000 homes in the region.

What are the lessons of the Spanish Fork wind project for future developers of sustainable energy? Did Livingston and Mikell make any mistakes? Are you surprised by the importance of local politics to the success of the project? What governmental policies might help in the development of sustainable-energy projects?

V. Carbon Capture and Storage

Many people believe that "clean coal" is also an important answer to the nation's energy concerns. As noted earlier, coal supplies the majority of electric power produced in the United States. More importantly, the United States is self-sufficient in coal, supplying all of our current coal use. The United States also has the largest coal reserves of any nation in the world, constituting about a quarter of the total known global reserves—enough to meet our energy needs for probably several hundred years. The remainder of the world's coal reserves is spread out among more nations than any other fossil fuel (more than 100 countries currently mine coal), so there is less concern with regional disruptions and volatility. Coal, furthermore, is currently less expensive per unit of energy than either liquid petroleum or natural gas. So coal looks quite good in terms of both energy security and economic prosperity.

The problem with coal is its environmental impact. Chapter 5 discussed the high SO_2 content of coal and its association with acid rain. The burning of coal also produces a variety of other dangerous air pollutants (including NO_x, ozone, particulates, and mercury emissions), and its mining negatively affects air, land, and water. Most importantly, coal has a higher carbon content per unit of energy than either petroleum (17% less carbon per unit of energy) or natural gas (43% less). About a third of the United States' CO_2 emissions are from coal, making coal one of the major contributors in the nation to climate change.

The tension between coal's climate impact, on the one hand, and its domestic abundance and low cost, on the other, has led scientists and policy makers to examine the opportunity for *carbon capture and storage (CCS)*. In CCS, companies capture CO_2 emissions from their facilities and then store it someplace where it is unlikely to escape into the environment, such as in deep geological formations. CCS is discussed most frequently as a way to capture and sequester carbon from coal-fired power plants, but it can theoretically be used to reduce the carbon emissions from any large point source. One study has estimated that there is enough storage capacity in North America to sequester carbon emissions at current rates for more than 900 years. Some proponents of CCS suggest that the CO_2 could also be used in productive fashions, such as injecting the CO_2 into petroleum fields to enhance recovery.

CCS is still in its experimental stage. Only four industrial-scale carbon storage projects are currently operating in the United States, all in conjunction with oil and natural-gas production. Under the 2009 Economic Recovery Act, the federal government committed $1 billion toward the development and construction of FutureGen, a first-of-its-kind coal-fueled, near-zero-emissions power plant, to be located in Illinois and to utilize CCS. Scientists are still not sure how well CCS will work under various conditions, and the costs of installing and operating CCS is likely to be very expensive (at least initially).

CCS raises a number of policy issues. First, to what degree should the government promote CCS? In the early, experimental stages of CCS, should companies that engage in CCS get credit in cap-and-trade systems for the carbon that they store? Should the government subsidize the development of CCS technology and projects? We have very little knowledge about how CO_2 behaves in deep underground formations and what types of approaches work best in constraining stored carbon over the long run. The temptation is to wait until we have more information before putting significant resources into CCS, but the best way to get more information is to operate and monitor CCS projects.

Second, who owns the right to store CO_2 in underground formations? Does the storage capacity belong to overlying landowners (following the traditional common law rule that landowners own everything underlying their property)? If so, and if a landowner has sold the mineral rights underlying his land to an oil company, does the landowner continue to hold the sequestration rights, or do those belong to the oil company? Because CO_2 does not stay in one place but flows within a formation, can an overlying landowner object to the injection of CO_2 anywhere in a formation? Must the developer of a CCS project get the approval of all overlying landowners before moving forward? Should the law recognize private rights at all to sequestration capacity? If the law does recognize such rights, should the government condemn the rights and then hold and use them for the general public benefit?

Third, what regulations should the government impose on carbon storage? The government will want to ensure that carbon storage is unlikely to leak and that it does not lead to any significant damage to groundwater, other neighboring resources, or surface activities. Governmental regulations will therefore need to address such subjects as the selection of sites for storing the carbon, injection protocols, and monitoring for surface leakage or unintended movement of CO_2 into groundwater or nearby oil or gas reserves.

Finally, CCS projects must constrain carbon not only now but for hundreds or thousands of years. How should the government ensure long-term monitoring and management of a project—and provide for remediation and mitigation if containment problems develop? The government could require private insurance, but insurance generally does not deal with such long-term risks, and there is currently insufficient data to calculate premiums for even short-term risks. Some analysts argue that the government should take over the monitoring and management of a CCS project a decade or so after the project has completed its injection of CO_2, with the cost paid for by the project developer, taxpayers, or some combination thereof. Other analysts have suggested that the government should require project developers to enter into "risk pools" that would provide funds for the life of their projects. An underlying question in choosing among these options is whether the cost of long-term monitoring and management should be borne by project developers (on a polluter-pays principle) or by the public (on the theory that CCS is solving a broad societal problem).

QUESTIONS AND DISCUSSION

1. Look back at the discussion of the "5 P's" in the environmental policy toolkit at pages 54–60. If you were designing an energy policy for the United States, what measures would you include in the policy?

2. Virtually all experts seem to agree that raising the price of fossil fuels to reflect their true cost would be good public policy. This has been a common policy in Europe. Why then has Congress shown no interest in raising the price of fossil fuels? Is there any way of making such a measure politically acceptable? What costs should be included in any tax or surcharge imposed on fossil fuels?

3. What criteria should governments use in setting energy efficiency standards for cars, appliances, and other products? Should governments weigh the costs and benefits of alternative standards? Should governments set the most rigorous standard that is technologically feasible?

4. How might the federal government address the various "risk-risk" problems associated with CAFE standards (see page 20)?

5. The Department of Energy projects that total ethanol production in the United States (mostly from corn) will be 10–14 billion gallons annually by 2030—approximately 10% of projected U.S. gasoline demand in the same year. Brazil can produce sugar-based ethanol for about $1 per gallon, much less than the cost of U.S. corn-based ethanol, but the United States imposes high tariffs on imported Brazilian ethanol. If these tariffs were reduced or eliminated, the low-priced imports would move the United States faster toward independence from oil. Should the United States change the tariff? Does your answer depend on the impact of Brazilian ethanol production on forests in Brazil? What else would you want to know in deciding on the wisdom of the tariff?

6. How should the United States balance the goals of reducing carbon emissions, increasing energy independence, and protecting the economy? Should the United States promote development of off-shore oil reserves if that would help in providing energy security, even if it would produce more carbon emissions and risk other environmental injury?

7. How should Congress address the "green versus green" conflict over the siting of renewable energy facilities and transmission lines?

8. What are the potential lessons of the Superfund program (discussed in Chapter 8) for the long-term monitoring and regulation of CCS?

9. What is the appropriate role for the national and state governments in the regulation of CCS? Is CCS regulation primarily a matter for state regulation (like the regulation of resource extraction)? A number of states have already adopted laws to promote and regulate CCS, and the Interstate Oil and Gas Compact Commission (IOGCC) has published a model regulatory framework for states. According to the IOGCC, the states have the necessary expertise and experience to regulate CCS because of their many years of experience regulating the underground storage of natural gas, as well oil and gas production. Or is CCS best regulated at the national level? The United States Environmental Protection Agency is currently developing rules for regulating the underground injection of CO_2 under the Safe Drinking Water Act.

Part 4

ENVIRONMENTAL IMPACT STATEMENTS

———

Chapter 12

THE NATIONAL ENVIRONMENTAL POLICY ACT

Passed in 1969, the National Environmental Policy Act (NEPA) was the first major statute of the modern era of environmental law.[1] A trail-blazer, NEPA took a fundamentally different approach than the patchwork laws that had preceded it and the more prescriptive national pollution statutes that would follow. NEPA does not seek to ensure environmental protection through technology-forcing standards or market instruments, nor does it mandate conservation of endangered species or wetlands. Rather, NEPA relies on information, forcing agencies to consider the environmental impacts of their proposed actions and alternatives. This approach reflects a New Deal faith in agency management—the belief that a bureaucracy will do the right thing if it considers the proper issues. Without question, NEPA's influence has been far-reaching, with its progeny in the statute books of 19 states (including CEQA in California, SEQR in New York, and SEPA in Washington state) as well as over 130 nations around the world.

NEPA requires that all federal agencies create an environmental impact statement (EIS) on a "recommendation or report on proposals for legislation and other major Federal actions significantly affecting the quality of the human environment."[2] Preparing an EIS is a considerable undertaking. Occasionally reaching the size of a large textbook, the EIS analyzes the environmental impacts across a range of proposed actions. This analysis considers both unavoidable adverse impacts and mitigation alternatives. For example, concerned over the amount of traffic in Yosemite Valley, the National Park Service might propose building a series of large parking lots throughout the Valley. Before undertaking this action, the Park Service must first prepare an EIS that considers not only the environmental impacts from this approach but also the impacts from a range of other actions— perhaps charging additional car fees to enter the Valley, a light-rail system, a tradable permit system for entry, or doing nothing at all. While laying out the environmental impacts of all these options, an EIS is agnostic and leaves the final choice to the decisionmaker.

NEPA also created the Council on Environmental Quality (CEQ) to oversee the NEPA process and its implementation.

---

[1] 42 U.S.C. §§ 4321 et seq.

[2] 42 U.S.C. § 4332(c); also known as NEPA Section 102(2)(c).

Perhaps surprisingly, the CEQ does not have (nor does NEPA provide for) enforcement authority. In practice, enforcement has come through citizen suits under the Administrative Procedure Act and federal question jurisdiction. In simple terms, NEPA cases generally raise one of two questions—should the agency have prepared an environmental impact statement and, if so, was the EIS adequate? The general remedy for a NEPA violation is a remand to the agency to stay its proposed project until it prepares and considers a satisfactory EIS.

Perhaps surprisingly, there have been thousands of NEPA suits. It might seem strange that NEPA's seemingly innocuous requirement of preparing an EIS has led to more lawsuits than any other environmental statute. What purposes does this requirement serve, and why are litigants so eager to enforce it?

As described above, the fundamental goal of NEPA is to *educate* decisionmakers, ideally by sensitizing them to environmental issues and helping the agencies find easy, inexpensive means of mitigating environmental impacts. From an *advocacy* perspective, an EIS can provide a source of leverage for internal agency opposition. A study by the National Science Foundation in the 1980s, for example, concluded that EISs give agency personnel a tool "to resist political importunities to pursue environmentally harmful measures." Moreover, it provides information that can be used by outside groups to fight an agency's decision in court, and the information is not easily dismissed. It's hard, after all, for an agency to explain why its own data in the EIS are incorrect. In relying on the EIS, in some instances litigants may be able to show that an agency action is "arbitrary and capricious" under the Administrative Procedure Act. From a *political* perspective, the EIS can be used to educate the public and provide information that can be used to fight the decision through the legislature or voting booth. Finally, NEPA litigation can *delay* a project (particularly if the EIS must be done again), allowing time to organize opposition and, in some cases, making the project so costly that it expires on its own.

I. NEPA Grows Teeth

Calvert Cliffs' Coordinating Committee v. U.S. Atomic Energy Commission was the first significant decision that interpreted NEPA, and it provides a useful insight into agencies' lack of environmental concern at the time of NEPA's passage.[3] In complying with the statute, the Atomic Energy Commission's proposed rules fully acknowledged that NEPA requires a "detailed

---

[3] *Calvert Cliffs' Coordinating Committee v. United States Atomic Energy Commission*, 449 F.2d 1109 (D.C.Cir.1971).

statement" to be "prepared" and to "accompany" the licensing application for a nuclear plant. And amazingly, this is exactly what would have happened. The agency's staff would prepare an environmental impact statement on the license application, and it would accompany the license throughout the process. In a brilliant example of form over substance, though, *the statement would never be read or considered by the licensing board*. It would simply go along for the ride. In his opinion, Judge Skelly Wright stated that the whole point of NEPA is to ensure that environmental considerations are taken into account by agency decision makers. Thus, to survive judicial review, agencies must prove that they have fully considered the detailed environmental statement "at every important stage in the decision making process."

In decisions that followed, particularly *Strycker's Bay Neighborhood Council, Inc. v. Karlen*, courts have gone to great lengths to make clear that NEPA is a procedural rather than a substantive statute.[4] Once an agency has made a decision subject to NEPA's procedural requirements, the judge may only consider whether the agency was arbitrary and capricious in failing to prepare an EIS or consider the relevant environmental issues. The judge cannot make the substantive decision on behalf of the agency. So long as the agency complied with the NEPA process and fully considered the EIS, the decision must stand *even if* the agency did not choose the environmentally preferable option. As the legal realists made clear long ago, however, the distinction between procedural and substantive review quickly breaks down. After all, how can the court take a hard look to determine if the agency complied with NEPA's procedural requirements (i.e., whether it fully considered the relevant factors) unless the court assesses the agency's final decision (a substantive analysis)?

CALVERT CLIFFS' COORDINATING COMMITTEE, INC. V. UNITED STATES ATOMIC ENERGY COMMISSION
449 F.2d 1109 (D.C. Cir.1971)

Baltimore Gas and Electric Company purchased property on the shores of Chesapeake Bay in Calvert County, Maryland, in 1966 with the intention of constructing a nuclear power plant. The company applied for a license and began construction in 1968. A group of scientists at Johns Hopkins University concerned about the impact of the plant produced and distributed a study setting out the potential adverse impacts of radioactive emissions and heated cooling water from the plant on the Chesapeake Bay

---

[4] *Strycker's Bay Neighborhood Council Inc. v. Karlen*, 444 U.S. 223 (1980).

ecosystem, particularly the blue crab population. Spurred by the study and concerned over the plant's construction, a group of environmental organizations formed the Calvert Cliffs' Coordinating Committee to challenge the plant's licensing.

Before the power plant could begin operation, it had to be licensed by the Atomic Energy Commission. In order to comply with the recently-passed NEPA, the Commission amended its licensing rules in 1970. The rules provided that a utility must submit an environmental report for a plant, but the Commission's hearing board was not required to consider the environmental impact of a plant unless a challenge was raised. The Calvert Cliffs' Committee challenged the new Commission rules as insufficient and a violation of NEPA's requirement for an EIS.

In this case of first impression, Judge Skelly Wright and the D.C. Circuit not only struck down the Atomic Energy Commission's rules implementing NEPA but made NEPA's requirements judicially enforceable by setting out the procedural and substantive requirements for agency compliance. Stressing the importance of pre-construction reviews, Wright made clear that NEPA's requirement of an EIS "mandates a particular sort of careful and informed decisionmaking process and creates judicially enforceable duties. . . . [If a substantive] decision was reached procedurally without individualized consideration and balancing of environmental factors—conducted fully and in good faith, it is the responsibility of the courts to reverse." The Court held that the Commission rules were inadequate and remanded them for revision.

Following the decision, the Atomic Energy Commission suspended licensing of all nuclear plants for eighteen months while it amended its rules. Baltimore Gas and Electric chose to pursue the Calvert Cliffs plant. It drafted a full environmental impact statement, which concluded that the project would not have major adverse effects on the environment. The plant received an operating license for its first reactor in 1974, and it came on line in 1975. In 2000, it became the first nuclear plant to receive a license extension, and its reactors are licensed to operate through 2034 and 2036.

II. When Must an Agency Prepare an EIS?

The logic behind preparation of an EIS is straightforward—a better informed agency will make better decisions. To conserve resources, time and avoid hassle, though, it's equally obvious why, given the choice, some agencies would prefer not to create an EIS that questioned its proposed action, at all. Recall that an EIS must be prepared for a "recommendation or report on proposals for

legislation and other major Federal actions significantly affecting"
the environment. The threshold questions for an agency deciding
whether it must create an EIS, then, are (1) whether it is dealing
with legislative recommendations or major federal actions and (2)
whether the environmental impacts are significant.

Most of the legal skirmishing has been over federal actions
rather than proposed legislation. In court decisions, federal actions
have been interpreted to include a wide range of activities—such as
approval of specific projects (e.g., construction of a road in a
national park), approval of rules, regulations, and other official
policies (e.g., adopting a new set of regulations for concessionaires
in national parks), adoption of formal plans or programs to guide
agency decisions (e.g., a plan to permit local rangers greater
discretion over their parks), and permitting or funding of private
projects (e.g., approval of a river crossing for a power line).

Of course, not all federal actions trigger NEPA. Some statutes,
such as the Clean Air Act and parts of the Clean Water Act, exempt
preparation of an EIS, and the EPA need not comply with NEPA in
other instances where EPA's decision-making process is
functionally equivalent to NEPA's requirements. Decisions *not* to
act do not trigger NEPA, either. Thus neither the decision by the
Department of Interior not to stop a planned wolf kill by Alaska nor
the decision by the Forest Service not to continue a decades-long
practice of using herbicides to control vegetation in a National
Forest triggered NEPA review.[5] Finally, an agency may provide
indirect support (e.g., partial funding for a local group that
undertakes a project with environmental impacts). In determining
whether indirect action should constitute a federal action under
NEPA, courts have considered whether the action could exist
absent the support of the federal government.

A. Major Actions

Deciding whether there is a federal action is a straightforward
judgment in most instances, but it can become complicated when
considering NEPA's qualifying adjectives—that the federal action
be *major* and that it *significantly* affect the environment. One could
certainly imagine a major federal action that does not cause a
significant environmental impact (e.g., providing a congressman for
the District of Columbia) but, for actions that are environmental,
one cannot practically determine if an action is major solely by
focusing on the resources involved and ignoring its impacts.

---

[5] *See Defenders of Wildlife v. Andrus*, 627 F.2d 1238 (D.C.Cir.1980) (holding
that the Secretary's refusal to stop the wolf-hunt was not a "government action"
requiring an EIS); *See also Minnesota Pesticide Info. & Educ. v. Espy*, 29 F.3d 442
(8th Cir.1994) (holding that because the National Forest Service did not act
affirmatively, it was not required to submit an EIS).

Consider, for example, an application for a federal right-of-way so a private power line can cross a navigable waterway. The crossing of the waterway will, in itself, have little environmental impact. But construction of the 67 mile power line will have significant impacts, and cannot be built unless it crosses the waterway.[6] This looks like a minor federal action with major consequential impacts and is known as a "small handle" problem, when federal permission or funding is only a small (though necessary) part of a much bigger non-federal project. Does it require an EIS? Small handle cases go both ways, with some courts focusing on the impacts of the entire project made possible by federal activity (EIS required) and others just focusing on the federal activity (no EIS).

Agencies may try to avoid NEPA's reach by dividing up or "segmenting" projects. At the extreme, for example, consider how the Forest Service might try to avoid preparing an EIS for its decision to build a 20-mile road in a National Forest. This 20-mile road certainly would seem to be a major federal action significantly affecting the environment. But what if, instead, the Forest Service transformed the project into twenty separate decisions to build 1-mile roads? By segmenting, the agency can transform major projects into innocuous minor ones. In isolation, none of these one-mile roads will likely trigger the requirements for an EIS. In scrutinizing examples like this, therefore, courts have asked whether the separate segments have independent utility. If the road segment along mile 16 makes no sense without miles 17 and 15, then they must be considered together.[7]

A related problem concerns attempts to divide up separate types of actions. Imagine, for example, that the Forest Service decides to build a small road providing access into a timber harvest area but does not prepare an EIS because the road will not have significant impacts. Soon after, the Forest Service approves two timber sales in the harvest area but does not prepare an EIS because the timber harvest will not have significant effects.[8] Should the impacts of the road and timber sales be considered together in a joint EIS? "Connected actions" are interdependent parts of a larger action and cannot proceed unless other actions occur before or simultaneously. The timber sale cannot occur without the road, and the road makes no sense without the timber sales. As a result, the CEQ has stated that such actions must be considered together and many courts have ruled against such segmentation efforts by

---

[6] *Winnebago Tribe of Nebraska v. Ray,* 621 F.2d 269 (8th Cir.1980).

[7] 40 C.F.R. § 1508.27(b)(7). *See Thomas v. Peterson,* 753 F.2d 754, 761 (9th Cir.1985) (holding that the impact of both the road and lumber sale should be considered together).

[8] *Marsh v. Oregon Natural Resources Council,* 490 U.S. 360 (1989).

agencies, stressing NEPA's role in having agencies consider broadly the impacts of their actions.

B.   Significantly Affecting the Human Environment

In determining whether an action significantly affects the human environment (such as filling 30 acres of wetland), CEQ has directed agencies to consider the "context" and "intensity" of the proposed action. Put another way, the significance of the impact depends on the overall setting, particularly if it is in an environmentally sensitive or valued area. As a real estate agent would observe—location, location, location. The rules for determining significance are, by necessity, far from bright lines and ultimately require agencies to consider a range of factors in making a judgment call. In considering intensity, is the action controversial or does it involve uncertain effects? Are its impacts short or long term? Does it involve endangered species or critical habitat? Moreover, the impact must primarily be physical rather than social or economic. In *Metropolitan Edison v. People Against Nuclear Energy*, for example, prior to restarting the companion reactor at 3-Mile Island, the Nuclear Regulatory Commission performed an EIS that considered the effects of fog from cooling towers, the possibility of low-level radiation, and the danger of an accident.[9] Plaintiffs demanded that the EIS also consider the psychological trauma on the community of restarting the reactor. The court rejected this claim, stating that even if psychological injuries are genuine, they are too remote from the challenged action. In other words, an EIS must consider the risk of harm to the environment but not the potential *psychological* harm caused by exposure to risk.

C.   Categorical Exclusions

All agencies, whether environmental or not, can avoid NEPA compliance if the action is "categorically excluded"—that is, if categories of actions are specifically excluded in the agency's approved NEPA procedures. The CEQ rules define a "categorical exclusion" as "a category of actions which do not individually or cumulatively have a significant effect on the human environment and which have been found to have no such effect in procedures adopted by a Federal agency in implementation of [NEPA's] regulations."[10] In other words, the agency can determine for itself whether similar types of activities can be excluded from NEPA analysis. This makes good sense for some of the categorical exclusions provided by the Department of Agriculture, for example,

---

   [9] *Metropolitan Edison Co. v. People Against Nuclear Energy (PANE)*, 460 U.S. 766 (1983).
   [10] 40 C.F.R. § 1508.4.

which cover "routine activities such as personnel, organizational changes, or similar administrative functions."[11]

Categorical exclusions, however, can also provide an attractive means for an agency to avoid preparing an EIS and have generated a great deal of controversy. The most recent dispute arose in the aftermath of the Deepwater Horizon disaster in the Gulf of Mexico, where a British Petroleum oil rig drilling the Macondo Well caught fire, killing eleven workers, blowing out its seabed drilling equipment, gushing oil into the Gulf for 87 days and ultimately releasing almost 5 million barrels of oil. The Minerals Management Service (MMS) had provided categorical exclusions for oil exploration plans in the central and western Gulf of Mexico. The Presidential Commission later examining the disaster concluded that "MMS categorically excluded from environmental impact review BP's initial and revised exploration plans," and as a result "MMS performed no meaningful NEPA review of the potentially significant adverse environmental consequences associated with its permitting for drilling of BP's exploratory Macondo well."[12] It cannot be known whether a more complete NEPA analysis would have resulted in more effective spill prevention, but the story provides a sobering view of what can happen when NEPA compliance runs up against a mission-oriented agency and strong external pressure to speed up energy exploration activities.

III. Timing

If it is unclear whether an EIS must be prepared, agencies will often first develop a much shorter Environmental Assessment (EA). An EA operates as a quick and dirty review and, if it suggests no EIS is necessary, the agency will issue a FONSI (Finding Of No Significant Impact). Agencies can often use the EA process to reach a finding of no significant impact by including mitigation measures, known as a "mitigated FONSI." The decision not to undertake an EIS can then be challenged in court as final agency action. If the agency proceeds to prepare an EIS, a draft EIS is distributed and made available for public comment for 45 days. The agency then prepares a final EIS as well as responds to categories of public comments. Once the EIS has been issued, there is a 30-day moratorium on agency action so that challenges can be filed. This timeline, however, says nothing about when the review process should commence.

---

[11] 7 C.F.R. § 1508.4.

[12] Deep Water: The Gulf Oil Disaster and the Future of Offshore Drilling 81–85 (2010).

THE NEPA DECISIONMAKING PROCESS
See 40 C.F.R. § 1501.4

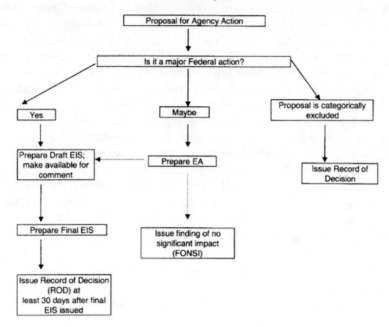

To prove useful, an EIS must be considered before the agency decides on an action, early enough that it can meaningfully contribute to the decision making process. Otherwise it simply serves as a *post hoc* rationalization for a decision already taken. Equally, the agency must have something fairly concrete in mind, otherwise the scope of potential EISs would be limitless. CEQ has taken a pragmatic view of timing, acknowledging that, even without a formal report or recommendation, an agency proposal may exist in fact. CEQ regulations require preparation of an EIS when the agency commences developing a proposal. This is before a report or recommendation, but after mere contemplation or study. In the context of connected actions, this means preparing an EIS before the first of the actions and assessing the cumulative impact. Challenging the timing of EIS preparation is difficult for parties outside the agency because, without inside knowledge, they really cannot know the status of various initiatives under consideration and whether so-called proposals have already become *de facto* decisions. To provide a bright line standard, courts have required that preparation of an EIS commence "before irreversible and irretrievable commitment of resources."[13]

---

[13] *Environmental Defense Fund, Inc. v. Andrus,* 596 F.2d 848, 852 (9th Cir.1979).

Another way timing plays out is in the context of scope. The case, *Kleppe v. Sierra Club*, for example, dealt with coal development policy on federal lands in the Northern Great Plains area.[14] It was clear to most observers during the Ford Administration in the mid-1970s that there was an ongoing plan to lease major areas in the northern Great Plains region to coal mining interests, but there was no official plan or announcement. The Department of Interior prepared EISs for its national coal leasing program and for individual leases. The Sierra Club, though, sued to force Interior to conduct a regional EIS, arguing that the national EIS was too general and the project-specific EISs too narrow to assess regional impacts. Impacts were greatest at the regional level and it was here that the Sierra Club argued alternative approaches should be considered. The problem from Interior's perspective, the government responded, was that there were many levels of decisionmaking at which one could reasonably prepare an EIS, and it was unreasonable to demand an EIS at every level.

The Supreme Court sided with Interior, stating that an EIS is required only where there is an actual report or recommendation on a proposal for major federal action. A comprehensive EIS is appropriate, the Court declared, when there are significant cumulative or synergistic environmental effects, but it is left to the discretion of the agency when this is the case. In other words, the Court defers to agency discretion over the proper scale of analysis. In practice, agencies have addressed this through the practice of "tiering," preparing successive EISs from broad scale to smaller. Thus an agency often prepares a "programmatic EIS" on an overall project, considering cumulative effects and overall alternatives, and then prepares site-specific supplemental EISs as they become appropriate. By tiering, an agency does not have to consider general effects each time it prepares an individual EIS, and does not need to be comprehensive in its programmatic EIS.

IV. Adequacy of the EIS

The issues raised above formed the basis for much of the early NEPA litigation. Much NEPA litigation focuses, as well, on the question of whether the EIS is adequate. A standard EIS will include an explanation of the purpose and need for action, a full description of alternative actions, an assessment of the environmental impacts of these actions, and possible mitigation measures to reduce adverse impacts of the proposed actions. In taking a hard look at such an EIS, courts have focused on questions of alternatives, adequacy, uncertainty, and new information. As we

---

[14] *Kleppe v. Sierra Club*, 427 U.S. 390 (1976).

shall see, this has resulted in a range of legal strategies to consider in challenging the adequacy of an EIS—the EIS did not set forth responsible opposing views or alternatives, it was not compiled in objective good faith, or it would not permit the decisionmaker to fully consider and balance the relevant factors.

According to CEQ regulations, the requirement that an EIS evaluate alternative actions is the "heart" of the EIS. This forces comparative assessment of the impacts and benefit of each action and, hopefully, shows the agency how it can achieve its objective in a less environmentally harmful manner. Obviously, though, there is an endless number of potential alternatives an agency could consider. To address this, courts have required that agencies consider an array of alternatives that fairly represent the *range* of alternatives. In *California v. Block*, for example, plaintiffs challenged the EIS informing the U.S. Forest Service's decision over which portions of a 62 million acre national forest should remain roadless and designated wilderness.[15] There was no lack of interest on the part of the public, and the Service's draft EIS drew 264,000 public comments. In its final EIS, the Service considered 11 alternatives, ranging from the extremes of all wilderness to no wilderness. So far, so good. In between the extremes, however, none of the alternatives considered allocating more than 33 percent of the roadless area to wilderness. In holding that this was inadequate, the Ninth Circuit emphasized that an agency need not consider every alternative or alternatives that are unlikely to be implemented for legitimate reasons but, equally, it must not ignore important alternatives or bias its evaluation by arbitrarily narrowing the range of options considered. While NEPA remains a procedural statute, this type of analysis skates a very close line to substantive review.

It goes without saying, but the quality of an EIS analysis is obviously subject to judicial review, as well. In practice, this means the agency has to address the issues seriously. In *Sierra Club v. U.S. Army Corps of Engineers*, for example, the Corps prepared an EIS for filling part of the Hudson River to build a highway.[16] The EIS described the area to be filled as a "biological wasteland," despite objections by EPA and the U.S. Fish & Wildlife Service. In requiring the Corps to prepare a supplemental EIS, the Second Circuit concluded that by ignoring the views of other expert agencies, and by not adequately compiling relevant data and analyzing it reasonably, the Corps had reached a "baseless and erroneous factual conclusion" that "cannot be accepted as a

---

[15] 690 F.2d 753 (9th Cir.1982).
[16] 701 F.2d 1011 (2d Cir.1983).

'reasoned' decision." In most cases, though, wary of appearing to engage in substantive review, courts are reluctant to reverse agencies on this ground. Thus in *Sierra Club v. Marita*, plaintiffs sued the Forest Service, claiming that its EIS needed to employ an ecosystems approach based on advanced principles of conservation biology.[17] Despite the testimony of thirteen distinguished scientists, the court rejected the plaintiffs' argument. According to the 7th Circuit, agencies must use "high quality" science and ensure the "scientific integrity" of their analysis. But it remains in their agency discretion and expert judgment which particular methodology to use.

As described in Chapter 2, scientific uncertainty is an unavoidable aspect of environmental decision making. This arises in the context of NEPA when agencies must decide what to do if there is insufficient information to predict the impacts of specific options. In particular, when do agencies have to conduct more research? CEQ regulations require that an agency make "reasonable efforts" to obtain relevant information, but obtain information that is "essential" to a reasoned choice among alternatives unless the overall costs of doing so are exorbitant.[18] In practice, this requires that agencies at least consider the tradeoffs between the costs of getting more information and the value of getting it. When possible, an agency should rely on credible scientific evidence and, if information is unavailable, admit that the effects are uncertain and unknown.

A related question is whether an agency must prepare a supplemental EIS when new information becomes available, perhaps significantly changing the range of impacts initially considered. Imagine, for example, that the area to be filled in the Hudson River really was a "biological wasteland." Soon after the filling of the river, though, a local fisherman caught an endangered species and it now appears that a population of the fish lives nearby. Must the Corps stop construction and prepare a supplemental EIS? Recall that NEPA's goal is to ensure the agency makes informed decisions. Thus CEQ regulations require preparation of a supplemental EIS if "significant new circumstances or information relevant to environmental concerns" becomes available.[19] As with other stages of the EIS process, this is subject to the rule of reason. Surely such a "post-decision" supplemental EIS is not necessary every time new information comes to light. Rather, an agency must look to the significance of the new

---

[17] 46 F.3d 606 (7th Cir.1995).

[18] 40 C.F.R. § 1502.02.

[19] 40 C.F.R. § 1502.9(c)(iii).

information, its value to the decision making process, and how much of the federal action remains to be completed.

And what if the predictions of the EIS, upon completion, turn out to be inaccurate or mitigation measures ignored? Consider the plight of Ms. Noe. She owned a bookshop that apparently was rattled to the core by the nearby construction of Atlanta's metro system, MARTA. She sued for a temporary injunction, among other remedies, asserting MARTA and its builders had failed "to stay within the noise levels predicted by the environmental impact statement."[20] Both the district and circuit courts, however, refused to imply a private right of action for Noe to sue under NEPA. As the circuit court explained, NEPA does not provide any protections or prohibitions regarding private conduct. "NEPA does not even require the protection of the environment. NEPA requires only that, prior to beginning construction of a project likely to affect the environment, an environmental impact statement be produced so that the individuals responsible for making the decision to go ahead with or stop the project do so on a well-informed basis."[21]

NEPA also applies to international actions when there are impacts in the United States. In perhaps the most creative of all NEPA challenges, in *National Organization for the Reform of Marijuana Laws (NORML) v. U.S. Dep't of State*, NORML alleged that a U.S.-supported narcotics program in Mexico that sprayed herbicide on marijuana and poppy plants would have significant health effects in the United States (by Americans smoking the herbicide-laden weed) and that an EIS must be prepared.[22] The government agreed to conduct an EIS. By contrast, an EIS is not required when environmental impacts occur *exclusively* in a foreign jurisdiction. The case law regarding environmental impacts in the global commons such as the high seas or Antarctica, though, is less clear.[23] President Carter signed Executive Order 12114 in 1979, providing for analysis of environmental impacts abroad from major federal actions, including impacts in the global commons.[24] The Order exempts, however, actions taken by the president or when national security is involved. Moreover, as with all Executive Orders, it does not create a cause of action and noncompliance cannot be challenged in courts. In Executive Order 13141, President Clinton required environmental reviews for major trade agreements, though the reviews need only focus on impacts from

---

[20] *Noe v. Metropolitan Atlanta Rapid Transit Authority*, 644 F.2d 434, 435 (1981).

[21] *Id.* at 438.

[22] 452 F. Supp. 1226, 1229 (D.D.C. 1978).

[23] *Environmental Defense Fund, Inc. v. Massey*, 986 F.2d 528 (D.C. Cir.1993).

[24] Exec. Order No. 12,114, 3 C.F.R. § 356 (1979).

increased trade in the United States, not in the territory of the trading partner or the global commons.[25]

V. Limiting the Reach of NEPA

Not all federal actions trigger NEPA. As noted above, actions mandated by some environmental statutes or taken by the EPA need not comply with NEPA. More problematic, however, have been recent efforts to exempt certain activities that clearly do have environmental impacts from NEPA's coverage.

Congress, for example, has passed a number of laws providing special exclusions. In the 2004 Energy and Water appropriations bill, for example, a rider mandated construction of a road in the Izembek National Wildlife Refuge in Alaska. The rider stopped short the NEPA alternatives analysis, requiring construction of Alternative 1, "notwithstanding any other provision of law."[26] NEPA has also been effectively amended through administrative action. The Bush Administration's "Healthy Forests Initiative," for example, exempted certain types of commercial logging projects through new categorical exclusions.[27] Congress has also passed legislation allowing the Forest Service and BLM to renew grazing permits without conducting an environmental review.[28]

The most difficult choices surrounding NEPA application involve national security. As a result of the increased concern with national security following the attacks of September 11th, there has been a vigorous debate over whether the Department of Defense's compliance with environmental laws compromises military readiness. The claim that NEPA indirectly weakens national security is a powerful charge and raises difficult trade-offs. Should the military be given special exemptions from NEPA and, if so, under what circumstances?

Such conflicts have been particularly contentious in the testing of active sonar by the U.S. Navy. In contrast to "passive" sonar, which listens for submarine engine noises, active sonar emits powerful sound waves and then listens for distinctive echoes to identify underwater objects. Animal rights and environmental groups have raised concerns that active sonar can damage marine mammal hearing and disrupt their communication, thus affecting their breeding, feeding and other social interactions. Congress addressed this issue by passing legislation that permits the

---

[25] Exec. Order No. 13,141, 64 FR 63169 (1999).

[26] Energy and Water Development Appropriations Act of 2004, Pub. L. No. 108–137, 132, 117 Stat. 1827 (2003).

[27] 68 Fed. Reg. 33813 (June 5, 2003).

[28] Pub. Law 108–108 (Section 325); Pub. Law 108–447 (Section 339).

Secretary of Defense to exempt any action from compliance with any requirement of the Marine Mammal Protection Act (MMPA) for a period of up to two years. No exemption was created for NEPA compliance.

In *Winter v. NRDC,* environmental groups requested a preliminary injunction to halt the Navy's use of active sonar in fourteen large-scale training exercises in Southern California.[29] The Navy had prepared an Environmental Assessment, concluding that the impacts were insufficient to require development of an EIS. In the face of litigation, the Navy subsequently agreed to prepare an EIS, but the plaintiffs moved for a preliminary injunction, trying to halt training exercises until the study was completed. The district court, agreed, finding that plaintiffs had demonstrated a probability of success on the merits. The Supreme Court, however, reversed. While acknowledging the seriousness of plaintiffs' concerns, the Court held that the balance of equities and public interest strongly tipped against an injunction, stating that "The public interest in conducting training exercises with active sonar under realistic conditions plainly outweighs the interests advanced by the plaintiffs. Of course, military interests do not always trump other considerations, and we have not held that they do." Justice Ginsburg's dissent argued that the Navy's fourteen training exercises would be completed by the time the EIS has been drafted.

The *Winter* decision leaves a number of unanswered questions. How, for example, can the Court conclude that the balance of interests (including potential harm to the marine mammals) favors the Navy and therefore use of active sonar should continue until the EIS is prepared, without the very information the EIS would provide? What pre-EIS evidence would plaintiffs need to have demonstrated in order to satisfy the Court?

VI. Does It Work?

Determining the effectiveness of NEPA is hard to do. Unlike the Clean Air Act or Clean Water Act, where one can simply measure air quality or water pollution over time, measuring the influence of environmental information on agency decision making is no easy matter. At one extreme, the EIS could simply serve as a *post hoc* rationalization for decisions already taken—simply going through the bureaucratic motions. And there certainly is reason to fear that this may happen in some instances. After all, conflicts of interest run to the very core of NEPA. Placing agencies in charge of conducting an EIS that may challenge their proposed actions, some have commented, is like placing the fox as guard of the hen house.

---

[29] 555 U.S. 7 (2008).

As Joe Sax has memorably commented on NEPA, "I think the emphasis on the redemptive quality of procedural reform is about nine parts myth and one part coconut oil."[30] Given the concrete statutory mission of an agency with dedicated budgets, organized lobbies, and congressional pressure, on the one hand, and the requirements of NEPA to consider environmental impacts of a range of actions, on the other, one might reasonably be doubtful of NEPA's influence. After all, there have traditionally been few political reward for forests not cut or range lands not grazed.

Despite all these reasons to dismiss NEPA, it has achieved a great deal and continues to do so. Compared to the state of agency transparency at the time of its passage, NEPA has played an important role in opening agency decision making to the public. NEPA has provided constant pressure on agencies to broaden their missions to consider and adopt environmental values. And it has spurred agencies to modify proposals and mitigate adverse impacts.

The experience of the Atomic Energy Commission, preparing an EIS and refusing even to read it, simply could not happen today. Environmental impact assessment has become a standard part of federal decision making. Moreover, mindful of what an EIS will likely show, many projects are dropped before even conducting an EA, thus escaping measurement. Talk to environmental group litigators about NEPA and many say it is critical in providing data on agency actions they could not otherwise obtain or use. Does NEPA ensure agency decisions will be environmentally responsible? No. But it does ensure they will be informed and, in a field with such strongly conflicting interests and values, that is no small feat.

QUESTIONS AND DISCUSSION

1. NEPA takes an informational approach to changing behavior. Information, however, comes at a cost. Agency resources spent preparing an EIS (both in terms of cost and time) are unavailable to spend on other pressing needs. How would you go about assessing the cost-effectiveness of NEPA and determining whether developing EIS are a good use of agency resources?

2. The EPA is excused from complying with NEPA. Why do you think the National Park Service or the U.S. Forest Service has not been granted the same NEPA exemption as EPA?

3. Perhaps surprisingly, NEPA does not require that the agency actually mitigate environmental harm, even if that mitigation can be accomplished at little or no additional cost. Should this be required?

4. The Presidential Commission report on the Deepwater Horizon stated that BP's oil response plan for its drilling operations in the Gulf had

---

[30] Joseph L. Sax, *The (Unhappy) Truth about NEPA*, 26 Okla. L. Rev. 239, 239 (1973).

discussed the potential impact on sea lions and walruses. Walruses likely have not been seen in the Gulf of Mexico since the last Ice Age. Why do you think the BP plan addressed the impact of an oil spill on this marine mammal?

5. What do you think of the institutional incentives of the NEPA process? Does it make sense, for example, for "action agencies" to write the EIS for the very actions they are proposing? In Canada, by contrast, the EIS process is directed by an independent agency with no interest in whether the proposed action goes forward or not.

6. In light of the *Winter* decision and the MMPA exemption passed by Congress, what do you think is the proper balance between marine mammal protection and military operations? What standard should a judge use in balancing the need for an injunction until an EIS has been prepared against the importance of particular Navy training programs to military readiness?

TABLE OF CASES

DEFINITIONS

Environmental law is, unfortunately, full of acronyms and obscure terms.
The list below sets out the most common of these and the page
numbers in the text where they are explained.

INDEX

References are to Pages